THE Prosecutors Deskbook

ETHICAL ISSUES

and

EMERGING ROLES

for

21ST CENTURY

PROSECUTORS

American Prosecutors Research Institute
99 Canal Center Plaza, Suite 510
Alexandria, Virginia 22314
(703) 549-4253
www.ndaa-apri.org
First edition published 1971.

Second edition published 1977.

Printed in the United States of America.

This publication was developed under a grant from the Office of Justice Programs,
U. S. Department of Justice. Point of view expressed herein are those of the authors
and do not necessarily represent the official position or policies of the Office of
Justice Programs or the Department of Justice.

TABLE OF CONTENTS

FOREWORD

The *Prosecutors Deskbook* addresses a broad array of topics of importance to prosecutors, identifying salient issues and developments that will aid prosecutors in their vital work. The many articles are not intended to be exhaustive, and the topics presented will require additional inquiry and research. Consequently, prosecutors must continually collect and synthesize new information and hone their prosecutorial skills.

During the past half-century, the role of the prosecutor has changed dramatically. Numerous changes have expanded the roles, responsibilities and capabilities of prosecutors and their offices. For example, increasing workloads result in growing numbers of prosecutors and staff and new evidentiary issues result from scientific and technological changes, such as the increased utilization of DNA evidence. These developments illustrate the impact of scientific and technological improvements. Other changes have resulted from the adoption of new prosecution approaches and the assumption of new prosecution roles, ranging from community crime and drug prevention activities, to the expansion of intermediate sanctions and treatment options. As a consequence of increasing needs and demands, prosecutors across the nation are constantly in need of new ideas, initiatives and resources.

In recent years, a number of developments in law and practice have contributed significantly to meeting important prosecutorial needs. In learning about these developments, prosecutors increasingly rely upon resources such as professional associations and organizations dedicated to enhancing their knowledge and skills, as well as assisting them to shape the profession's future. Some of these developments are: (a) the growth and maturation of criminal justice associations and organizations specifically dedicated to representing the interests and ideas of prosecutors; (b) improvements in prosecutorial training and technical assistance programs; (c) systematic refinements in the art of advocacy and enhancements of prosecutorial skills; and (d) the creation of new capacities for delivering training and sharing knowledge nationally. Below are descriptions of key professional organizations that have contributed to this progress and will continue to serve the needs of prosecutors.

NATIONAL DISTRICT ATTORNEYS ASSOCIATION

The National District Attorneys Association (NDAA) is the largest and most influential organization representing the interests and ideas of local prosecutors. Located in Alexandria, Virginia, just across the Potomac River from the District of Columbia, NDAA has provided valuable service and assistance to state and local prosecutors for more than half a century. Formed in 1950 as the National Association of County and Prosecuting Attorneys in response to increased crime and a need to protect citizens and communities, NDAA adopted its current name in 1959. That same year the association qualified as a nonprofit, tax-exempt institution for the purpose of receiving contributions and grants. NDAA represents the interests of prosecutors in the United States and its territories, including the Commonwealth of Puerto Rico and the U.S. Virgin Islands. NDAA members include full-time prosecutors from large and small metropolitan areas and part-time prosecutors from rural communities.

NDAA continues to be recognized as the premier association representing the perspective of the local prosecutors, those professionals who carry out the overwhelming percentage of the nation's criminal litigation. The organization serves as a forum to discuss public policy issues that affect the safety of America's communities and as a formidable voice in advocating prosecutorial views and interests. Chief prosecutors who are members of NDAA typically hold elective office and thus represent both major political parties. The organization maintains a bipartisan approach that has proven effective in influencing the formulation of national crime control and justice-related policies. In this regard, it is common that representatives and members of the organization share information and ideas with the White House, Congress, U.S. Department of Justice and other federal, state and local agencies and organizations.

State and local prosecutors share NDAA views and perspectives with decision makers in their own jurisdictions. Additionally, NDAA offers locally elected prosecutors and assistant prosecutors the opportunity to network with fellow prosecutors throughout the nation to enhance their knowledge, skills and influence. NDAA also partners with other prosecutorial groups to promote shared policies and practices. For example, NDAA partners with the National Association of Prosecutor Coordinators (NAPC) in various activities. The mission of NAPC is to provide a forum for the exchange of ideas and information for the mutual benefit of prosecutor coordinators and prosecutors.

AMERICAN PROSECUTORS RESEARCH INSTITUTE

In 1984, NDAA founded the American Prosecutors Research Institute (APRI) as a non-profit research and program development resource for prosecutors, with a special focus on local prosecutors. APRI has its own board of directors that includes representatives of the private sector. The organization has become a vital resource in training and assisting prosecutors, as well as a national clearinghouse for information on prosecutorial functions. APRI is committed to providing interdisciplinary responses to the complex problems of criminal justice. It is also committed to supporting the highest professional standards among officials entrusted with the crucial responsibility for public safety.

APRI has assembled a multidisciplinary staff that includes veteran prosecutors and researchers who are devoted to those programs that serve special needs in prosecutor offices. Access to comprehensive justice, medical and scientific data resources, including a nationwide network of working prosecutors, ensures that information provided by APRI is current, accurate and grounded in practicality. APRI staff members also conduct research on a broad range of criminal justice topics of interest to prosecutors. These topics range from assessing the impact of new legislation on the prosecutor's office, to the effectiveness of various criminal justice programs and reforms, to improving prosecutorial policies and practices.

Key APRI activities include such areas as training and curriculum development, technical assistance and consultation, publications and research. More specifically, APRI provides the prosecution community with such services as: specialized case law information, up-to-date information on legislation, detailed assistance for trial preparation, individualized support for trial presentation, access to experts and presenters, expert assistance with policy and program development, training on various stages of prosecutorial work, information on technology applications, assessments and evaluations of prosecutorial strategies and practices, technical assistance with grant development and administration, office management and organization guidance and assessments of office workloads and resource requirements.

NATIONAL COLLEGE OF DISTRICT ATTORNEYS

Now headquartered at the University of South Carolina Law School in Columbia, South Carolina, the National College of District Attorneys (NCDA) was created in 1970 to provide continuing legal education and training for prosecuting attorneys through programs specifically tailored to meet their needs. NCDA receives support from NDAA, the American College of Trial Lawyers, the American Bar Association and the University of South Carolina. It is devoted to providing continuing legal education to the nation's prosecutors. NCDA seeks to fulfill this important function nationally by continuing to train prosecutors, including training in the art of effective advocacy. The goal of NCDA training is to help prosecutors fulfill their responsibilities efficiently, effectively and ethically.

Over the last 31 years, the college has provided training to over 60,000 criminal justice practitioners. The cornerstone of the college's training is the two-week long Career Prosecutor Course. It concentrates on developing and refining prosecutorial expertise. Although the course includes intensive trial advocacy training, all aspects of a prosecutor's responsibilities are treated in small group discussion, demonstrations and lectures. The Executive Program (a course for prosecution leadership) has been presented annually since 1973. This course is directed to the elected prosecutor and policy making assistant prosecutors. It explores the various roles of a prosecutor: community leader, trial lawyer, administrator, legal advisor and law enforcement officer.

NCDA presents specialized courses around the country on subjects such as evidence, homicide, violent crime, drugs, forensic evidence, white-collar crime, investigation, office administration and representing local government in civil matters. For 10 years the college has sponsored a National Conference on Domestic Violence. This multi-disciplinary conference remains instrumental in keeping this issue in the forefront for government agencies, law enforcement and prosecutors.

In 1998 NCDA began conducting trial advocacy training at the National Advocacy Center under the direction of NDAA. The college also develops training programs for states and individual prosecutors' offices. In addition, the college develops publications on various subjects including ethics, office administration and trial advocacy and recently announced the establishment of the National Center for Prosecution Ethics, sponsored by NCDA and the University of South Carolina Law School. A resource center will be created to serve as an information hub where prosecutors will be able to collect and disseminate materials relating to rules, standards and guidelines, along with administrative and judicial opinions concerning the professional responsibility of prosecutors. All of these will be fully accessible around the country via the Internet.

NATIONAL ADVOCACY CENTER

The National Advocacy Center (NAC), funded through the U.S. Department of Justice, began training classes in April 1998. Situated on the University of South Carolina campus in Columbia, South Carolina, it is a joint venture of NDAA and the Department of Justice. The facility was built to train federal, state and local prosecutors and litigators in advocacy skills and management. More than 10,000 trainings occur there annually.

Several training organizations are located at the NAC. The Office of Legal Education of the Executive Office provides programs for federal personnel for U.S. attorneys, as does the National Bankruptcy Training Institute (NBTI) of the Executive Office for U.S. trustees. Programs for state and local prosecutors are provided by NDAA. For the first time, much of the training of state and local prosecutors has been centralized in a single, specially designed complex. In one wing of the complex, courses in trial advocacy as well as other specialized aspects of prosecutors' responsibilities are conducted by NCDA and APRI, under contracts with NDAA. The faculty includes leading authorities in prosecutorial fields as guest lecturers.

The NAC has 262,000 square feet of classroom, conference and hotel space. Approximately 45 Justice Department employees and 15 NDAA employees are currently assigned to the facility. The center includes two 50-seat lecture halls, one 75-seat lecture hall, two 190-seat lecture halls, a 440-person training area and 10 full-size courtrooms equipped with state-of-the-art audio and visual technology for training purposes. The NAC also includes a full-service hotel, operated exclusively for the advocacy center. It has 265 guestrooms for prosecutor trainees and visiting lecturers and an onsite restaurant and travel service for the convenience of trainees, faculty and staff.

NATIONAL ASSOCIATION OF ATTORNEYS GENERAL

The National Association of Attorneys General (NAAG) was founded in 1907. The mission of NAAG is to facilitate interaction among state attorneys general as peers, thereby enhancing the performance of attorneys general and their staffs to respond effectively to emerging state and federal issues. NAAG members include attorneys general and chief legal officers of the states, territories, the District of Columbia and the Commonwealth of Puerto Rico.

Each year, NAAG organizes federal-state working groups and sponsors seminars, conferences, summits, emerging issue forums and special events, involving a substantial number of attorneys' general staff members. NAAG publishes written reports, monographs and numerous newsletters on a wide range of substantive topics. NAAG also serves as liaison to the federal government, assisting state attorneys with appellate advocacy.

NAAG's vision, goals and activities include: (a) developing information related to the independence, scope and management of offices of attorneys general; (b) maintaining a network among the chief legal officers of the states and jurisdictions by providing a meeting ground for cooperation and learning; (c) promoting cooperation and coordination on interstate legal matters to foster more responsive and efficient legal systems for state citizens; (d) advising attorneys general and their staffs of significant legal developments and emerging trends occurring in the states and federal government; (e) increasing citizen understanding of the law and law enforcement's role; and (f) influencing the development of national and state legal policy through such means as advocacy training.

FUTURE CHALLENGES AND ISSUES

Future challenges and issues will likely create more opportunities for professional organizations to serve the prosecution community. Many prosecutors are becoming involved in activities not previously included in their traditional roles and responsibilities. This trend is illustrated by the advent and expansion of "community prosecution" practices, which attempt to foster partnerships with law enforcement, government agencies and community organizations to address public safety and quality of life issues in our nation's communities. Community prosecution is promoted nationally, locally and through federal grants, sometimes targeting special groups such as violent offenders who violate firearms laws.

In addition to improved and more collaborative prosecution practices, prosecutors increasingly partner with other law enforcement officials in a wide range of crime prevention and drug treatment activities. Recently, Congress has shown support for federal funding to enhance and expand such initiatives. As with most new initiatives, especially those receiving federal funds, prosecutors must carefully evaluate the results. Only by rigorously documenting successes and failures will prosecutors and others be able to identify the best prosecutorial strategies, techniques and the reasons for their success.

Finally, technological and scientific developments are creating new training and technical assistance needs. For example, the use of DNA evidence gives rise to new and significant questions and issues. When are defendants and convicted offenders entitled to such evidence and under what circumstances? Many observers predict that current reliance upon DNA evidence is relatively rare when compared to its potential future use. Another recent development associated with changing technologies is that of crime involving the use of computers, referred to as "cybercrime." Cybercrime includes focusing on old crimes committed in new ways, as well as new crimes that can result in widespread destruction and harm from computer hacking and viruses. Prosecutors are in need of highly specialized knowledge and skills to effectively deal with these crimes.

In summary, prosecutors across America are privileged to have numerous professional organizations that work to help prosecutors prepare for future challenges. Ideally, the substantial progress that is being made through research, training and technical assistance will continue. After all, American prosecutors truly serve as "the people's attorneys," by enhancing safety and justice for all. Continued support of this mission is vital to a better future. The *Prosecutors Deskbook* represents a valuable contribution to this effort.

NEWMAN FLANAGAN
Executive Director, National District Attorneys Association
President, American Prosecutors Research Institute
President, National College of District Attorneys

PREFACE AND ACKNOWLEDGMENTS

Perhaps the most significant development underlying the need for a new *Prosecutors Deskbook* is the ever-changing role of the prosecutor. Prosecutors are expected to punish crime, as they always have, but are now expected to prevent it as well. While prosecutors continue to represent citizens in their courtrooms, they are also increasingly providing leadership in community safety by promoting innovative programs that prevent and combat juvenile and adult crime and drug abuse. For example, prosecutors now advocate and direct efforts to promote victim protections, and community policing and prosecution activities. These concepts were unknown as recently as 20 years ago. Prosecutors' offices today increasingly rely on criminological and performance-based research to accomplish these missions, as citizens expect their prosecutors to anticipate rather than simply react to crime and quality-of-life issues. Citizens want their prosecutors to take the lead on such issues as community improvement and neighborhood renewal. These expectations represent momentous transformations to the prosecutor's role, with enormous potential for significant improvements to our communities.

Despite these promising changes, prosecutors often must face misperceptions and negative images of their activities communicated through the media. For example, allegations of "prosecutorial misconduct" too often surface as defense trial tactics that are superficially aired in the popular media. In truth, allegations of "prosecutorial misconduct" are rarely substantiated and are confused with occasional "prosecutorial error" which does not involve professional misconduct.

Another critical responsibility of today's prosecutor is, therefore, public education. The public is best served when the prosecutor operates at all times with good intentions and honest dealings; in short, when he or she conducts every aspect of prosecutorial action in an ethical manner, maintaining the appearance of fairness. The public needs to know that their prosecutors are searching for justice and truth; the prosecutor owes it to them to make this expectation a daily reality. Fairness and honesty are the best and most effective defenses against allegations of mistakes or misconduct.

In light of these trends, the *Prosecutors Deskbook* is designed to highlight and address key ethical and emerging issues of the 21st Century. The *Prosecutors Deskbook* was last revised in 1977, nearly a quarter of a century ago. This third edition is the product of the talents and dedication of many individuals. The importance and quality of the articles reflect the depth and understanding of these knowledgeable and experienced contributors.

Very instrumental to the work of this project was the inspiration provided by the members of the *Prosecutors Deskbook* Advisory Group. All prosecutors, these members developed and initiated the twin themes of this revised edition: emerging issues and ethical responsibilities of importance to prosecutors. The American Prosecutors Research Institute (APRI) is indebted to the many talented prosecutors who shared their expertise and experiences. APRI is especially appreciative for the truly extraordinary support, dedication and hard work invested by Nola Foulston (District Attorney, Sedgwick County, Wichita, Kansas) for her leadership in this project. Special thanks and recognition are also extended to John Brigham, Project Manager, APRI, for assisting the contributors and managing the project and grant. Among APRI staff who contributed to the completion and success of this project were: Steve Dillingham, Chief Administrator; George Ross, Director of Grants Management; D. Jean Holt, Publications Director; and Laura McKechnie, Editorial Assistant. Finally, special thanks is extended to the U.S. Department of Justice's Bureau of Justice Assistance and to grant monitors Bud Hollis and Jeannie Santos for the support and assistance that made this project possible.

MEMBERS OF THE *PROSECUTORS DESKBOOK* ADVISORY GROUP

Nola T. Foulston, Chairperson
District Attorney, Sedgwick County
Wichita, Kansas

Ted Booras
Chief Assistant State's Attorney, 15th Judicial District
West Palm Beach, Florida

Lawrence Brown
Director, California District Attorneys Association
Sacramento, California

Richard G. Callahan
Prosecuting Attorney, Cole County
Jefferson City, Missouri

Phyllis Gardner
Assistant District Attorney, Shelby County
Memphis, Tennessee

David LaBahn
Deputy Director, California District Attorneys Association
Sacramento, California

Barbara LaWall
County Attorney, Pima County
Tucson, Arizona

Mark Lee
Assistant District Attorney, Suffolk County
Boston, Massachusetts

Kenneth McCurry
Deputy, Criminal Appeals Division
Cook County State's Attorney's Office
Chicago, Illinois

Kevin P. Meenan
District Attorney, 7th Judicial District
Casper, Wyoming

David Sherman
Assistant County Attorney, Pima County
Tucson, Arizona

Thomas W. Sneddon
District Attorney, Santa Barbara County
Santa Barbara, California

Mike Thomas
Prosecuting Attorney, Saginaw County
Saginaw, Michigan

John Brigham
Prosecutors Deskbook Project Director and Grant Manager
American Prosecutors Research Institute

INTRODUCTION

The *Prosecutors Deskbook* contains valuable information on topics of special interest to prosecutors and identifies sources of information relevant to the profession. Finding and understanding the law, however, is only one aspect of being a prosecutor. Experienced prosecutors agree that professionalism is the hallmark of the successful American prosecutor. American prosecutors have been called ministers of justice, representatives of the people, quasi-judicial officers and the consciences of the criminal justice community. The responsibility rests squarely on the shoulders of prosecutors to represent the American people impartially, with only the interests of justice in mind. It has been said that the prosecutor's duty to ensure that innocent people do not suffer punishment is even greater than the duty to ensure that guilty people do not escape conviction.

Unlike private attorneys who advocate for the interests of their individual clients, the prosecutor has a broader clientele, the entire community, which must be served with the highest ethical and professional standards. The pursuit of the truth is the prosecutor's central mission. In some circumstances, the mission can place the prosecutor in an awkward or unpopular position. The media, public opinion and other pressures can place the prosecutor at odds with the electorate and other public officials. The pressure to heed the dictates of public opinion continually tests the professionalism of prosecutors. Still, the prosecutor must stand relentless in the pursuit of fairness and equal justice.

HISTORICAL ROOTS

The compelling need for an impartial administrator of justice had its roots in colonial America. Under English common law, private counsel represented the interests of the crown. The conflicts created by that arrangement were soon obvious. True impartiality, restraint in the discretionary exercise of government powers and fairness in the face of sovereign pressure exposed the flaws inherent in a system where advocates owed their allegiance to one party. The independent spirit of the early colonists demanded that a prosecutor serve the public interest in matters involving the public welfare and safety of citizens. Over time, American colonies replaced private counsels with public prosecutors, and the importance of having an impartial administrator pursue the guilty and protect the innocent became the backbone of the American system of criminal justice.

POWER AND DISCRETION

The role of the modern prosecutor is one of exercising power and setting the tone for the criminal justice system. The prosecutor decides who will be charged with an offense, who will not be charged and what charges are appropriate. Clearly, the power of the prosecutor is unparalleled in the criminal justice system. Prosecutors must discharge that power with care and the interests of all citizens firmly in mind.

Today, particularly in the media, questions are raised regarding the exercise of prosecutorial discretion. Unfortunately, prosecutors can sometimes be depicted as being politically motivated or pursuing a defendant for personal reasons, such as gaining publicity. These accounts call into question the factors that prosecutors should employ in exercising discretion. Permissible factors that influence prosecutorial decisions include: the strength of the evidence, the likelihood of successful conviction, impacts on citizens and the community, and the likelihood of a fair and just verdict and sentence. Accordingly, prosecutors must remain professional and diligent in their exercise of discretion.

THE PROSECUTOR AND THE POLICE

Prosecutorial professionalism and police professionalism are shared imperatives. The two professions have interlocking roles and responsibilities. A close and productive relationship between the prosecutor and police is beneficial to both and to society, as it promotes harmony and the effective administration of justice. Still, areas of conflict can arise and prosecutors are duty bound not to allow personal or occupational relationships to interfere with competing legal and ethical requirements.

Collaboration and communication between prosecutors and law enforcement should not be mistaken as unconditional support or approval. On occasion, prosecutors may assume an adversarial role with law enforcement. For example, the prosecutor may be obligated to make legal determinations regarding law enforcement actions and conduct. To avoid such conflicts, prosecutors and police should work closely on matters and ensure that their communications remain open and constant. Police need to know that they can call upon the prosecutor to provide sound legal advice when needed.

In sum, when the prosecutor enjoys a healthy relationship with the law enforcement community and accepts the role of legal advisor and educator, the community reaps the benefits and justice is enhanced. However, the prosecutor must always be prepared to render independent judgments when needed to promote the ends of justice.

THE PROSECUTOR AND THE COURT

Perhaps the truest test of professionalism for a prosecutor comes when dealing with the court. Respect for the judicial system and its representatives must be maintained at all times, even when the court appears not to reciprocate or to rule erroneously. The prosecutor should enjoy and promote a relationship of mutual respect with the court. The rule of law has no favorites and supports no personal agendas. The prosecutor must display dignity at all times when dealing with the court. The professional prosecutor speaks through legal arguments and briefs to appropriate appellate forums when differences of opinion occur. By maintaining dignity and respect at all times, the prosecutor furthers the ends of justice and represents the citizens more effectively.

THE PROSECUTOR AND THE DEFENSE

Special requirements and cautions apply when the prosecutor deals with defense counsel or the defendant. Generally, it is advisable to avoid communications with persons against whom you have filed charges. An interested party in a criminal proceeding cannot be treated with the same access as defense counsel. Prosecutors may find themselves subject to judicial scrutiny or bar association discipline if care is not taken in communications with defendants.

A distinction exists when the prosecutor is investigating a criminal matter and such communication is authorized. Grand Jury proceedings or other sanctioned inquiries may allow the prosecutor to deal directly with a defendant or targeted party, but care and caution should be taken to avoid placing the case and prosecutor at legal risk.

The relationship with criminal defense counsel is vastly different than that with defendants. The judicial system contemplates open, fair and candid communication between the prosecutor and the defense lawyer. There is no place for rancor or lack of respect for the opposing party. Recognizing that each lawyer has different clients and each plays different independent roles, the professional prosecutor should strive to open and maintain lines of communication with the defense attorney. The mutual goal is to further the ends of justice. Professionalism is demonstrated when the prosecutor can maintain a position of fairness and honesty regardless of the conduct of others.

THE EMERGING ROLE OF THE PROSECUTOR

The prosecutor's role has evolved into a powerful one within the criminal justice system, and it continues to gain prominence. Along with the need to exercise leadership comes the responsibility to discharge duties and authorities fairly. This also requires that the prosecutor conduct himself or herself in a manner that reflects well on the entire justice system. Added to this awesome responsibility is ever-increasing pressure for the prosecutor to take on expanded roles that now include such responsibilities as crime prevention, victim assistance and quality of life improvements.

All American prosecutors must understand that the prosecutor's role is far more than just prosecuting defendants. For example, he or she must understand and respond to issues of juvenile and domestic violence, drug use, gang behaviors, hate crimes and even cybercrimes. Every day poses new challenges and opportunities for prosecutors. For these and other reasons, prosecutorial professionalism and an unwavering commitment to be a "minister of justice" to all people are essential elements in safeguarding our system of justice in America.

In describing the many facets of being a "minister of justice," the *Prosecutors Deskbook* addresses a variety of topics and legal developments of importance to the prosecution community. The topics include: the role of the prosecutor, pretrial and trial practices, special topics, effective strategies, public policies and practical considerations. It is my hope that this tool will meet your needs and advance what I consider to be the noblest profession that one can ever aspire to undertake.

TOM CHARRON
Director of Education
National District Attorneys Association

THE ROLE OF THE PROSECUTOR

THE CHANGING ROLE OF THE PROSECUTOR

By Stephanie Anderson, District Attorney, Cumberland County, Portland, Maine

-Without justice, there can be no peace...

Introduction

American society has changed dramatically since the 1960s. The turmoil that has accompanied those changes has been reflected through the prism of the American criminal justice system as newer versions of older crimes clash with the established order. These changes have produced an overall increase in the crime rate, especially for juvenile crime, drug-related offenses and a host of newer crimes that are, at once, more serious, more complicated, often more violent and always more difficult to prosecute.

Because prosecutors are at the center of the American justice system, their work is profoundly affected by these developments. In addition, the public is rightly concerned. Increased crime heightens concerns about personal safety and, as in any system that seeks to be responsive to the public it serves, creates a growing expectation that the prosecutor ought "to do something" to deal with the problem. To meet this challenge, prosecutors are changing their focus—how they think, how they work, how they set priorities and how they relate to the needs of their constituencies.

This article will identify the fundamental characteristics of prosecutors and the various roles they assume in discharging their legal mandates and moral obligations. It will touch briefly on some of the changes that have occurred in American society over the past 40 years. Finally, it will discuss the need to evolve and expand traditional prosecutorial roles and the implications of that expansion.

CHARACTERISTICS AND ROLES OF THE PROSECUTOR

The American prosecutor enjoys powers that are unique and unparalleled elsewhere in the world. Vested with discretionary authority by state constitutions or statutes (and locally elected in all but a handful of jurisdictions in the United States), prosecutors are free to apply the laws of their jurisdictions to their constituencies as they believe best. They alone determine whether or not to charge someone with a crime and they alone determine the course of the prosecution. They have the power to reduce the charges, or even terminate the prosecution altogether, by simply filing a piece of paper with the court indicating that the state is no longer willing to pursue the charge. This discretion is (virtually) unreviewable, clothed with (virtual) immunity, and remains (virtually) absolute.

The United States has a system of public, as opposed to private, prosecution. This emphasis on serving the interests of the public might be easily taken for granted but the fact is that our legal predecessor, England, had a *private* system of prosecution until well into the late 19th century. Under this "private system," individual citizens hired lawyers to press prosecution of crimes they believed they had suffered. In practice, this system favored the wealthy and the powerful, and access to justice was not available to the poor and underprivileged. That experience, and the difficulties inherent in dealing with an arbitrary, distant and unresponsive government, where privilege reigned over principle, prompted our colonial forefathers to establish a government of laws based upon individual sovereignty and the principles of republican and representative government. Recall that our Declaration of Independence, in 1776, proclaimed that:

… (A)ll Men are created equal and were endowed by their Creator with certain inalienable Rights… that to secure these Rights, Governments are instituted among Men, deriving their just Powers from the Consent of the Governed…

The framers of the Declaration of Independence viewed freedom, civil liberties and the right of citizens to self-government as *God*-given rights that were devolved from men *to* their government. By implication, these rights originated by virtue of one's birth as an English citizen and *not* as a form of monarchical or parliamentary "privilege" that could be revoked at will. A bold ideal for the subjects of a constitutional monarchy to hold, it nonetheless represented the culmination of a philosophical evolution in British legal practice by men willing to forsake the security of life in England for the ardor, difficulties and freedom of life in the New World.

From a prosecutorial standpoint, this thinking first manifested itself with the adoption of a system of public prosecution by the colony of Connecticut in 1704. By emphasizing the importance of *public* (as opposed to governmental) accountability and by rejecting the concept of private prosecution as anathema to the emerging American concept of democratic process, Connecticut anticipated the radical notion of individual sovereignty some 70 years before the American Revolution. This demonstrated the belief in the radical idea that *all* persons should have access to justice, not just the privileged class. This idea found fertile ground in the new world, and took root. Over time, these changes were adopted by other colonies, and by the year 1789 and the adoption of the United States Constitution, the notion of a system of public prosecution was already firmly entrenched in American jurisprudence.

The prosecutor came to embody the very notion of legal sovereignty itself and, as the legal representative of the state, was held to a moral and ethical standard commensurate with that responsibility. In the words of Justice Sutherland in *Berger v. United States*, the prosecutor

> *... is the representative not of an ordinary party to a controversy, but of a sovereignty whose obligation to govern impartially is as compelling as its obligation to govern at all; and whose interest, therefore, in a criminal prosecution is not that it shall win a case, but that justice shall be done. As such, he is in a peculiar and very definite sense the servant of the law, the twofold aim of which is that guilt shall not escape or innocence suffer. He may prosecute with earnestness and vigor—indeed, he should do so. But, while he may strike hard blows, he is not at liberty to strike foul ones. It is as much his duty to refrain from improper methods calculated to produce a wrongful conviction as it is to use every legitimate means to bring about a just one.*[1]

It is one thing to have high ideals; however, it is altogether something else to implement them. On a practical level, American prosecutors share a number of fundamental characteristics: most are popularly elected public officials, endowed with complete and nearly unreviewable discretion in the discharge of their responsibilities that render them the chief administrators of justice and centers of power in the criminal justice system. They are also officers of the court, defenders of constitutional government, and, by virtue of their public election and almost unlimited professional discretion, representatives of the democratic conscience of their communities.

Organizing each of these varied and difficult responsibilities requires a unifying principle, and therefore many prosecutors' offices are governed by a mission statement— a concise statement identifying primary roles of the prosecutor, such as:

*The district attorney is committed to ensuring public safety and promoting pub-
lic respect for government through the prompt, effective, and compassionate prosecution of cases in a manner that advocates for the interests of all victims, respects
the law enforcement agencies, responsibly stewards public resources, and holds
offenders accountable while at the same time protecting the constitutional and
legal rights of the accused.*

These legal mandates and moral obligations are executed through a variety of roles
that prosecutors fulfill. First and most important, as the prosecutor of crimes within
their jurisdictions they must initiate and conduct all prosecutions of persons accused
of criminal offenses. Consistent with discharging these responsibilities, prosecutors
exercise broad discretion to select those cases that they believe warrant prosecution.
This discretionary action is long-standing in nature and today it is also necessitated
by a scarcity of investigative, prosecutorial and judicial resources, by muddled and
vague legislative mandates and by the ever-present requirement to consider the best
interests of justice for their particular jurisdictions.[2]

Through charging decisions and sentencing agreements they also help to determine—and adjust as circumstances dictate—the "costs of crime." This can be a
power of enormous reach, one with great influence on the civic culture—the business, economic and social life—of their communities. The fact that they serve as
elected public officials denotes clear responsibilities to the public and compels them to
be sensitive to, reflective of, and where necessary, willing to be educators of community attitudes and opinions on a myriad of social issues, such as, public safety, obscen-
ity, environmental concerns, domestic violence, police misconduct and capital punishment, to name a few. Prosecutors must, or should, strive to transform public *angst*
into positive reform.

There are other roles, however, in which their influence may not be as obvious but
where the effects can be quite profound. For instance, as the (elected and, hence,
accountable) chief law enforcement officer for their districts, they bear the ultimate
responsibility for the integrity of the criminal justice systems in their communities.
They set the justice priorities in their offices. In that capacity they act as advisors to,
educators of, and occasional prosecutors of their local law enforcement officials.
They are also chief executives and financial officers for their offices, and, as such, are
responsible for funding, for all personnel matters, for setting office policies and procedure and for the training and overall morale of their staffs.

Moreover, prosecutors have an obligation, in order to minimize retrials, to assist trial judges in avoiding reversible error. The prosecutor engages in a juggling act: representing the interests of the state; staying alert for police errors; and watching for defense counsel and judicial mistakes that might result in reversible errors. Prosecutors wear many hats.

Each of these roles also automatically qualifies prosecutors as leaders in the criminal justice system. By virtue of their community standing, they have opportunities to act as highly influential advisors to the legislature and the judiciary, with the objective of stimulating criminal justice reforms and worthwhile programs to solve community problems.

MAJOR CHANGES THAT HAVE AFFECTED THE ROLE OF THE PROSECUTOR

This section is not intended to be an exhaustive discourse on the changes in American society or an explanation of the problems that have arisen throughout the social fabric of our country. Rather, it identifies certain *major* changes and proposes that the ensuing problems can be understood and addressed only in the context of how they arose.

Destabilization of Family, Community and "Mediating" Institutions

Emergence of Single Parent Households

Since the 1960s, societal changes have deprived many children of adequate parental guidance and of the stabilizing influences that previous generations derived from family, neighborhood and community—the largely constructive influences that children depended on to help them make the right choices and become responsible adults. There has been a dramatic rise in the number of single-parent (and dysfunctional) households and a clear connection between these trends and household incomes, levels of education and family stability. And while many different explanations can be offered for this phenomenon, the fact remains that many children today have been deprived of the proper nurturing, structure and guidance they require to mature into responsible adults.

Elimination of Character Education from Public School Curriculum

The introduction of the so-called "decision-making" model of morals education that began to take hold and expand in the public education system[3] has contributed to a growing confusion among children about fundamental and previously unquestioned moral values. The "decision-making model" represented a rejection of and shift away from character education.

Character education is based on the idea that there is right and wrong, and that there are character traits that children ought to know. They learn these by example, and, once learned, the traits need to be practiced until they become second nature. Character education was criticized by some as dogmatic, naïve and prone to abuse. It was replaced by the decision-making model with good intentions: to help students think more independently and critically about values. The idea here was that young people would be more committed to self-discovered values than to ones that were simply imposed upon them by adults. The common feature of these curriculums is the assumption that children can learn to make good moral decisions without bothering to acquire moral habits or strength of character.

Unfortunately, however, by focusing students on self-acceptance rather than personal responsibility, young and impressionable minds can be happily and easily led into believing that their choices can never be wrong, so long as they are comfortable with them. Instead of encouraging virtuous behavior and providing students with effective tools for responsible adult citizenship, this method has caused confusion about moral values and has helped produce a significant number of young people unable to distinguish reasonable moral arguments from mere rationalizations.[4] This has resulted in an influx into the criminal justice system of youthful offenders who lack a moral compass and are often devoid of any remorse for their destructive behavior, let alone any sense of appreciation for the harm that they may have inflicted on their victims.

The Drug Epidemic
The drug epidemic of the 1970s and 1980s gave birth to a skyrocketing crime rate, and led to an overburdened court and probation system that was unable to address the problem. The increases in drug-related crimes affected not just the defendants, but also their families, friends and neighbors, and the social institutions around them. The crime and disorder associated with drugs and drug-related offenses had significant consequences for school environments, local commerce and for neighborhoods. The damage done placed great stresses on these institutions, making it difficult for them to deploy even basic services to their constituencies. As crime destabilized the institutions, neighborhoods declined and it became increasingly difficult for local people to execute the basic work of civic life: to educate and raise their children; move freely

about the neighborhood; work, shop or play unimpeded by crime, violence and disorder. The resulting public outcry for a strong law enforcement response led to drug interdiction programs and stiff, mandatory prison sentences. Soon, drug addicts filled the jails and prisons yet they were not "cured." Families were still destabilized, neighborhoods were still in decline and people still did not feel safe.

Declining Stabilizing Forces and Opportunities for Young People

As the drug culture infected society and social disorder increased, young males, traditionally that segment of society at highest risk for criminal behavior, were at the same time facing declining opportunities to learn through positive experience how to change and rehabilitate their lives. In addition, entrance standards were raised for the few opportunities—educational and employment related—that remained.

To use just one example, consider the impact of the steep decline in the number of young men serving in the armed forces brought about in part by the abolition of the draft,[5] the winding down of the Cold War and the resulting decline in defense spending. Military service diverted hundreds of thousands of young adult males (the largest potential criminal cohort) away from their neighborhoods and into a regimented, disciplined system characterized by respect for authority, a code of honor and an ethic of self-sacrifice and service to others. The very prospect of forced military service also motivated hundreds of thousands more to pursue college and university education. For the most part, those who emerged from military service (or the educational institutions they attended in place of the military) enhanced their self-esteem and fostered a sense of hope for their own future.

During the 1970s, 1980s and 1990s, the numbers of young men with military experience declined significantly. Today's young men continue to search for the camaraderie and sense of self-worth commonly associated with military service. The major difference is that they may now find this on the streets, in gangs, drugs, crime and other antisocial activities. As leaders in the criminal justice system and visionaries for change, prosecutors must contend with the increase in juvenile crime and, at the same time, take a leadership role in identifying and developing rehabilitation opportunities for children and young adults.

Technological Advances

Another change in the American criminal landscape has come with huge advances in information and forensic technology. While this technology provides prosecutors with more efficient case, data and office management tools, it also generates a new class of criminals and crimes. Crimes committed in cyberspace present the prosecutor with unprecedented challenges. Prosecutors and investigators have to become expert or at least proficient in computer technology, presenting a myriad of new training demands. At the same time, this technology allows offenders virtual invisibility as they perpetuate new kinds of crimes. The proliferation of child pornography and cyberstalking are only two examples of this phenomenon. The investigation and prosecution of these crimes is costly and labor intensive, placing greater demands on the resources of the prosecutor's office.

Surge in Immigration into the United States

Another impact on prosecutors has been a vast influx into the United States of immigrants and refugees from all over the world. While they can enrich our culture, they are often ill prepared to assume the rights and responsibilities of American citizenship and not properly educated about American laws and culture. Consequently, many frequently run afoul of it. The challenge of communicating with inhabitants who speak many different languages and dialects leads to an obvious increase in the need for interpreters with a resulting increase in the length and difficulty of hearings (not to mention the introduction of new and interesting cultural defenses at trial).

Stricter Scrutiny of the Police

Technical requirements placed on law enforcement agencies by the courts, particularly in the area of defendants' rights, have increased. Starting with the landmark decisions of the United States Supreme Court in *Escobedo*[6] and *Miranda*[7], the courts have imposed many new conditions on search and seizure, the right to counsel, electronic surveillance and related issues, all the while subjecting police and law enforcement agencies to stricter scrutiny. This scrutiny clearly enhances the quality of American justice, but it also increases the reliance the police place on prosecutors for legal and technical assistance, even at the early stages of an investigation. It also increases the complexity of criminal litigation. For example, prosecutors are frequently expected to review and provide uniform forms for search warrants, arrest warrants and surveillance requests.[8]

Expanding Federal Jurisdiction and Influence

The prosecutor has also been affected by the growth and expansion of the federal government's jurisdiction into areas of traditionally local concern. The result is an increased need for collaboration and cooperation with various, diverse and often remotely located agencies of the federal government, a time-consuming activity under the best of circumstances. Additionally, federal funding streams are so attractive to resource-deprived local prosecutors that offices often find themselves willingly placing greater demands on themselves in the form of increased bureaucracy, higher administrative costs and the imposition of federal policies in order to achieve the reward of increased federal funds. The complexity of these funding streams, particularly the increased reliance on federal dollars that results, can actually divert scarce resources *away* from core prosecutorial missions. Prosecutorial man-hours are often taken up with federal requirements for collaborative meetings, training sessions and all manner of report writing. In essence, the historically local orientation of the prosecutor, without careful discipline, could degenerate into a subsidiary of a distant federal government.

THE CASE FOR A SHIFT IN PROSECUTOR STRATEGY

Taken together, the social disruptions caused by the rise of a drug culture, declining educational standards, scarce economic opportunities for an at-risk population, an infinitely more complex cultural environment and technological and jurisdictional changes, as discussed above, have decreased civil order. They have weakened the vitality and efficacy of traditionally normalizing institutions (i.e., the family, the neighborhood, the schools and the social services) to mediate and regulate behavior and at the same time, made the day-to-day management of the prosecutor's office more problematic and complicated.

Prosecutors are vested with the moral and legal authority to affect meaningful change. As a result of these changes however, they should be far more innovative and they should develop a capacity for understanding the root causes of the disorders that they confront. They must evaluate how the management of their offices, and the public resources and authorities vested in those offices, can further the public safety goals of the communities they serve. In short, today's prosecutors ought to shift primary focus from that of simple case manager to that of innovator and coordinator of (often-complex) law enforcement strategies targeted to protect and revitalize community institutions. This requires prosecutors to expand beyond their traditional core mission—the prosecution and litigation of crimes—and forces them to adopt new and innovative strategies to strengthen their communities and actually reduce crime. This is not to say that there is only one right way, or one right strategy, for prosecutors to use in managing their offices. It is, and always will be, left up to individual prosecutors to fulfill their duties in the manner they deem best for the best interests of their jurisdictions.

This section will discuss two major operating models upon which prosecutors might focus their management styles: the Case Processing Model and the Strategic Problem Solving Model. The two models differ in the level of priority placed by the prosecutor on the internal operating procedures of the office, i.e., the way they react to, or "process" the caseloads. Certainly, each management method is concerned with protecting the public's safety.[9]

In the Case Processing Model, the prosecutor is focused primarily on dealing with caseloads in the most expeditious manner possible. Each case is handled and processed. Then the next case is dealt with. These prosecutors await each day's docket to arrive at their office; each case is handed from their law enforcement agencies over to them when the proper time comes. They then dismiss, amend, plead or try the case. Obviously, this is a reactive strategy.

In the Strategic Problem Solving Model, the sum total of overall office policies and office strategies, including the types of cases emphasized and the outcomes sought, can *proactively* affect the level of crime in the community. In the Strategic Problem Solving Model, the prosecutor also focuses on how best to manage the office but does so pursuant to a comprehensive strategy of community involvement. The overall objective is to actually attack crimes *before* they get to the courtroom or the station house.

In fact there are many variations of both strategies and at any given time, a prosecutor will likely use different strategies simultaneously within one office to most effectively address different types of problems.

Limits of the Case Processing Strategy

From a processor point of view, the prosecutor's aim is to move cases quickly through the system and to treat like cases and like defendants similarly. Charging policy guidelines are typically based upon the strength or value of the case: the quantity and quality of the evidence, the nature of the crime itself and the depravity and/or dangerousness of the defendant. Case strength or value is then balanced against the resources available. Once a case has been charged, plea-agreement policy guidelines generally reflect the strategic concern the prosecutor has for achieving particular outcomes for the victim and the community: crime reduction through general deterrence or incapacitation, restitution for the victim and, where possible, rehabilitation for the offender.

Concern for successful prosecution of crimes (defined as outcomes that result in conviction and punishment) is a commendable goal and is justified on several levels. It honors the rule of law and a just result serves as society's moral judgment on the nature of the conduct. Best of all, perhaps, the effectiveness of this strategy can be measured by objective criteria readily available to the prosecutor: what case came in, what went out, what happened to it and how long did it take? This strategy is attractive for prosecutors due in no small measure to the fact that, generally, prosecutors are not held directly responsible for the crime rate. Success can be objectively measured and expressed to the public in the form of a high conviction rate. So long as the cases are processing smoothly and the "biggest bad guys" are getting caught, convicted and sentenced to long prison terms, the prosecutor is respected by the public and is even occasionally hailed as a hero in the press.

But this strategy has very serious limitations. Except in the broadest sense of general deterrence, this type of strategy probably does little to *reduce* crime and disorder.

For example, the prosecutor may believe in the value of rehabilitation, retribution and restitution as legitimate aims of sentencing. Because the caseload is predicated on the enforcement and arrest policies practiced by the local police departments, however, prosecution efforts to improve crime control in accordance with a Case Processing Strategy are generally limited to establishing the "costs of crime" after the fact. This is determined through the verdicts, pleas or sentencing agreements that occur weeks, months or years after the crime.

Without reliable data about sentencing outcomes, the prosecutor's vision about the potential of crime control policies is constricted by the limits of the data. Ultimately, prosecutors are reduced to measuring success by how well their caseloads are managed. This is the only indicator available to them. Efficient "handling" is viewed as the goal, at the expense of larger social purposes such as overall crime control and community improvement.

With this approach prosecutors begin to wonder about what impact, if any, their policies have on reduction of crime. They look to program evaluations and other outcome measures, but their efforts are hampered by imperfect and inconsistent information. They remain uncertain whether certain sanctions do in fact send a deterrent signal, and if so, which ones and to whom. Nor are prosecutors certain how or why their sanctions will prevent future crimes. Because they are unable to precisely identify the impacts on deterrence and safety that result from their sentencing policies, they are limited to informed guesses and anecdotal evidence about the impact of those sentencing policies on their communities. The lack of empirical evidence to justify these policies makes prosecutors and their practices open to political attack. On any case in particular, victim and community responses may cause the prosecutor to question the approach taken, and the prosecutor may therefore adjust the handling of the case accordingly. Absent reliable empirical data, however, this reaction is by necessity subjective and imperfect. This dilemma is quite representative of prosecutors' daily responsibilities; they are frequently called upon to make decisions for which there are no clear guidelines and which can only be based upon one's experience and judgment.

Another problem with the Case Processing approach is that when dealing with cases individually and not collectively (in the context of the impact on the community), the policies of the prosecutor may unintentionally *increase* disorder and neighborhood crimes. For example, assume a prosecutor's response to a gang problem results in the arrest, prosecution and conviction of the gang's leaders. Removing them from the street may in fact cause gang incidents to *increase*. Why? Because locking up the leaders for lengthy periods of time might be an excellent outcome (under the Case Processing model), but the removal of gang leadership will often generate greater instability within the gang culture. The (unanticipated) result may be more crime, violence and disorder as other members attempt to demonstrate their capacity and strength in efforts to fill the new leadership vacuum.

Weaknesses of other government and community institutions often generate patterns of cases that may prevent the prosecutor from making charging decisions based on the Case Processing approach. Instead, prosecutors must take on marginal cases, sometimes in violation of their charging policies, largely because the offender needs to be persuaded or coerced into cooperating with the rehabilitative efforts of one or more social service agencies. In this situation, the prosecutor's office has been changed into, in effect, a social services placement agency but one with control of potentially severe criminal consequences for the offender in case he or she fails to meaningfully participate or comply with mandated treatment requirements.

This raises a number of distinct ethical issues, for instance:

- What are the consequences for the prosecutor of pressing de minimus (what could be essentially unprovable) cases in service of the larger purpose of coercing defendants into potentially beneficial programs and services that they would otherwise resist? These include, for example, juvenile services, substance abuse and drug treatment, mental health services and domestic violence intervention programs.

- What are the costs to the prosecutor's office, and ultimately to the public, of the diversion of prosecutor's resources away from prosecuting crime (in the traditional sense), towards providing the social services or the incentive for the social services that were once provided, and perhaps more efficiently so, by schools, churches and other private sector agencies and received on a voluntary, not a punitive, basis?

- To what extent do prosecutors, by performing in lieu of other governmental agencies that do not properly discharge their responsibilities (i.e., child welfare agencies, schools, parole boards, mental health hospitals) actually perpetuate the inefficiencies of those agencies and thereby contribute to the underlying problems those agencies are failing to control? Are our citizens best served by criminalizing what were previously aberrant but not necessarily dangerous habits and activities? By willingly assuming additional responsibilities are we not inculcating an incapacitating reliance on the part of those agencies? Wouldn't offenders, their families and their neighborhoods be better served if the social service intervention had occurred at some point before they reached the criminal justice system? And how are we to measure the sincerity of the "conversions" that offenders often undergo as a result of criminal sanctions?

These ethical questions underscore the importance of the delicate balance that exists between the recognized need to protect individual liberties (a need present at the creation of the idea of the office of the American prosecutor) against the recurring need of the state to maintain social order. If, in fact, a weakening of our families, communities and schools is occurring, shouldn't prosecutors be sensitive to the need to include within their professional focus those policies that would best revitalize and strengthen those community institutions? Prosecutors, even when focused on a

Case Processing Strategy, recognize the cumulative effect that crime has on society: weakening of social ties; increased feelings of powerlessness and loss of hope for the future; reduced individual participation in the social, economic and political life of neighborhoods and communities; and more crime and more disorder.

In response, prosecutors should expand their organizational boundaries and jettison obsolete ideologies. They should become problem solvers. Prosecutors should recognize that their policies and performance are vital to maintenance of the social and economic health of the community. This significant responsibility encompasses and eclipses the traditional, limited notion of the office's responsibility to ensure the public's safety. Prosecutors must secure neighborhoods against criminal disruption and thus, over time, allow other social institutions to once again regulate their own affairs. Reducing the pressure of crime and disorder upon the key institutions of the community—the family, schools, churches, local, private and public institutions—will strengthen civil society but this objective is far beyond anything that simple Case Processing Strategies can hope to accomplish.

THE PROSECUTOR AS STRATEGIC PROBLEM SOLVER

The prosecutor as Strategic Problem Solver looks to control crime at its source. Problem solvers marshal all available tools in the law enforcement and criminal justice systems. They think "outside the box," not limiting themselves to what they are familiar with. Their quest is to apply all of the authority, resources and competencies available to them to craft new approaches to remedy society's problems. They know that the quality of civic life is directly dependent upon the quality of neighborhoods. Vital neighborhood institutions are the key to social order. Without it, democracy itself is impossible.

In order to accomplish this, prosecutors should know more about the mechanics of crime and disorder, more about the sources of crime and more about the consequences of crime on institutions. Prosecutors should develop some understanding of the institutional sources of disorder and the impact that prosecutorial policies might have on this disorder. Their goals are to control crime at its source by identifying the root sources and causes of crime and then to attack these problems directly. Achieving this will require fundamental changes in the various roles prosecutors play: litigator, chief executive and financial officer, chief law enforcement officer, criminal justice system leader and community leader. These roles of the prosecutor will be affected by a shift in emphasis toward a more comprehensive, problem solving strategy.

Litigator

Litigators should consider the long-term interests of neighborhoods and families when estimating a case. They should adjust their charging policies accordingly to assess proper values for the public assets under threat. One example of where this redefinition of litigation (measuring the quantity and quality of the evidence, the nature of the crime and the dangerousness of the defendant but including an assessment of the cost to the institution under attack) has already occurred is with domestic violence cases. Prosecutors nationwide have revamped preexisting charging and prosecution policies in an attempt to regulate and realign the balance of power in the severely dysfunctional family. Prosecutors now routinely prosecute these cases without the full cooperation of the domestic violence victim and frequently in direct opposition to her (or his) wishes and stated preferences. (Interestingly, this practice would appear to conflict with *National Prosecution Standards 42.3*[10] and, presumably, with most statutory and constitutional victims' rights protections.)

Another example of a type of case that fails the traditional "case strength" test is a street level "buy and bust" drug case involving a minimal amount of a controlled substance. This would ordinarily be considered a minor crime but if the aim is to restore order to the community and if drugs are a major social problem that contributes to disorder, then those factors alone should substantially increase the value of this type of prosecution.

In addition to changing charging policies, the prosecutor as problem solver recognizes that law enforcement responses (investigation, prosecution and sentencing) have often proven ineffective in many crime-plagued areas. Therefore, the problem solver should be willing to merge criminal with civil remedies. For example, civil forfeiture statutes have tremendous potential to reduce crime: seizure of criminal assets interferes with criminal activity and deters others by making the activity potentially less profitable. Furthermore, civil forfeiture penalizes the criminal, prevents unjust enrichment and raises revenue for crime-reduction programs. Unfortunately, civil forfeiture statutes are under attack. Prosecutors, therefore, should work to protect these statutes. This effort may well require legislative interaction on the prosecutor's part.

There are other civil remedies that can be used effectively by prosecutors to reduce crime. Some of these are: injunctions, divestitures, trusteeships and suits for monetary loss or commercial injury. Again, if the prosecutor's objective is to deter conduct that threatens the welfare of the community—and not merely to process the cases as they come into the office—then, in the right situation, these tactics can be a valuable weapon in the prosecutor's arsenal. Often, these tactics can be more effective than traditional criminal sanctions.

Chief Executive and Financial Officer

As chief executive and financial officer, the prosecutor is motivated to efficiently use public resources and legal authorities to stabilize institutions in the interest of future safety. As previously mentioned, prosecutors already struggle with local public resources insufficient to confront heavy and often growing arrest and caseloads. It is not surprising that many prosecutors rely on federal funding to support operational budgets. As prosecutors devise more strategies to deal with the problems of crime at its source, they will have to look more and more to outside funding—from federal, state and private sources—to implement their strategies. This risks increasing administrative and bureaucratic complexity at a time when the office can least afford to take on extra burdens.

Adopting a strategic problem-solving model of office management may place greater responsibilities on the support staff. Technical and training needs in particular must be continually assessed.

Chief Law Enforcement Officer

As chief law enforcement officer, the prosecutor has the ultimate responsibility for the integrity of the criminal justice system. Maintaining public trust and confidence is, in large part, the prosecutor's primary duty. Police and prosecutors already work closely together. Shifting from an emphasis on case processing to an emphasis on strategically solving problems generates an even greater need for police and prosecution collaboration. For example, in many areas, police have started so-called community policing programs. These represent a dramatic shift away from a 911 response-oriented strategy to a problem solving oriented strategy. Many law enforcement agencies have established community-policing centers in afflicted neighborhoods. They work with members of the community to identify existing and potential vulnerabilities to crime and to invest human capital in solving the problems before they escalate. This is quintessentially active, indeed proactive, policy.

Unfortunately, community-policing programs are often developed absent an overall, inter-agency crime reduction strategy, even though this is one area where the combined forces of the prosecutor and the police should produce great value for the public. The prosecutor must be involved in all aspects of policing to provide strategic direction. And even though police and prosecutors may work together to devise strategies to stabilize neighborhoods, community policing must inevitably fail if handed off to the traditional case-processing model of prosecutor management.

For example, police and prosecutors can work together to devise strategies for opportunity blocking methods that reduce vulnerability to certain types of targeted criminal activity. An example of opportunity blocking is generating a "bad business atmosphere," through police presence and prosecutorial policies in an area victimized by prostitution. This can be accomplished relatively simply with increased police presence: more frequent patrolling, writing down license plates numbers of potential customers, giving them verbal warnings and making arrests. This strategy drives down the demand for the service and produces a supply-reduction effect on the prostitutes—they dwindle away because the business environment is hostile. The prosecution of these offenses gives strength and force to the police strategy, and, although prostitution and soliciting cases may not be considered serious under a traditional Case Processing case-strength analysis, they obviously acquire a higher value if the objective is to combat widespread community blight and disorder.

Criminal Justice System Leader

As a criminal justice system leader, the prosecutor should be concerned with stimulating systemic justice reforms, to include the complete spectrum—from the actual arrest of a suspect to the charging, prosecution, trial and, assuming conviction, sentencing and incarceration. From the vantage point of the strategic problem-solving model, the prosecutor should concentrate all the tools available in the criminal justice arsenal. This includes relationships with local, regional and state law enforcement agencies, the judiciary and other public and private community leaders. The overall objective is to monitor and revise existing public policy, or devise new ones and mount an overall assault on crime.

As Community Leader

As community leaders, prosecutors should be sensitive to the concerns and attitudes of their constituencies. They should use their power and opportunity to buttress their innovations. They can also muster the community's assistance for crime-reducing strategies. For example (by way of opportunity blocking), steering wheel locks can more effectively reduce car theft than apprehension and conviction of the car thieves themselves. Likewise, widespread use of holograms on credit cards deters more credit card thefts and fraudulent transactions than occasional prosecutions of forgers. The business community has strong financial incentives to reduce crime and can be a strong ally with the prosecutor in implementing opportunity-blocking strategies. Prosecutors can and do, for example, enlist the community's aid in cleaning up playgrounds and improving the lighting around them. This makes the environment less hospitable to drug dealers and vagrants and more hospitable to children and families. Likewise, the community can be called upon to help prosecutors add non-incarcerative punishment and rehabilitation capacities. The development of community restitution programs can provide sanctioning alternatives for offenders and at the same time return some value to victims and the communities.

Implications

Change is not easy and prosecutors are likely to meet resistance on many fronts. First, the results produced by adopting a Strategic Problem Solving Model require time and persistence, as opposed to standard criminal prosecutions that are comparatively swift. The results can be difficult to measure and quantify and sometimes do not lend themselves to objective data collection. Success is more likely to be measured by how safe people in the community feel, for example. This sort of valuation can be problematic; given the huge caseloads which prosecutors must deal with, the pressure to produce quick results (quantity rather than quality) can quickly derail broader strategic goals.

Second, change requires a long and demanding learning curve. Prosecutors should learn a great deal more about the causes and effects of crime on their communities. And unfortunately, while the quality of the research on strategic prosecution and problem solving is improving, there is currently little hard data available. What does exist is often conflicting. Research may not yet have established a reliable set of performance indicators for each and every new strategic approach the prosecutor may wish to undertake. Often, prosecutors must get their education informally, from the community. This may of necessity involve communication and coordination with an alarming number of sources and organizations. Prosecutors may have to rely on systematic surveys of target areas to identify community sentiment, host focus groups and become more involved with neighborhood organizations and associations. This of course diverts resources away from the traditional mission of processing cases (that must still be maintained) towards the cause of effectuating civil order.

Third, prosecutors are apt to get resistance from their staff members. Prosecutors, for the most part, are blessed with a cadre of young, brilliant, energetic, public-spirited and highly motivated personnel. But, assistant prosecutors may have been lured into the office by television and law school visions of jury trials and courtroom drama. They may not share an interest in the more mundane tasks of analysis and innovation and even less interest in becoming a community mediator or point of contact during their off-hours. They are much more interested in prosecuting burglaries than dealing with juvenile truants, even though they probably know that daytime truancy is directly related to burglary rates. Motivating one's staff to value the higher principles involved in an overall crime reduction strategy may be the most important and difficult task that a prosecutor undertakes.

Fourth, the public may look askance at these new strategies, especially if they make prosecutors appear to be "soft" on crime. For example, so-called drug courts and other strategies that divert criminals away from incarceration are often perceived by the public as being "soft." Traditional attitudes like these will persist, and, over time, the prosecutor's motivations for innovation may succumb to the expectation that only criminal penalties should be pursued. For this reason, it is absolutely essential that the community and public are educated about the great potential to reduce crime that these strategies can offer.

Fifth, expansion of organizational boundaries causes bureaucratic strife. Innovations by the prosecutor may be considered presumptuous or threatening by other agencies. For example, even if the simple act of cleaning up an overgrown playground reduces crime, the public works department may worry that their turf has been unduly infringed upon. In such circumstances, it is important for the prosecutor to communicate with other agencies and institutions. Remember that the goal is to fortify and not usurp them. They may need to be reassured.

CONCLUSION

This broader Strategic Problem Solving Model propels the prosecutor into untraditional roles. Without reliable methods to measure results of these roles, prosecutors may take enormous risks when breaking out of the mold. But, given the tremendous social problems they face, avoiding these changes may be riskier yet. It may appear safer to stick with the tried-and-true methods, but by focusing exclusively on a case-processing strategy, prosecutors may actually do nothing to really reduce crime. Then, they are mere functionaries processing whatever crime-of-the-day gets dragged into the office. While it would be best if the neighborhood and government institutions functioned as they are supposed to, the prosecutor may be best suited to tackle the problems of a disordered society and to help restore the integrity of social and governmental institutions so that they can once again regulate themselves. Prosecutors enjoy a level of confidence by the public and possess moral authority—the bully pulpit—so they can focus support for an issue in a way that no other branch of government can. Prosecutors are often believed to be politically conservative. This is an advantage, as the public will give them certain latitude when they propose solutions that appear to be unconventional. Prosecutors possess extraordinary legal authority to confront problems. They have the power in the criminal justice system to impose solutions. Prosecutors are uniquely situated to influence other agencies' decisions and, because they have the ears of the legislative, executive and judicial branches of government, have access to potentially significant political support. In short, prosecutors are now called upon to provide hope for our future. Fortunately, they are up to the task.

... And without hope, there can be no justice.

ENDNOTES

[1] *Berger v. United States*, 295 US 78 (1935).

[2] See the *National District Attorneys Association* (NDAA) *National Prosecution Standards*, Standards 42 and 43.

[3] For an in depth discussion of the impact of "decision making" model of moral education in our schools, see Kilpatrick, William, *Why Johnny Can't Tell Right from Wrong*, New York: Touchstone Books, 1992.

[4] According to Kilpatrick, due to this failed philosophy of moral education, character education is making a comeback in our schools.

[5] The draft also provided a strong incentive for young men who wanted to avoid military service to excel at higher education and stay there.

[6] *Escobedo v. Illinois*, 378 U.S. 478 (1964).

[7] *Miranda v. Illinois*, 384 U.S. 436 (1966).

[8] *National Prosecution Standards*, Standard 40.

[9] The concepts expressed in the discussions of the Case Processing Model and of the prosecutor as problem solver are inspired in large part by the work of Ronald Goldstock, director of the New York State Organized Crime Task Force and professor of law at Cornell University School of Law and from the "Summary of the Proceedings: Findings and Discoveries of the Harvard University Executive Session for State and Local Prosecutors," John F. Kennedy School of Government, Harvard University, 1986-1990.

[10] This standard, pertaining to charging decisions, states "the prosecutor should exercise discretion in screening for the purpose of eliminating matters from the criminal justice system in which prosecution is not justified or not in the public interest. Factions which may be considered in the decision include… reluctance of a victim to cooperate in the prosecution."

HIGH ETHICAL STANDARDS: THE FOUNDATION FOR EVERY PROSECUTOR

By Douglas R. Roth, First Deputy District Attorney,
Sedgwick County, Wichita, Kansas

Introduction

Traditionally in the United States the role of an attorney (in a civil trial, anyway) is adversarial. It is presumed that if there is full discovery and if both sides conduct the trial as competitive adversaries that the truth will emerge and the party that *should* prevail *will* prevail. While this process and presumption is the foundation of our legal system, it creates unique problems for prosecutors. Prosecutors' responsibilities are different from other attorneys and more specifically, they are distinctly different from those of criminal defense attorneys. A prosecutor's responsibility is not only to represent the state and society but also to discover and disclose the truth and seek justice. Defense attorneys, undoubtedly from time to time have such an obligation but the prosecutor has (or should have) this in mind in each and every case. A prosecutor is not an ordinary party to a controversy but a representative of a sovereign whose obligation to govern impartially is as compelling as its obligation to govern at all.[1] Justice White in *United States v. Wade,* described the unusual position prosecutors have in our judicial system, writing that:

> "Law enforcement officers have the obligation to convict the guilty and to make sure they do not convict the innocent. They must be dedicated to making the criminal trial a procedure for ascertainment of the true facts surrounding the commission of the crime. To this extent, our so-called adversary system is not adversary at all; nor should it be."[2]

It is within this complicated framework of competing and conflicting interests that prosecutors must successfully discharge their duties.

Prosecutors are seen as leaders of the criminal justice system and, whether elected or appointed, they should conduct their professional and personal affairs in accordance with the highest ethical standards. The *Prosecutors Deskbook* cannot teach the personal commitment necessary for prosecutors to judiciously conduct their professional and personal lives; the motivation to make that commitment must come from each individual. Rather, the intention is that this article will provide a basis from which prosecutors can properly address many of the ethical issues that will confront them. It cannot provide answers to all of the ethical dilemmas that prosecutors will face; those answers are dependent upon the facts of each individual situation. Instead, it hopes to provide guidance for recognizing the ethical issues and locating the necessary resources to address and properly resolve those issues.

The starting point for addressing ethical questions should be the state rules that establish ethical standards governing attorney conduct. Since the *Model Rules of Professional Conduct (MRPC)* has been adopted in 38 states, it will be the authority most often cited in this chapter. State ethical and disciplinary codes are the minimum standard to be used but not the sole source that can aid prosecutors. The *National Prosecution Standards, Second Edition*, published by the National District Attorneys Association is also an excellent resource.

At a time when their motives appear to be under increasing attack, prosecutors should ensure that established ethical codes of conduct are the cornerstone of each professional decision they are called upon to make. Many prosecutors believe that they are increasingly being accused of alleged prosecutorial misconduct in what may be fast becoming a standard trial tactic for some defense attorneys. Perhaps the situation should be referred to as "prosecutorial error." Perhaps prosecutors should recognize the term "prosecutorial misconduct" for what it really is—incorrect, misleading and unnecessarily pejorative. (After all, we do not refer to an incorrect ruling by a trial judge as judicial misconduct.)

Usually this charge comes in the form of allegations before the court at the trial level and on appeal. Occasionally, in a noteworthy case, it occurs in the news media. It is of concern that the increasing barrage of misconduct allegations will harm the reputation of prosecutors and eventually negatively affect juries and the courts. A single, widely publicized case of actual misconduct can undo the goodwill and reputation built upon thousands of appropriately handled cases. Once a prosecutor's reputation has been tarnished it can be difficult, if not impossible, to rebuild.

By employing a thorough working knowledge of applicable legal and ethical standards, a prosecutor should be able to avoid the pitfalls of a misconduct determination. Given the adversarial nature of the legal system and the resourcefulness of some defendants, it can be difficult to escape every alleged violation. However, this article will provide prosecutors with ideas and resources that can help them avoid fueling the allegations.

TRAINING: THE FIRST STEP

The first step in protecting oneself from an allegation of unethical conduct is prevention and that requires training. Appropriate education is an important ingredient in a prevention program. Ethics education should not be viewed as a necessary evil or as yet another requirement of a mandated continuing legal education program. Rather, it should be the cornerstone of an office-wide professional training program. It is better to anticipate, research and consider an ethical question before the issue arises than to respond without the benefit of a well-planned, thought-out approach. Anticipating and preparing ahead of time how best to respond to an ethical dilemma thrust upon the prosecution during the heat of trial should be part of trial preparation. An office-training program should include review and discussion of hypothetical ethical problems along with frank dialogue about possible solutions. An in-house review of policies and cases should be made periodically to ensure that office performance is above the ethical standards established by the state disciplinary authority.

A TWENTY-FOUR-HOUR JOB

Attorneys are governed by professional standards in every aspect of their lives. The ethical standards established to guide and govern the profession do not just apply to their duties as attorneys. Ethical standards govern all aspects of the prosecutors' work, whether they are serving as investigators and administrators, preparing budgets, supervising personnel or even running for elective office. "All aspects" means exactly that. For example, during a recent county prosecutor's race in Kansas an attorney made false allegations about his opponent's position on the legalization of marijuana. The allegations were later proven to be without merit. That attorney was subsequently disciplined for his false statements.[3]

SANCTIONS

Failure to employ the highest ethical standards in the prosecutor's professional and personal life can result in the loss of a good reputation. If lost, it is seldom if ever regained. A court can impose sanctions in an appropriate ethics case up to and including dismissal. In addition, a prosecutor can suffer loss of a job or an election, reduced immunity from civil suit, and even legal action or Bar discipline that could include the loss of one's license to practice law.

WINNING REALLY ISN'T EVERYTHING

Every staff member should understand that the highest goal in a prosecutor's office is not to win every case. The United States Supreme Court, in *Berger v. United States*, expressed the standard for prosecutors by stating that the responsibility "in a criminal prosecution is not that it shall win a case, but that justice shall be done."[4] In order to operate an office in compliance with high ethical standards a prosecutor should demand the highest level of ethical performance from employees. They should be required to search for the truth, engage in fair play, protect everyone's rights, err on the side of caution, reject a "winning at all costs" attitude and lead by example. The "ends justify the means" attitude should be totally rejected. The fact that this will sometimes result in a loss of a case may be difficult to accept, especially if the result allows a guilty person to escape accountability for a crime. A difficult situation is created when the public's expectation of and right to a safe community suffers because a prosecutor has taken action that protects a criminal's constitutional or statutory rights. However, the prosecutor's duty to protect everyone's rights, including a guilty defendant's, should prevail. The system requires this. It can be a harsh responsibility.

PUBLICITY AND THE MEDIA

Like it or not, a good working relationship with the news media is a necessity, especially in those jurisdictions that elect their local prosecutor. However, maintenance of a good working relationship with the media should be subordinate to the need to preserve the privacy rights of all citizens. A prosecutor should never talk to a representative of the media without first having a thorough working knowledge of the state's ethical guidelines governing the public dissemination of information about a case and the law governing the privacy rights of victims, witnesses and suspects. Absolute immunity from civil liability does not attach to a prosecutor's release of information.[5]

MRPC 3.6 attempts to make a reasonable balance between the need to disseminate information to the public and the protection of a suspect's right to a fair trial. It permits a limited public release of information. Attorneys are cautioned that the rule also governs the release of information to non-media, including speeches to civic groups and even private discussions with individuals. Attorneys are not to release prohibited information that has a "substantial likelihood of materially prejudicing an adjudicative proceeding." Discussions with friends about the evidence that supports a case may violate the rule, especially in smaller jurisdictions in which dissemination of case facts, i.e., the suspect's confession, may travel by word of mouth until it reaches potential jurors.

One possible protection from a potential ethical violation for improperly releasing information is the creation of an office policy prohibiting employees from discussing cases with non-employees. However, any restraint on speech, such as this one, should be closely tied to its intended purpose and it should be enforceable. A blanket prohibition may be neither. Furthermore, it is recommended that every prosecutor's office designate a trained employee to handle all media releases and contacts not specifically reserved by the elected or appointed chief prosecutor.

Under MRPC 3.8(e), prosecutors have an additional responsibility to exercise reasonable care to prevent law enforcement, employees and others associated with a prosecution from violating MRPC 3.6. Prosecutors know only too well that limiting in any way the statements of law enforcement agencies is one of their most difficult tasks. An example of an MRPC 3.6 violation they may have seen is a law enforcement press conference that displays guns, money and drugs seized during a raid along with the names and/or mug shots of suspects expected to be prosecuted. A prosecutor's presence at such an event only makes the violation worse, as it adds additional credibility to what at that point are only allegations.

Law enforcement agencies that wish to obtain publicity for a successful investigation should be told to wait until the prosecution is completed. To meet the responsibilities under MRPC 3.6 and 3.8(e), every prosecutor's office, at a minimum, should provide local law enforcement agencies with a copy and explanation of MRPC 3.6 and a request that it be followed. The state agency or organization charged with disciplining attorneys for unethical conduct should be consulted for its opinion on the minimum steps that should be taken by a prosecutor in order to comply with Rule 3.8(e).

DISCOVERY AND EXCULPATORY EVIDENCE

Allegations that a prosecutor has failed to provide appropriate discovery remain a much-litigated issue in criminal cases. Policies in prosecutors' offices related to defense discovery range from providing the minimum required by law to an open-file policy that produces everything that is not work product or privileged. No matter what the policy, the most challenging issue remains the definition and production of exculpatory material. Production of this material is not only a legal and ethical question; it is also a constitutional requirement.

In *Brady v. Maryland*, the U. S. Supreme Court held that a prosecutor has a constitutional duty to provide the defense with evidence that is favorable to an accused if it is material to guilt or punishment.[6] See also *United States v. Bagley*, (evidence is material if there is some reasonable probability that the result of the proceeding would have been different if the evidence had been disclosed);[7] *Kyles v. Whitley*, (reasonable probability of a different result is established if the withholding of evidence undermines confidence in the outcome of the trial); *Kyles v. Whitley, supra* (prosecutor has a duty to learn of any favorable evidence known to persons acting on the government's behalf, including the police);[8] *United States v. Agurs*, (the duty to disclose *Brady* material is present even if the defendant has made no request for the material);[9] *United States v. Bagley, supra* (in meeting *Brady* obligations there is no difference between exculpatory and impeachment evidence).

Some evidence is easily recognized as exculpatory but often the exculpatory nature is less clear. Attorneys and judges struggle when attempting to determine whether evidence is *Brady* material requiring disclosure or something less. All prosecutors should have a thorough working knowledge of *Brady*, *Bagley*, *Kyles* and other related cases.

Prosecutors should avoid the temptation of making a self-determination that the possible exculpatory evidence is not credible or admissible and therefore does not need to be disclosed to the defense. The test under *Brady* is not whether the evidence is admissible. Potentially exculpatory evidence should still meet all the standards for admissibility before a jury will learn of its existence. As with all evidence, admissibility is determined by the court. Production of potentially exculpatory evidence is not a concession to defense counsel or the court that it is admissible or that the standard for admission is somehow lessened. Even if the exculpatory evidence is not admissible a prosecutor should investigate its reliability to determine if the case should go forward. Given a prosecutor's duty to seek the truth and to not convict innocent persons, the firm belief that a particular defendant is guilty should always be subject to reasonable review and re-evaluation, if required.

MRPC 3.4 requires counsel to make a reasonably diligent effort to comply with legally proper discovery requests. It also prohibits an attorney from obstructing another party's access to evidence. This includes access to witnesses.

Prosecutors routinely encounter witnesses and victims who may not want to talk to defense counsel or investigators prior to trial. Sometimes, to avoid pressure, a witness will decline to be interviewed and then suggest that the refusal is pursuant to the prosecutor's instructions, leading to allegations that the prosecutor is hiding information or preventing the defendant from preparing an adequate defense. Unless required by court order or statute, witnesses usually cannot be forced to talk to defense counsel or prosecutors out of court. But under MRPC 3.4 an attorney cannot request that a person not give relevant information to another party. The best practice for prosecutors is to instruct witnesses, preferably in writing, that they *may* talk with defense representatives if they choose to but that they are not obligated to.

A prosecutor's duty to seek justice never ends. Therefore, the duty to provide exculpatory evidence is enduring in nature and does not end after conviction and appeal. When a witness changes his or her earlier testimony, and when this meets the *Brady* test, that alteration should be promptly reported to defense counsel and the court, even though this may result in additional post-trial litigation.

CONTACTS WITH REPRESENTED PARTIES

A prosecutor's ethical responsibilities during contacts with represented persons, whether suspects, defendants or witnesses, is one of the more problematic areas encountered. What may be constitutionally permissible activity for law enforcement officers may not be ethically permissible for prosecutors. Generally, an attorney may not communicate with a party represented by counsel about the subject matter of the representation without consent of counsel, unless the law otherwise authorizes the contact. See MRPC 4.2. A prosecutor is prohibited from knowingly violating the rule through the use or intervention of others, including law enforcement officers. See MRPC 8.4. While violation of MRPC 4.2 and 8.4 may not result in suppression of evidence, it may result in disciplinary sanctions.

Non-custodial communications with represented persons during the investigative stage before a criminal action has begun may not violate the ethical standards of the many states that prohibit contact with persons represented by an attorney. When those contacts are legally permissible they fall under the "authorized by law" exception contained in MRPC 4.2. A thorough review of constitutional and statutory law applicable to contact with represented persons should be made before a prosecutor travels into this controversial area. The wrong decision can result in suppression of evidence and/or disciplinary sanctions for ethical violations.

Recognition that a prosecutor cannot initiate contact with a represented witness, suspect or defendant regarding the subject matter of the representation is relatively easy. The more difficult (or tempting) situation involves a represented suspect who initiates and requests contact with a prosecutor or law enforcement officer. Ethically a prosecutor must decline the request to have contact. If notified by law enforcement officers of a similar request to them, a prosecutor should advise the officers to refuse the request. Unless the representation has been terminated, the contact may not take place. Furthermore, it may not be "suggested" by prosecutors or law enforcement officers that the representation should be terminated.

Frequently, law enforcement officers and prosecutors need to discuss with a defendant matters unrelated to a pending criminal charge against that particular defendant. This usually involves other crimes committed or witnessed by the represented person. Contact is ethically permitted if it concerns matters not covered by the representation. The critical issue to be resolved prior to the contact is the complete extent of the representation. Usually, with court-appointed counsel, it involves the case covered by the appointment and related matters. With retained counsel this determination becomes more difficult, especially if no case is yet pending or when there is a history of representation of the person by the same attorney. If there is uncertainty, it must be resolved before there is contact with the suspect or witness. Even if the matter to be discussed is unrelated to the representation it can quickly evolve into one that will involve the representation. The suspect or witness will usually want some type of consideration regarding the matter covered by the representation in return for his or her cooperation. The prosecutor must be prepared for this change in circumstances and be ready to immediately back out, if necessary, if the discussion with the represented person suddenly becomes related to the representation.

EX PARTE COMMUNICATIONS

Generally, *ex parte* communications with the court regarding a pending matter are prohibited. If this should occur, the communicating attorney must immediately notify the other parties of the nature and circumstances of the communication. Without vigilance by the court and the attorneys this is a prohibition that is easily broken, especially by those prosecutors and defense attorneys who appear daily before the same courts.

The situation becomes even more difficult if the court initiates the *ex parte* communication. What attorney wants to risk offending a judge by (correctly) telling the court that a matter should not be discussed because opposing counsel is not present?

Nevertheless, counsel must respectfully remind the court that defense counsel should be contacted and be given an opportunity to participate.

The nature of *ex parte* proceedings and communications keeps one or more parties from providing input to the court. For this reason, attorneys having permissible *ex parte* contact with the court have an expanded responsibility to make a full disclosure to the court of material and relevant facts, especially those that are adverse. For prosecutors, this issue most frequently arises when seeking search and arrest warrants. MRPC 3.3(d) addresses the issue for all attorneys by requiring lawyers to inform the court of all known material facts, even those adverse, that are needed by the court to make an informed decision. This includes evidence that tends to reduce or defeat probable cause for the search or arrest warrant. The obligation is on the prosecutor to present the court with exculpatory evidence at the *ex parte* probable cause determination. In addition to disciplinary sanctions against the prosecutor, the failure to provide the court with all known adverse material facts can result in a later suppression of evidence seized pursuant to the search warrant or obtained after the arrest.

In addition to losing credibility with the court for withholding evidence in an *ex parte* contact a prosecutor also can lose his or her immunity from civil liability. In *Burns v. Reed*, the U. S. Supreme Court ruled a prosecutor was entitled to absolute immunity for his participation in withholding material evidence from the court in an *ex parte* judicial hearing seeking a warrant.[10] However, a review of the *Burns* case and subsequent decisions reveal that had the prosecutor withheld the evidence in a non-judicial setting or advised the police to withhold the evidence, the absolute immunity would have been lost. Even if a prosecutor is able to escape liability based on immunity, he or she may still be subject to disciplinary sanctions. In fact, courts frequently regard disciplinary proceedings as an alternative sanction method for prosecutors who have engaged in improper or illegal actions but who nonetheless have immunity from civil liability for those same actions.

CANDOR

In order for the court to make correct decisions, it is important that it know all the relevant and applicable facts and law applicable to the matter under consideration. While it is not expected that attorneys will intentionally present evidence contrary to their client's position, it is required that they notify the court of known applicable law that is adverse to the client's position if opposing counsel does not make the notification. *See* MRPC 3.3. This candor is extended to *ex parte* hearings. Under no circumstances should a court be misled regarding the facts or the law. The court can be misled not only by a positive verbal or written representation but also by silence when there is a duty to speak.

Prosecutors drafting search warrant applications that use information provided by confidential informants should be careful to protect the identity of the informant from discovery. Providing too much information in the probable cause affidavit may enable suspects to deduce the informant's identity. However, at the same time the prosecutor has the duty to provide to the court all material and relevant evidence so that it can make an independent finding of probable cause, ethical considerations require the presentation of adverse evidence that may mitigate or negate that probable cause. Sometimes this requirement—to satisfy both legal and ethical considerations—increases to an unacceptable level and the likelihood is that the suspect will discover the informant's identity. In this circumstance, the prosecutor should not proceed without first reviewing the matter with law enforcement and the informant to determine if disclosure of the informant's identity is a danger and, if so, whether the search warrant request should be withdrawn.

The prosecutor may not misrepresent the facts in order to protect the identity of the informant. There is a huge distinction between providing general information in order to make it difficult to determine the identity of an informant, and making false representations to the court to protect that identity.

CONFLICTS OF INTEREST

The prohibition against an attorney's involvement in cases in which there is a conflict of interest can affect a part-time prosecutor. Many states and jurisdictions employ part-time prosecutors. Given the need to supplement a part-time salary, the prosecutor may be tempted to ignore the prohibition and get involved in a matter that conflicts with his or her position. Many conflict of interest situations can be resolved by obtaining from the clients a knowing waiver of the conflict. *See* MRPC 1.7. However, a prosecutor cannot waive, on behalf of the prosecutor's office, a conflict of interest that has arisen by virtue of the prosecutor's private civil practice.

A full-time prosecutor can encounter another conflict of interest problem when leaving government service for private employment. Involvement in cases one previously handled as a prosecutor is prohibited. Involvement by the former prosecutor's new firm is also prohibited unless the firm qualifies for a waiver of the conflict of interest. *See* MRPC 1.11. Of course, an attorney may not negotiate employment with the defendant or defense counsel during prosecution of the case.

THE PROSECUTOR AS WITNESS

Besides the obvious risk that the court and jury may not believe them, there are several reasons why prosecutors are prohibited from testifying in cases handled by them. In *United States v. Birdman,* the court discussed four reasons to prohibit the practice: the risk the prosecutor will not testify objectively; the risk the prosecutor's testimony will be improperly enhanced; the risk of giving the prosecutor's trial argument testimonial value; and, the risk that public confidence in the justice system will be undermined.[11] Under MRPC 3.7 a prosecutor is permitted to testify in a matter in which he or she is an advocate if it relates to an uncontested issue. However, state rules and court decisions should be consulted before embarking down this treacherous road. Realistically, there is seldom an uncontested matter in a criminal trial. Furthermore, expect the matter to become contested as soon as a prosecutor tries to testify. Even if it involves uncontested matters the practice is closely scrutinized by courts and risks the reversal of a conviction.

It is not unusual for a trial prosecutor to be placed in a difficult situation when a witness testifies about a material fact and that testimony is contrary to the witness's statement given earlier during the pretrial interview. The party hurt by the new, changed testimony may wish the prosecutor to testify about the prior inconsistent statement. (Remember, if the new, changed testimony hurts the defense, that prior inconsistent statement should be disclosed under *Brady.*) Unfortunately, there is no perfect solution to this dilemma. A smart trial attorney interviews witnesses *before* their testimony is offered in court. The best manner to reduce the risk of inconsistency is to always have a third person—an investigator or a police officer—present during that interview, especially when the case involves unpredictable, unreliable witnesses who will testify about material facts.

Generally an entire prosecutor's office is not disqualified from a case because one of the office's prosecutors is likely to be called as a witness. *See* MRPC 3.7. This rule, however, may vary from state to state.

THE RIGHTS OF THIRD PERSONS

Would it make the job easier if law enforcement officers and prosecutors did not have to obtain search warrants or subpoenas in order to obtain evidence from third parties? Perhaps. However, the easy way is usually not lawful. Meeting constitutional and statutory requirements and protections mandates the involvement of a detached magistrate. This obvious check on unbridled police power is a necessary burden. Sometimes prosecutors are approached by law enforcement officers with requests to proceed in a manner that bypasses or circumvents the involvement of a detached magistrate. This type of request often arises with requests to conduct a warrantless search of a third person's house or vehicle in order to obtain evidence that may incriminate a suspect who will probably lack standing to contest the search. It has also come as a request for permission to confront a business owner in order to obtain a suspect's records, i.e., medical, phone or financial records, without the use of a subpoena or warrant.

No matter what form the temptation to improperly or illegally expedite an investigation takes, the prosecutor should insist that only lawful means be used. Prosecutors are expected and required to act in a manner that does not violate the legal rights of third parties. They cannot engage in actions that have no substantial purpose other than to embarrass, delay or burden a third party. *See* MRPC 4.4.

Almost every action taken by a prosecutor will affect someone's legal rights. When that person is a suspect, an attorney will likely enter the case at some point to protect and assert his or her rights. Often that is not the case with third parties, who may be witnesses, friends, family, employers or businesses that are involved with the suspect, and prosecutors should be vigilant not to jeopardize their rights.

Another area that can create a problem for prosecutors is their relationship with victims. Victims can misinterpret the role of a prosecutor in "representing" them in a criminal case; they may feel that the prosecutor is "their" attorney. Therefore, caution should be taken to prevent any misunderstanding as to the identity of the prosecutor's true client. While many of the goals of the prosecutor and victim may be the same, the prosecutor is *not* the victim's attorney. In *State ex rel. Romley v. Superior Court of Maricopa County*, the defense claimed that the many rights extended to the victim along with corresponding duties imposed upon the prosecutor rendered the prosecutor the de facto victim's attorney.[12] The Arizona Court of Appeals ruled that a prosecutor does not "represent" the crime victim but instead represents all persons, including the defendant and his family. The victim or other third party in a criminal case should be instructed to consult with private counsel on any matters involving their legal rights or private causes of action.

SUPERVISORY ISSUES

Supervising attorneys should make reasonable efforts to ensure that subordinate attorneys act in an ethical manner. A supervising attorney is responsible for another attorney's ethical violation if he or she orders or ratifies the unethical conduct and furthermore has the obligation to take remedial action if the unethical conduct is discovered at a time when the consequences can be avoided or mitigated. *See* MRPC 5.1.

A lawyer is not excused from unethical actions because they were undertaken at the direction of another unless it was done at the direction of a supervising attorney as a reasonable attempt to resolve an arguable question of professional duty. *See* MRPC 5.2.

REPORTING MISCONDUCT

Although the requirements vary from jurisdiction to jurisdiction, attorneys have the general responsibility to report misconduct and ethical violations to whatever authority has the duty to investigate and discipline unethical conduct. Since to a large degree the integrity of the profession relies on self-policing, the responsibility to report violations should not be taken lightly. However, as a practical matter attorneys are often reluctant to report other attorneys, especially if it does not involve a major breach or prejudice their case.

This problem is especially difficult for prosecutors. No matter when or how a prosecutor reports unethical conduct to the disciplinary authority, defense counsel will attack the motives of the prosecutor who makes the report. If alleged unethical conduct is addressed while the criminal case is pending, defense counsel might claim the prosecutor is merely trying to intimidate the defendant and defense counsel so that they fail to mount an aggressive defense. If the conduct involves an alleged conflict of interest, defense counsel might proclaim an improper attempt to interfere with the defendant's choice of counsel and cause his or her removal. If the conduct is reported after the criminal case is concluded, defense counsel might assert that the prosecutor made the allegation to "get even" for an aggressive (or perhaps successful) defense.

In addition to having a thorough working knowledge of the state's misconduct reporting requirements, it is recommended that prosecutors also contact representatives of the entity empowered to investigate and discipline attorneys. Prosecutors should make themselves aware of that entity's preference for the type and timing of complaints.

After a prosecutor files a report of unethical conduct against a defense attorney, the respondent may counterclaim and allege that the prosecutor's office has also engaged in unethical conduct. This possibility should not dissuade prosecutors from reporting unethical conduct when called for. It should motivate prosecutors to ensure, through training and supervision, that their own "house" is in order.

As leaders of the criminal justice system, prosecutors should conduct their professional and personal affairs in accordance with the highest ethical standards. The starting point for addressing ethical questions should be state ethical and disciplinary codes that govern attorney conduct. From there, prosecutors should educate their staff to follow the ethical codes and make every effort to establish them as the cornerstone of all professional decisions.

ENDNOTES

[1] *Berger v. United States*, 295 U.S. 78 (1935); *Strickler v. Greene*, 527 U.S. ____ (1999).

[2] Justice White, *United States v. Wade*, 388 U.S. 218 (1967).

[3] *In re Johnson*, 729 P.2d 1175 (Kan. 1986).

[4] *Berger v. United States*, 295 U.S. 78 (1935).

[5] *Buckley v. Fitzsimmons*, 509 U.S. 259 (1993).

[6] *Brady v. Maryland*, 373 U.S. 83 (1963).

[7] *United States v. Bagley*, 473 U.S. 667 (1985).

[8] *Kyles v. Whitley*, 514 U.S. 419 (1995).

[9] *United States v. Agurs*, 427 U.S. 97 (1976).

[10] *Burns v. Reed*, 500 U.S. 478 (1991).

[11] *United States v. Birdman*, 602 F.2d 547 (3d Cir. 1979).

[12] *State ex rel. Romley v. Superior Court of Maricopa County*, 891 P. 2d 246 (Ariz. 1994).

The American Prosecutor in Historical Context

By Joan E. Jacoby, Executive Director, Jefferson Institute for Justice Studies, Washington, D.C.

Introduction[1]

The American prosecutor enjoys independence and a wealth of discretionary power unmatched in the world. With few exceptions, the prosecutor is a locally elected official and the chief law enforcement official of the community. The American prosecutor represents a local jurisdiction and his or her office is endowed with unreviewable discretionary authority. Nowhere else in the world does this combination of features define prosecution.

If there is no other prosecutor like this then where did the office come from and what was it that gave this position this unique set of features? There has been continuous interest—and even controversy—about the origins of the prosecutor. Historians have variously pictured the prosecutor as having descended from one of the three European nations that had a substantial impact on the early development of the American nation. They have claimed that the prosecutor descended from the English attorney general, the French *procureur publique,* and even the Dutch *schout.* Although a number of convincing arguments can be developed to demonstrate the influence of all three heritages on American criminal justice, no compelling theory has been forwarded that shows a direct line from any one European precursor to the American prosecutor. The fact is that while many features of these predecessors may be found in the American prosecutor, the role, powers and authority of the office reflect an amalgam of forces not exclusive to any of them.

The American prosecutor has the power, like the *procureur,* to initiate all public prosecutions; he or she is a local official of regional government like the *schout;* he or she has the power to terminate all criminal prosecutions like the attorney general. But as much as the prosecutor has these features, the roots of the office cannot be attributed to any single source. Rather, it reflects the same forces that fostered the American revolution, conquered the vast open spaces of the west and espoused the principles of democracy, namely, the right of the people to have a voice in the government process and a belief in a system of checks and balances.

This article traces the development of the American prosecutor, showing how the office came to assume its present role and examining the influences that produced the essential features of the modern prosecutor. It explores the historical context that changed the face of prosecution. Previous theories are presented about the origins of the American prosecutor that show how little is known about its historical development. It sets the stage for the birth of the American prosecutor by focusing on the first step that occurred when the colonies adopted a system of public, not private, prosecution.

It explores why prosecution is local in nature, not centralized at the federal level. It examines the forces that made the office of the prosecutor elective. Finally, it traces the controversial history of the prosecutor's discretionary power, namely the unreviewable authority to bring charges or dismiss them. By the end of the article, the hope is that all prosecutors will have a richer understanding of their roots and the history of events that created this uniquely American institution. By describing the dynamics of this development process, prosecutors may be better able to examine present day issues within a historical context.

PREVIOUS STUDIES ABOUT THE ORIGINS OF THE AMERICAN PROSECUTOR

In 1620, the estimated population of the colonies was 2,500. By the end of the century (1690) the colonial population had increased almost one hundred-fold, numbering about 213,500. Bear in mind, however, that the rapidly growing colonial population was dispersed over widely separated regions. In 1700, Boston had a colonial population of 7,000; New York, 5,000; Philadelphia reported 700 houses and Charleston, South Carolina had 250 families. [2]

By 1790, a new nation had been formed in North America. Following a revolution, a peace treaty and the election of our first American president, the first census estimated a population of 3.9 million that included 698,000 slaves and 65,000 free Negroes. During this period, the office of the American prosecutor was born and was given a set of characteristics that would ultimately make it unlike any other prosecutor in the modern world.

The prosecuting attorney did not descend from any one particular institution at any one time or place. While much remains unclear or undocumented, some facts are known. It can be safely said that: there was no figure like the prosecutor at

Jamestown or Plymouth; by the time of the revolution, an officer with some of his basic characteristics had appeared in various colonies; and, by the Civil War there were district attorneys quite like those in the present era.

The few attempts at recording the history and development of the American prosecutor have been inaccurate or incomplete. A summary published in the *Missouri Crime Survey* in 1926 was one of the first to describe the origins of the American prosecutor. The summary was not a scholarly study but simply stated that the American public prosecutor was descended from a "chief prosecuting officer in England... whose duties for centuries have been the prosecution of crimes and misdemeanors."[3] This assertion was inaccurate since England did not adopt a system of public prosecution of crimes until 1879, only 47 years before the publication of the *Missouri Crime Survey*.[4]

In 1931, the Wickersham *Report on Prosecution* attempted to clarify the forces influencing the development of prosecution. In a longer and more detailed report, the commission noted that American criminal justice differed from the English tradition in that the British used a system of private prosecution whereby individual citizens hired lawyers to press prosecutions of crimes they had suffered. The report concluded that the concept of a public officer to conduct prosecutions had been borrowed from the French after the American Revolution, when French institutions were in favor and British institutions were unpopular.[5]

Although this theory had some merit, it overlooked the facts that public prosecution had preceded the American Revolution and that public officers conducted prosecutions 75 years before the French influenced the young American republic. It also failed to account for crucial differences between the French *procureur* who was part of a national civil service hierarchy with very little freedom of action and the American prosecutor who, even then, was an independent, local officer.

Another highly provocative theory was forwarded in 1952 by W. Scott Van Alstyne writing in the *Wisconsin Law Review*.[6] Van Alstyne argued that the prosecuting attorney was an office that resulted from Dutch influence. Early Dutch settlers, scattered along the American seaboard from Delaware to Connecticut, had utilized a local prosecuting official called the "*schout*." Van Alstyne documented colonial records indicating the existence of the *schout* in at least five of the original colonies. Unfortunately, the Dutch settlements had a short life and their influence on criminal justice and prosecution could not be directly linked to the American prosecutor.

The most comprehensive study of the possible historical origins of the American prosecutor was prepared in 1976 by Jack Kress of the State University of New York.[7] Kress concluded that the truth about the three theories of development lay in a combination of factors and influences. His analysis suggested that the development of the prosecutor could be traced by integrating the various factors that influenced the evolution of the office rather than by trying to force the modern prosecutor into a narrow historical framework. Kress's approach is the one adopted for this study. The prosecutor and prosecution are presented within their historical context, i.e., within the legal institutions and choices available to the early American colonists.

It is the choices that produce the most interesting insights into the development of the American prosecutor. Why was one feature selected and not others? Were all the decisions deliberate or did some come about as a natural extension of our society's development? By examining the choices and the forces that made them acceptable, we can see how they combine into our modern system of prosecution.

PRIVATE VERSUS PUBLIC PROSECUTION

The fundamental, differentiating factor in American criminal law lies in the adoption of a system of public prosecution. The public prosecutor is not part of America's heritage from British common law. As Professor Kress stated, the district attorney appears to be "a distinctive and uniquely American contribution... whereas Americans typically describe their legal system as based upon English common law, in terms of both its procedural attributes and substantive penal codes, the public prosecutor is a figure virtually unknown to the English system, which is primarily one of private prosecution to this day."[8]

The origin of a public prosecutor presents something of a historical and social puzzle. What is clear is that private prosecution was inconsistent with the American concept of a democratic process. Although private prosecution prevailed in the English world at the time of the establishment of the first American colonies in Jamestown and Plymouth, it never took root in the colonies. By 1704, one colony, Connecticut, had adopted a system of public prosecution and all others would soon follow.

There are clear differences between a system of private prosecution and a public one both in concept and operations. The British system of private prosecution developed from a social and governmental environment that had its roots in medieval rather than modern social contracts and was designed to protect the monarch, not the individual. The court system that evolved was one that pitted individual against individual. English common law did not make the sharp division between civil wrongs and criminal wrongs. All violations of law were wrongs committed by an individual against an individual. As a result, English justice was a system whereby the individual protected himself and avenged himself in the courts because he could not rely on the strength and security of societal protection. It was a system designed to protect *property* in a society based on *property*. As a result it became a system of government "of the rich and by the rich" but then, so too was the medieval English society in which it first developed.[9]

As the English legal system developed and became more complex, the professional bar grew and adapted, serving as prosecutors for individual clients. No lawyer was elected or appointed to serve as a representative of the county, the court, the town or the government. Rather, individual solicitors and barristers were hired to prosecute individual cases in the same manner as they were for any other legal matter. The conduct of prosecution (until 1885) was never "in the hands of any special body of counsel dedicated to that particular class of work... there is nothing which corresponds to the District Attorney in the United States."[10]

The French had operated under a similar system beginning in the twelfth century; but, over the next three hundred years, they began to adopt public prosecution in progressive stages. Eventually, they abandoned the private system, retaining private complaint only as a method of correcting a neglectful prosecutor.[11] The Dutch and Germans adopted similar and related forms of public prosecution.

The idea of private prosecution is alien to modern America, as is its basic supposition that crime is essentially a private concern between the aggressor and the victim. The concept of criminal justice that developed in the United States proclaims the opposite view. The American system conceives the criminal act to be a public occurrence and society as a whole to be the ultimate victim.

There are few vestiges of private prosecution in the United States today. Few states allow the use of private prosecutors, and those that do restrict their participation to limited types of cases. The opposition to private prosecution has also been clearly and consistently demonstrated by court decisions. In several states, convictions were overturned in cases where private counsel was hired to pursue a prosecution.

In the opinion of the Wisconsin courts in the *State v. Peterson,* such practice was contrary to "state policy."[12]

In 1921, the Connecticut courts made the definitive statement in opposition to private prosecution in *Mallory v. Lane.* The opinion of the court stated, in part:

> In all criminal cases in Connecticut, the state is the prosecutor. The offenses are against the state. The victim of the offense is not a party to the prosecution, nor does he occupy any relation to it other than that of a witness, an interested witness mayhaps, but none the less, only a witness. It is not necessary for the injured party to make complaint nor is he required to give bond to prosecute. He is in no sense a relator. He cannot in any way control the prosecution and whether reluctant or not, he can be compelled like any other witness to appear and testify. The Peace is that state and sense of safety which is necessary to the comfort and happiness of every citizen and which government is instituted to secure.[13]

When the earliest settlers of America rejected the premise of private prosecution, they set in motion a series of events that ultimately produced a uniquely American prosecutor who was characterized by being a locally, elected official. This article documents how prosecutors emerged and became instruments of local governments that were firmly established in the colonies long before the American Revolution began and the United States was created.

THE EMERGENCE OF LOCAL PROSECUTORS

This section describes the forces that created the local courts and justice systems from which the local sheriff and the local prosecutor emerged. It examines the period from 1600 to 1750 when local governments waxed strong; English and Dutch judicial systems were adapted to meet local needs; courts were decentralized and grand juries were added. The result was to create two new faces in the justice system—local sheriffs and prosecutors.

From the beginning, the colonization of America fostered a spirit of independence among its new immigrants that was reinforced by the geographic dispersion of the colonies over more than two thousand miles along the eastern seaboard of North America. Although they shared British norms and traditions and a system of jurisprudence based on English common law, their isolation from each other and England sparked the emergence of strong and independent forms of local government. "The heritage of English ideas that went with the institutions was so rich and varied that Americans were able to select and develop those that best suited their situations and forget others that meanwhile were growing prominent in the mother country... The New England town, for example... set New Englanders off not only from Englishmen, but from Virginians."[14]

English royal power would increase the size of the colonies in the eighteenth century, but it could not control the emergence of a basic local populism that remained dominant until the American Revolution.[15] Influenced by geography, a spirit of independence and a rich cultural heritage, the early residents created local government bodies, established local courts and as part of this process, created a local public prosecutor.

In many ways, the rise of local independence was as much a result of neglect by the monarchy and the British government as it was an exercise of the independent nature of the colonists. British disinterest allowed the colonists to devise a judicial system that would be consistent with their beliefs and the assumptions of public prosecution that they had adopted at the outset. "The British government claimed the sole right to create courts, and the early courts except in the charter and proprietary colonies, were created by executive action. However, after the initial settlement, the judiciary received little attention from the King, and colonial courts were left to evolve without much thought or consideration. England never tried to make the judicial system in the colonies uniform."[16]

In the early 1600s, the first courts reflected the simple nature of colonial society with its small population. They were tribunals held by the governor of the newly formed colony with all procedure copied directly from the English common law. Prosecution of criminal offenses consisted of charges being brought to the attention of the courts by individuals who had been wronged and who sought redress. There was no formal system of advocacy, no trained bar and no public official to bring charges. Nor was there a separation of powers or functions. The first court was held in the Virginia colony, where after 1619, the governor sat regularly with his council and the elected burgesses to decide criminal cases. Their procedures mirrored the British government where there was substantial involvement by the executive and legislative branches with the judicial branch of government.

In 1636, the Massachusetts Bay Colony modeled its court system after the rural British justice of the peace courts.[17] With a larger population (numbering about seven thousand), the colony was able to support a professional judiciary even at that time. "The colonists' substantial adaptation of the machinery of criminal justice as administered by the English justices of the peace was apparently deliberate. It was what they were used to, and, as the system developed… it provided wide latitude for the exercise of magisterial discretion; consequently it comported well with the leaders' ideas about the functions of government and law."[18]

Some of the other colonies experimented for short times with more unorthodox alternatives to British law. For example, in the colony at Newport, Rhode Island, in 1639 there was a brief attempt at government by arbitration. However, by the time Newport City was founded in 1640, this had quickly given way to the simple justice of the peace court system.[19]

As the populations in the New World grew and settlements spread west, the courts reorganized. In 1691, the New York colony established a complex two-tiered system with courts of original jurisdiction in all outlying counties and an appellate court in New York. Maryland and Massachusetts made similar changes the following year; Pennsylvania followed in 1702; Virginia, in 1705; and South Carolina, in 1721.

The century's emerging justice system was also influenced by Dutch jurisprudence and would eventually produce a sheriff and a prosecutor. The Dutch colonies of New York and New Jersey were familiar with Dutch law and the duties of the Dutch judicial officer, the *schout*.[20] The first courts in New Amsterdam (1653) and Bergen (1661) consisted of a director general, three magistrates and a presiding officer, the *schout*, whose duties in the court were to present criminal charges against alleged criminals. The *schout* was a combination constable and court officer with limited discretion in charging. He presented the case against the defendant and notified all accused of the charges being leveled against them. He had some powers of arrest and was involved in the collection of evidence, but he served more as a central figure that controlled access to the court than as an officer who initiated prosecutions.

Early records of the New Amsterdam court show that the first *schout*, Cornelius Van Tienhoven, appeared as plaintiff in a criminal trial for the first time on February 17, 1653, and consistently thereafter in most criminal matters until his replacement in 1665. *Schouts* remained in office for the next 20 years and even weathered the change of flags over the colony. In 1664, the English captured the settlement in the name of the crown and the Duke of York. Under the interim code of law known as the "Duke's Law" the *schout* remained as an officer of the court.

In 1674 English common law was established in New York, New Jersey and in other former Dutch settlements in Delaware and Pennsylvania. Although the title of *schout* disappeared, his function as police-prosecutor was carried on through the office of the sheriff. When the propriety of this was questioned for lack of precedent in the English courts, "the Governor's council issued a plainly-worded reply which stated that the sheriff was to put the law into execution, apprehend and prosecute viola-tors."[21]

The separation of the police-prosecutor functions was not clearly distinguished in the early days. Records exist of an ordinance established by the English governor of Newcastle, Delaware, in 1676 directing the sheriff to act as principal officer in the execution of the laws. Subsequent records show him acting as the prosecutor in a notorious murder case in the Newcastle courts. In 1686 the Quaker communities of Burlington, New Jersey, and in 1687, the county of Philadelphia, both established the position of county prosecutor. Both towns were in close geographic proximity to former Dutch settlements in whose courts *schouts* had conducted prosecutions only 10 years earlier.

Still the Dutch colonies did not have hegemony over this new form of public prose-cution. Parallel changes were taking place in colonies where the English influence was primary. In these colonies, the office of the attorney general underwent adjustment. Virginia's first attorney general was an agent for the monarchy. In 1643 Richard Lee was appointed to the courts as a representative of the crown. Lee's primary responsi-bility in the court was advisory and most of his formal duties were corresponding with legal authorities in England to get opinions on certain points of law. Lee became involved in criminal matters only where an alleged violation of the law directly involved the royal interest, which was infrequent. So strong was his advisory role that he was not required to be at court. In fact, the attorney general of Virginia was not even required to live at the capital in Williamsburg, where court was held until 1670.

Change in his role was rapid. By 1670 the attorney general was ordered to appear in the Court of Oyer and Terminar during all trials and to relocate his residency to the capital. By 1687 Virginia had deputy attorneys general for courts in the outlying counties, and by 1711, both the attorney general and his deputies were handling all serious criminal trials, although less serious matters were still being handled summarily by the magistrate of the court.

In other colonies the role of the attorney general in criminal matters had been more active than was traditional in England or had been the case in Virginia from the beginning. William Calvert, the first attorney general of Maryland and the brother of the governor, assumed much more than an advisory responsibility.[22] Appointed in 1666, Calvert was responsible for presenting criminal indictments to the grand jury and sat on the court as a member of the Governor's Council during all criminal trials. In 1687, in the same year that Philadelphia County appointed its own prosecuting officer, the English governor of Pennsylvania appointed David Lloyd to be attorney general of the colony. Lloyd, in turn, appointed deputies for the county courts, each of whom had some limited responsibility for criminal prosecutions.[23]

New Hampshire existed for its first 45 years without an attorney general. The post was created in 1683 and, at once, the attorney general was charged with the responsibility for presenting all cases before the grand jury.[24] The Carolinas' Acts of 1738 created the post of attorney general and allowed for deputies in all county courts. Prosecutions were brought almost exclusively by these men. "There were important changes in the court's procedures for exercising its criminal jurisdiction. For the first time the court has a prosecuting attorney, a deputy appointed by the attorney general for each county."[25]

Once deputy attorneys general were assigned permanently to local county courts, it was not unusual for them to be considered instruments of local rather than central government. Part of this perception was due to the rampant march toward local government and local control; part stemmed from the inconvenience of servicing a centralized court system. For example, even after court reorganization in Virginia in 1705, it was not uncommon for a retinue of 10 to 20 citizens from an outlying county to spend days on the road traveling to Williamsburg for a serious trial. Without proper legal counsel and expert magistrates, the citizens were cautious about local trials where harsh punishment might be the result for the accused. So all serious cases were heard in Williamsburg; the occasion of the trial required that the prisoner, his guards, the local sheriff, the accuser, all witnesses and a jury of six or 12 men be sent from the rural counties to the capital.[26] Ultimately, the difficulty of the logistics favored local trials and supported the need for local legal expertise.

Some changes in the justice system were instigated by the increased use of grand juries that sparked requests for jury trials and the need for a professional buffer between the grand jury and the courts. In the early courts the magistrates or justices handled criminal offenses in a summary fashion. By the mid 1700s, however, presentment by grand jury was as common a method of bringing charges as were indictments and informations. But the power of the grand jury was often criticized for inflicting its personal biases and dislikes on the court and increasing the number of jury trials. "At Plymouth Colony, presentment by the grand jury was tantamount to conviction unless a traverse was had, and then there was trial by jury."[27] Jury trials had been uncommon in North Carolina prior to 1739 when the county court began to summon the grand jury and to "have criminal cases tried before a jury by a public prosecutor."[28]

In the formative years between 1650 and 1750, it did not take long for local public prosecutors to emerge either as officers of the court or representatives of the attorney general. Connecticut was the first colony to establish county attorneys as prosecutors. William Pitkin, the first prosecutor, was appointed at Hartford in 1662. In 1704 Connecticut also became the first colony to entirely eliminate the system of private prosecution by establishing public prosecutors as adjuncts to all county courts. The statute of 1704 states: "Henceforth there shall be in every county a sober, discreet and religious person appointed by the county court to be attorney for the Queen to prosecute and implead in the law all criminals and to do all other things necessary or convenient as an attorney to suppress vice and immorality."[29] By 1711 local men were being nominated from Virginia county courts to serve as deputy attorneys general.[30]

In New York other forces worked to strengthen local control of the courts, including local control of prosecution. By the beginning of the eighteenth century, sheriff/prosecutors had been replaced by deputy attorneys general who had much the same power and responsibility. But because of their status as assistants to the attorney general, the deputies were paid a percentage of the court fees collected and thus were the victims of uncertain wages. By 1732, however, the counties began to pay these officials through relief granted by the county grand jury under its common law powers. Recognition of an obligation to pay for the services of the prosecuting officer without duress indicates that by 1732, the deputies had become an integral part of the local court structure. This resulted in many attorneys settling into the county and becoming permanent members of the local bar.[31]

The nature of the offices varied. Some were county officials appointed by the courts; some were deputies of the attorney general but were nominated by the court and operated with little supervision; some were deputies of the attorney general operating directly under his purview. Often more than one form existed simultaneously such as in Philadelphia and Pennsylvania. In spite of these differences, prosecutors had in common that—unlike any judicial officer in England or Europe—they were a new breed created by the demands of a new society. It would not be until a century later that the prosecutor's status would change to that of an elected official. In the meantime, the foundation of our modern justice system had been established, and the task of winning independence from Great Britain would have little effect on it.

In retrospect the emergence of local public prosecutors long before the colonists declared their independence and fought a revolutionary war was the result of a series of important choices made by early settlers. The first was the rejection of the notion of a privileged class and the adoption of the principles of representative government. This created a system of public prosecution, not private. The second was the shift of some centralized powers and authority to local governmental entities. This hastened the decentralization of the lower courts and the creation of local court officers. Finally, the public's demands for law enforcement and public safety, and the court's need for professional representation to act as a buffer between them and the grand jury were satisfied by separating the powers and duties of the sheriff/prosecutor.[31] It was not until nearly 100 years after the Revolutionary War, during the age of Jacksonian democracy in the 1830s, that the prosecutor acquired elective status.

THE AMERICAN PROSECUTOR FROM APPOINTIVE TO ELECTIVE STATUS

This section examines the democratic movement during the period from 1789 to the Civil War that changed the local prosecutor from an appointed to an elected official. In these early days of the new republic, the country shifted from a limited democracy that was ruled by a few franchised citizens to a democracy that extended the vote to almost all citizens. At the same time, governing power continued to be decentralized as the state's influence over local authority declined and weakened. With the power of the vote, and the election of President Andrew Jackson in 1828, more and more offices became elective.

As Jacksonian democracy swept the land, sparked by the spirit of independence in the new states, two important changes occurred. The position of the local judge changed from appointed to elected, which in turn directly helped make the office of the local prosecutor elective as well. A separation of powers occurred that moved the prosecutor from the judicial branch of government to the executive. These two changes gave the American prosecutor a new set of responsibilities, power and authority. Ultimately they became the foundation for the independent discretionary authority that was to distinguish this office from that of any other prosecutor in any country in the world.

The Early Republic: A Limited Democracy: 1789-1820

The federal system of prosecution established in 1789 provides a freeze-frame of the trends and philosophies that were predominant in criminal prosecution at the beginning of the American nation. The U.S. attorney general was a weakened office with vague supervisory powers, acting in an advisory capacity, and with limited appellate jurisdiction. Primary responsibility for prosecution was delegated to state and local prosecutors. The concept of local prosecution was well established by 1789, with most of the states utilizing deputy attorneys general for prosecution.

Even though the attorney general was the nominal head of state prosecution, in reality the local prosecuting attorney was moving swiftly toward achieving his own localized power. Local courts and local appointments or recommendations hastened this trend and marked a concomitant decline in the centralized power of the attorney general.[33] Massachusetts, for example, had created the office of the district and county attorney in a statute of 1817 and placed it under the nominal supervision of the attorney general. By 1843 the position had become so independent that the attorney general's office was abolished as being unnecessary.[34]

In the first 30 years of the new republic there were few changes to the limited duties and responsibilities of the prosecuting attorney, and there was little alteration in the prosecutor's base of power. The appointive status was the major reason for this stability. The prosecutor could not make independent decisions or exercise choice and discretion without regard for the opinions and politics of those who appointed him (and in those days, unlike today, all prosecutors were male). Whether the appointee was the governor, as in Pennsylvania, the attorney general, as in North Carolina, the local judge, as in Connecticut, or the local court, as in Virginia, the prosecutor was subordinate to another official within a political process upon which his tenure depended.

Appointive status was not exceptional during this period; few offices were elective and few citizens were electors. There were strict limitations on the general franchise, and the nation was, by modern standards, a very limited democracy. Voting was regulated by age, sex, race and property ownership. Those actually allowed to cast ballots in the general elections constituted a very small proportion of the population.

A review of the first constitutions of the 13 states indicates just how limited democracy was. The only office that was elected by the people in all states was the position of legislator. The office of the governor was on the ballot in only six of the 13 states: Massachusetts, Rhode Island, Connecticut, Pennsylvania, Delaware and Maryland. In New York, New Jersey, New Hampshire, Virginia, North Carolina, South Carolina and Georgia, the governor was either appointed or elected by the legislature. Only five of the first constitutions, Massachusetts, New Jersey, Maryland, Virginia, and Georgia, mention the office of the attorney general. Even these states list the office in the judicial rather than the executive article of the constitution.

Most of the first state constitutions were silent about the elective status of local officials. New Jersey and Pennsylvania elected their county sheriffs and coroners at large, while Maryland elected only the sheriff. North Carolina made provision for these county offices but declined to say in the constitution whether they would be elected or appointed. In fact, they were appointed. Virginia had no provision for the election of local officers, but did say that they would continue, as had been the colonial custom, "to be nominated by their respective courts."

In North Carolina, South Carolina and Virginia, county and local officers were elected indirectly by the legislature. In New York, Massachusetts and New Jersey, they were appointed by the governor with the consent of the legislatures.

Only the state of Connecticut made mention of local prosecutors. Referring to the statute of 1704, its constitution states simply that "there is no attorney general, but there used to be a King's Attorney in each county; but since the King was abdicated, they are now attorneys to the Governor and company."

Expanded Democracy and Elected Offices: 1820-1860

The stature and power of the prosecuting attorney increased not as a result of changes to the legal code in the first 30 years of the republic but rather as an outgrowth of a broader political movement that began about 1820. It was highlighted by the presidency of Andrew Jackson and culminated prior to the Civil War.[35] The period of Jacksonian Democracy saw increased democratization of the American political process. Its effect was to redefine the political nature of officeholders nationwide. It caused a greater number of public officials to be popularly elected and it established local elections to elect local officials. These movements expanded and strengthened the concept of decentralized government, which had been the hallmark of colonial government. They eventually gave greater independence to elected officials and established positions that required the exercise of discretion.

This democratic upsurge, although affirming the basic populist spirit that had operated in the colonial period, was fueled by the westward expansion. As new states joined the union, more progressive constitutions hastened the addition of popularly elected offices. Vermont, Kentucky and Tennessee were the first three states to enter the union during the Washington administration and before the turn of the century. Vermont (1791) and Tennessee (1796) adhered fairly rigidly to the pattern of the original states by only providing only for the election of assemblymen. Kentucky (1792) adopted the more progressive examples of New Jersey and Pennsylvania that permitted county officers, most notably the sheriff and coroner, to be elected in their counties.

In several states formed out of the Northwest Territory, Ohio (1802), Indiana (1816) and Illinois (1818), the constitutions decreed the election of governor and numerous local offices. Although there was no mention of judicial elections or elections of the prosecuting attorney in any of their constitutions, such alterations were possible if the legislature so desired. For example, in 1821, the first prosecutor in Ohio, elected in and serving Cuyahoga County, was provided by statute.[36]

While none of these states mentioned the office of prosecuting attorney specifically, all included some mention of prosecution. Article 29 of the Vermont constitution required that all prosecutions be public and that indictments include the phrase "against the peace and dignity of the state." Kentucky provided for an attorney general that would appear for the commonwealth "in all criminal prosecutions and in all civil cases in which the commonwealth shall be interested in any superior court." Tennessee mentioned neither prosecuting attorneys nor an attorney general but did set limits on the amount of money to be paid for attorneys appearing "for the state in Superior Court."

The District Attorney as a Minor Judicial Figure

Although today the local prosecuting attorney is considered an executive officer and the primary law enforcement official in his or her district, in the early republic the prosecutor was viewed as a minor figure in the court. The position was primarily judicial and only quasi-executive. As a subsidiary of the courts, the prosecutor was considered an adjunct to the real powers of the courts, the judges.

There is much evidence to support this thesis. Most telling is the fact that the prosecuting attorney, whether district attorney, county attorney or attorney general, was originally mentioned in the judicial article of the constitution. Even in states where separate articles were written for local and county officers, the prosecuting attorney, for the first half-century at least, was relegated to a subsection of those articles establishing the structure and officers of the state court system. Never was the prosecutor listed as a member of the executive branch, nor described as an officer of local government. The prosecutor was, in the eyes of the earliest Americans, clearly a minor actor in the court's structure.

Greater deference and attention was given to two other officers of the county: the county sheriff and the county coroner. Their positions in the early American criminal justice system clearly outstripped that of the prosecuting attorney. Their importance is further substantiated by the fact that these were the first offices to gain independent status and to be locally elected.

The earliest literature and proceedings of the courts indicate that the sheriff was the foremost member of the criminal justice system as it existed before the Civil War, and no other office was in even close competition. In 1816 when a member of the New York Bar, John Tappen, prepared a manual describing the New York courts and government for junior and entering members, he gave an extensive treatment of the sheriff's office and the duties of 20 other offices.[37] He did not once mention the prosecuting attorney, even though New York had established a seven-district court system in 1796 and had placed an assistant attorney general in charge of prosecution in each district. In 1801 chapter 246 of the state laws provided for a district attorney for each district. Lack of even the most perfunctory attention by Tappen leads to the conclusion that the role of district attorney at that time was minor in the criminal justice hierarchy. Historians studying the Virginia courts in the early republic describe the sheriff's revered status but also make no mention of the prosecuting attorney.[38]

Gaining Elective Status and Separation from the Judicial Branch of Government

None of the early constitutional amendments affected prosecution until judges gained elective status. "In the colonial period, and for some decades thereafter, the prosecutor's office was in fact an appointive one, appointing being in some cases by the governor and in other by the judges… As with judicial offices, however, appointment almost everywhere gave way to popular election in the democratic upsurge of the nineteenth century; and it became the universal pattern in the new states."[39]

The popular election of judges was a key element in creating locally elected prosecutors. States revised their constitutions and increased the number of local elective offices. In May 1798, Georgia revised its constitution and became an innovator by allowing its citizens to elect not only local executive officials but also local judges. "Five justices of the inferior court shall be elected by the voters in each county, to preside in the inferior courts of the county; and justices of the peace shall be elected annually by the voters in every militia captains district."

Mississippi (1807) created the offices of attorney general and prosecuting attorney as separate entities. Prosecuting attorneys were indirectly elected in districts; that is, they were elected by voice vote of the assembly in session. Alabama adopted a similar procedure in 1819. Louisiana failed to provide for the election of judges in its 1812 constitution and, not unexpectedly, failed also to provide for elected prosecuting attorneys. It did, however, establish the office of prosecuting attorney separate and apart from that of the attorney general, another indication of the growing independence of the office from centralized authority.

After Andrew Jackson was elected in 1828, the trend toward more elective offices and an expanded franchise swept the United States, affecting the constitutions and statutes in almost every state. During the next 20 years, seven of the 13 founding states amended their constitutions to accommodate this new spirit. The attorney general became an elected position in Rhode Island and New York. Lower court judges and justices of the peace were elected in Rhode Island (1842) and New York (1846); and only justices of the peace in Pennsylvania and Delaware. Georgia, the state that had first provided for elected jurists, amended its constitution in 1839 to provide for prosecuting attorneys in each county to be elected by the general assembly.

In 1832 Mississippi became the first state to include in its constitution a provision for the popular election of local district attorneys. It also allowed for the election of all judges on the circuit and appellate levels. Fourteen years later in 1846, Iowa voted to hold popular elections for judges and county attorneys. In New York the prosecuting attorney became a constitutional office in 1846. The district attorney was established by the Pennsylvania legislature on May 3, 1850, a move that was motivated by "a wave of home rule sentiment in the country."[40]

The move to elect judges and prosecutors was not unanimously supported. As Professor Caldwell, a critic of judicial elections, stated: "Most of the reasons that militate against the popular election of judges also stand opposed to the popular election of the administrative officers of our prosecutive system. Every thinking person knows that election by popular vote is determined not by merit or ability but by popularity and that popularity is not always based on merit."[41] Despite these concerns, when the election of judges finally came so did that of prosecuting attorneys.

By the Civil War, public perception of the role and responsibilities of the public prosecutor had changed. For the first time, some of the new state constitutions listed the prosecuting attorney in the executive article along with other county officers including the sheriff, the coroner and the clerk. The prosecutor's new elective status and independence from the court was a major force in defining prosecutorial functions. The public began to recognize and ask for a clear and distinct separation between the duties and powers of the prosecutor and those of the courts.[42]

Roscoe Pound, writing about the influence of the French law and thought in the United States in the first half of the 19th century, described the changing nature of the public prosecutor. The public prosecutor's increasing independence during this period, the shift from appointive to elective, from judicial to executive status, exemplifies the French belief, dictated by Montesquieu, that there should be full and complete separation between the branches of government. In this respect, at least, the American local prosecutor is much more clearly descended from the *procureur publique* than from the king's attorney.[43]

By 1850 the trend was clear and irreversible. For the most part, the new states thereafter provided for a prosecuting attorney in their constitutions; those that did not, provided for one by law. By 1912, when New Mexico and Arizona were admitted, all 48 states had such an officer, 38 by constitution and 10 by law.[44] Only five states did not provide for locally elected prosecutors: Delaware, Rhode Island, Connecticut, New Jersey and Florida.[45]

It is interesting to note that the four states that did not provide for local elections of prosecutors were all original members of the Union, suggesting that they chose to preserve the colonial forms of early prosecution. Two of the states, Rhode Island and Delaware, are geographically so small that it was probably not feasible to operate a local system of prosecution.[46] In both these states the elected attorney general is the principal officer of prosecution.

The relationship between judicial elections and elected prosecutors appears to be one where the prosecutors rode the coattails of the judges to gain elective status. If the judges did not gain elective status then neither did the prosecutor. In New Jersey prosecutors represent local jurisdictions, but they are appointed by the governor with the advice and consent of the senate and are supervised by the attorney general. The same appointive procedure is followed for judges. In Connecticut local prosecutors were appointed by the local court until 1984, when Article 23 of the constitution was amended to take the prosecutor out of the judicial branch and place him in a newly created independent constitutional agency called the Criminal Justice Commission.[47] This independent agency is connected to the executive branch for administrative purposes only. The 12 Connecticut state's attorneys are appointed by the commission to eight-year terms. Deputy state's attorneys are also appointed by the commission after review by the state attorney.

Finally, of interest is the structure of prosecution in the two newest states. Alaska, the 49th state, was admitted to the union in 1959. Its constitution empowers the attorney general to conduct prosecutions through prosecutors in the local jurisdictions who are appointed by the attorney general. In Hawaii (also 1959) the position of attorney general does not exist. The prosecution function is divided between elected and appointed: the prosecutors in three of the four counties are elected while the mayor appoints the prosecutor for Maui.

By 1859 the office of the American prosecutor had been defined as a locally elected position with executive functions separate from the judiciary. Now the groundwork was laid for the final transformation in his identity. With elective status it was possible for him to claim and exercise discretionary power. Of all the powers of the prosecutor, his authority to bring charges and dismiss them is the most controversial and criticized. This authority was not gained easily or quickly as the next (and final) section on the development of the American prosecutor will show, but the addition of discretionary power to the office produced a uniquely American prosecutor.

THE AMERICAN PROSECUTOR'S DISCRETIONARY POWER

This section traces the controversial history of the prosecutor's discretionary power, namely his unreviewable authority to bring charges or dismiss them. It continues tracing the American prosecutor's journey after gaining elective status and becoming independent of the judiciary.

Twenty years after the Civil War, the prosecutor had become a unique amalgam of the offices and historical influences that had preceded him. Like the private citizen in the English system, or the *procureur* or the *schout*, he could initiate those prosecutions he chose. Like the English attorney general, he could terminate prosecutions by informing the courts that the state was unwilling to proceed further. Because he was a locally elected official, he was free to apply the laws to his jurisdiction as he felt they best served his constituency. And, because he had been conferred discretionary authority by state constitutions or statutes, his decisions were virtually unreviewable. It was these last two characteristics that made him a center of power in the American criminal justice system.

The controversy surrounding this discretionary power continues unabated even today despite a long history of case law in support of the power. Critics decry the weakening of the grand jury as an independent check on prosecution and oppose prosecution plea agreement (plea "bargaining") practices. However, their attempts to limit discretion in the form of legislated sentencing guidelines, mandated sentences, habitual offender statutes and the like have had just the opposite effect.

Constitutions, Statutes and the Court Uphold the Prosecutor's Discretionary Power

The freedom to "make a choice among possible courses of action or inaction," or unreviewable prosecutorial discretion, was in the end what truly set the American prosecuting attorney apart from all other members of the criminal justice system.[48] The discretionary power of the American prosecuting attorney had become indisputable in three crucial areas. The prosecutor alone had the power to decide whether criminal action would be brought; to decide the level at which an individual would be charged, and the prosecutor could not be prevented from terminating prosecution when appropriate and necessary.

The transformation of this once minor court figure is well demonstrated in case law. A series of court cases, beginning in 1883 and continuing to the present, has almost unanimously affirmed the prosecutor's unshared and unreviewable powers in this aspect of the criminal law.[49] By 1883 in *People* v. *Wabash, St. Louis and Pacific Railway*, the Illinois Court of Appeals voiced their strong interpretation of the powers of the prosecuting attorney: "He is charged by law with large discretion in prosecuting offenders against the law. He may commence public prosecutions in his capacity by information and he may discontinue when, in his judgment the ends of justice are satisfied."[50]

Attempts to compel the prosecuting attorney to proceed in cases where he felt criminal prosecutions were not warranted have persistently failed. In *Wilson* v. *County of Marshall*, the prosecutor was said to have "absolute control of the criminal prosecution."[51] In cases in New York,[52] New Jersey[53] and California,[54] the state courts declared that they lack the power to compel the prosecuting attorney to enforce the penal code. "The remedy for the inactivity of the prosecutor is with the executive and ultimately with the people."[55]

Further buttressing the prosecutor's discretionary power are court rulings that support the prosecutors' right to determine what crimes they will investigate, and under what circumstances. In a Wisconsin case, *State ex. rel. Kurkierewicz* v. *Cannon*, the family of an 18-year old who had been shot by a policeman under suspicious circumstances sought a *writ of mandamus* from the courts to compel the prosecutor to order an inquest into the causes of death.[56] The family cited an earlier Wisconsin case, *State* v. *Corbal,* in which the court had held that although the prosecutors' duties are discretionary, they remain subordinate to the will of the legislature.[57] Again, the court refused to interfere with the discretion of the prosecuting attorney. In *Wilson* v. *State*, a 1949 Oklahoma court decision defended the prosecutor's right to charge a defendant with a charge that was less than the evidence would support.[58] In several federal cases including *Howell* v. *Brown, Milliken* v. *Stone* and *Puglach* v. *Klein*, the courts ruled that similar unfettered discretion exists at the federal level.[59]

By 1912 when Arizona and New Mexico were admitted to the Union, the process of consolidating prosecutorial power and discretion in the local prosecuting attorneys was essentially complete. The local prosecutor was the primary representative of the public in the area of criminal law.

PROSECUTORIAL DISCRETION IS DISCOVERED: CHECKS AND BALANCE OR ABUSE OF POWER?

The long slow evolution to power culminated in the public's belated recognition and concern. By the 1920s, after almost three hundred years of existence, the office of the prosecuting attorney finally was to become the subject of a number of commission studies and reports focusing on their central role in the criminal trial process. The impetus for many of the studies was a whole new set of problems facing America after World War I—new technology and the automobile, society's rising expectations, increasing populations, new immigrants and prohibition, among others. Topping the list for concern was crime.

Most of the commissions attempted to define the local criminal justice system and assess its ability to cope with the stresses of the turbulent post war period. Some reports were politically motivated, as was the Chicago report of 1921, which was prepared by a political opponent of the Cook County state's attorney.[60] However, most reflected earnest attempts to remedy the then decaying law enforcement structure.

State and local crime commissions were formed in Baltimore and Chicago in 1921, in Cleveland in 1922[61] and for the state of Missouri in 1926. Commissions also met in Georgia, New York, Illinois, Minnesota, Pennsylvania and California before the end of the decade.[62] Almost all of them took a long hard look at the prosecutor. Most were shocked by the extent of his power and dismayed by his inability to control the crime situation. The California Crime Commission (1929) called for more attention to the "unsupervised area of plea-bargaining," and suggested that the power of the prosecutor in this area be diluted.[63]

In 1934 a National Commission on Law Observance and Enforcement (NCLOE) was formed to study the status of criminal justice in the United State under the leadership of the legal scholar, George W. Wickersham. The Wickersham Commission included some of the most notable legal minds of the day, including Wickersham, Roscoe Pound of Harvard University, Newman Baker of Northwestern and Charles Bettman, the author of the *Cleveland Crime Commission Study*. The commission concentrated an entire volume of its report on the duties and functions of the prosecuting attorney.

The report was highly critical of the situation in the criminal courts. The commission felt that the political nature of the prosecutor was detrimental to the best administration of justice and that the direct election of prosecuting attorneys provided neither qualified candidates nor a proper check on the prosecutor's discretionary practices.

About the same time, between 1933 and 1935, a comprehensive series of articles about the public prosecutor was published in the *Journal of Criminal Law and Criminology*. The series was co-authored by Newman Baker and Earl DeLong, also of Northwestern University. Baker and DeLong were the first to describe the paradoxes embodied in the local prosecutor: "The people of the United States have traditionally feared concentration of great power in the hands of one person and it is surprising that the power of the prosecuting attorney has been left intact as it is today."[64] Baker and DeLong were especially impressed with the power that the prosecuting attorney had attained. "Nowhere," they proclaimed, "is it more apparent that our government is a government of men, not of laws."[65] They pointed out that the prosecutor was shaped only by those who elected him and that popular election had meant that the local standards had come to determine how the law was applied. And this, they argued was the crucial factor in the effectiveness of the criminal laws. "The law is written by legislators, interpreted occasionally by appellate courts, but applied by countless individuals acting largely for themselves. How it is applied outweighs in importance its enactment or its interpretation."[66]

Other commentators had been wary of a power that was only checked at the ballot box and warned that it would lead to abuses. Judge William B. Quinlin of Wisconsin, speaking before a meeting of the state's district attorneys in 1921, exhorted them "not to legislate."[67] He pointed out that, in his opinion, the district attorney was duty bound to equitably prosecute all crimes brought to his attention. He feared that the voter was not likely to provide diligent checks on unlimited discretion. As another author has said: "To some extent (the prosecutor) derives his authority from statute, but more largely he relies on custom. The people look to him for results; they are not likely to ask whether he has stayed within the exact limits of his powers."[68]

Baker and DeLong, however, recognized that it was no accident that the prosecutor was allowed to exercise wide discretion and that he often enforced the laws as a

direct expression of local custom and sentiment. They knew that the system charac-
teristically produced satisfactory prosecutors for the majority of American jurisdictions and that there was too direct a connection between the voters and the office-
holder for any crime that was genuinely perceived as dangerous to the community
to go unprosecuted. At the same time, they noted that the rise of crime would force
the prosecutor to "steer a middle course" between initiating all actions and following
only his personal preferences. [69]

Despite the public's criticism and opposition to the prosecutor's discretionary
power, the courts did not agree. With little hope of changing case law, opponents
focused on procedures that allowed discretion to operate. Two issues generated
considerable interest: the weakening of the grand jury and the "abuse" of justice
through plea "bargaining."

Discretion, Accusatory Power and the Grand Jury

By the 1930s the grand jury was losing ground to the prosecutor, who had come to
"dominate the grand jury process" in his position of advisor and presenter of evidence. "The grand jury" said political scientist Austin MacDonald, "is poorly fitted to
perform its allotted tasks—it is virtually compelled to rely on the prosecutor for its
facts, witnesses and opinions."[70] Twenty-four states had by-passed the grand jury
process, and almost all criminal cases were being filed by means of prosecutor information. In other states, there was movement for similar change—for a procedural
recognition of a legal fact of life—that the power to charge no longer was controlled
by the grand jury. Charging was in fact a function of the locally elected prosecutor.

Raymond Moley argued that the use of the information rather than the indictment
system: "properly centers responsibility upon the prosecutor for actions which are
apparently largely under his control even when indictments only are used. He seems
to dominate the grand jury to such a degree that its actions are in reality his own,
and for that reason they should be his nominally as well as actually." [71]

Justin Miller, in a study published by the *University of Minnesota Law Review* agreed
with Moley and added that the use of informations was a fiscal boon to criminal
justice administration. His study showed that informations were more expeditious,
less expensive and more efficient, resulting in the initiation of fewer unsuccessful
prosecutions.[72]

Two factors helped save the grand jury. One was the subpoena and immunity power of the grand jury. The other was the secrecy of its proceedings and its value for reviewing sensitive, socially controversial or politically explosive cases. As a result, although the prosecutor controlled the flow of information and evidence to the members of the grand jury, he escaped the political consequences of an unpopular decision. He could claim that the power to indict or not to indict in that specific case had been in the grand jury's hands and not his.[73]

Despite its inherent value as a check and balance on prosecutor discretion, the grand jury's impotence became evident to the legal reformers of this century. In 1961 MacDonald wrote that, "the present trend seems to be toward the further expansion of the powers of the prosecuting attorney and the virtual abandonment of the grand jury system in ordinary criminal proceedings."[74]

Discretion and Plea Agreements

Plea agreements are not a new phenomenon. They apparently originated in 17th century England as a means of mitigating unduly harsh punishment. Indeed, it was noted that if a person accused of any crime chose to plead guilty and offer up his accomplices, the king "might grant him life and limb." If he failed to fulfil the conditions imposed upon him, he was hanged on his own condition.[75] Although plea bargaining was apparently widespread from the beginning of the Republic, studies did not confirm its pervasiveness until the 1920s. Few courts, however, discussed the practice and most of those that did, condemned it.[76]

The Wickersham report was particularly disturbed by the issue of plea bargaining, which was constantly referred to as an "abuse" of the process. The report expressed the opinion that the prosecuting attorney had gained too much power and too many responsibilities, recommending that the states institute a "systematized control of prosecutions under a director of public prosecutions or some equivalent official with secure tenure and concentrated and defined responsibility."[77]

Although the vast majority of cases are disposed by pleas and often times negotiated pleas, and the court system recognized it could not support the abolition of plea negotiation, the National Advisory Commission on Criminal Justice Standards and Goals (NAC) called for its end by 1978.[78]

As crime continued to increase and place even higher demands on the dwindling resources in the courts, however, abolishing plea bargains was simply not feasible. Moreover, new laws dealing with crime that, in effect, transferred power from the court to the prosecutor expanded its use. A notable example are the habitual offender laws that provided for enhanced sentencing of repeat offenders. As William McDonald of Georgetown University noted, "When mandatory sentences are involved, the charging decision becomes the sentencing decision... In short, when the penal code is such that the prosecutor's charging decision can make a major impact on the types of sentence to be served, the prosecutor's domain is expanded into the traditional judicial prerogative of sentencing."[79]

LOOKING TO THE FUTURE

In 1931 the Wickersham Commission wrote, "In every way the Prosecutor has more power over the administration of justice than the judges, with much less public appreciation of his power. We have been jealous of the power of the trial judge, but careless of the continual growth of the power of the prosecuting attorney."[80] According to Professor Newman Baker, his position was secure, because "the permanence of the prosecutor as he exists at present, is substantially buttressed by constitutional provisions in most of the 48 states and revision of such constitutional provisions comes slowly."[81]

In 1971 the National Association of Attorneys General commented that "there is little probability that the basic pattern (of increased power and prestige for local prosecutors) will be changed; there is every indication that it will be strengthened."[82]

One can only hazard a guess as to how the nature of the American prosecutor will change in the new century. There is little doubt that he or she will continue as a locally elected official. But there is some doubt as to whether his or her discretionary power will remain unchanged. No matter what the future holds, one fact is still clear. After three hundred and fifty years of existence, the American prosecutor is unique, and has been uniquely formed out of America's rich soil of diversity, innovation and willingness to change.

ENDNOTES

[1] Much of the material presented here was extracted from the first chapter of *The American Prosecutor: A Search for Identity*, authored by Joan E. Jacoby and published by Lexington Books, D.C. Heath and Company, 1980.

[2] *Missouri Crime Commission* (New York: McMillan, 1926).

[3] Patrick Devlin, *Criminal Prosecution in England* (New Haven, CN: Yale University Press, 1958).

[4] National Commission on Law Observance and Enforcement (NCLOE), *Report on Prosecution* (Washington, D.C.: U.S. Government Printing Office, 1931).

[5] W. Scott Van Alstyne, "The District Attorney - A Historical Puzzle," *Wisconsin Law Review* 1952: (1952), 125. *See also,* Douglass Campbell, *The Puritan in Holland, England and America* (1899), 438-467.

[6] Jack M. Kress, "Progress and Prosecution," *Annals of the American Academy of Political and Social Sciences* 423 (January 1976), 99-116.

[7] *Ibid.*, 100. This is no longer the case, however. The Prosecution of Offences Act of 1985 established the Crown Prosecution Service in England as an independent prosecution body. The statute says that no prosecution can be brought without the consent of the Crown Prosecutor.

[8] Glanville Williams, "The Power to Prosecute," *Criminal Law Review* (1955), 601.

[9] Patrick Devlin, *Criminal Prosecution in England* (New Haven, Conn.: Yale University Press, 1958), 25.

[10] *See* A.C. Wright, "French Criminal Procedure," *Law Quarterly Review* 44 (1928), 423.

[11] *State v. Peterson*, 195 Wis. 351, 218 N.W. 367 (1928).

[12] *Mallory v. Lane*, 97 Conn. 132, 138 (1921).

[13] John Blum et al., *The National Experience* (Harcourt, Brace and World, 1968), 59.

[14] Charles A. Beard and Mary R. Beard, *New Basic History of the United States*, (Doubleday, 1968), 84.

[15] Edwin Surrency, "The Courts in the American Colonies," *American Journal of Legal History* 11 (1967), 263.

[16] George Lee Haskins, *Law and Authority in Early Massachusetts* (New York: McMillan, 1960), 177.

[17] Oliver P. Chitwood, *Justice in Colonial Virginia* (New York: DeCapo Press, 1971), 120. A different view is taken by Arthur P. Scott, *Criminal Law in Colonial Virginia* (Chicago: University of Chicago Press, 1930).

[18] John T. Farrell, "The Early History of Rhode Island's Court System," in *Rhode Island History*, vol. 9: 65.

[19] *See generally* Julius Goebel and Raymond T. Naughton, *Law Enforcement in Colonial New York* (New York: 1944) and Harry B. Weiss and Grace M. Weiss, *An Introduction to Crime and Punishment in Colonial New Jersey*, (Trenton, NJ: 1960) 8-9.

[20] Van Alstyne, *op cit,* "The District Attorney," 137.

[21] Raphael Semmes, *Crime and Punishment in Early Maryland* (Baltimore: Johns Hopkins Press, 1938).

[22] John J. Poserina, "Appointed Attorney General's Power to Supercede an Elected District Attorney," *Temple Law Quarterly* 33 (1959), 78, 83.

23 Edwin L. Page, *Judicial Beginnings in New Hampshire* (Concord, NH: 1959), 60.

24 Paul M. McCain, *The County Court in North Carolina before 1750* (Durham, NC: Duke University Press, 1954), 18.

25 Scott, *op cit. Criminal Law*, 48-49.

26 Goebel and Naughton, *Law Enforcement*, 334.

27 McCain, *County Court*, 33.

28 Van Alstyne, *op cit.* "The District Attorney," 1125.

29 Chitwood, *op cit. Justice in Colonial Virginia*, 120.

30 Goebel and Naughton, *op cit. Law Enforcement*, 332-334.

31 Even today it is still possible for police to prosecute district court cases in Massachusetts, although the practice has mostly been discontinued by district attorney policy.

32 Newman Baker, "The Prosecuting Attorney - Provisions of Organizing a Law Office," *Journal of Criminal Law and Criminology* 23 (1932), 926, 957-959.

33 National Association of Attorneys General (NAAG), *Report on the Office of the Attorney General* (Raleigh, N.C): The National Association of Attorneys General, 1970), 15. *See also* Elliot Richardson, "The Office of the Attorney General: Continuity and Change," *Massachusetts Law Quarterly* 53 (1968),6.

34 NAAG, *Report,* 19.

35 Alfred Bettman, *Prosecution* (Cleveland,OH: Cleveland Foundation, 1921).

36 John Tappen, *The County and Town Officer* (Kingston, NY: 1816).

37 Isabel Ferguson, "County Courts in Virginia, 1700-1830," *North Carolina Historical Review* 8 (0000), 14.

38 Lewis Mayers, *The American Legal System* (New York: Harper and Row, 1964), 413.

39 John J. Poserina, "Appointed Attorney General's Power to Supercede an Elected District Attorney," *Temple Law Quarterly* 33 (1959), 83.

40 Newman Baker, "The Prosecuting Attorney," 962.

41 Presently, North Carolina is the only state that still defines the prosecutor as a member of the judicial branch of government.

42 *See* Roscoe Pound, "The Influence of the French in America," *Illinois Law Review* 3 (1908), 354. On independence of the U.S. attorney, see 85 F. Supp. 537, 540 (D. Nebraska, 1949).

43 *See* Baker, "Prosecuting Attorney," 955-959. The 10 states are Connecticut, Delaware. Maine, Rhode Island, Ohio, Missouri, Kansas, Nebraska, Wyoming and Minnesota.

[44] Florida later altered its procedures, and the prosecuting attorney is now locally elected.

[45] Rhode Island does not even have a county government structure.

[46] The commission is composed of two judges, two attorneys and one civilian appointed by the governor. The commission terms are co-equal with the term of the governor.

[47] Kenneth Culp Davis, cited in Kress, "Progress and Prosecution," p. 100. See *People v. Newcomber*, 284 Ill. 315, 120 N.E. 244 (1918).

[48] *See People v. Newcomber*, 284 Ill. 315, 120 N.E. 244 (1918) (*mandamus* denied to states attorney seeking to compel trial judge to accept *nolle prosequi*).

[49] 12 Ill. App. 263 (1883).

[50] 257 Ill. App. 220 (1930).

[51] *People v. Berlin* 361 N.Y.S. 2d 114 (1974).

[52] *See State v LeVien*, 44 N.J. 323, 209 A.2d 97 (1965). *See also State in the Interest of F.W.*, 26 N.J.Super. 513, 327 A.2d 697 (1974).

[53] *People v. Adams,* 117 Cal. Rptr. 905 (1974).

[54] *Milliken v. Stone*, 7 F.2d 397, 399 (S.D.N.Y. 1925).

[55] 52 Wis.2d. 368, 166 N.W.2d 255 (1969).

[56] 248 Wis. 247, 21 N.W.2d 381 (1946).

[57] 209 P.2d 512, 514 (Okla. 1949).

[58] *Howell v. Brown,* 85 F. Supp. 537 (D. Neb. 1949); *Milliken v. Stone*, 7 F.2d 397 (S.D.N.Y. 1925); *Pugach v. Klein*, 193 F. Supp. 630 (S.D.N.Y. 1961).

[59] John J. Healy, *The Prosecutor in Chicago in Felony Cases* (Chicago, 1921), 307.

[60] Alfred Bettman, *Prosecution* (Cleveland, Ohio: Cleveland Foundation, 1921), 56-60. The Cleveland survey included a complete description of the duties and responsibilities of the office of the prosecutor and included an attempt to statistically describe the functions of the office.

[61] *See* National Commission on Law Observance and Enforcement (NCLOE), *Report on Prosecution*. (Washington, DC, Government Printing Office, 1931).

[62] Baker, "The Prosecuting Attorney," 788-789.

[63] Baker, "Prosecuting Attorney," 934.

[64] Baker, "The Prosecutor —Initiation of Prosecution," *Journal of Criminal Law and Criminology* 23 (1933), 770, 771.

[65] *Ibid.*, 796.

[66] William B. Quinlin, "The District Attorney," *Marquette Law Review* 5 (1921), 190, 194.

[67] Austin F. MacDonald, *American State Government and Administration,* 6th ed. (New York: Tomas Crowell, 1961), 474.

[68] Baker, "The Prosecutor," 771.

[69] MacDonald, *American State Government and Administration,* 474-475. Notable exceptions to this are North Carolina, Virginia and Connecticut.

[70] Raymond Moley, "The Initiation of Criminal Prosecution by Indictment or Information," *Michigan Law Review* 29 (1931), 403.

[71] Ibid. *See* Justin Miller, "Information or Indictment in Criminal Cases," *Minnesota Law Review* 8 (1924), 379-408.

[72] *See* Moley, "Initiation," 403.

[73] Austin F. MacDonald, *American State Government and Administration,* 9. 474.

[74] Sir James Stephen, "Criminal Procedure from the Thirteenth to the Eighteenth Century," *Two Select Essays in Anglo-American Legal History* (1908), 485.

[75] James E. Bond, *Plea Bargaining and Guilty Pleas.* (New York: Clark Boardman Company (1975), 12.

[76] NCLOE, *Report on Prosecution,* 38. See also Kress, "Progress and Prosecution," 110-111; Roscoe Pound, *Criminal Justice in America,* American Constitutional and Legal History Series (New York: DeCapo, 1972); Compare with views of Raymond Moley, "The Initiation of Criminal Prosecution by Indictment or Information," *Michigan Law Review* 29 (1931), 403.

[77] Standard 3.1, *Task Force on Courts, National Advisory Commission on Criminal Justice Standards and Goals,* (Washington DC, Government Printing Office, 1973), 46.

[78] William F. McDonald, "The Prosecutor's Domain," *Criminal Justice Readings,* vol. 3, ed. by George S. Bridges, et al. (Pine Forge Press, Thousand Oaks, CA, 1996), 247.

[79] National Commission on Law Observance and Enforcement (NCLOE), *Report on Prosecution* (Washington, D. C.: U. S. Government Printing Office, 1931).

[80] Baker, "The Prosecuting Attorney," 927.

[81] National Association of Attorneys General (NAAG), *Report on the Office of the Attorney General* (Raleigh, N.C.: The National Association of Attorneys General, 1971), 103.

PRETRIAL PRACTICES AND SPECIAL TOPICS

THE STATE OF THE LAW AFTER BATSON

By Michael T. Conroy, Assistant District Attorney, Richmond County,
Staten Island, New York

Introduction

There is no right more fundamental in our criminal justice system than the right
of an accused to a trial by jury as guaranteed by the Sixth Amendment to the
United States Constitution. We first learn about this right early in our elementary
school education as we begin to study our nation's founding principles. However, all
too often, as adults and as attorneys, we lose sight of the reason our Constitution
contains this protection and the other fundamental protections that we cherish. It is
important to remember that these principles are firmly rooted in our history and
have helped us to achieve the freedom we enjoy today.

Fear of unchecked governmental power is the major reason. It is the very reason that
our founding fathers designed a system of constitutional checks and balances—to
ensure that no one governmental branch would overrun any other. In our criminal
justice system, jury trials reflect this distrust of centralized, unchecked power. We can
trace our jury system back to England. The concept was and is simple: an accused
can safely place more faith in a fair trial by 12 of his countrymen than by a judge or
a panel of judges, who owe their position, and hence their life, to the king or to
other government officials. It was the denial of this right to the English colonists in
America, among other grievances, which prompted our split from the British
Empire and led to the birth of this nation.

While the right to a jury trial has always been present in our Constitution for federal trials, it is only relatively recently that this right has been guaranteed at state trials
for serious crimes. In *Duncan v. Louisiana*[1] the Supreme Court recognized that this
right was so fundamental, so crucial to a fair trial that it must also be guaranteed to
the citizens of the states in state courts. As Justice White explained, "[p]roviding an
accused with the right to be tried by a jury of his peers [gives] him an inestimable
safeguard against the corrupt or overzealous prosecutor and against the compliant,
biased or eccentric judge."[2]

Unquestionably everyone, judges included, possesses certain biases and prejudices. Whether those biases and prejudices preclude them from being fair and impartial jurors is a question that attorneys seek to answer during jury selection. In the same way that we would rely on judges to exclude themselves if they believed they could not be fair and impartial during a jury trial, so too are potential jurors relied upon to reveal their biases. Unfortunately some potential jurors, while perhaps not outright perjuring themselves, may be less than truthful in their answers, or truly may not perceive their own biases. Few want to believe that they are not always fair. And then, of course, there are those jurors with an agenda who will intentionally perjure themselves to remain on the jury. The relief for this inequity lies in the peremptory challenge.

With its basis in the English common law, we developed a jury system in which peremptory challenges serve to ensure that both parties receive a fair trial. Peremptory challenges are not a right afforded a defendant under the Constitution but are viewed almost as reverently.[3] Peremptory challenges, by their very definition, do not require a stated reason but may be used on the basis of mere whim.[4] The challenges are designed "not only to eliminate extremes of partiality on both sides but to assure the parties that the jurors before whom they try the case will decide on the basis of the evidence placed before them, and not otherwise." [5]

Jury selection is clearly not a science. It is left to the attorneys to determine whether a particular juror can be fair. Easiest is the case where the venire member admits his or her inability to sit as a judge of another for whatever reason stated. More difficult, however, are the cases in which the potential jurors steadfastly maintain their sense of fairness. Do those jurors have any deep-seated convictions that will significantly affect their verdicts? It is up to the attorneys to decide, apart from the answers given in response to voir dire, whether based on some inflection, gesture or other not so obvious clue, if the potential juror will strive to be fair. The concern which arises is this: does counsel, whether for the prosecution or the defense, believe that a juror cannot be fair and impartial largely because of prejudice (for or against) that is grounded upon the race (or age or sex) of the defendant (or of the victim). The prejudice may be intentional or subliminal—the party may not realize that his strike is really racially motivated. Nevertheless, the courts cannot afford to tolerate racism in jury selection.

Batson v. Kentucky, 476 U. S. 79, 106 S. CT. 1712 (1986), was the first in a series of cases designed to eliminate racial discrimination from the jury selection process. Whether *Batson* has met its goal, and whether *Batson* has created more abuses, will remain the subject of vigorous debate. Nevertheless, *Batson* (and its progeny) remain the law of the land. If any change in this status quo is forthcoming it will most likely be the expansion of *Batson,* not its diminution.

This article is designed to address the state of the law after *Batson*. It is not designed to address the merits of the *Batson* analysis. Clearly the ultimate goal—eliminating racial discrimination from the jury selection process—is an extremely important one, but whether *Batson* is workable in actual practice (outside of the realm of appellate courts) is a viable question. Nevertheless, working prosecutors must have an understanding of *Batson*, as the consequence for doing otherwise is fatal: reversible error. Here we seek to provide the prosecutor with some guidance on how to handle *Batson* in day-to-day trial work.

THE *BATSON* LINE OF CASES

To deal with *Batson* on a regular basis it is necessary to first understand the legal reasoning that led up to *Batson* and how the Supreme Court has systematically expanded the doctrine. *Batson* has truly changed the definition of a peremptory challenge, forcing attorneys to provide reasons in support of their jury strikes and prodding them to analyze and, perhaps most importantly, to articulate in detail why they wish to strike a specific individual from a jury.

For too long discrimination based on race, gender and religion has tarnished our national history. Even though slavery was eliminated in this country over one hundred and thirty-five years ago, we know that racism continues. Racism in jury selection has also long been with us. The United States Supreme Court first addressed this problem in 1879, shortly after the enactment of the Fourteenth Amendment to the United States Constitution, in the case of *Strauder v. West Virginia*.[6] *Strauder* considered a West Virginia law that prohibited blacks from serving on the venire and it set the stage for subsequent cases addressing racism in the criminal justice system. But not until *Swain v. Alabama*, 100 years after *Strauder*, did the Supreme Court address racism in the selection of the petit jury, and it was not until *Batson* that the Supreme Court developed the doctrine that underlies our present system of peremptory challenges.

In *Strauder*, the Supreme Court struck down a West Virginia law that precluded everyone except for white males over 21 years of age from serving on juries. *Strauder*, an early case of equal protection analysis, found that the recently adopted Fourteenth

Amendment protected the defendant's rights to a jury of his peers.[7] Justice Strong explained the reasoning behind the decision: "We do not say that within the limits from which it is not excluded by the amendment that a State may not prescribe the qualifications of its jurors, and in so doing make discriminations. It may confine the selection to males, to freeholders, to citizens, to persons within certain ages, or to persons having educational qualifications."[8]

Although it seems reasonable to assume that the *Strauder* court probably did not intend by this language to provide anything like a roadmap for continued discrimination, it is clear from this language just how free the states remained after *Strauder* to direct their long-standing discriminatory practices. The newly freed slaves did not own land, nor were they educated, so they had little hope of satisfying any criteria that required evidence of freeholdership or education. *Strauder,* therefore, had little effect on existing jury selection processes and focused on the denial of the defendant's rights. As *Batson* and its progeny developed, there occurred a shift away from this exclusive concentration; post-*Batson*, it is the rights of the *juror* that will attract the scrutiny of the Supreme Court. Despite the muted impact of *Strauder*, however, the case did state an important principle that has withstood the test of time: that the Constitution does not guarantee a defendant a panel made up of persons of his own race.

The issue of discriminatory practices in selection of the petit jury first came to a head in *Swain v. Alabama.*[9] In *Swain* the Court addressed a prosecutor's use of peremptory challenges to strike blacks from serving on a black defendant's jury (Alabama employed a struck jury system, in which each litigant would alternately strike jurors from the venire until the number was reduced to 12). *Swain's* venire contained eight blacks, two were exempt from service and the prosecutor struck the remaining six. Further, no black had served on a jury in this jurisdiction since 1950.[10] Despite this information, the Court refused to delve into the reasons for the prosecutor's strikes. However, the Court did not outright preclude this possibility.[11] It merely stated that the defendant had failed to establish purposeful racial discrimination.[12] Justice White opined that, "[t]here is no evidence... of what the prosecution did or did not do on its own account in any cases other than the one at bar."[13] The *Swain* Court insisted that defendants must provide evidence of a systematic pattern of peremptory challenges, established through information from multiple cases, exhibiting purposeful racial discrimination.[14] This was a heavy burden to satisfy in order to show a violation of the Equal Protection Clause. *Swain* and *Strauder* represented the state of the legal reasoning concerning purposeful racial discrimination in jury selection at the time the Court agreed to decide *Batson*. *Batson* then made a radical and unexpected change in direction.

In *Batson*,[15] a black man was tried for second-degree burglary and the receipt of stolen goods. The prosecutor used his peremptory challenges to strike all four black venire persons, yielding an all white jury. The defendant was subsequently convicted. The trial court denied the defendant's motion for a hearing on whether the prosecutor's peremptory challenges violated the defendant's rights under the Sixth and Fourteenth Amendments.[16]

The *Batson* court proceeded to conduct an exhaustive review of the case law, with extensive discussion of *Swain* and *Strauder*. Justice Powell explained, "... the Equal Protection Clause forbids the prosecutor to challenge potential jurors solely on account of their race or on the assumption that black jurors as a group will be unable to impartially consider the State's case against a black defendant."[17] The Court recognized that this principle was clear from over 100 years of constitutional analysis. The *Batson* Court, however, departed from the requirement that placed the burden on the defendant to establish that the prosecutor had in fact injected racism into the proceedings.

Describing the defendant's burden of proof under *Swain* as "crippling,"[18] the *Batson* Court proceeded to simplify the defendant's evidentiary threshold. Instead of requiring defendants to prove repeated striking of blacks over multiple cases, *Batson* permitted the defendant to establish a *prima facie* discrimination case based on the facts of his case alone. Under *Batson* the defendant must demonstrate the following:

- that he is a member of a cognizable racial group;

- that the prosecutor's challenges removed from the venire members of that racial group; and

- that the prosecutor used these challenges to exclude the venire members on account of their race.[19]

The Court explained in establishing this third criteria that "the defendant is entitled to rely on the fact, *as to which there can be no dispute*, that peremptory challenges constitute a jury selection practice that permits 'those to discriminate who are of a mind

---

to discriminate.'"[20] The Court's dim view of peremptory challenges is clear from this language that apparently views peremptory challenges as inherently discriminatory. It is this analysis that underlies the subsequent decisions expanding the *Batson* doctrine.

Post-*Batson*, the establishing of a *prima facie* case of discrimination now shifts the burden to the prosecutor to provide a race neutral reason for the peremptory strike. After the neutral explanation is proffered, the trial judge must evaluate whether the defendant has established purposeful discrimination, ultimately creating a credibility evaluation.[21] *Batson* addressed *only* a defendant's challenge to the prosecutor's use of peremptory challenges against minority venire members of the same race; it focused on the *defendant's* rights.[22] *Batson's* impact later became truly wide-ranging in subsequent cases, when the focus shifted from the defendant's rights to that of the juror's.

Powers v. Ohio[23] presented a fact pattern that paralleled *Batson* in every aspect but one—the defendant in *Powers* was white. The first test established by *Batson's prima facie* case formulation was whether the defendant belonged to the same racial group as the juror. Accepting that the juror's equal protection rights were violated by racially motivated peremptory strikes, *Powers* addressed the issue of whether the defendant had standing to raise the issue of the equal protection rights of potential jurors. Accordingly, *Powers'* conclusion that there was standing opened the door to even more *Batson* challenges but, even in the cases that followed, the Court continued to focus on the actions of the prosecutor (an obvious state actor), not those of defense counsel.

The National District Attorneys Association (NDAA) officially opposed *Batson* and filed an *amicus curiae* brief on behalf of the Commonwealth of Kentucky outlining that position.[24] NDAA expressed two concerns. First, permitting inquiry into the prosecutor's reasoning was inconsistent with historical, accepted trial practice. Second, if the Court were to implement rules regarding jury selection, than any such rules should apply equally to both the prosecution and the defense. This first concern is still outstanding but the Court ultimately addressed the second concern. The rules now apply equally to both sides. However, the Court took a circuitous route before ultimately applying *Batson* to the defense.

The key to this process was the extension of *Batson* to civil litigation in *Edmonson v. Leesville Concrete Company, Inc.,*[25] where juror rights became the focus of the Court. State action in this case arose by the use of the peremptory challenge by the private litigants. According to *Edmonson*, the government, by allowing peremptory challenges at all, becomes involved in discrimination if or when judges grant improper race-based challenges.[26] Justice Kennedy concluded, "By enforcing a discriminatory peremptory challenge, the court 'has not only made itself a party to the [biased act], but has elected to place its power, property, and prestige behind the [alleged] discrimination.'"[27]

Finding that the court's granting of a racially based peremptory challenge created state action, the next step, extending the *Batson* prohibition on prosecutors to criminal *defendants* in *Georgia v. McCollum*,[28] was a logical conclusion.[29] *McCollum* made it clear that defendants may no longer use the powers of government to achieve racially discriminatory purposes when they ask a judge to enforce an improper challenge. As a result of *Edmondson* and *McCollum*, the prosecution may establish a *prima facie* case in the same manner as the defense, thereby forcing the defendant to provide a race neutral reason for the questioned challenge.

WHERE WILL *BATSON* LEAD US?

The open question is whether the extension of the *Batson* doctrine will lead to the eventual outright elimination of peremptory challenges. Today, *Batson* issues are commonly raised at trial. A review of the case law shows literally thousands of cases in both federal and state courts. It seems obvious that the resulting plethora of appeals might ultimately lead the Court to conclude that their guidelines have failed to achieve the desired result—purging the criminal justice system of racial discrimination. Perhaps this will lead the court to conclude that eliminating all peremptory challenges will absolutely end the issue.

It would seem a strange turn of history indeed if peremptory strikes—regarded for centuries as a right inherent in and necessary to the greater right to a trial by jury—become a casualty of the Court's search for another kind of freedom, the freedom from racial discrimination in the judicial system. But such a drastic result is not without precedent nor is it incredible. Justice White's concurring *Batson* opinion noted, "It appears that the practice of peremptorily eliminating blacks from petit juries in cases with black defendants remains widespread [after *Swain*], so much so that I agree an opportunity to inquire should be afforded when this occurs."[30] Justice Marshall did recommend the elimination of peremptory challenges, explaining, "the *inherent potential* of peremptory challenges to distort the process by permitting the exclusion of jurors on racial grounds should ideally lead the Court to ban them entirely from the criminal justice system."[31]

Already, *Batson*-type challenges are not limited to race. In *J.E.B. v. Alabama ex rel. T.B.,*[32] the Court expanded *Batson* beyond race to include gender, concluding, "gender, like race, is an unconstitutional proxy for juror competence and impartiality."[33] Again the focus was on the rights of the juror, not the defendant, and distrust of peremptory challenges permeated throughout the opinion: "[d]iscrimination in jury selection, whether based on race or gender, causes harm to the litigants, the community, and the individual jurors who are wrongfully excluded from the judicial process."[34]

The eventual reach of *Batson* may encompass more than race and gender. Eliminating jurors based on religion or organizational associations, as well as other race and gender-neutral reasons may one day fall within the rubric of *Batson* too. As Justice Clarence Thomas has proposed, "given the Court's rationale in *J.E.B....* no principled reason immediately appears for declining to apply *Batson* to any strike based on a classification that is accorded heightened scrutiny under the Equal Protection Clause."[35] The Court does not as yet appear ready to tackle these issues. Prosecutors need to keep in mind that new *Batson* applications are always possible and may turn up where least expected. The reason the Supreme Court has yet to venture into these areas is perhaps best explained by the Court's still ambivalent attitudes towards the issue of peremptory strikes based on attitudinal associations rather than on ideas about racial, ethnic or other societal stereotypes.

For instance, let us examine the case of a man accused of sodomizing a young boy. Among the potential jurors is a male who has admitted membership in the North American Man Boy Love Association (NAMBLA), an organization that espouses pedophilia. Clearly the potential juror is constitutionally entitled to freedom of association under the First Amendment. He unequivocally insists that he can be fair and impartial, and will apply the sodomy laws as charged by the judge. No bases for a challenge for cause apparently exists but certainly no prosecutor would leave this man on the jury, no matter how much he professed his ability to enforce the law. Membership in groups and associations, therefore, clearly provides insights into attitudes, and attitude is a basis to strike a potential juror, despite their insistence that they will be fair.

In other matters, say for example an auto larceny trial, this juror's NAMBLA membership should be of no issue. In fact, it would probably never arise. But let us say that we are selecting for an auto larceny trial and the prosecutor strikes this juror solely on the basis of his membership in NAMBLA. Have we now crossed from atti-

tude to race or stereotype? Does the context of the trial pose a problem? These difficult questions might seem to erect major intellectual and logical obstacles to the
spread of *Batson*, but bad cases make bad law.

BATSON AND THE PROSECUTOR AT TRIAL

What can prosecutors do to protect themselves from unfounded *Batson* challenges
while ensuring that defendants are not making improper challenges of their own?
The trial record is the key. It is the record that will be reviewed to determine
whether the trial court properly implemented a *Batson* analysis. It should be kept in
mind that from the prosecution's perspective the remedy for failure to do this is
fatal—reversible error, not subject to harmless error analysis. Therefore, the actual
handwritten record made by the trial prosecutor becomes very important.

In some jurisdictions the court reporter is not required to record the minutes of voir
dire and jury selection. Typically, trial lawyers go about the question and answer of
prospective jurors round after round. After many interviews one can easily forget
what answer, gesture or other factor influenced the decision against leaving a particular individual on a jury. Remember, it is not until the defense has made out a *prima
facie* case that the court must demand an explanation. Usually the court is looking
for a pattern of strikes—a pattern that may not have been developed earlier. The
court must go back and review the previous strikes and attempt to ascertain why
those jurors were struck. Absent good notes, the prosecutor is likely to have forgotten why he struck the venire members. It is unreasonable to hope that the court will
necessarily remember a specific individual if the lawyers cannot. Hence, good notes
as to all the reasons for striking venire members are crucial. These notes become
especially important if an appellate court subsequently finds that the trial court
improperly decided that the defense failed to make a *prima facie* showing of purposeful racial discrimination. The case will then be sent back to the trial court, in light of
this decision, to determine if the reasons in support of the strikes were race neutral.
Years later when the issue is raised on appeal, absent extremely good notes, this
becomes an impossible task.

Experience has demonstrated that defense counsel will usually employ a *Batson* challenge in the first instance, instead of waiting for a pattern. This situation creates a
dilemma for the prosecutor. At such an early stage there is clearly no basis for a *prima
facie* case. If the prosecutor decides to put his explanation on the record he may be
revealing his trial strategy, thus giving the defense a tactical advantage. However, by

stating the reasons early, the record about the prosecutor's reasoning is made while it is fresh in the minds of all parties, most especially the trial judge's, who at that point is more likely to remember how the juror appeared, behaved and responded. These are often subtle items the judge may not recall later and he or she may not ordinarily take notes. The judge may wish at this point to add his or her own observations to the record which, ideally, will help lend support to the accuracy of the prosecutor's observations of the venire member and thus give credence (on the record) to the prosecutor's explanation.

It should be noted that by *providing* a reason, the prosecutor has relieved the defendant of his burden to establish a *prima facie* case. Once an explanation is given, the trial judge and the appellate judges will look to see if it is race neutral. Therefore, even if a *prima facie* case was not made out by the defense, in the event the court finds that the prosecutor's reasoning was not race neutral or that there was intentional discrimination, the juror will be impaneled or the case reversed.

Just what is a race neutral reason? Has the defense made out its burden of proof? *Hernandez v. New York* [36] addressed this issue. The Court explained that a neutral explanation is one that is based on *anything* apart from the juror's race or gender. The reasoning will be considered race neutral as long as no discriminatory intent is present in the explanation.[37] The fact that the reason given, while not arising to justify a strike for cause, might parallel a valid cause challenge, will assist in demonstrating its race neutral character.[38] It must be remembered that the inquiry does not stop at the race neutral explanation. Once a race neutral explanation is proffered it is left to the judge to determine whether the moving party (the party challenging the strike) has met its burden of proof in establishing purposeful discrimination.

The Court clarified this issue in *Purkett v. Elem*,[39] where it noted that in determining whether an explanation is race neutral, facial validity of an explanation has no effect on race neutrality, as long as discriminatory intent is not inherent in the reason.[40] The determination that the reason proposed is race neutral does not mean the court will deny the movant relief. The trial judge must then consider whether the burden of proof is met, forcing the judge into making a credibility determination that will be deferred to by the appellate courts.[41] The trial judge will then review in his own mind what transpired. As noted *supra*, prosecutors should make their explanations as detailed as possible, providing *all* their reasons that support their peremptory strikes. Again, thorough notes taken during voir dire are critical. A prosecutor must therefore be attuned at all times to why the juror should be struck. This task becomes easier with practice.

CONCLUSION

Why prosecutors should seek to strike one individual and keep another is the subject of another article. Prosecutors should determine, before trial, the criteria they are looking for in a juror. Advanced preparation will assist them in later establishing concrete reasons to eliminate jurors. One area in which *Batson* has certainly been of assistance is in forcing prosecutors to be more analytical about what they look for in potential jurors. Prosecutors should never feel personally confronted when a *Batson* challenge is made against them. Remember, for some (or many) defense counsel this has simply become a standard practice used to create an appealable issue.

It is the prosecutor's duty to ensure that racial discrimination does not enter into the jury selection process. Striking someone because of his or her race or gender should simply never be done. To the same extent, prosecutors cannot allow the defense to interject racial discrimination into jury selection. It is their duty to seek justice, and in so doing they should be vigilant to protect citizens from being discriminated against on account of race. Accordingly, prosecutors should not be afraid to raise *Batson* issues in the context of a *prima facie* allegation that the defense is improperly challenging jurors because of race. Although *Batson* should never be used by either side as a tactical weapon to disrupt an otherwise proper jury selection, prosecutors can also make *Batson* motions, and often should. Too often the defense will raise a *Batson* challenge just to make sure it is present as an appealable issue without ever having a basis for the challenge. Prosecutors must do their best to ensure that this does not happen.

ENDNOTES

[1] 391 U.S. 145, 88 S.Ct. 1444 (1968)(White, J.)

[2] *Id.* at 391 U.S. at 156, 88 S.Ct. at 1451.

[3] "There is nothing in the Constitution of the United States which requires the Congress [or the states] to grant peremptory challenges," *Swain v. Alabama*, 380 U.S. 202, 219, 85 S.Ct. 824, 835 (1965)(White, J.) (*quoting Stilson v. U.S.*, 250 U.S. 583, 586, 40 S.Ct. 28, 30). The peremptory challenge is "one of the most important rights secured to the accused." *Pointer v. U.S.*, 151 U.S. 396, 408, 14 S.Ct. 410, 414 (1894).

[4] Peremptory challenges are described as an arbitrary and capricious right which must be exercised with full freedom or it fails its full purpose. *Lewis v. U.S.*, 146 U.S. 378, 13 S.Ct. at 139 (1892).

[5] *Swain*, 380 U.S. at 219, 85 S.Ct. at 835 (1965) (White, J.). In *Swain,* Justice White provided a legal history of the peremptory challenge system. *Id*. at 212-220, 85 S.Ct. at 831-836. *Swain* is discussed in further detail *infra*.

[6] 100 U.S. (10 Otto) 303 (Strong, J.).

[7] *Id*. at 308-310.

[8] *Id*. at 310.

[9] 380 U.S. 202, 85 S.Ct. 824 (1965) (White, J.).

[10] *Id*. at 205, 85 S.Ct. at 828.

[11] *Id*. At 224, 85 S.Ct. at 838.

[12] *See Id*. at 223-24, 85 S.Ct. at 837-38.

[13] *Id*. at 225, 85 S.Ct. at 838.

[14] *See Id*. at 226, 85 S.Ct. at 839.

[15] 476 U.S. 79, 106 S.Ct. 1712 (1986) (Powell, J.)

[16] More specifically the defendant raised the right to a jury chosen from a cross section of the community and the equal protection of the laws. *Id*. at 82-83, 106 S.Ct. at 1715.

[17] *Id*. at 89, 106 S.Ct. at 1719.

[18] *Id*. at 92, 106 S.Ct. at 1721.

[19] *Id*. at 96, 106 S.Ct. at 1723.

[20] *Id*. (*quoting Avery v. Georgia*, 345 U.S. 559 at 562, 73 S.Ct. at 892)(emphasis added).

[21] *Id*. at 98, 106 S.Ct. at 1724, and n. 21.

[22] *Id*. at 89, 106 S.Ct. at 1719, n. 12.

[23] 499 U.S. 400, 111 S.Ct. 1364 (1991)(Kennedy, J.).

[24] National District Attorneys Association, *National Prosecution Standards, Second Edition* 206 (1991).

[25] 500 U.S. 614, 111 S.Ct. 2077 (1991) (Kennedy, J.) The court's disdain for peremptory challenges was further demonstrated in *Edmonson*. The Court opined that the peremptory strikes otherwise eliminate someone who satisfies jury service requirements. *Id*. at 620, 111 S.Ct. at 2083.

[26] *See Id*. at 620-24, 111 S.Ct. at 2082-2085.

[27] *Id*. at 624, 111 S.Ct. at 2085.

[28] 505 U.S. 42, 112 S.Ct. 2348 (1992)(Blackmun, J.).

[29] Even Chief Justice Rehnquist, who filed a dissent in *Edmonson*, concurred in *McCollum*, agreeing that *Edmonson's* reasoning gave the Court no choice but to apply *Batson* to criminal defendants. *See Id*. at 59-60, 112 S.Ct. at 2359 (Rehnquist, C.J., concurring).

[30] *Batson*, 476 U.S. at 101, 106 S.Ct. at 1725 (White, J., concurring).

[31] *Id*. at 107, 106 S.Ct. at 1728 (Marshall, J., concurring).

[32] 511 U.S. 127, 114 S.Ct. 1419 (1994) (Blackmun, J.).

[33] *Id*. at 129, 114 S.Ct. at 1421.

[34] *Id*. at 140, 114 S.Ct. at 1427.

[35] *Davis v, Minnesota*, 511 U.S. 1115, 1117 (1994) (Thomas, J.) (dissent from denial of certiorari); *but see J.E.B.*, 511 U.S. at 141, 114 S.Ct. at 1428, n. 14 (such challenges "do not reinforce the same stereotypes about the group's competence or predispositions that have been used to prevent them from voting, participating on juries, pursuing their chosen professions, or otherwise contributing to civic life.")

[36] 500 U.S. 352, 111 S.Ct 1859 (1991) (Kennedy, J.) (plurality opinion).

[37] *Id*. at 360, 111 S.Ct. at 1866.

[38] *Id*. at 363, 111 S.Ct. at 1868.

[39] 514 U.S. 765, 115 S.Ct. 1769 (1995) (*per curiam*).

[40] *Id*. at 768, 115 S.Ct. at 1771.

[41] *Hernandez*, 500 U.S. at 364, 111 S.Ct at 1869.

THE POWER OF CHARGING DISCRETION

By Paul R. Wallace, Deputy District Attorney General,
Office of the Attorney General of the State of Delaware, Wilmington, Delaware

Introduction

It has long been held that the decision regarding whom to prosecute and for what offenses lies in the "own official discretion" of the prosecutor.[1] This power of the prosecutor includes the discretion to initiate and direct investigations, to decide whether to prosecute and to designate the crimes to be charged. As this authority is derived and unchanged from common law, prosecutors are deemed "entitled" to bring charges and to prosecute any such charge "as a right adhering to their office without leave of Court."[2] In turn, the only court-imposed or constitutionally-mandated restriction regarding the initiation of criminal proceedings is that criminal charges be brought by "formal and sufficient accusation"—an accusation formally made in the form of an indictment or presentation of a grand jury or by an information of the prosecuting attorney.[3] The responsibility of the prosecutor in "wielding" what has been referred to by at least one Supreme Court Justice as "th[is] most terrible instrument of government" is profound.[4] The manner in which a prosecutor exercises his or her charging discretion not only impacts individual offenders but shapes the perception of victims and communities regarding the effectiveness of the criminal justice system as a whole.

The tremendous power inherent in the autonomous ability to make criminal charging decisions comes with a heightened responsibility to exercise that discretionary judgment to best serve the prosecutor's client—the people. The decision to prosecute cannot be a mere mathematical application of criminal statutes to evidence of criminal wrongdoing. For "[i]f every policeman, prosecutor, every court and every post-sentence agency performed his or its responsibility in strict accordance with rules of law, precisely and narrowly laid down, the criminal law would be ordered but intolerable... [and] [l]iving would be a sterile compliance with soul killing rules and taboos."[5] Aside from the demoralizing effect that strict enforcement of each criminal law without individual prosecutorial decision-making would have, the stark reality is that not every crime *could* be prosecuted.[6] Only individualized attention by the prosecutor in each case can ensure just results that are within the bounds of applicable law and consistent with community needs. The most important tool in the proper exercise of this core prosecutorial function—the charging decision—is flexible discretion in screening, charging and diversion decisions.

WHAT GUIDES THE EXERCISE OF CHARGING DISCRETION?

As already noted, the power of a prosecutor to determine whether one should be charged with a crime is incredibly broad. Because the role of the courts in overseeing the exercise of that discretion is limited and the prescribed remedies for alleged inappropriate exercise of charging discretion are few, it is generally left to the individual prosecutor and prosecutorial agency to monitor these decisions.[7]

Certainly there are some checks in the criminal system that are outside the prosecutor's control and that can validate or reject his or her decision in charging. The grand jury must return a true bill or, eventually, at the end of a trial, the petit jury must determine whether the evidence supports the charge. However, the effect of a prosecutor's decision whether to charge or not affects a potential criminal defendant well before the petit jury ever sees the case. The prosecutor's initial decision to charge exposes the criminal defendant to the expense, anxiety and embarrassment of criminal proceedings. Further, assuming that the decision is made with sufficient evidentiary support to convict, the decision regarding the number and the nature of charges brought by the prosecutor may have a dramatic impact on the course of the trial or plea negotiations and it may affect the offender's ability or willingness to exercise statutory and constitutional rights. Lastly, depending on the judicial discretion available in sentencing, the initial charging decision can effectively determine the ultimate outcome and future liberty of the person charged. Aside from the concerns for individual offenders, the prosecutor should also be aware of the goals he or she presumably promotes when administering justice: the protection of society and the integrity of the criminal justice system. For these reasons alone, flexible discretion in charging decisions must be governed by the highest standards of ethics and appropriate restraint.

The first step, and therefore an integral part in the exercise of this discretion, is the screening phase of criminal matters. Prosecutors and their agencies should establish, maintain and follow appropriate guidelines to effectively regulate the exercise of discretion in screening criminal charges. Ethical standards for the screening function are best described in the National District Attorneys Association's *National Prosecution Standards*.[8] It is clear from those standards and the commentary regarding the prosecutor's charging decisions that uniform but flexible guidelines provide the most effective means of consistently meeting a prosecutor's ethical and legal obligations.[9] The existence of such guidelines promotes many of the goals a prosecutor seeks to further in exercising his or her office. Well-crafted guidelines take the common sense approach of treating serious criminal matters as such, ensuring that valuable resources are not wasted on lesser offenses and fostering a level of predictability in the criminal justice system that meets public expectations.

As the prosecutor exercises his or her discretion in deciding whether to prosecute and in determining the appropriate charges, there are two well-recognized sources of formal guidance: the ethical standards provided by the rules of professional responsibility and the constitutional guarantees of the Due Process and Equal Protection Clauses. It is left to the individual prosecutorial agencies to integrate the ethical and constitutional standards so as to guarantee fundamental fairness in charging decisions. The aim of charging is to address violations of law according to the goals of the criminal justice system. While in each case the weight of the various goals may vary, the charging decision generally reflects a desire to:

- Promote public safety and welfare;
- Hold the individual offender accountable;
- Restore the victim and society;
- Rehabilitate the offender;
- Seek adequate but reasonable retribution on behalf of the victim and society; and,
- Deter others from engaging in similar acts.

Only an individualized examination that weighs these various and oft-times competing considerations can insure an appropriate charging decision.

ETHICAL STANDARDS
The *Model Rule of Professional Conduct 3.8* (American Bar Association) and most state rules regarding the "[s]pecial [r]esponsibilities of a [p]rosecutor" provide only that "[t]he prosecutor in a criminal case shall refrain from prosecuting a charge that the prosecutor knows is not supported by probable cause."[10] The American Bar Association (ABA) and the National District Attorneys Association (NDAA) further provide that "[a] prosecutor should not institute, cause to be instituted, or permit to continue pendency of criminal charges in the absence of sufficient admissible evi-

dence to support a conviction."[11] *ABA Prosecution Function Standard 3-3.9* goes on to state, "the prosecutor is not obligated to present all charges which the evidence might support. The prosecutor may in some circumstances and for good cause consistent with the public interests decline to prosecute, notwithstanding that evidence exists which would support a conviction." Both the ABA and NDAA provide illustrative factors that can be used to formulate screening and charging guidelines. For instance, the *ABA Prosecution Function Standard* suggests the following considerations:

- The prosecutor's reasonable doubt that the accused is in fact guilty;
- The extent of the harm caused by the offense;
- The disproportion of the authorized punishment in relation to the particular offense or the offender;
- Possible improper motives of a complainant;
- Reluctance of the victim to testify;
- Cooperation of the accused in the apprehension or conviction of others; and
- Availability and likelihood of prosecution by another jurisdiction.[12]/[13]

Because the role of the prosecutor is one of great public responsibility, ethical standards and caselaw warn against consideration of factors that are strictly personal to the prosecutor.[14] These impermissible factors include:

- The prosecutor's rate of conviction;[15]
- The personal or political advantages or disadvantages that might be involved in bringing or foregoing prosecution in the case; and,[16]
- The pressure from a supervising attorney to make a decision inconsistent with the individual prosecutor's case evaluation and belief regarding his or her ethical obligation in the matter.[17]

Once the decision to charge is made, the nature and number of charges should be determined. Here, as with all other aspects of the prosecutor's charging discretion, courts generally refuse to substitute their own judgment as to what offenses appropriately address the criminal behavior.[18] As long as the conduct is proscribed by statute and the prosecutor does not make his or her decision in bad faith or because of some arbitrary classification, the nature and number of charges is wholly left to his or her discretion. Again, given this broad discretion and the ever-increasing number of enhanced penalty statutes, each prosecutor is ethically constrained to show reasonable restraint in charging.

The prosecutor is not obligated to bring all charges that the evidence in a case may support.[19] Instead, the prosecutor should only file charges that adequately encompass the offense or offenses believed to have been committed and rationally address the nature and scope of the criminal activity.[20] Given the power of minimum mandatory sentencing statutes, what must be scrupulously avoided is the tendency to "over-charge" or engage in inappropriate "leveraging" by using the charging decision *only* as a means of obtaining guilty pleas to lesser charges.[21]

All of the ethical considerations that have been discussed thus far are those which *should* be taken into account in developing case screening and charging guidelines. However, although they are minimal, there are legal or constitutional limitations the prosecutor *must* consider in making the charging decision.

CONSTITUTIONAL CONSIDERATIONS

While the law of criminal procedure does prescribe checks and balances on the prosecutors charging power—the grand jury, the preliminary hearing or the actual trial of the case—there are few judicially recognized avenues for challenging charging decisions. Put more simply, while a prosecutor may be successful or unsuccessful in eventually convicting one of a charge brought, his or her initial decision to bring that charge can almost never be reviewed for legal error.[22]

Selectivity in charging decisions is not only permissible but also requisite to meeting the many considerations already mentioned. Unless based on a constitutionally protected criterion such as race, religion, sex or for the purpose of suppression of constitutional rights, that discretion simply will not be judicially second guessed.[23] This hands-off approach taken by the courts in reviewing the discretion exercised in charging decisions gives almost unlimited latitude to the prosecutor. Unless a court can make specific findings of improper selectivity, the prosecutor's discretionary call will stand. The courts simply cannot review those discretionary calls out of a generalized desire to seek "fairness" for a defendant.[24] Courts likewise reject arguments that statutes under which charging decisions are made provide too much discretion to the prosecutor.[25]

The two constitutional arguments most often made when attacking a prosecutor's charging decision are based upon the guarantees of equal protection and due process.[26] While the equal protection and due process clause guarantees do limit charging discretion, few criminal defendants ever succeed when they invoke these provisions to challenge the decision to prosecute.[27]

Ensuring that prosecutorial discretion in charging is not exercised in a manner offensive to the equal protection clause—that is, in a manner discriminatory as to race, religion or the exercise of related constitutional rights—is not difficult, as the bounds of propriety are readily recognizable. Courts have long and consistently warned against a prosecutor's exercise of discretion based on impermissible factors.[28] The standards that counsel against the exercise of prosecutorial selectivity based on these impermissible classifications are relatively easy to integrate into charging policies and guidelines.

Due process considerations, however, are somewhat more nebulous. The guarantee of due process prohibits prosecutors from choosing to proceed against a defendant for exercising a statutory or constitutional right.[29] In the due process case, a defendant generally argues retaliatory prosecution based on improper motives. In such cases, courts have found vindictive prosecution where defendants were punished for exercising their statutory or constitutional rights that relate to the prosecution.[30]

It is generally in these cases that the prosecutor faces the more difficult ethical dilemma. Most prosecutors are aware that charging decisions based on race, religion or other similar arbitrary classifications are wholly inappropriate. The ethical or legal boundaries prohibiting such discriminatory practices are readily identified. Charging decisions that may be "retaliatory" or "vindictive," however, are less easily identified. A "retaliatory" charging decision is, by definition, one made in reaction to an adverse court ruling or some act of the defendant's that the prosecutor views as detrimental to the people's position in the criminal investigation or proceedings. In these circumstances, the prosecutor may mistakenly believe it is appropriate to regain the lost advantage through a tougher charging decision. This simply is not so, and there must be heightened sensitivity by a prosecutor in making charging decisions after plea negotiations have fallen through or when there has been some adverse ruling by a court.[31]

In sum, to address the legal restrictions of charging discretion, the prosecutorial agency can easily integrate standards that ensure compliance with the equal protection clause. Special care, however, must be paid to those individual cases that raise the specter of due process violations.

SPECIAL ISSUES IN CHARGING DECISIONS

Beside the decision as to whether or not to bring a particular criminal charge, there are related "charging" issues that adopt the same analysis and invoke the same ethical and legal considerations mentioned above.

Seeking the Death Penalty

There is no more critical decision by a prosecutor than deciding when to seek the death penalty. Although the consequences of this discretionary decision by the prosecutor are "irremediable," courts grant the same wide berth to a prosecutor's decision in these cases as with any other criminal matter. In fact, the United States Supreme Court has never required prosecutors to adopt any screening procedures or charging policies to guide these decisions.[32] Instead, individual prosecutors are left to make this decision in the same manner as all other charging decisions. Given the nature of the consequences of this decision, however, heightened scrutiny in the screening and charging in capital cases should be employed utilizing the same standards mentioned above.[33]

Enhanced Penalty or Habitual Criminal Cases

Statutes that authorize enhanced penalties on the basis of prior criminality are a powerful weapon in the prosecutor's arsenal. Many of these statutes require the prosecutor to file a form of petition or motion enhancing the penalty after certain convictions.[34] Again, courts do not generally review the discretion of prosecutors in seeking these enhanced penalties but analogize such to other "charging" decisions made by prosecutors.[35]

DIVERSION PROGRAMS

A recent development in criminal justice is the increasing adoption of diversion programs for offenders. This alternative permits the prosecutor to channel offenders into programs that may involve no incarceration and even dismissal of criminal proceedings. Decisions to divert cases in this manner almost always lie first with the prosecutor. The prosecutor should exercise his or her discretion to divert offenders only when he or she considers it to be in the best interest of justice and beneficial to both the community and the individual.[36] Some factors to be considered in this decision include:

- The nature or the severity of the offense;
- Characteristics of the offender: Is this a first time offender? Does he have any special needs or difficulties? Will he be cooperative and benefit from the program? Is the offender likely to recidivate?

• The availability of a program that is appropriate to meet the needs of the offender and address the offense appropriately;
• The opinions and recommendations of the victim and law enforcement agency involved; and
• The availability of restitution and community restoration. [37]

The "charging decision" analysis adopted by the courts is also used in examining a prosecutor's decision to agree to or forego diversion.[38]

CIVIL LIABILITY RELEASE AND DISMISSAL AGREEMENTS

There is strong disagreement among courts and commentators as to whether prosecutors may condition the withholding of criminal charges on an offender's agreement to waive potential civil rights or tort claims relating to the case. The United States Supreme Court has held that a voluntarily executed agreement for which the defendant relinquishes civil rights claims in return for dismissal of criminal charges is enforceable.[39] Other courts, however, have expressed concern that such agreements involve prosecutors in a conflict of interest and create an appearance of professional and ethical impropriety.[40] When courts with the full understanding of the legal efficacy of such agreements continue to express skepticism and hostility, the prosecutor should be especially sensitive to the negative public perception created by such agreements. Thus, the *ABA Standards for Criminal Justice* state that a prosecutor should not condition a decision to forego criminal charging on the relinquishment of a right to seek civil redress unless the accused has agreed "knowingly and intelligently, freely and voluntarily, and where such waiver is approved by [a] court."[41] Thus, prosecutors should generally take the same skeptical view of such agreements and only use them in limited circumstances. Factors that may permit use of a dismissal-release agreement are:

• The civil claim arises from the same incident as the criminal charge;
• The prosecutor has reviewed the matter and is convinced there are no serious civil rights violations involved in the matter;
• The prosecutor is assured that the defendant's participation in the agreement is informed and voluntary;
• The prosecution and defense seek judicial approval of the agreement; and
• The prosecutor is convinced that the agreement is in the public interest.

Lastly, the prosecutor should be particularly aware of the imbalance of power between his or her office and the defendant. Consequences to a defendant who does not enter into such an agreement are much greater than to the government agency that will benefit. Moreover, the prosecutor must always avoid activity that appears to use the threat of criminal proceedings to gain advantage in civil proceedings. Thus, although there may be judicial and ethical approval for the use of such agreements it must be done sparingly and with a great deal of sensitivity to the perception of impropriety that may be fostered.

CONCLUSION

In the face of long and sometimes boisterous criticism of prosecutors' broad discretion in bringing criminal charges, courts have been exceedingly reluctant to step in to regulate the process. Each prosecutor must insure that he or she carries out this unique function in a manner consistent with the law and the highest ethical standards. It is not only the individual defendants who are affected by the exercise of this discretion. Public confidence in the abilities of the criminal justice system to address the wrongs committed by offenders depends greatly on the prosecutor's initial decisions. These decisions must be the product of screening and charging standards that foster objectivity, predictability and the best interests of the public welfare.

ENDNOTES

[1] *State v. Whitlock*, 41 Ark. 403 (Ark. 1883).

[2] *Id.*

[3] *Albrecht v. United States,* 273 U.S. 1 (1927).

[4] *Martin v. Merola*, 532 F.2d 191, 196, n.1 (2d Cir. 1976) (Lumbard, J., concurring) (quoting Frankfurter, J., letter to the *New York Times,* March 4, 1941).

[5] Breitel, "Controls in Criminal Law Enforcement," *U. Chi. L. Rev.* 27 (1960): 427.

[6] ABA Standards *for Criminal Justice: Prosecution Function and Defense Function,* Third Edition, 1993 (hereinafter *ABA PROSECUTION FUNCTION STANDARD ___*).

[7] *See* Morton, Lyn M. " Seeking the Elusive Remedy for Prosecutorial Misconduct: Suppression, Dismissal, or Discipline?" *Geo. J. Legal Ethics* 7 (1994): 1083.

[8] National District Attorneys Association, *National Prosecution Standards* §§ 42.1- 42.4 (2d ed.1991) (hereinafter "*NDAA NATIONAL PROSECUTION STANDARD* § ___").

[9] *See* "Commentary," *ABA PROSECUTION FUNCTION STANDARD* 3-3.4; "Commentary," *NDAA NATIONAL PROSECUTION STANDARD* §§ 42.1- 43.6; Vorenberg, J. "Decent Restraint of Prosecutorial Power," *Harv. L. Rev.* 94 (1981) 1521, 1543-46.

[10] *See*, e.g., *DEL. LAWYER'S PROF. COND.* 3.8 (1998); SUPREME JUDICIAL COURT RULE 3:07, MASSACHUSETTS RULES OF PROFESSIONAL CONDUCT 3.8 (1999); NORTH CAROLINA STATE BAR RULE 3.8; *OKLA. ST. R. PROF. COND.*, R. 3.8 (1999).

[11] *ABA PROSECUTION FUNCTION STANDARD* 3-3.9(a); *NDAA NATIONAL PROSECUTION STANDARD* § 43.6(a); and, "Commentary," *NDAA NATIONAL PROSECUTION STANDARD* § 43.3.

[12] *ABA Prosecution Function Standard* 3-3.9(b)(i)-(vii).

[13] *See also NDAA NATIONAL PROSECUTION STANDARD* § 43.6.

[14] *See*, e.g., *In Re Ridgely*, 106 A.2d 527 (Del. 1954).

[15] "Commentary," *ABA PROSECUTION FUNCTION STANDARD* 3-3.9; *NDAA NATIONAL PROSECUTION STANDARD* § 42.4(a).

[16] *ABA PROSECUTION STANDARD* 3-3.9(d); *NDAA NATIONAL PROSECUTION STANDARD* § 42.4(b).

[17] *ABA PROSECUTION FUNCTION STANDARD* 3-3.9(c).

[18] *See*, e.g., *Wilson v. State*, 612 A.2d 159 (Del. 1992); *Albury v. State*, 551 A.2d 53, 61-62 (Del. 1988).

[19] *ABA PROSECUTION FUNCTION STANDARD* 3-3.9(b).

[20] *NDAA NATIONAL PROSECUTION STANDARD* § 43.2; *ABA PROSECUTION FUNCTION STANDARD* 3-3.9(f).

[21] *NDAA NATIONAL PROSECUTION STANDARD* § 43.4; "Commentary," *ABA PROSECUTION FUNCTION STANDARD* 3-3.9. *See also*, Vorenberg, *Harv. L. Rev.* 94: 1560-61.

[22] *Newman v. United States*, 382 F.2d 479, 480 (D.C. Cir. 1967).

[23] *Oyler v. Boles*, 368 U.S. 448 (1962).

[24] *State v. John P. Krueger*, 588 N.W.2d 921 (Wis. 1999).

[25] *See People v. Conat*, 605 N.W.2d 49 (Mich. Ct. App. 1999).

[26] *Albury v. State*, 551 A.2d at 61, n . 13.

[27] *See e.g., Wayte v. United States*, 470 U.S. 598, 610 (1985).

[28] *Yick Wo v. Hopkins*, 118 U.S. 356 (1886) (race); *Cleveland v. Trzebuckowski*, 709 N. E.2d 1148 (Ohio 1999) (age). *See also United States v. Falk*, 479 F.2d 616 (7th Cir. 1973) (en banc) (exercise of first amendment right); *People v. Walker*, 200 N.E.2d 779 (N.Y. 1964) (same).

[29] *Blackledge v. Perry*, 417 U.S. 21 (1974).

[30] *See*, e.g., *Osborne v. Commonwealth*, 992 S.W.2d 860 (Ky. Ct. App. 1999); *see also*, Vorenberg, *Harv. L. Rev.* 94: 1541-42.

[31] *See*, e.g., *State v. Antonio Marti*, 732 A.2d 414 (N.H. 1999).

[32] *See State v. Barnett*, 980 S.W.2d 297 (Mo. 1998).

[33] Demay, J. "A District Attorney's Decision Whether to Seek the Death Penalty: Toward an Improved Process," *Fordham Urb. L. J.* 26 (3) (1999): 767.

[34] *See* e. g. 11 *Del.C.* §4215 (Supp. 1999); see also Marshall, Nancy J. "The Constitutional Infirmities of Indiana's Habitual Offender Statute," *Ind. L. Rev.* 13, 597, nn. 1 & 25 (1980) (listing state habitual criminal statutes).

[35] *See, Ward v. State,* 414 A.2d 499 (Del. 1980); *Rollinson v. State,* 743 So.2d 585 (Fla. Dist. Ct. App. 1999); *McKnight v. State,* 727 So.2d 314 (Fla. Dist. Ct. App. 1999).

[36] *NDAA NATIONAL PROSECUTION STANDARD* § 44.4.

[37] *Id.*

[38] *See State v. Harris,* 1999 WL 357344 (Tenn. Ct. App. 1999).

[39] *Town of Newton v. Rumery,* 480 U.S. 386 (1987).

[40] *Cowles v. Brownell,* 538 N.E.2d 325 (N.Y. 1989).

[41] *ABA PROSECUTION FUNCTION STANDARD* 3-3.9(g). Compare with NDAA *NATIONAL PROSECUTION STANDARD* § 43.5 (counsels more strongly against such agreements).

PROPER PROCEDURES FOR CONSULAR NOTIFICATION

By Darrell Mavis, Assistant District Attorney, Los Angeles County, Los Angeles, California

Introduction

The Vienna Convention on Consular Relations ("Vienna Convention"), which defines consular privileges and duties and facilitates the exercise of consular functions relating to foreign nationals, has been referred to as "undoubtedly the single most important event in the entire history of the consular institution."[1] In 1969, the United States, along with over 130 other nations, signed the Vienna Convention, and it became the "law of the land" under the Supremacy Clause of the U.S. Constitution.[2] This chapter first examines the obligations of U.S. law enforcement under the Vienna Convention, and then discusses how prosecutors should respond to defense motions based on a failure to provide consular notification upon the arrest and/or detention of a foreign national.

U.S. LAW ENFORCEMENT OBLIGATIONS UNDER THE VIENNA CONVENTION

Article 36 of the Vienna Convention provides that consular officials shall be free to communicate with, and have access to, nationals of their country.[3] Similarly, nationals of a foreign country shall have the same freedom with respect to communication with and access to consular officials of their country. Article 36(1)(a) states:

> Consular officials shall be free to communicate with nationals of the sending state and to have access to them. Nationals of the sending state shall have the same freedom with respect to communication with and access to consular officers of the sending state.[4]

When a foreign national is detained by U.S. law enforcement, Article 36(1)(b) provides that competent authorities shall, without delay, inform a national that his consular officials may be notified of his detention:

> If he so requests, the competent authorities of the receiving state shall, without delay, inform the consular post of the sending state if, within its

consular district, a national of that state is arrested or committed to prison or custody pending trial or is detained in any other manner. Any communication addressed to the consular post by the person arrested, in prison, custody or detention shall also be forwarded by the said authorities without delay. *The said authorities shall inform the person concerned without delay of his rights under this sub-paragraph.*[5]

Article 36(1)(c) grants consular officers the opportunity to visit, converse, correspond and arrange for legal representation for a foreign national who is detained:

Consular officers shall have the right to visit a national of the sending state who is in prison, custody or detention, to converse and correspond with him and to arrange for his legal representation. They also shall have the right to visit any national of the sending state who is in prison, custody or detention in their district in pursuance of a judgment. Nevertheless, consular officers shall refrain from taking action on behalf of a national who is in prison, custody or detention if he expressly opposes such action.[6]

Thus, U.S. law enforcement officials should notify detained foreign nationals, including those with lawful permanent resident alien (i.e. a "green card") status, of their opportunity for consular access. If the detainee so requests, the United States must notify the relevant consulate of the detainee's arrest or detention.

The U.S. Department of State has prepared a booklet entitled *Consular Notification and Access: Instructions for Federal, State, and Local Law Enforcement and Other Officials Regarding Foreign Nationals in the United States and the Rights of Consular Officials to Assist Them* that outlines the procedures law enforcement officials must take and includes detailed instructions and translations of suggested consular notification statements in 13 languages.[7]

A law enforcement official should offer, without delay, to notify the foreign national's consular officials of the arrest or detention. He should advise the following:

As a non-US citizen who is being arrested or detained, you are entitled to have us notify your country's consular representatives here in the United States. A consular official from your country may be able to help you obtain legal counsel, and may contact your family and visit you in detention, among other things. If you want us to notify your country's consular officials, you can request this notification now, or at any time in the future. After your consular officials are notified, they may call or visit you. Do you want us to notify your country's consular officials? [8]

If the detainee requests that consular notification be given, the law enforcement officials must then notify the nearest consulate of the country in question without delay. The law enforcement officials should keep a written record of the provision of notification and actions taken. Pursuant to other bilateral agreements, over 50 nations require notification of the arrest or detention of their nationals, regardless of detainee's wishes.[9] This duty is referred to as "mandatory notification."

Once U.S. law enforcement has determined the nationality of a detained foreign national, they must determine if that country is on the mandatory notification list. If a detained foreign national's country is on the list of mandatory notification countries, then law enforcement should notify the country's nearest consulate office, without delay, of the arrest and/or detention. The foreign national who is arrested and/or detained should be informed as follows:

> Because of your nationality, we are required to notify your country's representatives here in the United States that you have been arrested or detained. After your consular officials are notified, they may call or visit you. You are not required to accept their assistance, but they may be able to help obtain legal counsel and may contact your family and may visit you in detention, among other things. We will notify your country's consular officials as soon as possible.[10]

RESPONDING TO DEFENSE MOTIONS BASED ON THE FAILURE OF LAW ENFORCEMENT TO FOLLOW THE VIENNA CONVENTION

Foreign nationals who have not been advised of their opportunity to contact their consular officials increasingly put forth this failure as a basis for suppressing statements and fruits of searches; for undermining convictions; and for seeking new sentencing hearings.[11] Foreign nationals have raised these claims in federal and state cases at all stages—in pre-trial, appeal and post-conviction habeas corpus proceedings. Several foreign governments, including Paraguay and Canada have formally complained of U.S. failures to notify their consulates and have backed their nationals in seeking judicial remedies. The failure of consular notification is an affront to the treaty partner, however, not to the rights of the individuals under the United States law or the Constitution. Thus, the prosecutor should successfully argue that the failure to provide notification should not result in a judicial remedy to the defendant.

When the Defendant Must First Raise the Failure of Consular Notification

The defendant must first raise the issue of a failure of consular notification in a trial court. Absent a clear and express statement to the contrary, the procedural rules of the forum country govern the implementation of an international treaty in that country.[12] Article 36(2) of the Vienna Convention affirms this principle by stating "the rights of the convention are exercised in conformity with the laws and regulations of the receiving state."[13] Thus, when an issue regarding the Vienna Convention arises in the United States, both international law and the Vienna Convention dictate that the procedural laws of the U.S., as the forum state, govern.

If the defendant does not assert his Vienna Convention claim in a trial court, he fails to exercise his rights under the Vienna Convention in conformity with the laws of the United States and therefore is procedurally barred from raising the claim. Generally, assertions of error in criminal proceedings must first be raised in the trial court in order to form the basis for relief in habeas claims.[14] Claims not so raised are waived.[15] The U.S. Supreme Court held in *Breard v. Greene*,[16] that a defendant could not successfully raise the failure of consular notification on federal habeas review. In Oklahoma, for example, the Oklahoma Court of Criminal Appeals denied a defendant's claim of error when he failed to raise the consular notification issue in the trial court.[17] Therefore, according to case law and the Vienna Convention, a defendant must first raise the issue of consular notification in a trial court.

Standing To Assert A Violation

According to international principles of standing, international agreements do not create private rights enforceable by individuals. The general rule on standing is that "international agreements, even those directly benefiting private persons, generally do not create private rights or provide for a private cause of action in domestic courts."[18] Rather, international treaties deal with the rights and duties of nation states; rarely do they address the rights of individuals. Under international law, it is the contracting foreign government that has the right to complain about a [treaty] violation."[19] The federal courts have held that international treaties are generally not judicially enforceable by individuals.[20] Treaties that do create individual rights typically are ones concerning disputes of a commercial nature between individuals or corporations. Therefore, the general rule of standing is that international agreements do not create private rights enforceable by individuals.

In addition, a prosecutor should argue that the Vienna Convention itself does not create private judicially enforceable rights. The Vienna Convention is based on the premise that "an international convention on consular relations, privileges and immunities contributes to the development of friendly relations among nations, irrespective of their differing constitutional and social systems."[21] The Convention expressly provides that "the purpose of [the] privileges and immunities [discussed in the Convention] is not to benefit individuals but to ensure the performance of functions by consular posts on behalf of their respective states."[22] The treaty language should control unless application of the words of the treaty according to their obvious meaning affects a result inconsistent with the intent or expectations of its signatories.[23]

However, some courts have held that the Vienna Convention creates individual rights that are enforceable in court proceedings.[24] In fact, the text of Article 36 has been interpreted to suggest persons have individual notification rights.[25]

The prosecutor should argue that the purpose of Article 36 is to facilitate the performance of consular functions by consular officials, which, in turn, may benefit a foreign national. Article 36 of the Vienna Convention, like its preamble, begins with the express statement that its provisions, including the requirements of consular notification at issue, are established "with a view to facilitating the exercise of consular functions relating to nationals of the sending state."[26]

Additionally, Article 36 appears in Chapter II of the Vienna Convention which is entitled "Facilities, Privileges and Immunities Relating to Consular Posts, Career Consular Officers and Other Members of a Consular Post." This section relates to the foreign national's *country*, not the foreign national. Also, Article 36 is specifically found in a section of the Vienna Convention entitled "Facilities, Privileges and Immunities Relating to a Consular Post."[27] The facilities, privileges and immunities of individuals are dealt with in a later section.[28]

The majority of federal courts have declined to decide whether the Vienna Convention creates judicially enforceable individual rights to consular notification and access.[29] At least one state court has gone as far as explicitly stating that no individually enforceable rights are created under the Vienna Convention.[30] Thus, where Article 36 is violated, the aggrieved party is the foreign national's country because it is the country whose consular operations have been hindered by the violation. The Vienna Convention does not provide for a judicially enforceable private right. Therefore, the prosecutor should successfully argue the defendant does not have standing to assert a violation of the Vienna Convention.

REMEDIES FOR A VIOLATION OF THE TREATY

The Vienna Convention does not provide a right to remedy a violation of Article 36 either in the parties' domestic courts or in any international forum. Rather, the U.S. Supreme Court has stated that diplomatic negotiations are the state's redress.[31] A state court, for example, has held that rights under the Vienna Convention are not constitutional in dimension and therefore do not provide grounds for relief.[32]

Similarly, U.S. citizens should not expect violation of the Vienna Convention in a foreign country to be remedied by the foreign country's judicial system. In the *Foreign Affairs Manual* of the U.S. Department of State, U.S. consular officers are instructed about consular notification procedures in foreign nations. While the *Foreign Affairs Manual* insists on timely notification, it does not suggest that failure of consular notification should be addressed through the host country's criminal justice system. Rather, the only remedy mentioned for violation of consular notification is diplomatic protest at various levels of the foreign country's government. The *Foreign Affairs Manual* explains that the purposes of such protests include:

> Protecting American prisoners against further abuse or violation of their rights; impressing the host government that the U.S. government is seriously concerned about the welfare and rights of its citizens and will not condone or tolerate their violation; protecting future American detainees against similar maltreatment; and improving the general level of treatment of U.S. citizens arrested and detained in foreign countries.[33]

Therefore, neither foreign nationals nor U.S. citizens in foreign countries should expect criminal proceedings to remedy a failure to provide consular notification.

Motions to Exclude Evidence

A foreign national may seek to exclude evidence that is obtained after he was arrested and not provided consular notification. Prosecutors should respond that exclusion of evidence is a remedy designed solely to safeguard constitutional rights.[34] Federal courts have recognized that the exclusionary rule was not created to vindicate a broad, general right to be free of agency action not authorized by law but rather to protect certain, specific, constitutionally protected rights of individuals.[35] Thus, non-constitutional violations should not warrant suppression of evidence under the exclusionary rule.[36] The Vienna Convention does not create any fundamental, constitutional rights.[37]

Absent an underlying constitutional violation, a statutory violation warrants suppression of evidence only where the statute expressly calls for that remedy.[38] One could argue a treaty violation is comparable to a statutory violation in this regard.[39] Since the Vienna Convention does not expressly provide for suppression of evidence as a remedy, exclusion of the evidence is not warranted under a statutory violation theory either.[40] Therefore, because the Vienna Convention does not create constitutional rights and does not warrant suppression of evidence as a remedy, the exclusionary rule is not an appropriate remedy for violations of the Vienna Convention.

Prejudicial Evidence Versus Showing Prejudice

Assuming the Vienna Convention creates an individual, judicially enforceable right from which there is a remedy and that the defendant raises the issue in the trial court, the defendant must still show that he has been prejudiced by the failure to provide consular notification. The burden of proof to show this prejudice is on the defendant.[41] A violation of the Vienna Convention is not prejudice per se.[42] Rather, the showing of prejudice must be a prejudice from the violation of the Vienna Convention, not a showing of prejudicial evidence to the defendant.[43] After all, a prosecutor is usually only seeking to introduce prejudicial evidence against a defendant.

Showing prejudice will be very difficult for the defendant to do. First, a foreign national must show he would have admitted to being a foreign national to trigger the notification process. Fear of deportation could provide an incentive to lie. Additionally, a foreign national from a non-mandatory notification country must show that he would have wanted his consular officials notified. Fear of adverse consequences from his country might cause him to decline to make his country aware of his custodial status.

If the foreign national is familiar with the U.S. laws and customs because he has lived in the U.S. for a while or has been arrested or been on probation before, then the foreign national's ability to show prejudice is even more difficult.

Assuming the defendant's consular offices were notified, the defendant must show that his consulate has the resources, at all hours of the day and night, to provide every citizen with immediate consulate services. Moreover, the defendant must show what the consulate officials would do at the time he was arrested and interviewed. The services offered by the consular officials vary tremendously but may include: explaining the legal system in broad terms; assisting in obtaining legal counsel; monitoring the progress of the case; seeking to ensure that the foreign national receives a fair trial; ensuring that the foreign national is being treated humanely; forwarding mail; and bringing reading material, food, medicine or other necessities.[44]

The function of the consulate official is not to advise every foreign national arrested: don't talk to the police. This so-called advisement is not the purpose of the Vienna Convention: it would strain relations between countries and would interfere with the separation of powers clause as contained in the Constitution. Because the Vienna Convention bars consular representatives from rendering any kind of legal assistance, the foreign national cannot claim prejudice on the grounds that the consulate would have told him not to talk to the police.[45]

Finally, even assuming the defendant could make all the showings articulated above, he still would not be able to justify suppressing a statement. The Vienna Convention does not require that the consular notification opportunity be given prior to advisement of *Miranda* rights.[46] Nor does the Vienna convention require that questioning stop while a foreign national's consulate is notified. The intent of the Vienna Convention is not to thwart a state's investigation by delaying a police interview that could possibly prevent destruction of evidence. Therefore, if a foreign national expresses a desire to contact his consulate, this is not an invocation for *Miranda* purposes and questioning under *Miranda* may continue. Nothing in the Vienna Convention provides that once law enforcement officials have notified the consulate, they must delay an interview until the arrival of consular officials.[47] Thus, the defendant needs to show that he would not have continued talking to the police while they notified the consulate.

In sum, the defendant must show a prejudicial effect from the violation of the Vienna Convention, not that there is prejudicial evidence against him.

CONCLUSION

The United States has an obligation to notify a foreign national of his opportunity to contact his consulate. With foreign nationals of countries that require mandatory notification of arrest or detention, law enforcement should notify the appropriate consulate regardless of the detainee's wishes. After all, the purpose of the Vienna Convention is to ensure that foreign governments can extend appropriate consular services to their nationals in the U.S. and that the U.S., in turn, may enjoy full, reciprocal access to U.S. nationals detained in foreign countries.[48] When the U.S. meets its obligations to other countries, it is in a better position to insist upon access to its nationals detained abroad.[49] A failure to be notified of the opportunity to consular access, however, is not a violation that should be remedied through the judicial system of any country.

ENDNOTES

[1] Luke Lee, CONSULAR LAW AND PRACTICE 27 (2d ed., 1991).

[2] *See* U.S. Const. art. VI, cl. 2.

[3] Vienna Convention on Consular Relations, Apr. 24, 1963, 21 U.S.T. 77 (hereinafter Vienna Convention).

[4] *Id.* at art. 36, para. 1(a).

[5] *Id.* at art. 36, para 1(b) (emphasis added).

[6] *Id.* at art. 36, para. 1(c).

[7] This booklet is available by telephoning (202) 647-4415 or on the Internet at http://www.state.gov. Direct access is found at http://www.state.gov/www/global/legal_affairs/ca_notification/.

[8] CONSULAR NOTIFICATION AND ACCESS: INSTRUCTIONS FOR FEDERAL, STATE, AND LOCAL LAW ENFORCEMENT AND OTHER OFFICIALS REGARDING FOREIGN NATIONALS IN THE UNITED STATES AND THE RIGHTS OF CONSULAR OFFICIALS TO ASSIST THEM, U.S. Department of State (1998) 7.

[9] Antigua and Barbuda, Armenia, Azerbaijan, The Bahamas, Barbados, Belarus, Belize, Brunei, Bulgaria, China (not Taiwan), Costa Rica, Cyprus, Czech Republic, Dominica, Fiji, The Gambia, Georgia, Ghana, Grenada, Guyana, Hong Kong, Hungary, Jamaica, Kazakhstan, Kiribati, Kuwait, Kyrgyzstan, Malaysia, Malta, Mauritius, Moldova, Mongolia, Nigeria, Philippines, Poland (nonpermanent residents), Romania, Russia, Saint Kitts and Nevis, Saint Lucia, Saint

Vincent/Grenadines, Seychelles, Sierra Leone, Singapore, Slovakia, Tajikistan, Tanzania, Tonga, Trinidad and Tobago, Turkmenistan, Tuvalu, Ukraine, United Kingdom, U.S.S.R. (passports may still be in use), Uzbekistan, Zambia, Zimbabwe.

[10] *See* CONSULAR NOTIFICATION AND ACCESS, *supra* note 9.

[11] Information for the Office of Investigative Policy, *Consular Notification and Access*, U.S. DEPARTMENT OF STATE, (March 24, 1999) 1.

[12] *See Sun Oil Co. v. Wortman*, 486 U.S. 717, 723 (1988); *Volkswagenwerk Aktiengesellschaft v. Schlunk*, 486 U.S. 694, 706 (1988); *Societe Nationale Industrielle Aerospatiale v. United States District Court for Southern District of Iowa*, 482 U.S. 522, 539 (1987).

[13] Vienna Convention, *supra* note 4, art. 36, para 2.

[14] *See Wainwright v. Sykes*, 433 U.S. 72, 75 (1977).

[15] *Id.*

[16] 523 U.S. 371, 537 (1998).

[17] *See Martinez v. Oklahoma*, 984 P.2d 813, 817 (Okla. 1999).

[18] RESTATEMENT (THIRD) OF FOREIGN RELATIONS § 907, cmt. a (1987).

[19] *United States v. Rosenthal*, 793 F.2d 1214, 1232 (11th Cir. 1986), *cert. denied*, 480 U.S. 919 (1987). *See also Head Money Cases*, 112 U.S. 580, 598-99 (1884).

[20] *See e.g. Argentine Republic v. Amerada Hess Shipping*, 488 U.S. 428, 442 (1989); *Goldstar v. United States*, 967 F.2d 965, 968 (4th Cir. 1992); *Mannington Mills, Inc. v. Congoleum Corp.*, 595 F.2d 1287, 1298-1299 (3d Cir. 1979).

[21] Vienna Convention, *supra* note 4, Preamble.

[22] *Id.*

[23] *Sumitomo Shoji America, Inv. v. Avagliano*, 457 U.S. 176, 180 (1982); *Maximov v. United States*, 372 U.S. 49, 51 (1963).

[24] *See Breard, supra* note 17; *United States v. Salas*, 168 F.3d 484 (4th Cir. 1998); *United States v. Alvarado-Torres*, 45 F. Supp.2d 986, 990-991 (S.D.Cal. 1999); *United States v. Chaparro-Alcantara*, 37 F. Supp.2d 1122, 1125 (C.D. Ill 1999); *United States v. Hongla-Yamche*, 55 F. Supp.2d 74, 78, 83 (D. Mass. 1999); *United States v. Superville*, 40 F. Supp.2d 672, 675-679 (D.V.I. 1999); *United States v. Torres-Del Muro*, 58 F.Supp.2d 931, 933 (C.D. Ill. 1999); *United States v. $69,530.00 in U.S. Currency*, 22 F. Supp.2d 593 (W.D. Tex. 1998); *Breard v. Netherland*, 949 F.Supp. 1255, 1263 (E.D. Va. 1996).

[25] *See Chapparo-Alcantara, id.*

[26] Vienna Convention, *supra* note 45, art. 36, para. 1(a).

[27] *Id.* at Section I, Chapter II.

[28] *Id.* at Section II, Chapter II.

[29] *See United States v. Rodrigues,* 170 F.3d 881 (9th Cir. 1999); *United States v. Kevin,* 165 F.3d 20 (4th Cir. 1998); *Murphy v. Netherland,* 116 F.3d 97, 99 (4th Cir. 1997), *cert. denied,* 521 U.S. 1144 (1977); *United States v. Salameh,* 54 F.Supp.2d 236, 279 (S.D.N.Y. 1999); *United States v. Tapia-Mendoza,* 41 F. Supp.2d 1250, 1253 (D.Utah 1999); *United States v. Esparza-Ponce,* 7 F.Supp.2d 1084, 1095-1096 (S.D. Cal. 1998).

[30] *See Kasi v. Commonwealth,* 508 S.E.2d 57, 64 (Va. Ct. App. 1998), *cert. denied,* 119 S. Ct. 2399 (1999).

[31] *See Breard, supra* note 17.

[32] *See Ohio v. Loza,* 1997 Ohio. App. LEXIS 4574 (October 13, 1997).

[33] U.S. Department of State, 7 Foreign Affairs Manual 415.1.

[34] *See United States v. Leon,* 468 U.S. 897, 906 (1984); *Massiah v. United States,* 377 U.S. 201, 204 (1964); *Mapp v. Ohio,* 367 U.S. 643, 649 (1961); *United States v. Alvarado-Torres, supra* note 25; *United States v. $69,530 in U.S Currency, supra* note 25.

[35] *See United States v. Hensel,* 699 F.2d 18, 29 (1st Cir. 1983); *United States v. Harrington,* 681 F.2d 612, 615 (9th Cir. 1982).

[36] *See United States v. Caceres,* 440 U.S. 741, 754 (1979).

[37] *See United States v. Ademaj,* 170 F.3d 58, 67 (1st Cir. 1999), *cert. denied,* 120 S.Ct 206 (1999); *Waldron v. INS,* 17 F.3d 511, 518 (2d Cir. 1993); *Alvarado-Torres, supra* note 25; *Murphy v. Netherland, supra* note 30, cited with approval in *United Mexican States v. Woods,* 126 F.3d 1220 1224, n.2 (9th Cir. 1997); *Salameh, supra* note 30; *Torres-Del Muro, supra* note 25; *$69,530.00 in U.S. Currency, supra* note 25, 595; *Esparza-Ponce, supra* note 30.

[38] *See United States v. Ani,* 138 F.3d 390, 392 (9th Cir. 1998); *United States v. Edgar,* 82 F.3d 499, 510-511 (1st Cir. 1996); *United States v. Daccarett,* 6 F.3d 37, 52 (2d Cir. 1993); *United States v. Thompson,* 936 F.2d 1249, 1251 (11th Cir. 1991) *cert. denied,* 502 U.S. 1075 (1992); *Hensel, supra* note 36; *Harrington, supra* note 36; *Alvardo-Torres, supra* note 25, 994; *Chaparro-Alcantara, supra* note 25.

[39] *See Breard, supra* note 17.

[40] *See* Vienna Convention, *supra* note 4, art. 36; *Ademaj, supra* note 38; *Alvarado-Torres, supra* note 25, 994; *Chaparro-Alcantara, supra* note 25, 1125-26; *Tapia-Mendoza, supra* note 30, 1255; *Torres-Del Muro, supra* note 25.

[41] *See United States v. Rangel Gonzales,* 617 F.2d 529, 532 (9th Cir. 1980).

[42] *See Ademaj, supra* note 38.

[43] *See Breard, supra* note 17, 537.

[44] Consular Notification and Access, *supra* note 9, 22.

[45] *Alvarado-Torres, supra* note 25, 993.

[46] *Miranda v. Arizona*, 384 U.S. 436 (1966).

[47] *Chapparro-Alcantara, supra* note 25, 1126.

[48] Information for the Office of Investigative Policy, *supra* note 12.

[49] *Id.*

THE PROSECUTOR IN JUVENILE JUSTICE: ADVOCACY IN THE COURTROOM AND LEADERSHIP IN THE COMMUNITY

By James C. Backstrom, County Attorney, Dakota County, Hastings, Minnesota and Gary L. Walker, Prosecuting Attorney, Marquette County, Marquette, Michigan[1]

Introduction

Juvenile justice is the most challenging and complex area of practice for prosecutors in America today. During the 1980s and continuing until 1995, there was an unparalleled increase in the number of juvenile criminal offenses in this country. Arrests of juvenile offenders for murder skyrocketed between 1985 and 1993, rising approximately 150 percent.[2] Juvenile arrests for aggravated assault rose dramatically by over 120 percent between 1983 and 1994.[3] Total arrests of juveniles for serious violent offenses increased by 67 percent between 1986 and 1995.[4] Arrests of juveniles for weapons offenses rose by 93 percent during this same time frame.[5] In many areas of our country, substantial growth has also occurred in nonviolent juvenile crime[6] but the growth rates in juvenile crime between 1985 and 1994[7] have far outpaced the rate for adults, which began to decline in most categories beginning in 1992.[8]

These alarming statistics cover youth from all backgrounds. Rising rates of juvenile crime have occurred not only in the urban areas of our country but also in suburban and rural areas. Perhaps the most significant example of the encroachment of juvenile violence into rural America in recent years has been the rash of tragic school shootings in Littleton, Colorado; Jonesboro, Arkansas; Stamps, Arkansas; West Paducah, Kentucky; Pearl, Mississippi; Bethel, Alaska; Moses Lake, Washington; Blackville, South Carolina; and Redlands, California.[9] These school shootings that occurred between 1995 and 1999 left 35 children dead and many others seriously wounded.[10] Such multiple killings by children between the ages of 11 and 18 were unheard of even a decade ago and while they are not reflective of typical juvenile violence in America today, they do represent an alarming trend that cannot be ignored.[11]

Fortunately, our nationwide rates of violent juvenile crime fell slightly in 1995 for the first time in almost a decade.[12] Decreases in overall levels of juvenile crime in the United States continued in 1996 and 1997.[13] This decline is obviously good news and hopefully predictive for the future although the actual decrease in juvenile crime may not be significant enough to offset an ominous prediction for the decades ahead. Estimates in a 1998 Bureau of the Census report reflect a growth in juvenile population of approximately 22 percent between 1990 and 2010.[14] Given these population predictions, the overall number of juvenile crimes committed may be dramatically higher in the next 20 years, unless we start large-scale, community-wide efforts to address this problem. We can ill afford to sit back and wait.

The challenge for prosecutors dealing with juvenile crime is not just a reflection of increasing caseloads. No longer do prosecutors serve merely as the gatekeepers to the juvenile court system by determining which juveniles should be charged with crimes, who should be diverted from prosecution and whether or not efforts should be made to seek waiver or transfer to adult criminal court. To cope with the sharp rise in juvenile crime between 1980 and 1994 and the foreboding predictions for the future, today's juvenile prosecutors should do far more. Greater expertise is required to address the increased levels of violence and the new laws dealing with victim rights, transfer to adult court and expanded juvenile court jurisdiction. Today's juvenile prosecutors serve not only as advocates for justice, for the victim and for community values but also as negotiators and dispositional advisors in juvenile cases. Additionally, today's juvenile prosecutors must go outside the courthouse and become community leaders and teachers working with civic and social groups, churches and schools to prevent juvenile crime before it occurs. This article addresses both the core functions and the expanding challenges facing today's juvenile prosecutors.

ORGANIZING THE PROSECUTOR'S OFFICE TO RESPOND MOST EFFECTIVELY TO JUVENILE CRIME: ASSIGNING EXPERIENCED AND TRAINED JUVENILE PROSECUTORS IS CRITICAL

Working with juvenile cases may be the most important work prosecutors will do during their careers. It is vital that prosecutors assigned to juvenile cases receive appropriate training and are selected on the basis of their skill and competence.[15] The chief prosecutor should look to qualities such as "knowledge of juvenile law, interest in children and youth, education and experience" in determining which assistants should be assigned to handle juvenile court matters.[16] Prior criminal trial experience and adequate training to develop trial skills are also important.[17]

The practice of assigning juvenile court cases to entry-level prosecutors—historically the pattern in many prosecutors' offices—should change. In today's world, juvenile cases are clearly as important and can be more complex, than those involving adult offenders. Tomorrow's adult criminals are appearing in juvenile court today. Juvenile cases often pose technical difficulties not always seen in adult cases. Furthermore, the presentation of evidence and dispositional alternatives requires expertise that the new, undertrained or less experienced prosecutor may lack. Juveniles who commit criminal offenses require special attention. The chances of successful rehabilitation with juvenile offenders may be greater than with most adult offenders. Therefore, "it is vital to have a single, trained, experienced deputy who can evaluate the case, the juvenile's criminal and social history," and the dispositional alternatives in the effort to obtain justice.[18]

Vertical Prosecution of Juvenile Cases Should Occur Whenever Possible

Vertical prosecution (assignment of the same prosecutor to the same case from initial charging through disposition) ensures continuity in the handling of juvenile cases. The lack of continuity resulting from using different prosecutors in the same case may reduce the opportunity for obtaining meaningful consequences and successful rehabilitation. "Vertical prosecution provides a message that the prosecution will stand firm,"[19] both to the juvenile's attorney and to the court. It is beneficial to have one person applying consistent criteria in an effort to hold juveniles accountable for their behavior. "Continuity will also be accomplished by assigning all probation violations and future cases to the same prosecutor" who handled the initial prosecution, whenever possible.[20] In larger jurisdictions, vertical prosecution may not be possible for those cases waived or transferred to adult court to be prosecuted by the adult prosecution unit.[21] However, the adult unit prosecutor should discuss all of the details surrounding the juvenile's background with any juvenile prosecutor who has previously dealt with the youth, to ensure the most effective prosecution and the most appropriate sentence.

Juvenile Cases Should Be Processed As Quickly As Possible

"Time is a major consideration in handling juvenile cases. Children often fail to remember what actions they took yesterday, let alone several months earlier."[22] The longer it takes to complete a juvenile case, the more likely the child will lose the long-term message.[23] Speedy processing of all juvenile cases is the goal, but a timely response is most important when dealing with serious, violent or habitual offenders.[24] These offenders serve as an example to other juveniles. "Therefore, the juvenile justice system needs to demonstrate that the community has expectations of behavior, will not tolerate violations of those expectations and will swiftly sanction any violations."[25] When the crime is far removed from the ultimate disposition of the case, such a demonstration cannot be made.[26]

THE PROSECUTOR SERVES AS THE GATEKEEPER TO THE JUVENILE JUSTICE SYSTEM

The Charging Function

"The discretionary decision to charge or not charge is the heart of the prosecutorial function."[27] The exercise of appropriate prosecutorial discretion is as essential in juvenile court as it is in adult court. "Such discretionary decisions require legal expertise, consistency of purpose and accountability."[28] The decision as to which charges, if any, are appropriate or whether the juvenile should be diverted into a program designed to ensure accountability without charging should be based upon all of the available facts and evidence in a case. While the prosecutor's primary duty is to seek justice and to protect the public safety, it is also appropriate to consider the special interests and needs of the juvenile to the extent that this can be done without compromising "the safety and welfare of the community."[29]

A juvenile prosecutor should have the right to screen cases to determine whether the facts of each case are legally sufficient for prosecution.[30] Legal sufficiency exists only in those cases in which a prosecutor reasonably believes the charges can be proven by admissible evidence at trial. In other words, the prosecutor should determine that there is sufficient probable cause to believe that a delinquent act was committed and that the juvenile accused committed it.[31] If not, no charges should be pursued.[32]

In some jurisdictions in this country, the prosecutor's office does not have the responsibility by law or practice to initiate juvenile court prosecutions. The National District Attorneys Association (NDAA) believes that such a system is inappropriate[33] and sets forth the following reasons for this conclusion:

- Prosecutors have a responsibility to represent the state in court on juvenile cases and therefore, should have the right to determine what cases are filed in that court;

- Prosecutors are unable to utilize an effective prosecution policy or effectively implement prosecution standards without control over the charging decision;
- Prosecutors are trained on the legal aspects of the charging process;
- Prosecutors give public safety a high priority in their decision making process;
- Prosecutors take into consideration the interests of the victim and have a process for giving and receiving information from victims;
- Prosecutors have access to both the criminal and social background of the juvenile; and
- Prosecutors are more easily accountable to the public than are other individuals in the juvenile justice system.[34]

Because of the need to maintain appropriate separation of powers, charging is an executive function that the judicial branch should not perform. Furthermore, because of the need to ensure proper legal review of the sufficiency of the evidence to proceed, charging is not an appropriate police or corrections department responsibility.[35] Prosecutors are governed by ethical standards that are not applicable to police or corrections officials. The decision to charge someone with a crime is appropriately a decision that should be made by an independent prosecutor who serves in the executive branch of government.

Development of Charging and Disposition Guidelines

Many prosecutors' offices have adopted written charging and disposition guidelines. In Minnesota, prosecutors are required to do so by law.[36] Adopting such guidelines does not limit the discretion of a prosecutor's office in the charging and disposing of cases, but does assure the public that prosecutors are exercising this discretion by looking at fair, non-discriminatory and appropriate factors. Therefore, charging and disposition guidelines for juvenile cases should be developed by the prosecutor's office.

Diversion

The decision to divert a case from prosecution is also a charging decision. It is a determination that sufficient evidence exists to file a charge in court but that the goals of prosecution can be reasonably reached through diversion. Prosecutors should consider establishing diversion programs for appropriate first-time or low-level juvenile offenders who pose no apparent danger to the public safety. Diversion programs should contain criteria to insure that the diverted juvenile offender is held accountable for his or her actions and that restitution is made to the victim of the crime where appropriate. In the event an agency other than the prosecutor's office coordinates a juvenile diversion program, the prosecutor should be involved in establishing the eligibility criteria and other guidelines for the program. Any diversion program should contain provisions to insure that diverted juveniles who do not successfully complete the program are referred back to the prosecutor's office for prosecution.[37]

The NDAA's "National Prosecution Standards for Juvenile Justice" addresses the factors that should be taken into consideration by a prosecutor in determining whether to charge juveniles formally or to divert them from prosecution. These factors include:

- The seriousness of the alleged offense;
- The role of the juvenile in that offense;
- The nature and number of previous cases presented by the police or others against the juvenile and the disposition of those cases;
- The juvenile's age and maturity;
- The availability of appropriate treatment or services;
- The juvenile's admission (or denial) of guilt or involvement in the offense charged;
- The threat posed by the juvenile to persons or the property of others;
- The provision for financial restitution to the victim; and
- The recommendations of the referring agency, the victim and advocates for the juvenile.[38]

As with charging and disposition guidelines, the use of diversion program guidelines promotes public confidence that eligibility standards for the program are fair, nondiscriminatory and appropriate. These guidelines will also assist juvenile offenders, their attorneys and parents in clearly understanding who is eligible for the program and what the program requirements will be.

Prosecution of Juveniles in Adult Criminal Court

Juveniles who commit crimes are usually subject to the jurisdiction of juvenile court. In certain situations, depending upon the seriousness of the crime, the threat to public safety, the age of the juvenile, the juvenile's criminal history and other relevant factors, the juvenile offender may be tried in adult criminal court. The process by which this is accomplished is commonly referred to as transfer, waiver or certification, depending upon the jurisdiction. Whether or not a juvenile offender should be prosecuted in adult court is one of the most critical decisions to be made in the juvenile justice system.[39]

A number of states have adopted or are considering changes in laws pertaining to the process of certifying serious, violent and habitual juvenile offenders to adult court. Minnesota and Michigan have both adopted such changes.[40] Three main categories exist under the laws in various states regarding how the decision of whether a juvenile should be prosecuted as an adult are made:

- The legislature mandates the transfer of a juvenile case to adult court;
- The prosecutor is vested with the discretion to determine whether to transfer a juvenile case to adult court; or
- The juvenile court judge is vested with the discretion to determine whether a juvenile case should be transferred to adult court.[41]

Most jurisdictions follow a process similar to the third category in which the juvenile court judge makes the final decision on whether a case should be transferred to adult court. However, in most of these jurisdictions, it is the prosecutor who has the discretion to determine whether the process should be initiated. In exercising that discretion, "the primary factors affecting this decision should be the seriousness of the crime and the threat to the public safety," and not what is in the best interests of the child, which has long been the standard applicable in most juvenile court proceedings.[42]

Many would argue that those juveniles who commit serious or violent crimes and who are over a certain age should automatically be prosecuted as adults. A number of states are considering the enactment of legislation to this effect. Minnesota has adopted this automatic, adult prosecution standard for youth who are at least 16 years old and charged with first-degree murder. In Michigan the waiver decision for juveniles over the age of 14 rests with the prosecutor in certain enumerated offenses.[43] NDAA has adopted a policy recommending that for serious, violent and habitual offenders 14 years of age and older, prosecutors should be given the discretion to file such cases in adult court without judicial intervention.[44]

Furthermore, NDAA believes that once a juvenile case has been transferred to adult court for prosecution, if there is a finding of probable cause for that offense,[45] then prosecutions for all further crimes committed by the youth should also occur in adult court regardless of the seriousness of the offense.[46] "In those situations where a prior case in which a juvenile is being tried as an adult has not been completed, additional charges filed against this juvenile in unrelated cases should also be dealt with in adult court."[47]

THE PROSECUTOR IS AN ADVOCATE FOR JUSTICE, THE VICTIM AND COMMUNITY VALUES

It is easy in a juvenile justice system that has long looked to the best interests of the child as its primary purpose for prosecutors to lose its focus on the need to serve as advocates for justice. While prosecutors should consider the special interests and needs of a juvenile when handling a case, they should never lose sight of their primary duty to seek justice and protect the safety and welfare of the community.[48]

Juvenile prosecutors should ensure that crime victims are properly notified of important decisions in the case, including charging and disposition matters, in the same manner as in adult prosecutions. Victims should be notified of and offered the opportunity to attend all hearings in a juvenile case and should be contacted prior to the acceptance of a plea agreement. The prosecutor should also ensure that victims have the opportunity to address the court prior to disposition. Furthermore, the prosecutor should make efforts to ensure that restitution is paid so that victims can, to the greatest extent possible, be made whole and not suffer financial losses as a result of the criminal activity.[49]

Juvenile prosecutors should keep in mind that they serve the interests of all the citizens in the community and their actions should be consistent with community values. To ensure awareness of these values, juvenile prosecutors should participate in community meetings and other activities concerning juvenile crime or crime prevention within their jurisdictions. By doing so, they will hear firsthand the feelings of the public concerning juvenile crime and its consequences.

In reference to the pursuit of justice, the prosecutor should keep in mind the concepts of fairness and accountability. The punishment for an offense, whether it is through court disposition or a diversion program, should be applied fairly to all defendants under similar circumstances and should hold juvenile offenders accountable for their actions. The prosecutor may elect to exercise discretion and dismiss a case that is technically sufficient but that lacks prosecutorial merit from a policy or economic standpoint.[50] The prosecutor may dismiss a case at any time in the proceedings if it is determined to be in the best interests of justice. However, care should be made to conform to appropriate guidelines in making these decisions. As mentioned above, prosecutors should adopt written charging and disposition guidelines that are available to the public to ensure both internal consistency and public accountability.

THE JUVENILE PROSECUTOR MUST SERVE AS A TRIAL AND DISPOSITIONAL ADVOCATE AS WELL AS AN EFFECTIVE NEGOTIATOR

The prosecutor should take an active role in all phases of a juvenile case, including both adjudication and disposition.[51] The prosecutor should ensure that decisions involving juveniles are made in a timely fashion to protect their rights to a speedy disposition of their cases. Cases requiring the detention of a juvenile offender should receive priority treatment. As previously mentioned, the timely resolution of juvenile cases is even more important than it is in the adult criminal system. A timely disposition that holds them appropriately accountable helps juveniles to understand clearly the harmful nature of their actions, whereas a disposition occurring many months after the juvenile's act will not have the same impact. Prompt determinations also promote public confidence in the system and fairness to the victim and to the community.[52]

The juvenile prosecutor should assume the traditional adversary role in the adjudicatory hearing recognizing, however, the particular vulnerability of child witnesses. All juvenile witnesses, including suspects should they testify, should be treated fairly and with sensitivity in direct examination, cross-examination and throughout the process.[53]

The prosecutor should also be involved in all plea negotiations with a juvenile or the juvenile's attorney. In negotiating a plea, the prosecutor should follow appropriate guidelines for the disposition of cases to ensure fairness and public confidence in the decision. As mentioned above, efforts should be made (in most jurisdictions, *must* be made) to contact the victim, prior to entering into any plea agreement, to obtain the victim's comments and/or concerns.

The prosecutor should be consulted in all decisions affecting the disposition of a case. No case should be dismissed without providing the prosecutor with notice and an opportunity to be heard.[54] Juvenile prosecutors should take an active role in the dispositional hearing in a juvenile case and make recommendations to the court as to what should be the appropriate disposition.[55] The prosecutor should review all reports prepared by the corrections department and others before making this recommendation. The prosecutor should also take into consideration what the penalty for the crime would be if an adult had committed it.

The prosecutor should be familiar with and able to provide input on the most appropriate dispositional program alternatives while periodically evaluating the effectiveness of such programs from the standpoint of the public's and the youth's interests.[56] A program that does not accomplish the goals for which it was created is a waste of taxpayer resources and will likely have little positive effect on the juvenile offender. New and more appropriate resources should be sought out and, if nonexistent, they should be created through diversion programs coordinated by the prosecutor's office.[57]

Age alone should not be a mitigating factor in the prosecutor's recommended disposition or the court's sentencing order for cases involving serious, violent or habitual juvenile offenders. The prosecutor's dispositional recommendation, in the final analysis, should focus upon the prosecutor's primary role of protecting public safety and welfare, holding the juvenile appropriately accountable for the crime committed and meeting the needs and interests of the juvenile offender.[58]

Regardless of whether the juvenile or adult justice system is used to adjudicate serious, violent or habitual juvenile offenders, meaningful sanctions should apply. Unfortunately, many states do not have sufficient resources to ensure that serious, violent or habitual offenders are placed in a correctional setting. Such resources are needed. Probation alone is not an appropriate sanction for serious, violent or habitual juvenile offenders. NDAA has concluded that the primary factors affecting a juvenile's sentence should be the protection of the community from harm and the offender's accountability to the victim and the public. Factors such as the seriousness of the prior criminal history should also be considered.[59]

Additionally, NDAA believes that juvenile codes that establish the best interest of the child as the primary consideration of sentencing should be repealed. As to less serious offenders, while there is a need to rehabilitate the juveniles, an important aspect of rehabilitation includes punishment. There needs to be adequate resources for the court to impose punishment through the use of appropriate and effective sanctions.[60]

The prosecutor's role does not end with a disposition hearing. The prosecutor should continue to represent the state's interests in all appeals, as well as in hearings concerning revocation of probation, modification of disposition and other collateral proceedings attacking orders of the court.[61] The prosecutor should also take steps to inform the juvenile court if its orders are not properly executed.[62] This follow-up by the prosecutor to ensure that dispositions are properly carried out also helps maintain public confidence in the system of juvenile justice. "Failure to provide consequences for noncompliance of parole or probation conditions endangers the public, creates a negative image of the system and increases the likelihood that juvenile offenders will become more violent or habitual in their behavior."[63]

THE PROSECUTOR'S ROLE IN CHILD ABUSE AND NEGLECT CASES

The prosecutor's role in cases involving the abuse and neglect of children is as important as his or her role in juvenile justice and delinquency. The protection of those in communities who are the most vulnerable and unable to defend themselves is of obvious concern. Further, the clear correlation between the abuse and neglect of children and their likelihood to engage in future criminal behavior[64] suggests that the safety of the community—the primary goal—will be well-served by an aggressive approach to these problems.

In Michigan and Minnesota, the prosecuting attorney and the county attorney, respectively, have clearly defined roles in child protection proceedings.[65] They are required to appear in court to present evidence and advocate for appropriate disposition in cases involving child abuse or neglect.

There are good reasons, however, that the prosecutor should assume a role that is broader than courtroom representation. Often the social service agencies charged with the investigation of child abuse lack adequate training in the investigative process or the standards of evidence necessary to successfully present cases in court. Experienced prosecutors can provide training and guidance in these areas. For example, prosecutors should draft the petitions with allegations of abuse or neglect because they are familiar with burden of proof, evidentiary standards and legal sufficiency.

The prosecutors should also assume an active role beyond the factual adjudication or finding by the court that abuse or neglect has occurred. Dispositional recommendations by the social service agency and court worker should be reviewed as a routine function. If necessary, an independent recommendation from the prosecutor should be presented to the court when it appears that the policy of the state agency is drawn by economic or other considerations that may not coincide with the best interest of the child. Remember: The prosecutor is the voice of the community.

Obviously, taking an aggressive role in child abuse and neglect cases necessitates a prosecutor who is dedicated to his or her role in juvenile court. It takes time and experience to become familiar with all of the dispositional programs and alternatives and to tailor them to each individual case. Prosecutors are in a unique position, however, to discover instances of abuse or neglect as the focal point of adult and juvenile criminal cases. An in-depth examination of a child delinquency or incorrigibility case may find that the behavior is occasioned by an abusive home. Domestic violence between adult partners may also involve the couple's children. Cases of criminal sexual abuse of a child should be examined to determine if an abuse or neglect petition is appropriate in addition to criminal charges.

Even if a state does not give prosecutors jurisdiction in cases of abuse and neglect of children, they should approach cases involving children with an eye toward making referrals to the appropriate agencies. Also, if a jurisdiction does not permit involvement, the prosecutor should consider lobbying to become involved, both for the protection of the children and ultimately of society as a whole.

THE PROSECUTOR SHOULD BE INVOLVED IN COMMUNITY OUTREACH EFFORTS TO ADDRESS JUVENILE CRIME

Perhaps the most important role for juvenile prosecutors today occurs outside the courthouse. If they are to solve the juvenile-crime crisis facing society, then education, prevention and early intervention will be the keys to their success. "Education and prevention go hand in hand with effective law enforcement and prosecution efforts."[66] Hence, prosecutors should become directly involved in these activities. However, police and prosecutors cannot solve the juvenile crime problem alone. It will take the united efforts of everyone to solve these problems, including parents, youth, teachers, school administrators, faith communities, civic and business leaders, law enforcement officials and community-based organizations.[67]

Prosecutors can play a valuable role in educating the public concerning juvenile justice issues by taking the opportunity to address these important matters in public speeches and presentations. They can actively participate in juvenile crime prevention programs within their communities.[68] As public leaders, prosecutors are in an ideal position to help coordinate prevention efforts by facilitating the creation of programs designed to help reduce juvenile crime and to promote health and safety. Prosecutors throughout our nation have been creative in establishing programs for suitable first-time or low-level juvenile offenders,[69] as well as a number of prosecutor-led truancy intervention programs.[70] Courtrooms to Classrooms is an innovative prosecutor-led education program, first implemented by the Denver District Attorney's Office, that involves a prosecutor working with schools to help elementary or middle school students understand how our criminal justice system works and to provide them with a positive role model.

NDAA believes in the importance of funding proven crime prevention initiatives, recognizing that programs that keep kids from becoming criminals in the first place are some of the most powerful weapons in law enforcement's arsenal against crime. Fight Crime: Invest In Kids, a group led by over three hundred police chiefs, prosecutors and crime survivors nationwide, actively promotes the importance of funding proven crime prevention initiatives. Included in these initiatives are programs aimed at providing early childhood care, preventing child abuse and neglect, and ensuring that quality childcare and after-school activities are available for America's youth.

Scientific research supports the effectiveness of these programs and their role in reducing criminal behavior. In Ypsilanti, Michigan, the High School Educational Research Foundation randomly admitted half of the at-risk three-and-four-year-old applicants to its quality preschool center and provided their parents with in-home coaching and parenting skills for an hour-and-a-half per week. Twenty-two years after this program ended, the children who received these services were just *one-fifth as likely* as at-risk kids denied the services to become chronic lawbreakers.[71]

In another study in Syracuse, New York, at-risk kids provided with early childhood services and a high quality preschool program were only *one-tenth as likely* as kids denied these services to be delinquent by age 16.[72] Other research has shown that programs that serve even a limited number of children have significantly reduced juvenile victimization during after-school hours. One study has shown that with intensive recruiting, after-school programs have cut crime by as much as 75 percent in some high crime neighborhoods.[73] Another study concluded that participants in after-school programs are more likely to do well in school, to treat adults with respect and to resolve conflicts without violence.[74]

Youth who are neglected or abused in their early years run a significantly greater risk of acting out violently when they become teenagers. With reports on record of almost three million abused or neglected American children in 1995, we need to make sure that child protection professionals have sufficient resources to identify and treat them. Studies in this area have once again shown the importance of reducing violence and criminal behavior. The Prenatal and Early Infancy Project[75] provided half a group of at-risk mothers with visits by specially trained nurses for coaching in parenting skills and other advice and support. Such a program was shown not only to *reduce child abuse by eight percent* in the first two years, but showed that 15 years following the completion of services, these mothers had only *one-third* as many arrests, and their children were *only half as likely* to be delinquent.

A similar Healthy Start program[76] in Hawaii offered at-risk mothers preventive health care and home visits by para-professionals who coached them in parenting skills and child development and offered family counseling. It was found that over a four-year period those who had not received such services were more than *two-and-one-half times as likely* to have a confirmed instance of child abuse within their families.

Truancy is one of the most important predictors of juvenile delinquency and a common factor that runs through the background of almost all juveniles who find their way into court. Effective truancy intervention programs are essential. Furthermore, prosecutors need to work hand-in-hand with the school districts and the social workers to ensure that children are in school and receiving the education that they need to become productive and law-abiding citizens. Also, the use of alcohol and drugs is often a precursor to crime and delinquency. The importance of alcohol and drug abuse programs aimed at youth cannot be ignored.

When elementary school children display disruptive behavior, it may be a warning signal for future criminal behavior. Prosecutors should be part of the effort to identify troubled and disruptive children at an early age and provide these children and their parents with appropriate counseling, social skills training and other help to ensure their future success. Once again, this is an area where studies have already shown the importance of early intervention. A Montreal study[77] showed that providing disruptive first and second grade boys with services like these *cut in half* the odds that they would be placed in special classes, be rated highly disruptive by a teacher or peers or be required to repeat a grade in school. Mentoring programs allowing youth access to positive adult role models are also extremely important, so that youth do not look to gang leaders for the support they need.

Prosecutors should continue to do everything they can to validate positive qualities in youth throughout America. There are far more kids in this country who are good role models in their communities than there are delinquents that are committing criminal offenses. These youth should be recognized and their positive assets promoted to enable them to become valuable role models for their peers in the community. These youth can also serve as resources to help identify problems and problem kids in the schools and in the communities.

It is important, however, to keep in mind that prevention should not come at the expense of the prisons and juvenile detention facilities necessary to house serious, violent and habitual offenders or at the expense of police, prosecutors, courts and corrections departments. The juvenile justice system in America should not be denied the funding it needs to carry out its primary responsibilities of investigating, convicting, adequately punishing and monitoring juvenile criminal offenders. There is no substitute for getting dangerous criminals off the street and behind bars. Nevertheless, the message of programs such as Fight Crime: Invest In Kids is a compelling one that should not be ignored.

A balance between law enforcement and prevention efforts should be maintained for the justice system to survive and adequately cope with the rising numbers of juvenile offenders who will be flooding its gates in the twenty-first century. Prosecutors and other law enforcement officials should step beyond their traditional roles and become involved with these types of crime prevention programs. Efforts like these can pay many dividends in the long run by helping to reduce crime.

CONCLUSION

As NDAA noted in its "Resource Manual and Policy Positions on Juvenile Crime Issues," "prosecutors are in the unique position of acting as society's voice in the juvenile justice system."[78] They are entrusted with ensuring that those who violate the laws are brought to justice and held accountable. To do so, adequate laws should exist to ensure that violent and repeat juvenile offenders are appropriately dealt with by the juvenile justice system. Such laws may provide for adult prosecution for serious, violent and habitual offenders or for some form of blended sentencing law[79] that provides adequate accountability and protection of the public safety.[80] Prosecutors should also be sure never to underestimate the importance of dealing with low-level criminal behavior appropriately and aggressively in an effort to prevent the occurrence of more serious behavior later on. Very few youth are apprehended for acts of violence who have not had some prior contacts with police, schools or social workers over non-violent activities like alcohol abuse or truancy. Anti-social behavior should be addressed and appropriately dealt with from its onset.

To deal most efficiently with juvenile crime, prosecutors should also become involved in prevention and early intervention efforts in their communities. "A balanced approach to juvenile justice is clearly warranted—one which emphasizes the enforcement, prosecution and detention of juvenile offenders, to protect the public safety and ensure accountability," and the importance of pursuing prevention and intervention initiatives aimed at crime prevention.[81] Prevention and prosecution are not incompatible. To the contrary, they should be pursued with equal vigor to help reduce juvenile crime in America.[82] Prosecutors should not only continue to be effective advocates in the courtroom but should also look beyond their traditional roles and become community leaders, establishing programs and participating in initiatives aimed at reducing juvenile crime before it begins.

ENDNOTES

[1] Mr. Backstrom is a vice president of the National District Attorneys Association (NDAA). Mr. Walker is also a vice president of NDAA. They have served as co-chairs of NDAA's Juvenile Justice Advisory Committee since 1995.

[2] See Bureau of the Census, U.S. Dep't Of Commerce, *Statistical Abstract of the United States 1997*, 209 (1997) [Hereinafter Statistical Abstract].

[3] See Howard N. Snyder, "Juvenile Arrests 1996," *Juv. Just. Bull.* 5 (Nov. 1997).

[4] See *Statistical Abstract, supra* note 1, at 209.

[5] See *Id.*

[6] See Federal Bureau Of Investigation, U.S. Dep't Of Justice, *Uniform Crime Reports for the United States 1994*, At 221 (1995) [hereinafter *Crime Reports 1994*].

[7] See *Id.*

[8] See Federal Bureau Of Investigation, U.S. Dep't Of Justice, *Uniform Crime Reports for the United States 1993*, At 225 (1994) [hereinafter *Crime Reports 1993*]; *Crime Reports 1994, supra* Note 5, At 212; Federal Bureau Of Investigation, U.S. Dep't Of Justice,

Uniform Crime Reports for the United States 1995, At 218 (1996) [hereinafter *Crime Reports 1995*]; Federal Bureau Of Investigation, U.S. Dep't Of Justice, *Uniform Crime Reports for the United States 1996,* At 226 (1997) [hereinafter *Crime Reports 1996*]; Federal Bureau Of Investigation, U.S. Dep't Of Justice, *Uniform Crime Reports for the United States 1997,* At 214 (1998) [hereinafter *Crime Reports 1997*].

[9] *See* Richard Lacayo, "Toward the Root of the Evil," *Time,* Apr. 6, 1998, Vol. 151 No. 13, at 38.

[10] *Id.*

[11] *Id.*

[12] *See* Snyder, *supra* note 2, 4.

[13] *See Crime Reports 1995, supra* Note 7, at 222; *Crime Reports 1996, supra* Note 7, at 230; *Crime Reports 1997, supra* note 7, at 218.

[14] *See* Bureau of the Census, U.S. Dep't Of Commerce, *Population Projections of The United States By Age, Sex, Race, and Hispanic Origin: 1995 To 2050,* at 72, Tbl. 2 (1996); Bureau of the Census, U.S. Dep't Of Commerce, *U.S. Population Estimates By Age, Sex, Race, and Hispanic Origin: 1990-1997,* at 28, Tbl. 1 (1998).

[15] *See* National District Attorneys Association, *National Prosecution Standards* § 92.1d, at 251 (2d Ed. 1991) [hereinafter *National Prosecution Standards*].

[16] *Id.*

[17] *See Id.*

[18] National District Attorneys Association, "Resource Manual And Policy Positions On Juvenile Crime Issues" 3 (1996) [hereinafter *Juvenile Crime Issues*].

[19] *Id.*

[20] *Id.*

[21] *Id.*

[22] *Id.*

[23] *Id.*

[24] The National District Attorneys Association (NDAA) has defined serious, violent and habitual offenders as follows:
- A serious offender is one who is caught for the first time having committed multiple felony offenses, a major economic crime, repeated misdemeanor crimes of violence, or other offenses defined by a local jurisdiction as serious;
- A violent offender is one who was involved in the commission of a felony crime of violence; and,
- A habitual felony offender is one who was found guilty of at least two prior felonies. *Id. at* 1-2. None of these categories is mutually exclusive.

[25] *Id.* at 4.

[26] *Id.*

[27] *Id. (citing Brown v. Dayton Hudson Corp.,* 314 N.W. 2d 210, 214 (Minn. 1981)).

[28] *Id.* at 4.

[29] *National Prosecution Standards, supra* note 14, §92.1b, at 250.

[30] *Id.* § 92.2a, at 251.

[31] *Id.* § 92.2b, at 251.

[32] *Id.*

[33] *See id. §92.2, at 251-254; Juvenile Crime Issues,* supra *note 17, at 4-5.*

[34] *Juvenile Crime Issues, supra* note 17, at 4-5.

[35] *See id.* at 5.

[36] *See* Minn. Stat. Ann. § 388.051, Subd. 3 (West 1997). A copy of the Charging and Disposition Guidelines of the Dakota County Attorney's Office for either adult or juvenile offenses may be requested by calling (651) 438-4440.

[37] *Juvenile Crime Issues, supra* note 17, at 5.

[38] *National Prosecution Standards, supra* note 14, §92.2g, at 253 (1991).

[39] *Juvenile Crime Issues, supra* note 17, at 6.

[40] *See* Minn. Stat. Ann. §260.125 MS 1998 Repealed, 1999 c 139 Art 4 s 3 260.125 Subdivision 1. Ms 1949 Renumbered 242.01 (Copyright 1999 by the Office of Revisor of Statutes, State of Minnesota (http://www.revisor.leg.state.mn.us/stats/260/125.html) and Michigan Compiled Laws Annotated 712A.4 (West 1999).

[41] *Juvenile Crime Issues, supra* note 17, at 6.

[42] *Id.* at 7.

[43] *See* Minn. Stat. Ann. §260.015, Subd. 5(B); *Id.*§ 260.111, Subd. 1a And Michigan Compiled Laws Annotated 600.606(1).

[44] *See Juvenile Crime Issues, supra* note 17, at 7.

[45] The notion of "probable cause" was added to the policy concerning this issue to address those situations in which a juvenile who is prosecuted as an adult is acquitted for the most serious crime but convicted of a lesser offense. In such a case, the acquittal on the more serious charge should not be grounds to keep future offenses involving the youth out of adult court, because a finding of probable cause concerning the commission of the more serious offense previously was made by a court or grand jury. Obviously, if evidence is brought forth resulting in the dismissal of such charge before trial, or if evidence brought forth at trial leads a judge to conclude that probable cause no longer exists as to the more serious offense in question, this same logic would not hold. Thus, no automatic presumption of adult prosecution in future cases should apply under those circumstances. Id.

[46] *Id.*

[47] *See Id.*

[48] *See National Prosecution Standards, supra* Note 14, § 92.1b, at 250 (1991).

[49] *See Juvenile Crime Issues, supra* Note 17, at 16.

[50] *See National Prosecution Standards, supra* note 14, § 92.2, at 251-54.

[51] *See Id.* §92.5-92.6, at 256-57.

[52] *See Id.* §92.2(2), at 253.

[53] *See Id.* § 92.5b, at 256.

[54] *Id.* §92.5d, at 256.

[55] *Id.* §92.6a, at 256.

[56] *Id.* §92.6d, at 257.

[57] *See Id.*

[58] *Juvenile Crime Issues, supra* note 17, at 10; *see also National Prosecution Standards, supra* note 14, § 92.6c, at 257 (stating that prosecutors must consider various interests before making a recommendation).

[59] *Juvenile Crime Issues, supra* note 17, at 10.

[60] *Id.*

[61] *National Prosecution Standards, supra* note 14, §92.7a, at 257.

[62] *Id.* §92.7b, at 257.

[63] *Juvenile Crime Issues, supra* note 17, at 10.

[64] "... children's exposure to violence has tremendous negative consequences—for them and for all the rest of us. A child who experiences serious violence is 50 percent—50 percent—more likely to be arrested as a juvenile, and nearly 40 percent more likely to be arrested as an adult. If you want to keep the crime rates going down you have to do more to break the cycle of violence to which children are exposed."

[65] *Legal Consultant to Department.* On request of Michigan department of social services or of an agent under contract with the department, the prosecuting attorney must serve as a legal consultant to the department of social services or agent under contract with the department at all stages of a child protective proceeding. Michigan Court Rules 5.914(c)(1). Minnesota's Child Protection Provisions of the Juvenile Court Act provide that: "[e]xcept in adoption proceedings, the county attorney shall present evidence upon request of the court. In representing the agency, the county attorney shall also have the responsibility for advancing the public interest in the welfare of the child." Minn. Stat. §260C.163, subd. 4. *See also* Rule 39.03 of the Minnesota Rules of Juvenile Procedure.

[66] *Juvenile Crime Issues, supra* at 17.

[67] *Id.*

[68] *See Id.*

[69] Examples of prosecutor diversion programs of this nature can be found in the Denver District Attorney's Office, Denver, Colorado; the prosecuting attorney's office in Thurston County, Olympia, Washington; and the Dakota County Attorney's Office, Hastings, Minnesota.

[70] Examples of prosecutor-led, truancy intervention programs are found in Los Angeles, California; St. Paul, Minnesota; and Marquette, Michigan.

[71] Schweinhart, L.J., H.V. Barnes and D.P. Weikart, *Significant Benefits: The High/Scope Perry Preschool Study Through Age 27* (Ypsilanti, MI: High-Scope Press, 1993).

[72] Lally, J.R., P.L. Mangione and A.S. Honig, "The Syracuse University Family Development Research Program: Long Range Impact of an Early Intervention with Low-Income Children and Their Families" in D.R. Powell, ed., *Parent Education as Early Childhood Intervention: Emerging Directions in Theory, Research and Practice* (Norwood, NJ: Ablex Publishing, 1988).

[73] Jones, M.B. and D.R. Offord, "Reduction of Antisocial Behavior in Poor Children by Nonschool Skill Development," *Journal of Child Psychology and Psychiatry and Allied Disciplines* 30 (5) (1989), 737-750.

[74] Miller, B.M., *Out-of-School Time: Effects on Learning in the Primary Grades* (Wellesley, MA: School-Age Child Care Project [now called the National Institute on Out-of-School Time], Center for Research on Women, Wellesley College, 1995); and Posner, J.K. and D.L. Vandell, "Low-Income Children's After-School Care: Are There Beneficial Effects of After-School Programs," *Child Development* 65 (2) (Society for Research in Child Development, 1994) 440-456.

[75] Olds, D.L., et al., "Long-term Effects of Home Visitation on Maternal Life Course and Child Abuse and Neglect: Fifteen-year Follow-up of a Randomized Trial," *Journal of the American Medical Association,* Vol. 278, No. 8, August 27, 1997, pp. 637-643. and Olds, et al., "Long-term Effects of Nurse Home Visitation on Children's Criminal and Antisocial Behavior: Fifteen-Year Follow-up of a Randomized Controlled Trial," *Journal of the American Medical Association,* 280:14, (October 14, 1998) 1238-1244.

[76] National Institute of Justice, "Helping to Prevent Child Abuse – and Future Criminal Consequences: Hawaii Healthy Start" (October 1995).

[77] Tremblay, R.E., McCord, J., LeBlanc, M., Boileau, H., Charlebois, P., Gagnon, C., and Larivee, S., "Can Disruptive Boys Be Helped to Become Competent?" *Psychiatry* 54:148-161 (1991).

[78] *Juvenile Crime Issues, supra* note 17, at 20.

[79] Blended sentencing laws have recently been adopted in a number of states. These laws provide for the "blending" of juvenile and adult sanctions for certain juvenile offenders. An excellent discussion of blended sentencing, with reference to different laws within various states, is included in Patricia Torbet et al, *State Responses To Serious And Violent Juvenile Crime* (Washington, D.C.: Office of Juvenile Justice and Delinquency Prevention, U.S. DEP'T OF JUSTICE, 1996, *11-16* (1996).

[80] Minnesota adopted such a blended sentencing law in 1995 by including a category for "Extended Juvenile Jurisdiction" (EJJ). *See* Minn.Stat.Ann. Sec. 260.126 (West 1998). This statute provides for dual jurisdiction over certain juvenile offenders who commit crimes that carry automatic prison sentences if committed by an adult. *Id.* EJJ juveniles are given an adult prison sentence that is stayed on the condition that they complete their juvenile disposition. *Id.*, Subd. 5. Upon completion the adult sentence is discharged. *Id.* This is just one example of new laws aimed at ensuring appropriate accountability for juvenile offenders committing serious offenses.

[81] James C. Backstrom and Gary L. Walker, "A Balanced Approach to Juvenile Justice: The Work of the Juvenile Justice Advisory Committee," *The Prosecutor*, July/Aug. (1998) 36.

[82] *Id.*, 38.

THE EFFECTIVE PROSECUTOR: ASSISTING CRIME VICTIMS WITH SPECIAL NEEDS

By Mary L. Boland, Assistant State's Attorney
Karen McKenna, Deputy Director, Victim Witness Assistance Program
Marilyn Baldwin, Victim Witness Appellate Specialist
Kelly Pierce, Victims with Disabilities Specialist
Nicole Kramer, Hate-Crimes Specialist
State's Attorney's Office, Cook County, Chicago, Illinois

Introduction

Over the past two decades, prosecutors have adopted a wide range of strategies designed to increase crime victims' participation in the criminal justice process, including coordinated interviews and investigations, fast-tracking of cases and vertical prosecution, early presentation of victim testimony and "on call" status for victims. Certain victim populations, however, face special barriers that require consideration. Child and senior victims, persons with disabilities, homicide survivors and victims of domestic violence, sexual assault and hate crimes present compound challenges to prosecutors and require the application of individualized strategies to effectively prosecute their cases. The average prosecutor's office nationwide has less than 10 members; victim-witness staff members generally make up only five percent of office personnel. However, this chapter will address basic considerations that *all* prosecutors—regardless of the size of office or availability of specialized staff—can adapt to assist victims with special needs to become key members of their prosecution teams.

Victims with special needs have often experienced life-shattering occurrences. Victimization destroys fundamental assumptions about fairness and belief in a safe and just world. Victims may react with fear, anger, embarrassment, shame, frustration, helplessness and depression. Many who survive prolonged or repeated victimizations may suffer from post-traumatic stress disorder, trauma analogous to that experienced by combat veterans. Others may experience hypertension, vigilance and distrust, and many report disruptions in sleep and concentration. Their ability to cope with work, school, relationships and life activities is often impaired. To attempt to regain some of the control lost in the victimization, victims often withdraw from their routine activities, such as work or school. It is not uncommon for persons victimized in their homes to move. Victims of hate crimes may feel outraged because of the nature of the crime and harbor bitterness not only toward the individual who committed the crime but also towards the perpetrator's entire race. In addition, over six million victims every year are seriously injured as a result of crime, in some cases suffering permanent physical disabilities. The victim's physical injuries may require medical care or hospitalization with attendant medical expenses. The victim may also experience loss of property, valuables and income.

Certain crimes, such as sexual assault, may hold such a stigma for family and friends that they isolate the victim, withholding their emotional support. Loved ones may avoid the victim to cope with their own trauma resulting from the crime. Others may blame the victim or distance themselves from the crime to maintain their own beliefs that this crime cannot happen to "good and decent" people like themselves.

Homicide survivors often experience overwhelming feelings of sorrow and grief. Those deeply affected by the loss of a friend or loved one to a violent crime include not only the family and significant others but also close friends, neighbors, schoolmates and coworkers. Mourning is compounded by the stress of involvement with the criminal justice system. Most of these survivors feel devastated and endure a long period of emotional strife while they struggle to reconstruct their lives.

Beyond the commonality of the trauma and loss shared by crime victims and survivors of crime, their effective participation in the criminal justice system requires that prosecutors tailor strategies to address their special concerns. For example, child or senior victims, victims with disabilities and victims of sexual assault or domestic violence are most often victimized by family members, acquaintances or persons who have power over them, such as caretakers or trusted adults. Victims' fears of retaliation are very real and threats of retaliation should be carefully assessed and addressed to increase protection for victims in all these cases.

Communication is a factor. Young children may lack the verbal skills necessary to recognize their victimization or to report it. Persons with disabilities have limitations in sight, hearing, physical movement or comprehension and need assistance in communicating the details of the crime or other considerations related to their disabilities. Seniors as victims are especially vulnerable to fraud, financial exploitation and other crimes of manipulation, may be very reluctant to proceed against a perpetrator upon whom they have grown dependent. Hate crime victims may need translators or may be ambivalent about their participation and role in the criminal justice system. Survivors of homicide may need intensive support services to participate. Moreover, the great numbers of sexual assault and domestic violence cases that have begun to enter the criminal justice system present unique challenges related to the dynamics of the crimes.

Perhaps the most valuable strategy that all prosecutors can adopt in working with all crime victims is to communicate appropriate information in a sensitive way and to seek out resources to help victims obtain crime victim counseling and court support through trained victim assistance personnel. Every prosecutor's office should continually update a list of informative suggestions and referral resources on restitution, counseling and support groups for victims. Additionally, through referral and networking agreements, prosecutors should seek to work with community service providers to avoid duplication of victim services and to prioritize and focus limited resources. Finally, to protect victim privacy in the criminal justice process, victims should be informed that they may refer all media inquiries back to the prosecutor.

Although there is no boilerplate checklist for helping victims to participate in the criminal justice system, the following strategies can maximize the participation of victims with special needs and thereby enhance the potential for success in their cases.

CHILD VICTIMS

Sadly, children today are just as likely to become victims of crime as adults. To work effectively with child victims requires special training and commitment. Counseling support for children and their families should start at the time the victim is identified and should continue for as long as it is feasible. Referral to professionals or agencies that will deal with the child's trauma is essential to the child's recovery. Successful strategies combine medical and legal investigative strategies with vertical prosecution to maximize rapport with the child and minimize the number of interviews. Today, many prosecutors work with child advocacy centers as part of the interview process. Anatomically correct dolls and drawings are used to assist children in explaining their victimizations.

It is important for the prosecutor to understand the developmental stages of children when working with a child victim. For example, while young children may not have the words to describe what has happened, older children may be embarrassed to use their words to describe the criminal acts. The prosecutor should learn how to communicate with young children through the use of drawing techniques and audio visual aids when they have difficulty expressing themselves. Even if the child is not qualifiable as a witness, a young child may provide valuable information in an interview. Also, the child's hearsay statements may be admissible.

Before interviewing a child, it is helpful to establish a rapport with the child and his or her family. After an introductory period, the prosecutor should interview the child away from the family members to avoid potential pressures or concerns the child might have about their presence. To build on the rapport with the child, perhaps start the interview by asking about his or her hobbies, pets or interests before turning to the subject of the crime. Let the child know that you have helped other children in similar circumstances. This will help the child recognize that he or she is not alone in this experience. Begin with simple, open-ended developmentally appropriate questions before moving to more specific, objective questions. To avoid confusion, use the child's own terms to describe body parts or specific acts.

For a young child to testify, the prosecutor may be required to prove competency. In qualifying the child, it should be demonstrated that the child knows the difference between telling the truth and a lie, and the significance of taking an oath to promise to tell the truth. It is also important to show that the child has the ability to recall and recount facts. Several studies have shown that children as young as five can appropriately answer objective questions concerning simple concrete events. Children are more likely to correctly answer questions about central actions than questions about peripheral information or about the offender's description. Keep in mind that a child's ability to answer objective questions may depend upon the difficulty of the question in relation to the age of the child. For example, some young children may have difficulty answering objective questions that involve units of measurement, such as height, weight and age, or that require abstract inferences, such as questions seeking motive or "why" answers.

To prepare children for court, the prosecutor should take them to an empty courtroom, preferably to the room in which they will testify. Walk them through the courtroom. Let them sit in the witness seat. To reduce intimidation, try to familiarize them with the court surroundings. For example, introduce them to courtroom personnel by name. Some prosecutors have established court orientation programs or "court schools" for this purpose.

In preparing children to testify, advise them to tell the truth (to avoid defense inferences). Explain that defense attorneys may try to confuse or upset them. Explain that they are not at fault and that the case does not rest on their testimony. Let them know that you are there to protect them and then do that in court by making your objections while they are on the stand. Reassure children that they will be safe.

In many jurisdictions, the testimony of a child may be taken *in camera* or through the use of a child shield consistent with the guidelines set forth by the United States Supreme Court. If you do choose to have the child testify in open court, remember that in eliciting testimony courts often permit a certain number of leading questions of child witnesses. After the testimony, help rebuild the child's self-esteem by praising the child on his or her courage.

SENIOR VICTIMS

Although statistically speaking seniors are victimized less often than younger people, the number of reported crimes against seniors is growing. The impact of crime on seniors is great. As part of old age, most seniors are forced to accept declining health; the loss of loved ones such as family, friends and neighbors who have died or moved away; the loss of jobs or income; and the loss of the ability to drive. Senior victims may have great difficulty coping with the additional losses incurred by crime. Violent crimes are particularly devastating. While most seniors are not likely to be physically injured in the commission of crimes, when injuries are suffered, aged victims may only recover partially or not at all

Sexual assaults against older females can cause serious injuries from which they never recover. This crime is so overwhelmingly humiliating to senior victims that they may have great difficulty in reporting the sexual act or participating in medical exams. They may fear that family members and neighbors will find out about the assault or that the media will publicize the crime. The prosecutor should take special care to protect elder victims of sexual assault from media attention. Secure waiting areas and escorts for such victims should be arranged.

Senior victims of fraud crimes frequently lose trust in their own judgment and in others. They may feel a sense of betrayal, especially if the perpetrator is someone they know. Often they hesitate to tell family members, friends or colleagues about their victimization for fear of criticism. If family and friends have been exploited by the same fraud, victims might feel guilty and suffer further isolation. Fraud crimes can destroy the elder victim's financial security as well as that of their loved ones.

If the elder victim has suffered financial loss, the victim may be unable to maintain his current lifestyle or restore his financial position. For example, losing even a small amount of money in a burglary may mean that the victim on a fixed-income goes without food, medication or other necessities. Financial hardship may also arise from costs incurred to restore property damage and other losses resulting from a crime. Ultimately, if the victim is unable to recover losses, the victim may even face the loss of independence as a result of the crime.

It is important to have information on compensation programs readily available for the elderly victim. When suggesting counseling, explain that it is useful in helping people deal with the stress caused by crime and is not a suggestion that they suffer from mental illness. As always, do not hesitate to utilize local and national elder assistance programs, including adult protective services, city and police elder abuse units and attorney general programs.

Senior victims, as witnesses, can pose special challenges to prosecutors. Although it is important to avoid the assumption that the victim's age automatically causes diminished sensory, cognitive or physical capacities, some seniors may become confused by everyday details and disoriented by new terminology, technology and procedures. Moreover, senior victims may not be aware of their diminished capacity or know how to raise this issue with the prosecutor.

Declining vision is a very common physical challenge of old age; difficulty in distinguishing certain colors, inability to change focus rapidly, sensitivity to glare and difficulty in adjusting to changes in lighting are common. Constriction of peripheral vision—the outer portion of the field that is highly sensitive to motion, light, darkness and varying shapes and sizes of objects—may be present. A loss of depth perception may cause difficulties in accurately estimating distances or the speed of vehicles. Almost one-quarter of seniors experience some hearing loss. Most often, deterioration is gradual and the victim may not be aware of the degree of loss.

For the interview, pick a quiet setting and tell the victim what to expect during the investigation. Arrange seating so that the victim is not facing the sun or bright light. Allow the victim to describe the incident in his or her own words. Be patient and reassuring. Some older people, particularly those in crisis, may need time to collect their thoughts and may need to take frequent breaks. Acknowledge the victim's anxiety and try to discern its cause. Keep questions short, clear and simple. Ask open-ended questions that encourage further discussion. Avoid interruptions that may cause the victim to lose the train of thought. Use the victim's terminology and language for acts, body parts, etc.

Even if the victim appears to be somewhat confused, do not automatically discount the information. If you feel that the victim needs assistance or is having difficulty understanding or communicating, ask if he or she has someone who can help but make every effort to obtain the answers to your questions from the victim before relying on information from others. If you need to have another person assist in communicating or providing information for the victim, conduct the conversation in the victim's presence and look for signs of corroboration from the victim (e.g., nodding in agreement).

Keep in mind that some victims may not drive or may not be able to travel alone on public transportation. Arrange safe, adequate transportation. Whenever possible, arrange court dates to avoid interfering with any medical care or treatment. Before trial, walk the victim through the courtroom. Prepare the witness to testify on the day of trial so that the information is fresh in his or her mind. Allow extra time for the victim to adjust to the surroundings. Changes in lighting conditions between the conference room and courtroom and the unfamiliar surroundings of these settings may cause the victim to appear confused or uncertain, raising credibility issues. During questioning, stand directly in front of the witness and reduce your pacing and movements. If there is hearing loss, increase the volume of your voice. Speak clearly and eliminate, if possible, background noises like fans and air conditioners. Create a deliberately slow pace in questioning to facilitate the senior's pace in answering questions.

VICTIMS WITH DISABILITIES

The odds are great that prosecutors will encounter cases involving victims with disabilities, for millions of American are fully or partially disabled. Some crime victims are so injured by the crime that they then join the ranks of persons with disabilities. The impact of the crime on a person with existing disabilities intensifies the challenges already faced and compounds the stress on the victim. The victim who is disabled as a result of the crime faces permanent life changes and the traumatic impact on this individual is profound.

Strategies for working with victims with disabilities will differ according to the nature and degree of the disability. As soon as possible, the victim's needs should be assessed to adjust for difficulties. A prosecutor should seek technical assistance from organizations, associations and agencies in the community that have expertise on disabilities. These resources can assist in making necessary adjustments, which may include: transportation by medi-car or ambulance, communication by qualified interpreters and use of TDD (Telecommunication Device for the Deaf) or TTY (Teletype) machines or relay service contracts. Ideally, basic protocols and materials will be agreed upon in advance of the case.

Treat adults as adults. Address people who have disabilities by their first names only when extending that same familiarity to all others. Do not patronize them. When meeting a person with a visual impairment, always identify yourself and others who may be with you. When conversing in a group, remember to identify the person to whom you are speaking. When introduced to a person with a physical disability, it is appropriate to offer to shake hands. People with limited hand use or who wear an artificial limb can usually shake hands. Shaking hands with the left hand is an acceptable greeting. If you are unsure, ask the victim how you should act or communicate most effectively with him or her. Ask also if he or she has any needs that will require special services or arrangements, and then make every attempt to provide for those needs. You may offer physical assistance, such as offering your arm if the need arises but do not assume the victim will need it or accept it. If you offer assistance, wait until the offer is accepted, then listen to, or ask for, instructions.

When interviewing a person with a disability, maintain eye contact and speak directly to that person rather than through a companion or to a sign language interpreter who may be present. Deliberately averting your gaze is impolite and can be uncomfortable, increasing the victim's tension. When speaking to a victim in a wheelchair or one who uses crutches, place yourself at eye level in front of the person to facilitate the conversation. Because a wheelchair is considered part of the personal body space of the person who uses it, leaning or hanging on to the wheelchair is generally considered annoying.

Tap the victim who is deaf or hard of hearing on the shoulder or wave your hand to get his or her attention. Look directly at the victim and speak clearly, slowly and expressively to establish if the person can read your lips. Most people with a hearing impairment cannot lip-read; therefore, a sign language interpreter should be arranged.

Listen carefully when talking with a person who has difficulty speaking. Be patient and wait for the person to finish, rather than correcting or speaking for the person. If necessary, ask short questions that require short answers, a nod or shake of the head. If you are having difficulty understanding, repeat what you have understood and allow the victim to respond.

Persons with cognitive disabilities may not be easy to identify. Among the many characteristics they may have are a difficulty understanding rapid speech or complicated sentences; they may have difficulty expressing themselves or be unable to read or write; they may be slow in responding, give inappropriate responses, have difficulty making choices; or they may not understand money, be confused by a transaction, not know their own address or act younger than their age. When scheduling interviews or testimony, it is essential for the prosecutor to consider the victim's energy and cognitive limits. Some victims cannot stay focused and alert for lengthy periods. In interviewing victims with cognitive disabilities a prosecutor should speak clearly and slowly and use simple, concrete words. Simplify written instructions and signs and use pictures or symbols. If possible, reduce the number of interviews of the victim.

Prior to trial, familiarize the victim with the courtroom and setting, and allow additional time for necessary adjustments. During trial preparation, minimize trial-related stress by explaining to the victim any prosecutorial strategies you will employ to highlight the limitations and diminished quality of life the victim faces as a result of the crime. Also explain why you will do this: to convince a judge and jury of the severity of the victim's physical and psychological impairments.

DOMESTIC VIOLENCE VICTIMS

Domestic violence might more properly be termed "family violence" because victims are found in all varieties of "families." Most often, however, reported victims of domestic violence are women attacked by their spouses or intimate partners. Although males can be victims, every prosecutor knows, even without statistical data, that the rate of domestic violence is immensely higher for adult female victims than for adult male victims. Intense scrutiny of this type of violence has also identified numerous secondary victims, such as children who witness violence directed at their mother and seniors.

Domestic violence is often a state of cyclical victimization. It may begin with emotional forms of control and move to physical restraint and battering followed by sexual assault and even homicide. To control or instill fear in their victims, offenders may stalk their victims before, during and after the relationship ends. Because domestic violence victims face overwhelming life changes by the time they reach the prosecutor's office, these cases present prosecutors with a myriad of challenges.

Domestic violence cases are perhaps the most victim-intensive of prosecutions. Victims often waver in their decisions to prosecute. The victim's decision to end the violence by escaping is the first step in the decision to prosecute but by the time the case reaches the prosecutor, the victim may have already tried but failed to obtain assistance or to take some self-protective action to prevent the violence. This failure can contribute to the victim's depression and indecision. She may not be able to predict the violence and thus try to avoid it. She may come to believe that she has no control over her destiny. The victim may feel trapped and less capable of escaping the relationship. Common factors that prosecutors should recognize in domestic violence victims are:

- Lack of control over finances even though she may be employed;
- Panic attacks as a result of stress and anxiety;
- Isolation from family and friends;
- Feeling of responsibility for abuser's behavior, or guilt;
- Low self-esteem and excessive criticism of self and others;
- Experience of or witness to childhood abuse;
- Rationalization of the violence and perhaps denial of the seriousness of her situation;
- Deference of power to others to make choices; and,
- Depression, use of alcohol or drugs to cope, and perhaps attempts at suicide.

Prosecutors should also be aware that the act of leaving the home might be especially dangerous for the victim. Women who attempt to leave their abusers are at greater risk of experiencing an escalation in violence. Researchers call this "separation violence." These victims need considerable reassurance in their efforts to seek justice. They typically initiate proceedings and then attempt to drop the case more than once. The victim may recant statements and express hostility at the prosecutor. Building rapport with the victim is the key to continued participation by these victims, and vertical prosecution of domestic violence cases is most effective. It is essential that prosecutors consider the protection needs of these victims at all stages of the prosecution and notify the victim of any change in status of the offender (bail amount and conditions, release, escape).

At the outset, domestic violence victims should have an individualized safety plan. The basic elements of a safety plan include: rehearsed escape routes in the event of an emergency (doors, windows, exits, elevators, stairwells), the telephone number and location of a safe place (safe home of a friend or relative, motel or hotel, or shelter) and emergency items to take (cab fare, clothes, keys, identifications, medical information, bank, credit and asset documents, personal protection orders). The victim should also think about how she will become independent of the abuser. The safety plan will necessarily be customized. For example, the plan might include starting a bank account for the victim, with statements sent to a safe address. Contact your community service providers or one of the resources at the end of this article for prepared materials to give to these victims.

The domestic violence victim also faces numerous life challenges in participating in the prosecution of her case. She may have temporary living arrangements, have difficulty with transportation to and from court, and may need child care assistance. In addition to crime victim counseling and compensation referrals, these victims may benefit from education and employment referrals while proceedings are ongoing.

Prosecutors may also work with children who have witnessed the violence and other friends or family members that are witnesses in the case. These witnesses will also have safety concerns and fears of retaliation that should be addressed to obtain their fullest participation.

While there is no single or perfect strategy in these cases, prosecutors have made great strides in improving prosecution through victim-intensive strategies. Many prosecutors' offices now have domestic violence protocols in place to assist in these prosecutions. Protocols cover referral to social service agencies, court preparation, accompaniment of the victim, charging options, reduction of risk strategies, mandatory arrest, personal protection orders, the use of photographs to document injuries, prompt victim statements, no contact orders as conditions of bail and sentencing strategies designed to improve victim protection and enhance public safety. Some prosecutors have created specialized domestic violence units with specially trained victim advocates, victim-witness staff, investigators and prosecutors and a referral structure for the victim's civil legal needs (divorce, housing). In the Chicago area, the creation of an expedited processing unit cut the lifespan of cases in half and resulted in a 25 percent increase in convictions, with a reduction in pretrial crimes.

SEXUAL ASSAULT

The criminal justice system has historically viewed sexual assault cases with suspicion. Although reform legislation has made it easier to prosecute, many victims still feel stigmatized by these crimes and are reluctant to participate. Victims also fear that family, friends and neighbors will find out about the attack and blame them. They greatly fear retaliation for reporting and proceeding with the prosecution. Finally, victims are often ambivalent about the ability of the criminal justice system to protect them and bring the offender to justice.

Children can be frequent targets of sex offenders. The impact of these crimes on a child can range from low self-esteem to serious mental health problems. Many children are manipulated in sexual abuse and as a result may feel some guilt or responsibility for the crimes. Young victims of pornography have lost control over their images and may be very concerned about privacy. The overwhelming majority of adult violent sex offenses involve males assaulting female victims. Adult females account for a small percentage of known offenders and adult males account for a small percentage of victims. Same sex cases make up a very small percentage of cases. Victims and offenders are likely to have had a prior relationship as family members, intimates or acquaintances.

One implication for prosecutors from these statistics is that in the majority of cases the offender is known to the victim. Therefore, the prosecutor should prepare the victim for defenses of false allegation and consent as often as misidentification. Many prosecutors also coordinate medical rape protocols with law enforcement investigative efforts to identify and gather evidence and to reduce interviews; they use vertical prosecution; and they obtain special training in sexual assault case management. Larger prosecution offices have specially trained sexual assault units.

Sexual assault victims need a great deal of support to participate fully in the criminal justice process. Prosecutors should encourage the victim to have a supportive person, such as a relative, friend or victim advocate, accompany the victim to all court proceedings. Prosecutors should always request that court cases involving rape be closed to media coverage and that appropriate measures be taken to protect the victim's identity from the media and the public. The victim's right to notification in all phases of the criminal justice process should be explained to the victim and the procedures by which the victim obtains information should be provided.

Sexual assault victims are extremely fearful of retaliation by the offenders. "No-contact" and other protective orders should be sought when appropriate. Prosecutors should explain to the victim that rape shield laws in every jurisdiction prevent the defense from delving into the victim's past sexual history. Also, in appropriate cases, medical and mental health experts can testify to the victim's physical injuries and the presence of rape trauma syndrome.

The laws in many states require victim input prior to any plea agreement; this is always a good practice. In cases of plea agreements, victim impact statements are particularly important. If a defendant pleads to a lesser assault charge, it is important for the court to know the extent of the physical, psychological and financial damages the victim endured, regardless of the plea bargain. Prosecutors should include special conditions of sentencing requested by the victim, such as protective orders, restitution, testing for HIV (with the results provided to victims in states that allow this by statute) and sex offender treatment where appropriate. Sex offender registration information and how to obtain such information should also be provided to the victim.

SURVIVORS OF HOMICIDE

Over the past two decades approximately 500,000 persons were murdered in the United States. This is more than eight times the casualties suffered during the entire Vietnam War.

In ordinary mourning, the bereaved initially experience shock and numbness; they may be stunned by the loss and their functioning may become impeded. They may have difficulty making judgments and have limited concentration. This may give way to anger or guilt and a period of disorientation and disorganization. The bereaved may experience physical or psychosomatic illness and have a desire to flee from the reality of the loss. Eventually, through concentrated grief work, which may take a period of one or two years or longer, the bereaved reorganize their lives. They begin making decisions, have renewed energy and integrate the loss into their life experiences.

Those left behind in the wake of homicide, however, experience sudden, overwhelming grief but are denied the opportunity to work through the various stages of mourning. Instead, they are immediately thrust into the criminal justice system. The forced postponement of grieving can cause devastating consequences and requires commitment and compassion by the prosecutor to avoid compounding the survivors' trauma.

The criminal justice system demands much of the survivors. They are expected to sit and listen quietly and calmly in a courtroom, however great the internal outrage and pain. They may feel out of control and powerless. The rage they experience when they first encounter the defendant is both human and natural but, in a court setting, expression of that rage is unacceptable and in fact could impede the outcome of the trial or of future appeals. Suffering in silence, stifling tears and "being strong" may be useful for the criminal justice process, but these avoidance mechanisms repress the grief response. Their grief continues unabated.

Prosecutors handling homicide cases should familiarize themselves with grief responses, and be prepared for the expression of a range of emotions and responses. Guard against the expectation that the survivors will "get over it." Grief is not something to be overcome but to be experienced. Recognize, too, that the feelings of the family may fluctuate over the course of time and throughout the court proceedings. Initial shock may give way to anger. Initial acceptance may turn into hostility. Sometimes that anger and hostility may be directed at you, because you are their link to the court system. Familiarize yourself with available community resources, crisis lines and homicide survivor support groups for the family to contact, and provide those numbers at the earliest opportunity. During court proceedings, arrange for a room away from the courtroom and the defendant's family where the survivors can wait.

Consistent contact with the victim's family is essential. If you commit to calling at a certain time or day, do so. Always return calls, even if you have only a few minutes to talk. The family may need to talk about the deceased with you. They may need to show you pictures, tell you stories and show you personal effects. Take the time to look and listen. The family may also have a number of questions. In responding, prosecutors should be as knowledgeable as possible about the case before answering questions. Refer to the victim by name. If you are not sure of an answer, offer to find out and then follow up with your response.

Listen and be empathetic; do not try to be sympathetic. For example, do not say, "I understand," when you do not. However, do tell survivors that you are sorry the murder happened and that it is horrible that someone killed their loved one.

Homicide survivors may not be able to assimilate information or explanations in one sitting. Put victims' rights information in writing, and be prepared to explain court proceedings to them more than once. Assist survivors to complete necessary forms for funeral bill reimbursement and follow-up victim notification.

Recognize that perhaps the only time that they will get to "speak" about the crime to the court will be in a victim impact statement. This is an extremely important process for these survivors and sufficient time should be given to the preparation of the statement. It will be useful early on in the case to suggest that the survivors begin a journal. This helps them express feelings and frustration with the system. They may also want to draw upon their entries, such as those around anniversaries or other significant days, in developing their victim impact statement.

In states that have a death penalty, the lengthy criminal justice process compounds the stress and pain of the survivors who keep the case open in their minds and hearts awaiting the closure that comes with the end of the process. Long periods may pass between actions on appeals, yet consistent communication with these survivors at appropriate points is critical. One excellent resource for prosecutors is the *National Protocol* (listed in the references section of this article), which identifies a model for survivor services in these challenging cases.

Although prosecutors are neither social workers nor grief counselors, their ability to work with the special needs of homicide survivors greatly impacts the prosecution of a case. Survivors report that the single most important contributing factor to their recovery and well-being was the ongoing attention, concern and resources offered by the prosecutor.

HATE CRIMES VICTIMS

Victims who have been targeted for their personal beliefs, cultural, religious or sexual preference, gender or physical or mental capabilities, suffer severe emotional impact from the hate crimes perpetrated against them. Furthermore, hate crimes impact entire communities, and the prosecutor should respond to the needs and problems that result from these crimes with a community perspective. Perhaps the best institutional strategy that prosecutors can adopt is to cultivate and maintain productive and communicative relationships with diverse community organizations. These relationships build mutual trust and will be indispensable in the prosecution of hate crimes.

Racially motivated hate crimes can be psychologically debilitating to the victim who may feel bitter not only toward the offender but also toward the entire race or cultural group of the offender. For example, African-American victims may have a strong distrust of the criminal justice system as unresponsive to their community, a sentiment that presents additional challenges to a prosecutor who must establish trust to gain the victim's participation in the prosecution. Another dynamic of racially motivated hate crimes is that they sometimes engender retaliatory crimes by the victimized group.

Victims of hate crimes who are recent immigrants sometimes associate government officials with the authoritarian regimes from which they fled to the United States. Or, they may not hold secure residency papers. As a result, victims and witnesses will often disclose only a limited amount of information regarding the crime. Prosecutors should provide these victims and witnesses with appropriate referrals for information on immigration laws and agencies that can help answer questions they have about the process. Prosecutors should expect to do detailed follow-up investigations in these cases. It is also important to provide this victim population with repeated explanations of the judicial process. For example, the concept of bail or bond may be confusing. Upon learning that their attacker gave a certain amount of money to the judge and left jail, some immigrant victims may conclude that the case was dismissed as part of a bargain. They may not realize that the prosecution is still pending.

Hate crime victims who are targeted because of their ethnicity or national origin may not possess competence in the English language. A prosecutor should be sensitive to the need for translators throughout the investigation and trial. Community groups may be able to arrange for translator services.

Persons targeted for religiously motivated hate crimes may experience a powerful sense of fear, vulnerability and isolation. Such victims may confide more readily in community and spiritual leaders. Prosecutors should consult with such leaders for assistance in gaining the cooperation of the victims in the prosecution of their cases. Also, prosecutors should be aware that the investigation and handling of physical evidence might pose unique problems when religiously significant objects or structures are damaged in a hate crime. For example, religious law or custom may dictate special handling of damaged items. Whenever possible, prosecutors should be sensitive to these religious laws or customs in considering the evidentiary requirements of the prosecution.

Victims of anti-gay hate crimes may have confidentiality concerns. Their family, friends or coworkers may not know that they are gay or lesbian. Prosecutors should be aware of legal privacy protection available to keep these victims' names or other personal information from the media. Prosecutors should also explain to these victims if sexual orientation will be an issue at trial.

In some jurisdictions, gender-based crime can be charged as a hate crime. In these cases, where the victim has had a prior relationship with the offender, prosecutors should enlist the assistance of domestic violence or sexual assault community resources.

PRINT RESOURCES

General

Alexander, E.K. and J.H. Lord. *A Victim's Right to Speak, A Nation's Responsibility to Listen*, National Victim Center, Mothers Against Drunk Driving, and American Prosecutors Research Institute: grant from the U.S. Department of Justice, Office for Victims of Crime, Arlington, National Victim Center, 1994.

Beatty, D., S. Smith Howley, and D. G. Kilpatrick. *Statutory and Constitutional Protection of Victims' Rights: Implementation and Impact on Crime Victims, Sub-Report: Crime Victim Responses Regarding Victims' Rights*. Arlington: National Victim Center, 1997.

Bureau of Justice Statistics. "Prosecutors in State Courts 1996," *BJS Bulletin*. Washington, D.C.: U.S. Department of Justice, July 1998 (1996 national survey of prosecutors).

National Association of Crime Victim Compensation Boards. *Program Directory: 1999*. Alexandria, 1999.

National Center for Victims of Crime. *Focus on the Future: A Systems Approach to Prosecution and Victim Assistance, A Training and Resource Manual*. Arlington: 1994.

Office for Victims of Crime. *New Directions from the Field: Victims' Rights and Services for the 21st Century*. Washington, D.C.: U.S. Department of Justice, 1998.

President's Task Force on Victims of Crime, Final Report. Washington, D.C.: U.S. Government Printing Office, December 1982.

U.S. Department of Justice. *Serving Crime Victims and Witnesses*. 2nd Edition. Washington, D.C. 1997.

Office for Victims of Crime. *Victim Assistance: National Resource Directory 1999*. Washington, DC; U.S. Department of Justice, 1999.

Young, Marlene. *Victim Assistance: Frontiers and Fundamentals*. Dubuque, Iowa: Kendall/Hunt Publishing Co., 1993.

Child Victims

For an excellent overview of child sexual abuse victims, see "Symposium on Child Sexual Abuse Prosecutions: the Current State of the Art," *U. Miami L. Rev.* 40 (1996) 167 and specifically articles therein: Lucy Berliner, "The Child Witness: the Progress and Emerging Limitations" (at 171), and Gail S. Goodman and Vicki S. Helgeson "Child Sexual Assault: Children's Memory and the Law" (at 181).

Kilpatrick, D., and B. Saunders. *Prevalence and Consequences of Child Victimization*, Crime Victims Research and Treatment Center, Medical University of South Carolina, Research in Brief, National Institute of Justice, 1997.

Senior Victims

National Center on Elder Abuse. *The National Elder Abuse Incidence Study: Final Report.* U.S. Dept. of Health and Human Services, September 1998.

Police Executive Research Forum (PERF). *Improving the Police Response to Domestic Elder Abuse.* Washington, DC: U.S. Department of Justice, Office for Victims of Crime, 1993.

Victims with Disabilities

Rubin, P. *The Americans with Disabilities Act and Criminal Justice: An Overview.* Research in Action, Washington, D.C.: National Institute of Justice, 1993.

Tyiska, Cheryl G. "Responding to Disabled Victims of Crime," *NOVA Network Information Bulletin*, Issue No. 8-12. Washington, D.C.: National Organization for Victim Assistance, 1990.

Domestic Violence

Boland, Mary L. *Domestic Violence: A Prosecutor's Guide.* Cook County State's Attorney's Office, Chicago, IL, October 1996.

Clark, Sandra J., Martha R. Burt, Margaret M. Schulte and Karen Maguire. *Coordinated Community Responses to Domestic Violence in Six Communities: Beyond the Justice System.* The Urban Institute, October 1996.

Fagan, Jeffrey. *The Criminalization of Domestic Violence: Promises and Limits.* Research Report, National Institute of Justice, January 1996.

National Institute of Justice and American Bar Association. *Legal Interventions in Family Violence: Research Findings and Policy Implications.* Research Report, National Institute of Justice, July 1998.

Bureau of Justice Statistics. *Violence by Intimates: Analysis of Data on Crimes by Current or Former Spouses, Boyfriends, and Girlfriends.* U.S. Department of Justice: Bureau of Justice Statistics, March 1998.

Sexual Assault

Greenfeld, Lawrence A. *Sex Offenses and Offenders: An Analysis of Data on Rape and Sexual Assault*, U.S. Department of Justice, Bureau of Justice Statistics, February 1997.

Kilpatrick, D., C. Edmunds, & A. Seymour. *Rape in America: A Report to the Nation.* The National Women's Study. Washington, DC: National Institute of Drug Abuse, National Victim Center and National Crime Victims Research and Treatment Center at the Medical University of South Carolina, April 1992.

Homicide Survivors

National Organization for Victim Assistance. *Crime Victims as Witnesses to an Execution: A National Protocol: A Report of First National Symposium on Crime Victims as Witnesses to an Execution* (ed. Mary Achilles) 1999.

Young, Marlene A. "Death and Dying," *The Community Crisis Response Team Training Manual*, National Organization for Victim Assistance, 1994 (2nd Ed.).

Hate Crimes

Anti-Defamation League. *Hate Crimes: ADL Blueprint for Action*, New York, 1997 and *1998 Hate Crimes Laws*, New York, 1997.

Cook County State's Attorney's Office. *Hate Crime: A Prosecutor's Guide.* 1998 (2nd Ed.).

Debbie N. Kaminer. *Hate Crime Laws.* Anti-Defamation League, New York, 1997.

Office for Victims of Crime. *Resources for Responding to Hate Crimes.* U.S. Department of Justice, Washington. D.C.

Wessler, Stephen. *Addressing Hate Crimes: Six Initiatives That Are Enhancing the Efforts of Criminal Justice Practitioners.* U.S. Department of Justice, Office of Justice Programs, Washington, D.C., February 2000.

VICTIM-RELATED CONTACTS

Government

ADA Information Line (800/514-0301), www.ojp.usdoj.gov/crt/ada/adahom1.htm, provides information, publications and technical assistance regarding the Americans with Disabilities Act.

Administration on Aging, (AoA) (Eldercare Locator - to find services for an older person in his or her locality: (800) 677-1116), AoA is the federal focal point and advocate agency for older persons and their concerns. It provides information, referral and outreach efforts at the community level.

Hate Crime Statistics, http://www.fbi.gov/publish/hatecrime.htm, includes FBI reported hate crimes statistics by year.

National Criminal Justice Reference Service (NCJRS)(800/851-3420), www.ncjrs.org, includes specific information on victims, permits key word searches of NCJRS publications, and links to other criminal justice pages. Many publication resources are free.

U.S. Dept. of Justice, Community Relations Service, http://www.usdoj.gov/crs/crs.htm, a specialized federal conciliation service available to state and local officials to help resolve and prevent racial and ethnic conflict, violence, and civil disorders. CRS helps local officials and residents tailor locally defined resolutions when conflict and violence threaten community stability and well-being. CRS conciliators assist in identifying the sources of violence and conflict and utilizing specialized crisis management and violence reduction techniques that work best for each community.

Violence Against Women Office (VAWO), www.ojp.usdoj.gov/vawo/, includes grant-funding opportunities for programs combating violence against women.

Other Service/Community Victim-Related Links

American Bar Association Center on Children and the Law, www.abanet.org/child/home; its mission is to improve children's lives through advances in law, justice, knowledge, practice and public policy. The center is involved with a national network of universities and other organizations doing research related to laws and government policies affecting vulnerable children.

Compassionate Friends, www.compassionatefriends.org, provides support to families who have experienced the death of a child through nearly 600 local chapters.

Court Appointed Special Advocates (CASA), www.casanet.org, (312) 433-4928 volunteers provide case management, courtroom support, school interventions and evaluations.

Disability and Business Technical Assistance Centers (DBTACS), www.icdi.wvu.edu/tech/ada.htm, (800) 949-4232, network of agencies that provide technical assistance to agencies and businesses regarding their responsibilities and duties under the ADA.

Mothers Against Drunk Driving (MADD)(800 GET-MADD or (877) 539-8255 - general information,) www.grannet.com/madd/madd.htm, provides ongoing information and support for families of victims of vehicular homicide or serious injuries caused by driving under the influence of drugs or alcohol.

National Children's Alliance, www.nncac, formerly the national Network of Children's Advocacy Centers, (800) 239-9950, provides training, technical assistance and networking opportunities to communities seeking to plan, establish and improve Children's Advocacy Centers.

National Center for Victims of Crime (NCVC) (800-FYI-CALL), www.ncvc.org/, provides victim-related research and information, and referrals. It includes a comprehensive database of legislation, reports emerging trends, publishes a newsletter and documents to improve crime victims.

National Coalition Against Sexual Assault (NCASA), www.ncasa.org/, (717) 728-9764, a feminist organization that provides leadership to the movement to end sexual violence through advocacy, education and public policy. It sponsors a national conference for members.

National Coalition Against Domestic Violence (NCADV), www.webmerchants.com/ncadv/default.htm, (303/ 839-1852), a national network for state coalitions and local programs serving battered women and their children, public policy at the national level, technical assistance, community awareness campaigns, general information and referrals and publications on the issue of domestic violence. It sponsors a national conference every two years for battered women and their advocates.

National Organization for Victim Assistance (NOVA), (202) 232-6682, www.try-nova.org, advocates for compassionate treatment of crime victims, provides direct assistance, training and technical assistance. It sponsors a national conference yearly for victim assistance professions.

Parents of Murdered Children, (513) 721-LOVE, www.POMC.org, support for families who have lost a child or sibling to violent crime.

Partnerships Against Violence Network (PAVNET), www.pavnet.org. *PAVNET Online* is a "virtual library" of information about violence and youth-at-risk, representing data from seven different federal agencies. It is a one-stop, searchable, information resource to help reduce redundancy in information management and provide clear and comprehensive access to information for states and local communities.

HOTLINES

American Association of Mental Retardation: (800) 424-3688

American Council for the Blind: (800) 424-8666

Americans with Disabilities Act (ADA) Information Hotline: (800) 949-4232

Childhelp USA/Forrester National Child Abuse Hotline: (800) 422-4453

Mothers Against Drunk Driving (MADD): (800) 438-6233

National Association for Hearing & Speech Action Line: (800) 638-8255

National Center for Missing and Exploited Children: (800) 843-5678

National Center for Stuttering: (800) 221-2483

National Center for Victims of Crime (NCVC): (800) 394-2255

National Clearinghouse for Alcohol and Drug Information: (800) 729-6686

National Clearinghouse on Child Abuse and Neglect: (800) 394-3366

National Criminal Justice Reference Service: (800) 851-3420

National Domestic Violence Hotline: (800) 799-SAFE (7233)

National Down's Syndrome Hotline: (800) 221-4602

National Fraud Information Hotline: (800) 876-7060

National Hearing Aid Helpline: (800) 521-5247

National Organization for Victim Assistance (NOVA): (800) 897-8794

Office for Victims of Crime Resource Center (OVCRC): (800) 627-6872

Rape, Abuse & Incest National Network: (800) 656-HOPE

TRIAL PRACTICES AND SPECIAL TOPICS

FOOTPRINTS IN THE SNOW: THE PROSECUTION OF ARSON CRIMES

By Karin Horwatt Cather, Assistant Commonwealth's Attorney,
Fauquier County, Warrenton, Virginia

Introduction
Definition of Arson for Purposes of this Article

For purposes of this article, arson is the burning or damaging, by explosive device, of a structure, with malice aforethought.[1] However, arson[2] may not always be the primary offense in a given transaction or occurrence. For example, a deliberately set fire may be the intentional or unintentional cause of death in a homicide or an attempt to cover up a homicide. However, this article is intended to be useful to the prosecutor who must prove that a fire or explosion at a structure was incendiary in nature and that a particular person caused the fire or explosion regardless of the primary identity of the offense.[3] The scope of this article is limited to an overview of the evidentiary and ethical issues unique to the prosecution of arson cases and the resources available to the arson prosecutor.

ARSON PROSECUTION IS AN INTERDISCIPLINARY UNDERTAKING

Proving an arson case requires a variety of expert witnesses and evidence from a broad array of sources that challenge the ordinary funds of knowledge and experience of the average prosecutor. The prosecutor is called to the scene of a fully involved house fire. It burns to the ground. Is the fire deliberate, and if so, did the defendant set it? The law presumes that the fire was accidental. The prosecutor must rebut this presumption and prove beyond a reasonable doubt that the fire was incendiary and not accidental.

Arson is a furtive crime. Eyewitnesses are rare, unless they are co-defendants.[4] To one unfamiliar with arson investigation and prosecution, the crime scene may appear to be of no help. Once the firefighters extinguish the fire, what remains will confound the uninitiated. The origin-and-cause[5] expert will see clues in the shape of a light bulb, the spalling of concrete, the obvious multiple points of origin, and the absence of valuable furniture in an expensive house. Arson leaves footprints, not only in the structure itself but also in the financial records of the perpetrators and on the bodies of the dead. The prosecutor of arson crimes must know how to find these footprints, both to evaluate the strengths of a case and to prepare the experts for trial.

Assume, for example, that a man in financial and marital difficulties shoots his wife in the head for her life insurance, removes some valuable items from the house and property (including, perhaps, some purebred animals), sets the house on fire and collects insurance on his wife and the house. Perhaps he marries another woman only days after the funeral. The footprints leading to the proof of arson can consist of such quanta of proof as:

- A charred piece of wood from the dwelling house;
- Bank records and credit history documents establishing that the owner of the property was experiencing severe financial difficulties in the months preceding the fire;
- Insurance documents establishing that the owner had increased the fire insurance on the structure and the life insurance on his wife;
- Testimony of a forensic chemist establishing the presence of accelerants [6] in the structure;
- Photographs establishing that the dwelling had been emptied of the best pieces of furniture prior to the fire;
- Testimony from the medical examiner [7] establishing that the cause of death for the owner's wife was a gunshot wound to the head and that, prior to the fire, the victim was already dead;
- Testimony from a origin-and-cause expert [8] about the existence of pour patterns, the fire's multiple points of origin and the integrity of the electrical system;
- The absence of any accidental causes; and
- For good measure, the relevant pages of the local newspaper documenting that the sky was clear and that there was no lightning at the time of the offense.

Complicating the mixture may be the presence of an informant or even a co-defendant on your witness list, which may also include a forensic accountant, several firefighters and rescue personnel and possibly even physicians.

Arson may be the objective of a perpetrator, or it may be the means to cover up or commit other criminal acts. For example, the motive [9] for an arson may be fraud, revenge or jealousy, the cover-up of a homicide, burglary or other crime or an act of civil disobedience or terrorism. Arson may also be a thrill-seeking act, a perverse act of sexual gratification or a means by which a perpetrator, by attempting a rescue, can appear heroic.[10] The perpetrator may even be a firefighter, searching for thrills.[11]

The interdisciplinary nature of arson prosecution cannot be overemphasized. The prosecutor must be willing to be educated by expert witnesses as to the subject matter of their testimony, but this is not enough. The prosecutor must also be sufficiently prepared to cross-examine the defendant's stable of paid experts who will range from honest professionals with a legitimate difference of opinion to the rankest of defense mercenaries.[12] Some of the "expert testimony" attempted by the defense will involve subject matter that is not science but science fiction.

For all of these reasons, it is highly recommended that any attorney who undertakes arson prosecution attend the week-long course sponsored by the Bureau of Alcohol, Tobacco and Firearms entitled "Arson for Profit for State Prosecutors."[13]

SPECIAL CONSIDERATIONS IN ARSON TRIALS

Search and seizure law, co-defendant testimony and the issue of parallel criminal and civil cases arising from the same transaction and occurrence constitute special issues unique to the prosecution of arson cases. Furthermore, certain strategic considerations arise from the extent to which expert testimony or large volumes of financial data are present in the case. The scientific testimony, the battle of the experts and, possibly, the reams of documentary evidence can confuse or bore the jury. The prosecutor should remind the jury members of the events that brought them to the courthouse in the first place. Otherwise, the consideration of a defendant's guilt might become an intellectual puzzle or a personality contest rather than a real life trial within the minds of the jurors. The prosecutor must regularly bring the jury back to the reality of the fire and the damage (or deaths) it has caused. Finally, the prosecutor must be acquainted with the insanity defense because it is a common defense to arson crimes.

Demonstrative Evidence

The physical condition of the structure and the items contained within the structure constitute evidence of arson. It is essential that the prosecutor present to the fact finder photographic documentation of the scene as demonstrative evidence, so that experts can easily show the jury the pour patterns, doors, windows, glass, light bulbs, multiple points of origin and the clear absence of accidental causes. An easily over-looked but essential piece of evidence is the recording of the call for emergency assistance—the 911 tape. These tapes, usually erased after 30 to 60 days depending on the agency, can document the emotional state of the caller.

To convey to the jury the reality of the fire and the destructive nature of the arson, hand them a charred piece of wood or other burned portion of the structure, assuming that the local jurisdiction allows potentially hazardous materials in the court-room. Videotapes of the burning structure (if a neighbor videotaped the incident with a hand-held video camera) and photographs of the victims, if any, will give the jury sights and sounds to take to the jury room with them.

Do not let the jury forget what fire can do. Call bystanders and neighbors as witness-es to describe their evacuation from their own homes, to recall how quickly the fire spread and to estimate how far they had to stand from the burning structure to avoid the intense heat. Give the jury a sense of the dangers that the firefighters faced. Have a firefighter describe the protective equipment they wear and testify to the fact that the protective equipment is necessary to protect against the heat and the lethal gases that fires generate. Point out if any firefighters were injured and let them explain how long it took to extinguish the fire and what specifically was required. At sentencing, elicit from the appropriate witnesses the extent to which the fire set by the defendant increased the response time to other fires in the area because of the diversion of per-sonnel to fight the defendant's fire. And to make the scientific evidence understand-able to the jury, make your witnesses explain terms of art to them.

Arson cases are often circumstantial evidence cases. Ironically, even prosecutors dis-miss circumstantial evidence cases as less compelling than direct evidence cases. The phrase, "it's just circumstantial" is part of the popular lexicon in a jury pool that has been conditioned by prime time television to believe that one must have the murder weapon in order to convict a defendant. But, a circumstantial evidence case is often more credible and more inexorable than a direct evidence case because physical evi-dence does not lie.

Illustrate the point with the jury using analogy. You are alone in the house with your four-year-old son, Adam and your six-year-old daughter, Betty. A blanket of fresh snow, untouched by footprints, surrounds the house. Your children have clean faces.

The cookie jar is full of chocolate chip cookies. You leave the room to fold clothes and return 20 minutes later to find the cookie jar empty. The snow around the house has not been disturbed. Betty points to Adam and says, "He took the cookies from the cookie jar." That is direct evidence against Adam. Adam's face, however, is still clean, while Betty's face is covered with chocolate chip cookie crumbs and she has chocolate chip cookie on her breath. That is circumstantial evidence against Betty. Which case is stronger?

The above analogy also illustrates that sometimes a lie is better than a confession in the prosecution of a crime. Why did the defendant file a claim form with his insurance company indicating that a 40 thousand dollar heirloom antique sofa with rich Corinthian leather burned in the fire when later police located the sofa in his storage shed? A defendant may attempt to recant a confession, but it is nearly impossible to recant a lie.

SEARCH AND SEIZURE LAW

Comprehensive exploration of the nuances of search and seizure law in arson prosecution is beyond the scope of this article but a casual exploration of the topic can reveal some specific issues to keep in mind. The initial entry by firefighters into the dwelling and the initial determination of cause and origin are covered under the exigent circumstances doctrine. However, if an origin-and-cause investigator enters and then leaves a putative scene of arson after a period of time, he may need a warrant to re-enter.[14] Sometimes, law enforcement may obtain an administrative warrant, which does not require probable cause to believe that a crime has been committed.[15]

PARALLEL CRIMINAL AND CIVIL PROCEEDINGS

Frequently the same transaction and occurrence that gives rise to arson prosecution precipitates litigation between the defendant and an insurance company. Parallel criminal and civil cases create benefits and difficulties. For example, an insurance company may deny coverage if the insured declines to cooperate with their investigators. Hence, the insured likely consents to an interview with the insurance investigators.[16] This same insured/suspect/defendant may have invoked *Miranda* when approached by law enforcement.[17]

The prosecutor may then subpoena the insurance investigator who interviewed the defendant to testify as to any statements made by the defendant, with a subtle constitutional advantage. The interview between the insurance investigator and the insured is an interview between private parties (i.e., the insurance investigator is not a state actor) that is by definition non-custodial, because a private insurance investigator does not have arrest powers and accordingly is not subject to the strictures of the *Miranda* decision. There is a considerable body of law[18] that addresses the issue of when a private entity becomes an agent of the state for purposes of search and seizure law, for purposes of *Miranda* and for purposes of establishing the voluntariness of confessions, consents to search and other waivers.[19] To the extent that, for example, an insurance investigator acts at the behest of or under the instructions of a state actor, this may for constitutional law purposes be deemed to be acting as an agent of the state.

If there are parallel proceedings, prosecutors and law enforcement officials involved in the criminal prosecution must be wary of sharing information with the parties to any civil action.[20] First of all, prosecutors are protected by sovereign immunity[21] when they are acting within the scope of their employment. Sovereign immunity protects a prosecutor from being sued by the defendant for prosecuting the case even if the charging decision causes the defendant to lose his or her job or causes injury to his or her reputation. This is so even if the defendant is acquitted. On the other hand, if a prosecutor assists a party to a civil action by providing information gained in the course of a criminal investigation, that prosecutor is not acting within the scope of employment and will not be covered by sovereign immunity.

Furthermore, if the criminal defense attorney learns that the prosecutor is sharing information with the parties in a civil case that are adverse to the defendant, the prosecutor's objectivity may be called into question before the trial judge. The prosecutor who shares information with a civil attorney risks attacks on his or her objectivity and needlessly jeopardizes what should be an impartial prosecution. A prosecutor maintains the right to view a particularly heinous crime with the appropriate degree of outrage and to view the perpetrator with contempt. Still, a prosecutor who shares information with civil litigants, risks the integrity of the criminal case.[22]

Differing rules of discovery in criminal and civil matters worsen the effect of this impractical and unethical decision to share information with any civil parties.[23] Frequently, rules of discovery in civil cases are much broader than in criminal cases. More importantly, evidence that is discoverable under civil rules may be privileged in the arena of a criminal prosecution, especially if the prosecution's case involves an anonymous tipster. *Roviaro*[24] and its progeny delineate a privilege that protects the identity of a confidential informant in instances where the informant was not a participant in the crime. *Roviaro* does not explicitly distinguish between civil and criminal cases but if the prosecution hands over files to a civil attorney, that civil attorney may not have standing to raise the issue of the informant's privilege.[25]

As a final note on the issue of parallel proceedings, the insurance company may have its own origin-and-cause expert who has investigated a fire that is the subject of parallel criminal and civil cases. In determining whether to call that expert as well as the state expert, the prosecutor should evaluate the strength of his own expert witness and the nature of the financial stakes involved in the civil matter. If the insurance company's expert has vastly superior resources and experience, is widely respected in the field and is a particularly charismatic witness, and if the prosecution's expert is relatively inexperienced or inarticulate as a witness, then the prosecutor may have no alternative. However, the prosecutor must be prepared to rebut defense arguments[26] that the insurance expert (or the company who pays the expert's salary) has a financial stake in the outcome of the criminal case and in the finding of arson.

CO-DEFENDANT TESTIMONY

As has been said, arson is a furtive crime. All too frequently the only eyewitness is a fellow perpetrator. When the prosecutor can only prove the case against one perpetrator by securing the testimony of a co-defendant, several ethical pitfalls arise. Why should the co-defendant be believed when she may have every reason to lie?[27] The prosecutor should first consider if there is any corroborating evidence to support the co-defendant's claim. Why would a prosecutor want to treat leniently a defendant against whom the prosecution has a strong case in order to convict a co-defendant against whom no other evidence exists? If the prosecutor intends to prosecute a suspect under circumstances where the pivotal evidence against that suspect is uncorroborated co-defendant testimony, then the prosecutor should have satisfied himself or herself beforehand of the credibility of the co-defendant.

Regardless of the existence of corroborating evidence—whether it is the defendant's false alibi, financial footprints or a bystander's description consistent with, but not unequivocally that of the defendant—it is essential that the prosecutor analyze for veracity the co-defendant's statement against the rest of the evidence in the case. For example, suppose the co-defendant informs the police or the fire marshal's office that he witnessed the defendant commit arson in a business. The co-defendant admits to being present, to knowing of the defendant's intentions and to assisting the defendant afterwards in disposing of the gas can containing accelerants. The co-defendant claims that he stood at the threshold of the business while the defendant entered with a gas can. He explains the path that the defendant took inside the building, describing the several discrete locations on different floors where he emptied the can and perhaps he lists specific items that the defendant removed from the business.

After a visit to the scene, or upon examination of a crime scene diagram, the prosecutor might note that the co-defendant could not have seen the defendant engaging in any of the specific actions he describes in his statement to police. How would the co-defendant know that the defendant emptied the can beside a file cabinet in an office on the second floor of the structure and on a throw rug in the hallway on the third floor unless he was present? And if he was present, should not the prosecutor at that point assume that he (the co-defendant) was the sole perpetrator? If such discrepancies exist between the statements of a co-defendant and the other evidence in a case, perhaps the lack of trustworthiness of the co-defendant should preclude anything but prosecuting the co-defendant by himself and affording him no consideration.

THE BATTLE OF THE EXPERTS

The Manual

There are a number of manuals and textbooks extant to guide origin-and-cause experts in their fields. These manuals detail methodologies for investigating suspicious fires.[28] You and your expert should be familiar with these manuals. Of course, your experts will have developed their own methodologies over time, so they will not follow these textbooks and manuals as if they are instructions for putting together an automobile. Even a pastry cook who is preparing a particularly complicated confection will deviate from a recipe occasionally and still produce excellent results. The defense attorney, however, will have the manuals available and will attempt to impeach the expert by suggesting that, because he does not follow the book by rote, his testimony should be discounted. The expert must be able to withstand cross-examination with this subtext. If the expert agrees that a given manual is the sole authority in the field—a veritable Bible on the subject, to be followed to the letter—the prosecution's case will be in jeopardy even though it is logical that few investigators will ever follow any manual to the letter. The expert should be prepared to respond that conducting an investigation requires the exercise of judgment that the mindless, automatic following of a manual does not permit. Otherwise, when the defense establishes that the prosecution's expert did not follow his "Bible" to the letter, then the expert's credibility is damaged goods—as is the prosecutor's case.

An intelligent, experienced expert will agree that certain textbooks or manuals may be good guides, but that they are merely guides. Under no circumstances should an expert concede that a manual or a textbook is *authoritative.*[29]

On redirect, the prosecutor should examine the text that the attorney is using in cross-examination to make sure it has applicability to an arson case. If the manual actually pertains to the proper response to, say, a hazardous material spill and not to the investigation of a suspicious fire or if it was actually published in the mid-seventies, the prosecutor will not know that unless he examines it. If the prosecutor can establish that a given manual raised on cross is inapplicable to the case, so much the better.

Negative Lab Results

It is neither uncommon nor fatal to the case when a laboratory examination of articles submitted from the crime scene produces negative results, even when all of the physical evidence points to an arson fire caused by an accelerant. There are several reasons for such results and the prosecutor must be prepared with testimony to explain them:

- There may have been no flammable or incendiary material involved;
- The flammable or incendiary material was not recovered in the sample that was sent to the laboratory;
- Too much time elapsed between the fire and the recovery of evidence;
- Too much time elapsed between the recovery of evidence and the analysis of the evidence;
- The wrong analysis of the evidence was conducted;
- The results were in error; or
- There was poor communication between the investigator and the laboratory.

If the perpetrator started the fire with combustibles such as newspaper or old boxes, the lab report would be negative for accelerants. Conversely, if the fire was particularly widespread or intense, it may have consumed all of the accelerants. If the fire was extinguished with large quantities of water, the accelerants may have been washed away. The accelerants may have been indistinguishable from other residues of combustion or simply missed, or there may have been no rational relation between the points of origin and the spread of the fire and the location of the samples taken. The remaining accelerant may have evaporated, or the sample may have been placed in a non-airtight container or with substances that absorb or degrade the sample.[30]

The Defense Expert

The credibility of the defendant's expert may range from that of a responsible professional with a legitimate difference of opinion to a defense mercenary whose testimony is for sale to the highest bidder. If time permits, research the defense expert. Call neighboring jurisdictions. If the expert has a reputation as one whose testimony is available to the highest bidder and if the case is serious enough, then (depending upon local rules), the prosecutor might obtain a subpoena *duces tecum* of the expert's financial information. By locating prior customers, the prosecutor can then investigate the nature and veracity of the expert testimony.[31]

The prosecution will rarely be able to demolish the defense expert on the stand. However, the prosecutor should be mindful of the defense witness's claimed area of expertise. If the defense witness is a chemist, then simply establishing that he is not an origin-and-cause expert may go far in reducing the impact of his testimony before the jury. The prosecutor should also be ready to object lest the defense expert testify to areas beyond his area of expertise. If the witness is a chemist, for example, do not let him impeach the medical examiner's findings. It is beyond his area of expertise.

If the expert is a mental health expert, the prosecutor should be armed with the Diagnostic and Statistical Manual of Mental Disorders/4th Edition (DSM-IV). Frequently, an expert will diagnose a defendant with a particular mental illness. A quick consultation of DSM-IV will show that antisocial behavior such as setting fires is not within the scope of the specific diagnosis.[32]

The Insanity Defense

Because of the complexity of the subject, this article can only provide a rudimentary overview of the insanity defense. Nevertheless, not-guilty-by-reason-of-insanity

(NGRI) is a common defense to arson,[33] and it is essential for the arson prosecutor to become familiar with it. The prosecution's effective rebuttal to a NGRI plea begins with a thorough investigation. Actually, an effective rebuttal to a NGRI defense can begin with a decent case report of an average investigation.

Determine the Standard

It must be noted from the outset that a NGRI plea pertains to the defendant's mental state *at the time of the offense.* The more remote in time from the offense the expert interviews the defendant, the less reliable the expert's conclusion.[34] Likewise, the more remote in time the prosecution's preparation for the NGRI plea, the less ammunition the prosecutor has to meet it.

Check the law in your jurisdiction to determine the standard for a finding of NGRI and the procedures that govern the plea.[35] There are three common tests for insanity:[36]

- The M'Naghten Test. The defendant (i) suffers from a disease of the mind (ii) such that he is unable to appreciate the nature and quality of his acts *and* (iii) he does not know that what he is doing is wrong;
- The M'Naghten Test, Disjunctive. The defendant (i) suffers from the disease of the mind (ii) such that he is unable to appreciate the nature and quality of his acts, *or* (i) the defendant suffers from a disease of the mind (ii) such that he does not know that what he is doing is wrong; and
- Irresistible impulse.[37]

Usually, insanity is an affirmative defense, which means that a person is presumed sane unless the defendant proves otherwise to the satisfaction of the jury. Many jurisdictions require pre-trial notice to the prosecution of defense counsel's intent to raise the defense. This notice, along with the standards of proof that the insanity defense requires, are significant factors for the prosecution. The notice provision is especially important because it usually triggers a reciprocal discovery requirement and likely gives the prosecution the right to have the defendant evaluated by a prosecution expert. And frequently, defendants will attempt to introduce mental state evidence that does not conform strictly to jurisdictional standards for insanity, i.e. voluntary intoxication ("I was so drunk/high/stoned that I had no idea what I was doing.") and diminished capacity.[38] It is important that the prosecutor have law from the jurisdiction close at hand to preclude such testimony. Some of such testimony will actually constitute an impermissible invasion by an expert into the ultimate issue of fact—that is, the issue of intent.

The Evidence: Following the Footprints

A defendant suffering from an epileptic seizure finds that she cannot control her foot on an accelerator because her muscles are beyond her control. This appears to be a classic case of irresistible impulse. A defendant suffering from Alzheimer's disease, who believes when he lights his wife's dress on fire with a stick from the fireplace that he is lighting a torch, is unable to appreciate the nature and quality of his acts. His is a clear NGRI case.[39]

On the other hand, the defendant who waits until the cover of darkness with a can of gasoline to break into a home, carefully picks a lock, pours the gasoline and lights the match without being detected or burned, carries out a series of actions that take conscious deliberation. Such a series of well-planned and executed actions circumstantially show that the defendant knew what she was doing and knew it was wrong. Furthermore, that same defendant who gives a false alibi might as well have confessed to the whole world that she knew what she was doing and knew that it was wrong. And of course, there is a difference between not being able to differentiate between right and wrong and not caring.

A defendant—enraged at catching his wife in bed with his best friend—runs out the door, grabs the gasoline from the garage, pours the gasoline at the foot of the stairs and lights it. He ultimately kills his wife, her paramour and a bystander who tries to rescue them. Such a defendant was clearly enraged but he would be considered temporarily insane only in a soap opera or based on the testimony of a hack expert.

There are defense experts who are prepared to testify that any of the above four defendants are considered NGRI. Therefore, the arson prosecutor should be prepared to address an NGRI defense well before trial, no matter how remote the defense is from the truth. The best evidence available to the prosecution in an NGRI case is the 911 tape—if the defendant was the caller. In the *Herbin* case (see footnote 37), the defendant took the position that he had snapped, lost control and was temporarily insane when he stabbed the victim three times and then sexually assaulted her.[40] In the 911 tape his voice was controlled and calm. Furthermore, he told the dispatcher that the victim had tripped on a knife in the kitchen, so he is caught on tape attempting to cover up his crime. This is evidence that he knew that what he did was wrong.

The second-best evidence are taped statements of the defendant—including any denial statements. In the context of an NGRI plea, a lie is much, much better than a confession from the prosecution standpoint.[41]

The third-best evidence is the testimony given by law enforcement officers and bystanders about the defendant's statements made at the scene. For some reason, many suspects view the officer that transports them from point A to point B as a mere taxi driver and will reveal things to the police officer/driver that they will reveal to no one else. They often drop their guard and reveal essential clues about their mental states. They may respond rationally to the freezing cold weather by asking for a coat. They may engage the driver in a discussion of the nationally televised baseball game the previous evening. They may deny outright that they set the fire. The attending officer should be alerted to the fact that his or her observations of the suspect's behavior in the informal encounter may be useful to the prosecution. The officer should note if the suspect responds to questions rationally and if he or she manifests emotions appropriate or inappropriate to the situation. Is the defendant crying because he's been arrested? Does she laugh while discussing the death of a beloved pet? Is he laughing because his estranged wife is dead? (Such responses may be crass and inappropriate but they are not, standing alone, insane).

It is essential that the attending and transporting officers be interviewed as soon as possible after the interactions because the observed behavior will be easily forgotten.[42] Ironically, the more unremarkable the officer's encounter with the defendant, the more essential the evidence of such an encounter becomes to your case and the more likely it is that the officer will forget the encounter. Such evidence should be obtained within hours. Even something handwritten on a napkin and photocopied could be sufficient to jog an officer's memory when at trial. The prosecution can do serious damage to any credible NGRI defense if there is a witness who can truthfully testify to notes even as concise as: "Transported defendant. Discussed Dallas game. Talked about this morning's blizzard. Said he was hungry. Said he didn't set the fire. We both were from New York and discussed the city. No further. Officer I.B. Goode, #0767."

The Expert

If the background and identity of the expert are unknown to the prosecutor, it would be wise to check with the Expert Witness Clearinghouse (footnote 32, *supra*) to check the expert's reputation and to determine his or her specialty. If this expert will provide a *curriculum vitae*, then the prosecutor should research the accuracy (or not) of the information. If an opportunity presents itself to speak with the expert ahead of time, prosecutors should listen but should avoid "cross-examination." [43] Doing so would help the expert prepare for cross-examination on the witness stand. Obtain and read the expert's publications, whenever possible.

Almost all professional organizations (e.g., your state bar, the American Psychological Association) have a code of ethics or professional guidelines that in some cases may be the law in the local jurisdiction.[44] Observe whether the expert's methodology departs from these standards[45] and determine who is paying for the expert testimony. If there is a parallel civil proceeding, inquire whether he or she serves as an expert in both cases.

Next, assuming the law in the jurisdiction requires the defendant to provide the defense expert's report in advance, the prosecution should review the expert's report and analyze the conclusion. Does the conclusion conform to the legal standard for insanity in the local jurisdiction, or does it simply diagnose the defendant? If the report concludes, without more, that the defendant is *currently* manic-depressive, for example, then a motion *in limine* may be in order to prevent the expert from testifying. That conclusion is irrelevant, if it does not conform to the local jurisdiction's standard for insanity.

If the conclusion of the report conforms to the legal standards for insanity, then determine whether the diagnosis—which might be an alcoholic blackout or legal intoxication—is considered a "disease of the mind" in the local jurisdiction. If the diagnosis is alcoholic blackout, be aware that a blackout is an absence of memory of an event caused by intoxication, not a state of unconsciousness during the event. The fact that the defendant does not remember the incident does not make him legally insane; it makes him have a memory problem. Another motion *in limine* may be in order.

Next, determine if the defendant's behavior is consistent with the definition of the disease in DSM-IV, and if anything about his or her behavior belies the conclusion of NGRI. For example, did he lie about the offense, give a false alibi, flee the police or increase his wife's life insurance prior to the fire? The offense may show evidence of planning that is inconsistent with the NGRI diagnosis.

Consider the information used to reach the expert conclusion: the length of the interview, the tests administered, the time-lapse between the date of the offense and the date of the interview, other people interviewed and the tests *not* administered such as those to rule out malingering. Consider to what extent the evaluator's conclusions are inconsistent with the evidence provided by bystanders' reports. If the defendant reports no memory of the offense then why does the evaluator believe him?[46]

To the extent that the offender's version is inconsistent with that of the police officer's notes, then the evaluator should account for the inconsistency. If the evaluator finds insanity even if the defendant's account is directly inconsistent with the police report without offering an adequate explanation, then this demonstrates rank evidence of bias. For example, the police may have noted that minutes after the offense the defendant was lucid, denied setting the house on fire and commented appropriately on the weather. In contrast, the evaluator may report that the defendant claimed to be out of control in a frenzied rage and completely subverbal due to post-traumatic stress disorder in the moments after the offense. If the evaluator accepts the defendant's version, this is bias. Getting an evaluator's admission of bias on the stand is ideal but just pointing out to the jury the fact that the expert chooses to ignore the observations of those people who had the opportunity to observe the defendant in a time frame much closer to the offense will speak volumes. All of the above issues are fruitful subjects for cross-examination.

When a defendant is found NGRI, depending on the diagnosis and prognosis and the law of the local jurisdiction, he or she is usually committed and entitled to a review after a set period of time. A truly NGRI defendant may spend more time behind four walls than a defendant who pleads guilty with no agreement as to disposition.

The Mentally Ill Defendant Who Is Not NGRI

Sometimes a prosecutor will be pressured into dropping charges by the argument that the defendant is mentally ill and the offense is a medical problem that psychiatrists and psychologists can best address. Do not be swayed into dropping charges either by the defendant's mental illness or by the threat of an NGRI plea.

It is probable that the law in the local jurisdiction provides for the triggering of specific events by a finding of NGRI—and one of them is an involuntary commitment for the defendant (a plus for public safety). This is not an attractive alternative for either the truly NGRI defendant or the mentally ill defendant who is not truly NGRI. The defense counsel may even attempt to convince the prosecutor to drop the charges by promising that the defendant will be handily committed and will therefore not constitute a risk to public safety.

However, outside a finding of NGRI, the standard for involuntary commitment is high. Generally, a defendant must pose an imminent danger to the safety of herself or others. Not only is that standard difficult to meet, but once the defendant no longer meets that standard she must be released even if her condition has not stabilized.

As another approach, the defense attorney may tell the prosecutor that the offender suffers from a disease of the mind that can be "treated" with psychoactive medication. Included will be an explanation that at the time of the offense, the perpetrator had stopped taking medication, and the prosecutor will receive a promise that the defendant, his family or his physician will ensure that he takes the medication in the future. However, unless the defendant is on bond or on probation to a court there is no guarantee of the defendant's continued medication compliance. Or more precisely, the prosecution has no remedy—such as a probation violation hearing or a finding of contempt by a court—for the defendant's noncompliance. Not only is medication compliance a serious treatment problem, no one can ensure that the medication will continue to be effective.[47] Finally, it is important to remember that a person may have a disease of the mind and still be perfectly capable of committing a crime, even down to the formation of criminal intent. Such a person constitutes a direct threat to the safety of others, especially if a defendant is committing arson crimes.

The prosecutor has a duty to act on behalf of victims of arson and protect the public from future victimization. A person who sets fires belongs behind four walls. Even assuming a department of corrections has no special facilities for a mentally ill inmate (a question that can be resolved with a phone call), "warehousing" a defendant sick enough to set fires, send letter bombs or assemble explosive devices (and who is not NGRI) does have the end result of protecting the public. In addition, it teaches the offender that there are consequences to anti-social behavior. If the defendant does not conform to the standard for NGRI and has committed a crime, the criminal justice system does a disservice to the public by pretending that the crime is a medical problem.

In the course of a NGRI trial, the prosecutor must educate the jury that a finding of NGRI answers a very narrow, very specific question, and that question is not, "is the defendant crazy?" In fact, much of the battle for the prosecutor is to fight the "anyone who'd do a thing like that *must* be crazy" conclusion that many slack-minded persons might come to. Just because someone commits a crime that is outrageously vile, wanton, horrible or inhuman does not make that person mentally ill. And mental illness, alone, does not mean a defendant is NGRI.

CONCLUSION

Arson prosecution is a challenging and fascinating specialty. On the surface, arson can appear to be an impenetrable subject area but with proper education, the specialty is approachable, interesting and effective for the prosecutor.

RESOURCES

Reference Books:

American Psychiatric Association, *Diagnostic and Statistical Manual of Mental Disorders, 4th Edition* (1994).

Gavin de Becker, *The Gift of Fear; Survival Signals that Protect Us From Violence* (1998).

Hervey Cleckley, M.D., *The Mask of Sanity: An Attempt to Clarify Some Issues About the So-Called Psychopathic Personality* (1988).

Physician's Desk Reference 2000 (54th Edition).

Web Sites:

Bureau of Alcohol, Tobacco and Firearms: http://www.atf.treas.gov/
Federal Bureau of Investigation: http://www.fbi.gov

International Association of Arson Investigators: http://www.fire-investigators.org/
List of prosecutors across the country: http://www.co.eaton.mi.us/ecpa/proslist.htm
Bureau of Justice Statistics: http://www.ojp.usdoj.gov/bjs
Bureau of Justice Statistics Publications: http://www.ojp.usdoj.gov/bjs/pubalp2.htm
United States Fire Administration's National Fire Incident Reporting System and
National Repository Data provided by the AFT: http://ows.atf.treas.gov:9999/

Legal research links: http://knowhow.com/Research/bookmark.htm

A fire investigation site: http://www.interfire.org/

EXPERT WITNESS

Jurisdiction: _____

Prosecutor: _____

Phone Number: _____

Fax Number: _____

E-mail Address: _____

Expert: (Please indicate)   (Defense)   (Prosecution)

Type of Case   (i.e. Insanity, DWI, Child Abuse):

_____

Name:_____

Title:_____

Organization: _____

Address: _____

_____

Phone Number: _____

Fax Number: _____

E-mail Address: _____

Summary of Testimony:_____

_____

_____

_____

_____

Information maintained in your office (i.e. transcripts, CV, literature): _____

_____

_____

_____

48

_____

ENDNOTES

1 For the offense to be arson, the *structure*, not items within the structure, must suffer charring or burning.

2 State laws differ greatly on the extent to which the presence or absence of certain variables will remove a particular act from the ambit of the arson statute. These variables include, but are not limited to, the ownership of the property by the perpetrator, the presence of persons in the structure and the nature of the structure in question. For a URL that provides access to the majority of state statutes, see http://www.law.cornell.edu/topics/state_statutes.html. The states differ as to whether the perpetrator's ownership of the property, without more, may take the offense out of the ambit of the arson statute. *Cf.* ARK. STAT. ANN. Sec. 5-38-301 (1987); GA. CODE ANN. Sec. 16-7-60 (1982); KAN. STAT. ANN. Sec. 21-3718 (1994). For example, most states agree that, even if the perpetrator is the owner of the structure, he may be convicted of arson if his intent was to defraud an insurance company or if it was reasonably foreseeable (or intended) that the act of arson would endanger the life of another. In some states, the perpetrator may be convicted of arson whether he is the owner of the structure or not, regardless of his intention in committing the arson. *See, e.g.,* VA. CODE. ANN. Sec.18.2-77 (1994). Some codes specifically address danger to firefighters. *See, e.g.,* ALASKA STAT. ANN. Sec.11.46.400. Consult the statutes in your jurisdiction for the particulars.

3 For purposes of this article, "person" or "perpetrator" includes an individual, corporation, partnership, association, company, business, trust, joint venture or other legal entity. *See, e.g.,* Va. Code Sec. 1-13.19; *see also,* NFPA 921 (1998 edition).

4 *See infra* Section IID.

5 Over the years, the term "cause and origin" has been replaced with "origin and cause," since one must find the origin of the fire if one wants to determine the cause. NFPA 921-1998; Sgt. Karl Mercer, Henrico County, VA, Police Explosive Ordnance Disposal Unit and Captain of the Law Enforcement Training Section, Virginia Fire Marshall Academy, personal communication, February 23, 2000.

6 An accelerant is any material used to initiate or promote the spread of a fire. The most common accelerants are flammable or combustible liquids. Whether a substance is an accelerant depends not on its chemical structure but on its use.

7 In some states, this individual is known as a "coroner."

8 The origin-and-cause expert will likely be a fire marshal or firefighter with special expertise in the cause and origin of fires. This expert in your jurisdiction may be an invaluable resource to the uninitiated (or even expert) arson prosecutor.

9 It is important for the prosecutor not to allow the jury to confuse *motive* and *intent*. Motive may contribute circumstantial evidence of the identity of the perpetrator, but a prosecutor may prove a case without any evidence of motive. On the other hand, *intent* is an essential element of the offense. It is important that the jury understand the distinction, especially in those cases with no apparent motive where there is no real factual issue with regard to intent. Otherwise, the jury may decide that, because they cannot find motive, they cannot convict.

10 A good sourcebook for arson prosecutors—which contains an excellent section about motives in arson—is John E. Douglas, Ann W. Burgess, Allen G. Burgess, and Robert Ressler, *Crime Classification Manual; A Standard System For Investigating and Classifying Violent Crimes* (1997).

11 Arson defendants may have seemingly-unrelated convictions for such sex offenses as indecent exposure or peeping tom violations.

12 In anticipation of which it would be helpful to be aware of the standard for admissibility of scientific testimony in your jurisdiction. *See, e.g., Daubert v. Merrill Dow Pharmaceuticals, Inc.,* 509 U.S. 579 (1993) and its progeny; *Keesee v. Donigan,* __ Va. __, ___ S.E.2d ___ (Rec. No. 990181, Decided 1/17/00); *Thorpe v. Commonwealth,* 223 Va. 609, 292 S.E.2d 323 (1982); *Cotton v. Commonwealth,* 19 Va. App. 306, 451 S.E.2d 673 (1994). *See also Kuhmo Tire Co. v. Carmichael,* 526 U.S. 137 (1999), which discusses the admissibility of a technical expert's opinion and clarifies *Daubert.*

13 For more information, see http://www.atf.treas.gov/breaking_news/state_local_training/index.htm or contact the center by telephone at (202) 927-2140 or by fax at (202) 927-3179. The Federal Law Enforcement Training Center (FLETC) maintains a website at http://www.treas.gov/fletc that contains course information. The National Center for State and Local Law Enforcement Training of FLETC has a toll-free number as well: (800) 743-5382. *Arson for Profit* is also offered at various other locations nationwide. The BATF Program Coordinator for state and local training can be reached at (202) 927-3098.

14 The seminal cases are *Michigan v. Tyler,* 436 U.S. 499 (1978) and *Michigan v. Clifford,* 464 U.S. 287 (1984).

15 *See, e.g.,* VA. CODE ANN. SEC 27-32.1 (1994) *et seq.*

16 It is important at this juncture for the prosecution to remember that while the agenda of the insurance company may coincidentally intersect with that of the prosecutor, such is not always the case. The insurance company may investigate a suspicious fire and make a determination of arson; to that extent and under those circumstances the agenda of the prosecutor and the insurance company coincide. On the other hand, the general counsel's office of the insurance company may decide against contesting a claim because the cost of litigation may outweigh the cost of paying the claim. Furthermore, if in the course of civil litigation the insurance company comes into possession of evidence that is exculpatory, the duty of the attorney for the insurance company to disclose such evidence is limited to ethical prohibitions against perpetrating a fraud upon a tribunal. The prosecution's duty under *Brady v. Maryland,* 373 U.S. 83 (1963) and its progeny are much broader.

17 The insurance company may also be in possession of some or all of the following information or documents: the insurance policy (and any amendments to the policy, such as any increases in coverage), the application for the insurance policy, correspondence from the insured, memoranda documenting communications from the insured to the agency, proof of loss statements provided by the insured (which may be inconsistent with the evidence found at the crime scene), statements under oath by the insured, letter of declination (denial of claim), appraisals or surveys of the property, payment history of the premium by the insured, copies of checks used to pay the premium, property insurance loss (PILR) reports, public/private adjuster investigative files, public adjuster's contract, and information from the attorney retained by the insurance company.

18 *See, e.g., United States v. Jacobsen,* 466 U.S. 109 (1984); *Mills v. Commonwealth,* 418 S.E.2d 718 (Va. Ct. App. 1992); *Mier v. Commonwealth* 407 S.E.2d 342 (Va. Ct. App. 1991); *Duarte v. Commonwealth,* 407. S.E. 2d.41 (Va.Ct.App.1991).

19 *Dickerson v. United States,* __ US __, __ S Ct __ (Rec. No 99-5525, Decided June 26, 2000), held in an intellectually-strained decision that 18 U.S.C.A. Sec. 3501 (West 1985), which overturned *Miranda v. Arizona,* 384 U.S. 436 (1966), was unconstitutional. The Fourth Circuit in *Dickerson* had ruled that Section 3501, rather than *Miranda,* governs the admissibility of confessions in federal court. 166 F.3d 667 (4th Cir. 1999).

20 Your jurisdiction may have reciprocal immunity statutes that may affect these considerations.

21 For cases on sovereign immunity, malicious prosecution and Section 1983 actions, see *Imbler v. Pachtman,* 424 U.S. 409 (1975); *Buckley v. Fitzsimmons,* 509 U.S. 259 (1993); *Albright v. Oliver,* 510 U.S. 266 (1994) and their progeny within your jurisdiction.

22 There is nothing to prevent a prosecutor from calling the insurance company's attention to public documents or public hearings so that the insurance company may avail itself of information that is available to the general public.

23 Parties to a civil litigation may enjoy immunity through arson-reporting immunity legislation. The Insurance Committee for Arson Control, at (212) 669-9245, publishes a STATUS REPORT ON ARSON-REPORTING IMMUNITY LEGISLATION that covers the status of the immunity laws in each state. Statutes vary across the 50 states, but all provide civil immunity; most provide criminal immunity; many permit agencies to obtain the requested information without a subpoena; and, indeed, many statutes *require* companies to report arson to law enforcement. *See, e.g.,* CALIFORNIA INS. CODE 1875 *et seq.* (West 1994); FLORIDA STAT. SEC 633.175 (1)-(8) (1996); N.Y. INS. LAW SEC. 319, 401, 405 and 406 (McKinney 1997); VA. CODE ANN. Sec 27-85.3 *et seq.* (1994). Alternatively, law enforcement officials may obtain their information pursuant to search warrant or subpoena *duces tecum.*

[24] *Roviaro v. United States,* 353 U.S. 53 (1957).

[25] The prosecution's standing to raise an informant's privilege arises from the fact that the identification of an informant directly affects the ability of law enforcement to investigate and/or prosecute cases.

[26] Whether grounded in fact or not.

[27] In fact, in some jurisdictions, the practice may be illegal or a violation of your state bar's disciplinary or ethical rules. *See, e.g.,* CAL. PENAL CODE SEC. 1111.

[28] Such as NFPA 921. It is advisable to view the Proposals and Commentary for revision of NFPA 921 because they contain a number of controversial proposals, such as the elimination of negative corpus determination. In other words, if the investigator eliminates all accidental and providential causes, the revised NFPA 921 would recommend against a finding of arson. *See* Proposals and Commentary to NFPA 921 at http://www.nfpa.org/index.html. The Report on Proposals is no longer available on the web site. For additional information, contact Lee Cram at the library: telephone (617) 984-7445; fax: (617) 984-7060; e-mail: lcram@nfpa.org.

[29] In fact, a proposal for an amendment to the NFPA 921 to this effect was rejected by the NFPA Committee on Fire Investigations. *See,* Report of the Committee on Fire Investigations—Proposals for Adoption of Amendments to the NFPA 921-1998. Proposals and Commentary to NFPA 921 at http://www.nfpa.org/index.html. See above note for #28, Log #27, p. 1397; Submitter: David A. Row, Oakland, MI Sheriff Dept./Rep. Oakland C. Association of Arson and Fire Investigators; Recommendation: Add text to read as follows: **However, this document [i.e., NFPA 921] should not be considered as authoritative in nature, but as reference information to be used in the furtherance of said technology and education.** Substantiation: Recently, efforts within the legal industry have attempted to modify by court proceeding, the scope and purpose of this document and its nature. Individuals doing so are creating a condition where the document itself comes into question. These people, in trying to call this an "authoritative document," are attempting to degrade the ability of investigators to do their job, which is in opposition to the scope and purpose of the document. The purpose is well outlined as a reference guide and makes suggestion as to how investigations should be handled. Of course, only in a perfect world could all investigations be handled using every step outlined in this document. My fellow fire investigators and I utilize this document as reference material, just as we refer to 10-12 other documents and publications written by a variety of authors. Members of the 921 Technical Committee should be aware of the misuse of this document, despite their good intentions in writing an adequate scope and purpose for the guide.
Committee Action: Reject.
Committee Statement: Though the Committee intends the document to be an authoritative text, it is not within the purview of the document to decide whether or not it is authoritative. The authoritative nature of any document is decided by the peer review community or the courts.

[30] It is possible to have a positive canine response and a negative laboratory finding. It has been hypothesized that the dog's nose is more sensitive than the laboratory's equipment. NFPA 921's Proposals and Commentary has suggested that a positive canine finding in the context of a negative laboratory finding be discounted.
See Proposals and Commentary to NFPA 921 at http://www.nfpa.org/index.html.
See January 1998 Standards Council Meeting Minutes at:
http://www.nfpa.org/current_codes_and_standards/standards_council/standards_council_minutes/january_1998/january_1998.html).
Research in this area is needed, since such a hypothesis can be proven or disproven through scientific tests.

[31] The Prince William County Commonwealth's Attorney's Office, located in Manassas, Virginia, is compiling an expert witness clearinghouse about experts of all specialties who are either good for the prosecution or who are defense mercenaries. Since many of these experts—both legitimate and illegitimate—testify in many states, this clearinghouse may have information useful to prosecutors across the United States. To determine if the clearinghouse has information about a particular expert that is useful to your jurisdiction, contact Assistant Commonwealth's Attorney Sandra Sylvester, at the Office of the Commonwealth's Attorney, Prince William County, 9311 Lee Avenue, Manassas, Virginia 20110-5594; phone (703) 792-6050; fax (703) 792-7081; e-mail ssylvester@pwcgov.org. **This office is actively seeking as well as volunteering**

information on expert witnesses. At the end of this chapter is a form that prosecutors with information about an expert can fill out and submit to the clearinghouse.

32 For example, defendants frequently cite depression as the disease of the mind giving rise to the insanity defense, but a review of DSM-IV (Major Depressive Disorder, 296.xx) shows that the standard requires that the patient display five (or more) of nine specific symptoms. None of those symptoms include homicidal ideation or homicide attempts or a specific plan for committing a homicide or any related attempts to destroy the property of others. Thus, it can be shown that a defendant who burns his house down with his wife inside may be depressed, but it was not his depression which caused him to commit the offenses.

33 NGRI is not a common defense. Out of thousands of felony cases, perhaps a few hundred may request to be evaluated with an end toward a possible NGRI plea. Out of those, only a bare handful actually plead NGRI. Such a plea is risky to the defendant who was not NGRI but wishes to escape culpability because the procedural effect of such a plea is to say, "I did it, but I was crazy." If he cannot prove he was NGRI, then all that is left is "I did it...." But of the half-dozen so not-guilty-by-reason-of-insanity (NGRI) pleas this author has encountered in nine years of felony prosecution, the three legitimate pleas involved either arson or attempted arson. The pleas were justifiable based on the facts—which showed that the perpetrators were not only floridly psychotic at the time of the incidents based on the police reports but also clearly incapable of understanding the nature and character of their actions. Furthermore, based on their mental statuses, they were more likely to spend more time behind four walls after an NGRI plea then if they pled guilty to the offense and were sentenced by the court.

34 It is not uncommon for the mental state of a defendant to deteriorate while he is in custody pending preliminary hearing or trial—for any number of reasons, such as the effect of arrest and incarceration on the self-concept of a particularly grandiose defendant or even from the mere stress of incarceration—so that the defendant might appear to the evaluator much more ill than he was at the time of his crimes. Usually, under those circumstances, a defendant may be transferred to a secure mental institution to be stabilized. Of course, the alternative of releasing the defendant poses an untenable risk to public safety.

35 *See, e.g.*, CAL. PENAL CODE SECTIONS 25(a), 1016(6) and 1026(a); NY CRIM PROC. LAW SECTIONS 125.25 AND 250.10-250.40; TEXAS CRIM. PROC. ANN. ARTICLE 46.03 SECTION 1; TEXAS PENAL CODE ANN. SECTION 8.01; VA. CODE ANN. SECTIONS 19.2-167 *et seq.*

36 *See, e.g., Shannon v. United States*, 512 U.S. 573 (1994); *Foucha v. Louisiana*, 504 U.S. 71 (1992) for good discussions of the various standards. A Virginia case is *Stamper v. Commonwealth*, 228 Va. 707, 324 S.E.2d 682 (1985).

37 A Virginia case that defines "irresistible impulse" is *Herbin v. Commonwealth*, 28 Va. App. 173, 183, 503 S.E.2d 226, ___ (1998) in which the author was lead counsel in the trial court. In Virginia, the irresistible impulse defense is available "where the accused's mind has become 'so impaired by disease that he is totally deprived of the mental power to control or restrain his act.'" *Godley v. Commonwealth*, 2 Va. App. 249, 251, 343 S.E.2d 368, 370 (1986)[citations omitted.]. Irresistible impulse "is to be distinguishable from mere passion or overwhelming emotion not growing out of, and connected with, a disease of the mind." *Thompson*, 193 Va. at 717, 70 S.E.2d at 291-92 (quoting 14 Am. Jur. Criminal Law 35, at 793); *see also Breard*, 248 Va. at 83, 445 S.E.2d at 679 (citing Thompson, 193 Va. at 717, 70 S.E.2d at 291-92) (holding that the diseased mind requirement is properly included in an "irresistible impulse" jury instruction). In order to prove irresistible impulse, a defendant must show that although understanding his or her actions, the defendant was unable, due to a disease of the mind, to control or restrain these actions. *See Thompson*, 193 Va. at 718, 70 S.E.2d at 292.

38 California, among others, has abolished the diminished capacity defense. CAL. PENAL CODE SEC. 25(a) and specifically makes mental state evidence outside an insanity defense otherwise inadmissible. CAL. PENAL CODE SEC. 28(a).

39 For purposes of illustration, we are presupposing the truth of these hypotheticals. In real life, a prosecutor should be skeptical. For example, one would not find that the epileptic in the first hypothetical would also have an irresistible impulse to steer the automobile in the precise direction of his mother-in-law; and the Alzheimer's patient would have other deficits in his repertoire of behaviors to corroborate his claim.

[40] The defendant was evaluated by both the Commonwealth's expert and his own and decided to go forward without calling either expert to bolster his claim; the Commonwealth did not call either in rebuttal because without any testimony as to a disease of mind there could be no instruction on the insanity defense.

[41] Also be mindful of the extent to which the defense has been fabricated from the beginning. Does the defendant act one way when he feels that he is not under observation and then feign some sort of mental illness when he is being recorded?

[42] It should be a matter of routine for any law enforcement officer in any felony case who has any contact with a suspect whatsoever to submit a report of such to the investigator in the case, even if the report is a one-liner that says nothing more than "Defendant silent the whole time." The need for such a report skyrockets as high as the stakes in the case.

[43] Also, be aware that any evidence provided to him to assist him in reaching his conclusion will be likely made available to the defendant.

[44] *See, e.g.,* The American Medical Association: http://www.ama-assn.org/ethic/ceja.htm; The American Academy of Psychiatry and the Law: http://www.cc.emory.edu/AAPL/index.html; American Psychiatric Association: http://www.psych.org; American Psychological Association: http://www.unl.edu/ap-ls/; www.apa.org._

[45] For example, if the expert is the defendant's therapist, his duty is to his patient. If he violates that duty in order to provide evidence to the fact finder that is detrimental to the defendant, then he damages the therapist-patient relationship; if he does not, and fails to disclose evidence to the fact finder that is harmful to the defendant, then he violates his oath as a witness. If the expert's role is merely an expert witness, then his theoretical duty is to the fact finder. Because the duty as therapist and duty as expert witness can be (and often are) mutually exclusive, the therapist should not serve as an expert witness in the case.

[46] The "I-Don't-Remember Defense" (also known as "I Blacked Out") usually has the defendant remembering everything in vivid detail until the micro-millisecond before the offense when "The last thing I knew, my probation officer was on fire." An honest psychiatrist will say that it is nearly impossible for a defendant to lose memory for a specific discrete period of time encompassing an offense under those circumstances.

[47] Medication compliance is a problem for everyone not just mental health patients. For example, many persons stop taking their antibiotics after they start to feel better; moreover, a quick look through the *Physician's Desk Reference* and the listings inside for the most commonly prescribed psychoactive medications will show that the side-effects alone almost guarantee that the defendants will not comply with their medication regimes. But in contrast to the case of the person with an ear infection who stops taking his antibiotic once the symptoms disappear, the consequences for non-compliance do not constitute a gamble for just the patient in the case of someone sick enough to set a fire or send a letter bomb.

In Rem Civil Asset Forfeiture: An Old Solution to a New Problem

By Dale R. Lee, Assistant District Attorney, 19th Judicial District, Baton Rouge, Louisiana

Introduction

The manner in which modern *in rem* civil asset forfeiture has developed is both lengthy and complicated. Recently, this type of forfeiture has become an important tool in the war on drugs. Some have advocated that *in rem* forfeitures are a useful method of attacking "financial facilitators" in the drug trade.[1] Asset forfeiture can also be useful to deter any offense that generates income for an offender or that facilitates an offender in the commission of a crime. Examples of some of these offenses include bribery, burglary, property damage, extortion, pornography, prostitution, some firearm offenses and even some environmental crimes. The general concept is that a criminal enterprise is difficult to maintain without the assistance of certain professionals, i.e., bankers, lawyers, real estate agencies.

In the context of drug crimes, these facilitators have little direct role in the physical distribution of illegal drugs and are not necessarily criminals. Their activities, however, allow drug dealers to launder ill-gotten money and convert it into useable and tangible assets such as vehicles, real estate for use as drug labs and distribution centers and weapons. By providing a disincentive to the facilitator, i.e., loss of profits, it is hoped that an important link in the chain can be eliminated.

Forfeiture statutes have been described as a weapon in the war on drugs. They are both preventative and deterrent-oriented measures and they include some controversial aspects.[2] As prosecutors have become more aggressive in their use of forfeiture statutes, it is inevitable that controversies would arise and that the courts would be called upon to resolve important procedural and constitutional questions. After several such cases, a distinct thread can be discerned.

What has developed has been a re-affirmation that *in rem* civil asset forfeiture is separate and distinct from punishment in the criminal sense. Thus, it is not improper for prosecutors to seek forfeiture in cases where the owner may also be guilty of a crime. Nor is it improper to seek forfeiture from a person who may have committed no crime. In either case, *in rem* forfeiture provides a means of disrupting the flow of capital into a criminal enterprise.

To fully appreciate the scope of modern forfeiture statutes, one needs to consider the historical development of *in rem* civil asset forfeiture, to recognize the goals of *in rem* civil asset forfeiture, and to comprehend the distinctions between the various types of forfeiture. Once understood in proper context, it will be apparent that *in rem* civil asset forfeiture is both useful and necessary in the effort to contain the growth of the drug industry.

HISTORY OF ASSET FORFEITURE

Although recent years have seen an increase in the number and types of asset forfeiture cases, the legal concept that a person may be divested of certain types of property is as old as written law. Asset forfeiture is found in some form in many ancient legal systems. Perhaps the first written requirement that property be forfeited appears in the Old Testament of the Bible. After delivering the Ten Commandments to the Israelites, Moses addressed many other legal matters. In particular, Exodus 21:28 provides that, "If a bull gores a man or a woman to death, the bull must be stoned to death, and its meat shall not be eaten. But the owner of the bull will not be held responsible." There is a clear dichotomy between the forfeiture of the offending property and the criminal punishment of the individual. In fact, in the next verse of Exodus it states that if the owner were aware that the bull had a habit of goring and did not take steps to prevent his escape, then both the bull and the owner were subject to death. In the first example, only the offending property was subject to forfeiture while in the second example, not only was the property forfeited, but the owner was subject to punishment for his conduct as well. A similar dichotomy exists in modern forfeiture statutes.

The traditions that led to the establishment of the American legal system had their roots in several cultures. Many if not all of these cultures had laws that provided for asset forfeiture. Examples may be found in Greek[3] and Roman[4] law. Later, several types of forfeiture developed in, first, Anglo-Saxon and, later, English law. Among them are: statutory forfeiture, forfeiture consequent to a criminal conviction and attainder and deodand.[5] The deodand, which means "to be given to God,"[6] may be seen as the precursor to modern forfeiture statutes. It required the value of an instrument of a crime to be forfeited to the king in the belief that the king would provide money for masses to be said in honor of the dead man's soul.[7] Over time, the deodand lost its religious connotation and became a source of revenue for the crown. The practice was amended in the Magna Carta to allow the king to hold real property for non-treasonous offenses for only a year and a day. After that time, the property reverted to the landlord. All personal property escheated to the crown.[8] Ultimately, the deodand was abolished with the passage of Lord Campbell's Act, which created a cause of action for wrongful death.[9]

Although the scope of forfeiture was limited somewhat in the United States by the Constitution and legislation,[10] the First Congress did enact laws that authorized *in rem* civil forfeitures and criminal prosecutions for the same conduct.[11] Coincidentally, this was the same Congress that proposed and passed the Bill of Rights. Early legislation in this country provided for the forfeiture of slave ships,[12] pirate ships[13] and for those who attempted to evade import duties.[14]

One of the earliest cases to discuss the role of *in rem* forfeiture in the United States was *The Palmyra*.[15] The ship was captured as a pirate vessel, and after it was forfeited, the owner sought damages. A criminal conviction was unnecessary to the resolution of the forfeiture claim, however. In that case, it was noted that "[m]any cases exist, where there is both a forfeiture *in rem* and a personal penalty."

Modern forfeiture statutes fall into one of several main types including: summary forfeiture, civil administrative forfeiture, civil judicial forfeiture and criminal judicial forfeiture. Summary forfeiture involves proceedings to confiscate and destroy contraband. Administrative forfeitures are intended to be cost-effective alternatives to judicial forfeitures where the property has limited value and the forfeiture is uncontested, or where the claimants who accept the administrative process do so with the understanding that defenses and the right to appeal an adverse action are limited. Civil forfeitures are usually proceedings against the property itself. Criminal forfeitures are *in personam* actions against the individual that usually necessitate a criminal conviction prior to forfeiture.[16] The primary focus in this article is on the civil judicial type, often referred to by the courts as *in rem* civil asset forfeiture.

The basic premise underlying these various types of forfeiture is that wrongdoers should not profit from their criminal endeavors. Thus, the remedy of *in rem* forfeiture can be likened to equitable remedies designed to prevent "unjust enrichment."[17] This concept—rather than punishment—should be viewed as the objective of any *in rem* civil forfeiture action.

ASSET FORFEITURE STANDARDS

The National District Attorneys Association drafted the "National Code of Professional Conduct for Asset Forfeiture." It provides ethical and professional standards for prosecutors to apply when dealing with asset forfeitures. Specifically, the code provides the following guidelines:

> Law enforcement is the principal objective of forfeiture. Potential revenue must not be allowed to jeopardize the effective investigation and prosecution of criminal offenses, officer safety, the integrity of ongoing investigations or the due process rights of citizens.

> No prosecutor's or sworn law enforcement officer's employment or salary shall be made to depend upon the level of seizures or forfeitures he or she achieves.

> Whenever practicable, and in all cases involving real property, a judicial finding of probable cause shall be secured when property is seized for forfeiture. Seizing agencies shall strictly comply with all applicable legal requirements governing seizure practice and procedure.

> If no judicial finding of probable cause is secured, the seizure shall be approved in writing by a prosecuting or agency attorney or by a supervisory-level official.

> Seizing entities shall have a manual detailing the statutory grounds for forfeiture and all applicable policies and procedures.

> The manual shall include procedures for prompt notice to interest holders, the expeditious release of seized property where appropriate, and the prompt resolution of claims of innocent ownership.

> Seizing entities retaining forfeited property for official law enforcement use shall ensure that the property is subject to internal controls consistent with those applicable to property acquired through the normal appropriations processes of that entity.

> Unless otherwise provided by law, forfeiture proceeds shall be maintained in a separate fund or account subject to appropriate accounting controls and annual financial audits of all deposits and expenditures.
>
> Seizing agencies shall strive to ensure that seized property is protected and its value preserved.
>
> Seizing entities shall avoid any appearance of impropriety in the sale or acquisition of forfeited property.[18]

These guidelines are generally self-explanatory and practical. Most of the provisions reflect the notion that prosecutors who handle forfeited property act as public trustees. As such, both the manner in which the property is forfeited and the manner in which the property is handled require prosecutors to be above scrutiny and accountable at all times. These standards have been strongly recommended by the United States Justice Department as an appropriate method "to enhance the integrity of the federal equity sharing program so that it will continue to merit public confidence and support."[19]

IN REM FORFEITURES AND DOUBLE JEOPARDY

From *U.S. v. Ursery* in 1996 came the analysis with which the United States Supreme Court attempted to reconcile the various decisions that had cast doubt on the viability of forfeiture statutes in light of the Double Jeopardy Clause of the Constitution.[20] *Ursery*[21] held that civil forfeitures do not constitute "punishment" for purposes of the Double Jeopardy Clause.[22] The Court reviewed its prior decisions of *Halper*,[23] *Austin*[24] and *Kurth Ranch*,[25] noting that these three cases were not *in rem* civil forfeiture cases. *Halper* was a civil penalty case; *Austin* involved the Excessive Fines Clause of the Eighth Amendment; and *Kurth Ranch* involved a state tax on confiscated property.[26] In *Ursery*, the Court stated that:

> Civil forfeitures, in contrast to civil penalties, are designed to do more than simply compensate the Government. Forfeitures serve a variety of purposes, but are designed primarily to confiscate property used in violation of the law, and to require disgorgement of the fruits of illegal conduct. Though it may be possible to quantify the value of the property forfeited, it is virtually impossible to quantify, even approxi-

mately, the non-punitive purposes served by a particular civil forfeiture. Hence, it is practically difficult to determine whether a particular forfeiture bears no rational relationship to the non-punitive purposes of that forfeiture. Quite simply, the case-by-case balancing test set forth in *Halper*, in which a court must compare the harm suffered by the Government against the size of the penalty imposed, is inapplicable to civil forfeiture.[27]

Furthermore, the Court re-affirmed the two-part test to apply when considering *in rem* civil forfeiture cases that was initially announced in *89 Firearms*.[28] First, courts should consider the legislative intent to determine whether the statute in question is a remedial civil sanction. Since *in rem* forfeitures have been traditionally viewed as remedial in nature, the Supreme Court found little difficulty in concluding that the statute in question was remedial. If the statute is remedial, courts should next consider whether the statutory scheme was so punitive either in purpose or effect as to negate the legislature's intention to establish a civil remedial mechanism. Thus, from *89 Firearms* it appears that the focus should not be on how the forfeiture affects the individual but rather on the legislative intent.

Since *in rem* civil forfeitures are remedial in nature and designed to remove instrumentalities used in the drug trade from the hands of those who benefit from the drug trade, it may be of little moment that the owner of the property was innocent of a crime.[29] In fact, there are numerous instances where the owner was either adjudicated to be innocent of the crime or was never prosecuted.[30]

As noted by Justice Thomas in a concurring opinion in the *Bennis* case:

> Improperly used, forfeiture could become more like a roulette wheel employed to raise revenue from innocent but hapless owners whose property is unforeseeably misused, or a tool wielded to punish those who associate with criminals, than a component of a system of justice. When the property sought to be forfeited has been entrusted by its owner to one who uses it for crime, however, the Constitution apparently assigns to the States and to the political branches of the Federal Government the primary responsibility for avoiding that result.[31]

The *Bennis* case provides an example of the ethical dilemma that prosecutors face when pursuing forfeiture proceedings. In that case, the husband had engaged in sexual activity with a prostitute. The vehicle was forfeited as a public nuisance for the crime committed by the husband. Although the wife did not commit a crime or knowingly support the criminal enterprise, forfeiture of the vehicle did not violate her due process rights.

If the purpose of the forfeiture is to deter the conduct giving rise to the forfeiture and to remove the instrumentalities and proceeds of such conduct, then returning the property to the certain owners appears counter-intuitive. The responsibility to ensure that the property is not being used in a criminal manner rests on the owner. As between the owner and the government, the owner is in the better position to prevent, discover, disclose and ultimately stop the offending conduct.[32] Thus, to return the property that was used in a criminal manner to family, close friends or associates of the wrongdoer fails to remove the financial incentives. Likewise, such a policy could lead to fraudulent claims of ownership in order to destroy the government's efforts to remove the property from the hands of those who benefit from the drug trade.[33]

The decision whether to pursue a forfeiture that may affect an innocent owner should be determined on a case-by-case basis. As noted by Justice Thomas, the responsibility to ensure that forfeiture statutes are not abused rests with the state agencies charged with enforcing them. This is a daunting task that must be accomplished with a sense of justice and fair play. In each instance, careful consideration must be given to the goals sought by the forfeiture, the public interest served by pursuing the forfeiture and the relationship of the innocent person to the property to be forfeited.

A discussion of double jeopardy in the context of asset forfeiture would be incomplete without an examination of *Hudson v. U.S.,*[34] a 1997 decision that repudiates the Court's procedures for analysis used in *Halper*. Hudson has important ramifications for any process in which parallel criminal and civil or administrative actions are brought based on the same transaction or conduct.[35]

The Court's analysis in *Usury* distinguished *Halper*. Prior to *Halper*, a traditional analysis had been used that looked to the face of the statute authorizing the civil sanction, to determine whether that sanction was, in fact, a punishment criminal in nature.[36] In

Halper, the Court recognized that whether the Double Jeopardy Clause precluded a subsequent punishment would depend on whether that subsequent punishment was, in fact, criminal. In doing so, the Court virtually disregarded the traditional analysis discussed above and relied instead upon a case-by-case analysis to determine whether a civil sanction implicates the Fifth Amendment Double Jeopardy Clause. After such an analysis, the Court ruled in *Halper* that the civil sanction could not be said to serve a remedial purpose only but, rather, could be explained only as serving the traditional goals of punishment—retribution or deterrence—thus constituting punishment for double jeopardy purposes.[37]

In *Hudson,* however, Justice Rehnquist delivered the opinion of the Court, writing that:

> We hold that the Double Jeopardy Clause of the Fifth Amendment is not a bar to the later criminal prosecution because the administrative proceedings were civil, not criminal. Our reasons for so holding in large part disavow the methods of analysis used in *United States v. Halper,* 490 U.S. 435, 448, 104 L. Ed. 2d 487, 109 S. Ct. 1892 (1989), and reaffirm the previously established rule exemplified in *United States v. Ward,* 448 U.S. 242, 248-249, 65 L. Ed. 2d 742, 100 S. Ct. 2636 (1980).[38]

Justice Rehnquist further stated:

> Our opinion in *United Sates v. Halper* marked the first time we applied the Double Jeopardy Clause to a sanction without first determining that it was criminal in nature.[39]

The *Hudson* Court also discussed how its analysis in *Halper* substantially deviated from the traditional double jeopardy doctrine by remarking that *Halper's* "deviation from longstanding double jeopardy principles was ill considered… (and)… has proven unworkable. We have since recognized that all civil penalties have some deterrent effect."[40]

Simply put, under *Halper,* where a criminal action follows a civil forfeiture action based on the same transaction, the subsequent criminal action would be precluded under double jeopardy principles as a subsequent punishment. Because civil administrative forfeiture actions often require less time to complete than the concomitant criminal action, law enforcement was often in the position of having to choose between a civil administrative forfeiture action or a criminal prosecution. *Hudson*, therefore, corrected this situation. The Court returned to the traditional analysis, as described in *Ward* and other cases, to reason that subsequent criminal prosecutions were not precluded by the Double Jeopardy Clause due to prior civil administrative action.[41]

CONCLUSION

There can be no doubt that *in rem* civil asset forfeiture is a valuable and necessary tool for fighting the war on drugs. Not only does it provide a financial disincentive to the criminal by removing assets from the hands of those who unjustly profit from the drug trade, it has the added benefit of placing those profits in the hands of agencies charged with actually fighting the war on drugs. Modern forfeiture statutes follow a long history of similar laws.

Although many ethical concerns should be addressed before and during the forfeiture process, the focus should remain on doing what is necessary to affect proper law enforcement goals. Courts have recognized that *in rem* civil asset forfeiture is a remedial measure designed to divest assets that are connected to a criminal enterprise. By removing the assets and placing them in the hands of the government, society, in effect, rights a social wrong. The responsibility and obligation to ensure that these statutes are not abused falls on those charged with enforcing them. The public has entrusted prosecutors with a powerful tool. Prosecutors should be vigilant to ensure that this trust is not misplaced.

ENDNOTES

[1] Cameron H. Holmes, *Forfeiture Achieves Proper Purposes By Appropriate Means*, 39 N.Y.L.S.L.R. 335, 338-339 (1994). "Financial facilitators" are typically professionals who assist the ongoing criminal enterprise by manipulating financial transactions to enable the enterprise to continue.

[2] National District Attorneys Association (NDAA), *National Prosecution Standards*, § 49 Commentary, 2d Ed. (1991) (citing 84 A.L.R 4th, Drug Forfeiture-Real Property as subject to Forfeiture (1990). And see THE PROSECUTOR, *Asset Forfeiture Talking Points; National District Attorneys Association Guidelines for Civil Asset Forfeiture,* Volume 27, Number 2, May/June 1993 (NDAA).

[3] Oliver W. Holmes, Jr., *The Common Law* 34 (1881) (discussing the use of forfeiture in ancient Greece).

[4] 7 *Twelve Tables 1,* translated in 1 Scott, *The Civil Law 69* (1932).

[5] *See Calero-Toledo v. Pearson Yacht Leasing Co.*, 416 U.S. 663, 680-683, 94 S.Ct. 2080, 2090-2092, 40 L.Ed.2d 452 (1974) (tracing the historical beginnings of forfeiture).

[6] Steven L. Kessler, *Civil and Criminal Forfeiture*, § 1.02 (1993).

[7] *Calero-Toledo*, 416 U.S. at 681, 94 S.Ct. at 2090-2091.

[8] Kessler, *Ibid.*

[9] *Calero-Toledo*, 416 U.S. at 681, 94 S.Ct. at 2091, fn. 19.

[10] U.S. Const. Amend.V (due process clause); U.S. Const. Art. III, § 3, cl. 2 (prohibiting forfeiture "except during the life of the person attained in cases of treason); and Act of April 30, 1790, § 24, 1 Stat. 117 (to prevent the common law practice of forfeiture of estate).

[11] *See U.S. v. Ursery*, 518 U.S. 267, 274, 116 S.Ct. 2135, 2140, 135 L.Ed.2d 549 (1996), citing Act of July 31, 1789, ch. 5 § 12, 1 Stat. 39 (goods unloaded at night or without a permit subject to forfeiture and persons unloading subject to criminal prosecution); § 25, *id.*, at 43 (persons convicted of buying or concealing illegally imported goods subject to both monetary fine and *in rem* forfeiture of the goods); § 34, *id.*, at 46 (imposing criminal penalty and *in rem* forfeiture where person convicted of re-landing goods entitled to drawback.

[12] Act of Mar. 22, 1794, 1 Stat. 347 (authorizing the forfeiture of ships that were used to deliver slaves).

[13] *See United States v. Cargo of the Brig Malek Adhel*, 43 U.S. 210, 2 How. 210, 11 L.Ed. 239 (1844) (upholding the forfeiture of a vessel engaged in acts of piracy despite the innocence of the owner).

[14] Act of July 31, 1789, §§ 12, 36, 1 Stat. 39, 47. *Boyd v. United States*, 116 U.S. 616, 623, 6 S.Ct. 524, 29 L.Ed. 746 (1886).

[15] *The Palmyra*. 25 U.S. 1, 14-15, 12 Wheat. 1, 6 L.Ed. 531 (1827).

[16] National Criminal Justice Association, *Assets Seizure & Forfeiture: Developing & Maintaining a State Capability*, pp. 7-8 (1988).

[17] Cameron H. Holmes, *ibid.* 39 N.Y.L.S.L.R. at 350.

[18] National Code of Professional Conduct for Asset Forfeiture, National District Attorneys Association, Alexandria, VA (1993).

[19] Attorney General Janet Reno, forward to *A Guide to Equitable Sharing of Federally Forfeited Property for State and Local Law Enforcement Agencies*, U. S. Department of Justice, Washington, D.C. (1994).

[20] U.S. Const. Amend.V.

[21] *United States v. Ursery* , 518 U.S. 267, 116 S.Ct. 2135, 135 L.Ed.2d 549 (1996).

[22] *Ursery*, 518 U.S. at 287, 116 S.Ct. at 2147.

[23] *United States v. Halper*, 490 U.S. 435, 109 S.Ct. 1892, 104 L.Ed.2d 487 (1989).

[24] *Austin v. United States*, 509 U.S. 602, 113 S.Ct. 2801, 125 L.Ed.2d 488 (1993).

[25] *Department of Revenue of Mont. v. Kurth Ranch*, 511 U.S. 767, 114 S.Ct. 1937, 128 L.Ed.2d 767 (1994).

[26] *Ursery*, 516 U.S. at 279-282, 116 S.Ct. at 2143-2144.

[27] *Ibid.*, 2145.

[28] *United States v. One Assortment of 89 Firearms,* 465 U.S. 354, 104 S.Ct. 1099, 79 L.Ed.2d 361 (1984).

[29] Please note that the Civil Asset Forfeiture Reform Act of 2000 (H.R. 1658) became public law 106-185 upon the president's signature on April 25, 2000. The act provides what supporters call more just and uniform procedures for federal civil forfeitures. In general, the act clarifies and in some respects substantially increases the burden on the prosecution regarding civil forfeitures. The majority of the reforms are related to creating a higher burden of proof on the part of the government to forfeit an asset and on lowering the burden required for "innocent owners."

[30] For instance, *see The Palmyra*, 25 U.S. 1, 14-15, 12 Wheat. 1, 6 L.Ed. 531 (1827) (recognizing that there are instances where there are proceedings *in rem* and no penalty *in personam* and that there are cases where there is both a forfeiture and a personal penalty. However, the two classes of cases are not dependent on one another); *Bennis v. Michigan*, 516 U.S. 442, 116 S.Ct. 994, 134 L.Ed.2d 68 (1996) (holding that forfeiture of innocent wife's share of a vehicle was permissible even though she did not know her husband would violate the law).

[31] *Bennis*, 516 U.S. at 456-457, 116 S.Ct. at 1003 (concurring opinion by Justice Thomas).

[32] National District Attorneys Association, *National Prosecution Standards,* § 49 Commentary, 2d Ed. (1991).

[33] *Ibid.*

[34] *Hudson v. U.S.*, 522 U.S. _____, 139 L. Ed. 2d 450, 118 S.Ct. _____ (Dec. 10, 1997).

[35] *See* David G. Savage's article on *Hudson*, "Double Trouble—Ruling Is Bad News for Sex Offenders, White-Collar Criminals," *ABA Journal*, February, (1998) 39.

[36] *See* e.g. *U.S. v. Ward*, 448 U.S. 242 (1980) and *Kennedy v. Mendoza-Martinez*, 372 U.S. 144 (1963).

[37] *See Hudson*, 139 L. Ed. 2d at 460.

[38] *Ibid.*, 456-457.

[39] *Ibid.*, 459.

[40] *Ibid.*, 460-461.

[41] *Ibid.*, 461-462.

CHARACTERISTICS OF COMPUTER-RELATED CRIME

By Frank White, Assistant District Attorney, Sedgwick County, Wichita, Kansas

Introduction

To some people, computer crime means crimes committed using a computer. To others, computer crime is the unauthorized entry into a computer or network of computers or the misuse of a computerized point of purchase connected to a retail sale system. While most computer crimes are *economic* in nature, and this article deals primarily with material relating to economic crimes, much of the information will apply to all computer-related crimes. As a brief overview, this article is intended to direct attention to the major concerns and obstacles encompassing the investigation and prosecution of computer crimes and the search and seizure of computers.

From the outset, those prosecuting crimes involving computers should have a working knowledge of the technology and the terminology. Excellent materials can be found at various Internet sites. For example, the Computer Crime and Intellectual Property Section (CCIPS) of the U.S. Department of Justice (DOJ) Web site[1] contains a wealth of information on the subject and is a convenient first step in developing a working knowledge of computers and the prosecution of computer crime. The DOJ manual *Federal Guidelines for Searching and Seizing Computers* as well as updates on laws and policies can be downloaded from the CCIPS web page. A directory of other computer crime Web sites and training organizations is provided in the appendix.

WHAT IS COMPUTER CRIME AND WHAT LAWS PROHIBIT IT?

For purposes of this article, the definition of "computer crime" is the use of a computer as an instrumentality of crime and as a location for the storage of evidence of crime.

Most jurisdictions have specific statutes defining computer crime that relate to intrusion into or modification of information on computers belonging to others. For example, Kansas State law K.S.A. 21-3755[2] defines computer crime as:

- Intentionally and without authorization accessing and damaging, modifying, altering, destroying, copying, disclosing or taking possession of a computer, computer system, computer network or any other property;
- Using a computer, computer system, computer network or any other property for the purpose of devising or executing a scheme or artifice with the intent to defraud or for the purpose of obtaining money, property, services or any other thing of value by means of false or fraudulent pretense or representation; or
- Intentionally exceeding the limits of authorization and damaging, modifying, altering, destroying, copying, disclosing, or taking possession of a computer, computer system, computer network or any other property.[3]

Besides the intrusion and modification of data, computers are also used to produce and store financial records related to criminal activity, to plan crimes, to harass and to threaten and to communicate with co-conspirators. Hard drives may contain digital copies of correspondence used in carrying out a crime. Furthermore, criminals obtain the personal and financial identity of individuals for fraudulent purposes through the use of computers. Only the criminal imagination and the practical limitations of the hardware and software restrict the unlawful use of computers.

UNIQUE ISSUES IN COMPUTER CRIME

The growth of computer and Internet (or cyber) crime has required law enforcement to develop a new set of tools for detection, investigation and prosecution of crime. For decades, criminals have used a variety of schemes to separate victims from their money, and virtually all have migrated to the Internet. Everything from envelope stuffing to securities fraud is pedaled via cyberspace. Through the Internet, stalkers can function anonymously. A hacker can obtain financial records and steal identities, and overnight, a victim's life becomes a financial nightmare. Investigation of such crimes usually requires an investigative specialist and the issuance of search warrants or subpoenas for the collection of evidence. The Fourth Amendment rules that apply to all searches apply to recovery of computer evidence. In addition, there are federal statutes and unique issues that significantly affect searches and seizures in computer cases.

The Privacy Protection Act and the Electronic Communications Privacy Protection Act

The Privacy Protection Act of 1980 (PPA),[4] which establishes guidelines for obtaining evidentiary material from publishers (i.e., newspapers and news media) created a minefield of sorts for investigators and prosecutors. In a sweeping update of the Omnibus Crime Control and Safe Streets Act of 1968, Congress extended privacy protection to electronic mail, cell phones, computer transmissions and private communications carriers with enactment of the Electronic Communications Privacy Act (ECPA) of 1986.

Congress passed the PPA in response to a U.S. Supreme Court ruling in *Zucher v. Stanford Daily*,[5] a case in which police investigators issued a search warrant and seized unpublished newspaper photographs of an illegal activity believed to be evidence of crime. The newspaper argued that the material was part of a work in progress and enjoyed First Amendment protection. Ultimately, the Supreme Court ruled that the material was not protected and could be seized. PPA requires that prosecutors issue subpoenas and give notice to publishers in order to obtain such material. A search warrant, however, cannot be used to obtain works in progress that might be published. The PPA permits the use of a search warrant if:

- The material to be seized is contraband, the fruits of or instrumentality of the crime;
- There are exigent circumstances (i.e., the material may be destroyed unless seized forthwith, or without notice); and
- There is probable cause to believe the person possessing the material has committed or is committing a crime.[6]

Violation of the act, i.e., the use of a warrant instead of a subpoena, may not result in suppression of the evidence but can result in civil penalties awarded to the aggrieved party. In *Steve Jackson Games, Inc., v. U.S. Secret Service*,[7] investigators had obtained and served a warrant and seized computers from Steve Jackson Games after tracing a hacker of a Bell South computer to the company. Jackson advised the Secret Service that the computers included a book that was being prepared for publication and requested the return of contents. The Secret Service ignored Jackson and continued to hold the computers and the contents of the hard drives. No charges were ever filed and after several months, the computers were returned.

Jackson filed suit, alleging violation of the PPA and ECPA. Although the Court found there was no violation at the time of the seizure, the agents had later been notified of the violation and could have confirmed Jackson's claims. The Court upheld the judgment for and a substantial award to the plaintiff. Violation of the PPA can result in a suit against the United States, against states that have waived sovereign immunity and against *each individual officer or employee acting within the scope of or under color of their office and employment*, in any state that has not waived sovereign immunity.

The ECPA[8] provides for civil penalties and criminal penalties in the event of a violation although good faith reliance on a warrant or court order is a defense to any civil or criminal action by an aggrieved party. ECPA has extensive requirements and should be studied. A copy can be obtained and downloaded from the CCIPS web site.

Under the ECPA, an Internet service provider (ISP) is prohibited from voluntarily disclosing contents of the electronic or wire communications it stores or maintains. Under limited circumstances, content can be revealed to law enforcement if the ISP inadvertently obtains the information and it appears to be related to a crime. Rules differ for "delivered" and "undelivered" e-mail and for account information. An e-mail message, for example, is protected as a "stored electronic communication" until the receiver opens it, at which time, the message ceases to be protected.

The ECPA allows the government to obtain electronic information in the following way:

- If the message has been in electronic storage for 180 days or less, a *search warrant* must be obtained and served on the provider;
- If in storage more than 180 days, or once delivered to the recipient, the material can be obtained by warrant (no notice to the account owner), subpoena or court order (with notice);
- Subscriber or transactional information (excluding content) can be obtained by search warrant, subpoena or court order. Material obtainable without a warrant includes name, address, local and long distance telephone toll billing records, telephone number or other subscriber number or identity and length of service of a subscriber, together with types of service provided. When the subpoena or court order is used, the provider is required to notify the customer. When a search warrant is used, the provider is *not* required to notify the customer. In many cases, it may be preferable to obtain a search warrant to obtain this type of information. [9]

Capture of Key Strokes or Real Time Communication

Most investigators and prosecutors understand that without an appropriate order allowing an interception, telephone communication cannot be intercepted or "tapped." Software is available, however, that can clandestinely intercept computer communications and remotely monitor computers. Some investigators and prosecutors may not realize that such a capture by a third party qualifies as a wiretap and violates the computer crime statutes of most states. Excepting the legitimate right of the employer to monitor staff computer activity or telephone use, wiretap and wiretapping laws generally apply to everyone, obviously including law enforcement, and can only be authorized by court order.

SEARCH AND SEIZURE OF COMPUTERS AND COMPUTER DATA

In order for Fourth Amendment protections to apply in search and seizure cases, there must be an actual expectation of privacy and the expectation must be one recognized by society as reasonable. Like most traditional search and seizure law, Fourth Amendment protections also apply to computers and their contents. Generally, a computer is considered a "private zone" for the user, as is a person's home or car. A computer used in one's employment, on the other hand, (despite an *expectation* of privacy) might not be protected. If protections apply, the computer may only be seized and searched in compliance with the requirements of the Fourth Amendment. Compliance is achieved by obtaining a valid search warrant or by finding an exception to the warrant requirement that allows the evidence to be seized and admitted in a court of law.

Exceptions to the Warrant Requirement

Of the recognized exceptions to the Fourth Amendment warrant requirement, consent searches have perhaps the most common practical application to computer searches and seizures. Although the remaining exceptions might sometimes apply, consent is the most often recurring and regular consideration in this type of search and seizure. A valid consent requires that the consenting person has authority to give the consent, the consent is voluntary and the consent is intelligently given. Furthermore, the consent must be written in language understandable to the person giving the consent.

It is particularly important when drafting consents in computer crime cases to include language that authorizes the seizure and subsequent search of the computer. If months pass from the time of seizure and the computer has not been forensically examined, it may be advisable to obtain a warrant rather than rely on the consent. Peripheral items such as disks, CDs, external disks and disk drives, backup tapes or other memory devices found with the computer should be specifically listed as part of the consent. In the event that important information has been omitted, it would be wise to obtain a search warrant before proceeding with a forensic examination. A sample consent form is included in the appendix of this article.

Search Warrants for Computers and Computer Data: Preliminary Matters

Before preparing the search warrant, obtain all the information available. Is the computer being used as a container; that is, are records or correspondence sought that may be stored in it? Is the computer used for legitimate, in addition to criminal, purposes? Is it networked? If it is networked, is it possible that the sought after data is stored at a remote location? Build on the information obtained. It is important to involve technical personnel early in the process to insure that the right things are requested. What type of equipment is used for different computing tasks? What hardware or software should be seized? Should the computer be examined on site or seized for later examination at the police lab? Should a forensic copy of the storage devices be made on site and the computer left with the owner? Are peripherals and related equipment attached? If so, the affidavit must include facts justifying the removal of equipment and peripherals. [10]

Particularity

The warrant must have particularity: a particular place where the equipment and data are located. As with all search warrants, the location should be as specific as possible, to include specific computers and equipment. While not too broad, the description should be broad enough to include those items that are reasonably expected to be at the location.

To adequately describe the items that might be included in a seizure, consider the following list: electronic data processing and storage devices, computers and computer systems including central processing units; internal and peripheral storage devices such as fixed disks, external hard disks, floppy disk drives and diskettes, tape drives and tapes, optical storage devices or other memory storage devices, peripheral input/output devices such as keyboards, printers, video display monitors, optical readers and related communications devices such as modems, together with system documentation, operating logs and documentation, software and instruction manuals.

Particular Records

A warrant for seizure of records of business or criminal activity should specify the items that are reasonably expected to be found. Consider, for example, "any and all records in any form, including but not limited to written, recorded, printed or electronically stored material relating to the business activity of (the name of company and the individuals, etc.) or that show a business connection among them, whether stored on paper, on magnetic media such as tape, cassette, disk, diskette or memory storage devices such as optical disks, electronic address books, or any other storage media, together with indicia of use, ownership, possession, or control of such records."

The Affidavit

The affidavit must contain information that will justify the seizure of all items listed in the warrant. There is a tendency when drafting an affidavit relating to computer crime and the recovery of data to use overly technical terminology. Every effort should be made to use language a magistrate with no technical training will understand. In the event that an adequate explanation of the case requires a highly technical affidavit, consider adding a glossary of terms. If an affidavit is attached, its validity should be substantiated in the body of the text. Helpful language for these affidavits is available in the *Federal Guidelines for Searching and Seizing Computers*. See the appendix.

Internet Service Providers

Subscriber and account information and history, payment history, detailed billings, "buddy list" content, "delivered" and "undelivered" e-mail and any other information maintained by the Internet service provider (ISP) can be obtained by search warrant. The ISP usually gathers the electronic data and gives it to the agency serving the warrant. The warrant must be obtained from a magistrate in the jurisdiction where the ISP stores the data. Preparation and execution of the affidavit and search warrant may require the cooperation of multiple jurisdictions. Many ISPs have subpoena/search warrant coordinators or departments that have established rules and procedures for responding to warrants, subpoenas and court orders. They are generally cooperative and many forensic computer investigators maintain a list of active ISP contacts. The Internet is also an excellent source of information about ISPs.

Follow-up Warrants

Forensic examiners often discover evidence of crimes not anticipated in the affidavit and search warrant. At the time of discovery and prior to expanding the search to include the additional types of evidence, a follow-up search warrant should be obtained that authorizes an expanded search. The inadvertent discovery of evidence not covered by the warrant will not require suppression, even though some portion of the material was viewed without the warrant. An expanded search without an additional search warrant, however, can result in the suppression of *all* the newly discovered evidence.[11]

CONCLUSION

Computer crime is an emerging area of law. It is essential that prosecutors obtain the assistance they need to properly draft warrants and affidavits and avoid the potential problems posed by federal legislation designed to protect the privacy of individuals.

ENDNOTES

[1] Computer Crime and Intellectual Property Section, U.S. Department of Justice, Washington D.C.: www.usdoj.gov/criminal/cybercrime/index.html

[2] K.S.A. 21-3755, Kansas, (1997).

[3] *Ibid.*

[4] U.S. Code Title 42, Sec. 2000a, (1980).

[5] *Zucher v. Stanford Daily,* 436 U.S. 294 (1967).

[6] *Ibid.*

[7] *Steve Jackson Games, Inc., v. U.S. Secret Service,* 816 F. Supp 432 (W.D. Tex 1993, *affirmed* 36 F.3d 457 (5th Cir. 1994).

[8] U.S. Code Title 18, Chapter 121, (1986).

[9] *Ibid.*

[10] *U.S. v. Upham,* 168 F.3d 532, (1st Cir. Me.) (1999).

[11] *U.S. v. Patrick Carey,* 172 F.3d 1268 (10th Cir. (Ks) 1999): *U.S. v. Grey,* ___ F. Supp.2d ___, (1999) WL 1251836 (E.D. Va).

APPENDIX

Internet Sites:

- U.S. Department of Justice, Computer Crime and Intellectual Property Section: www.usdoj.gov/criminal/cybercrime/index.html.

- National White Collar Crime Center. Source of training and information. Can provide Internet resource bookmarks: http://www.iir.com/nwccc.html.

- Computer Crime Research Resources. Source of information about key computer crime cases. Also very complete bibliography of computer crime books: http://mailer.fsu.edu/~bfl553/ccrr/.

- National Cybercrime Training Partnership: http://www.nctp.org.

Books
Rosenblatt, Kenneth S., *High Tech Crime*, KSK Publications, P.O. Box 934, San Jose, CA 95108

CONSENT TO SEARCH

I, _____ (print name), understand and state the following:

1.   That _____ (name of law enforcement officer), of the _____ Police/Sheriff/Law Enforcement Department/Agency, has requested that I consent to a search of my home, and more specifically, the seizure and complete forensic examination of my computer and all related computer disks and electronic equipment.

2.   I understand I have the right to refuse to allow the seizure or search of my property, absent a search warrant issued by the Court.

3.   Notwithstanding my right to refuse, I am hereby consenting to the search of my home located at _____(City), _____(State), and further consent to seizure of any property, including but not limited to my computer and all related computer disks, software and electronic equipment, and to the complete forensic examination of the computer, computer disks and all related equipment seized.

4.   This consent is given by me to the above named detective/officer of the _____ Police/Sheriff/Law Enforcement Department/Agency, or their designees, and no threats, inducements or promises have been made to cause me to give consent and/or to sign this consent form.

_____   _____
(Signature of person granting consent)   (Date)

_____   _____
(Signature of person requesting consent)   (Date)

CONSIDERATIONS IN THE PROSECUTION OF STALKING AND CYBERSTALKING CASES

By Diana M. Riveira, Senior Attorney and Program Manager,
American Prosecutors Research Institute, Violence Against Women Program,
Alexandria, Virginia, and Kimberly Pace, Assistant Commonwealth's Attorney,
Fairfax County, Fairfax, Virginia

Introduction

Over the last 20 years, the media, the public and legislators have increasingly focused attention on issues related to violence against women. The enactment of the Violence Against Women Act (VAWA) by the U.S. Congress in 1994 provided federal protection and remedies for female victims of violent crime. VAWA funding helps state and local agencies to establish policies and protocols and to hire additional staff to address issues related to these crimes, including stalking and, most recently, cyberstalking.

The high profile stalking and murder of actress Rebecca Schaeffer by Robert Bardo[1] in 1990 prompted the state of California to pass the first piece of stalking legislation. All 50 states, the District of Columbia, and the United States Congress have followed suit. New York was the last state to pass a stalking statute in 1999, having had only a criminal harassment statute up to that point.[2]

With the advent of computers and the Internet, traditional techniques of stalking are being supplemented with high-tech methods. States have reacted by adding provisions to their stalking legislation that criminalize stalking by electronic means or the use of computer equipment. Currently, 26 states have made harassment through electronic communications and e-mail illegal, and many other states have such bills pending in their legislatures.[3] On the national level, the Stalking Prevention and Victim Protection Act of 1999, which passed in the U.S. House of Representatives (H.R. 1869) and has been referred to the U.S. Senate, contains language that can be read to classify threatening e-mail communications as stalking behavior.[4]

Regardless of the level of technical complexity, stalking and cyberstalking cases pose unique challenges for prosecutors. How does a prosecutor prove that the defendant knew that his (and, to be fair, her) actions would place the victim in fear? How can a prosecutor demonstrate to a judge or jury that threatening e-mails were actually sent by the defendant and not by someone posing as the defendant?

The following article addresses these and other issues that come into play at all stages of stalking and cyberstalking prosecution. Prosecutors should come away with an enhanced understanding of the many considerations related to these cases that will be useful in avoiding potential pitfalls.

STALKING CASES

To adequately address the needs of stalking victims, prosecutors should first under-stand their own state's stalking legislation and be aware of the actions that make up stalking behavior. Approximately 1,400,000 Americans are victims of stalking every year.[5] The majority of those cases, over one million, involve female victims, with one in every 12 women stalked in their lifetime.[6] The disproportionate representa-tion of female victims is due to the strong connection between stalking and domes-tic violence and sexual assault cases. Many victims of domestic violence and sexual assault have also been stalked in varying degrees by their abuser.[7] As a result, the majority of stalking cases before state prosecutors are those involving female victims and male perpetrators.[8]

Only 13 percent of female stalking victims interviewed in the National Violence Against Women survey reported that their stalkers were criminally prosecuted.[9] Of the defendants charged in those stalking cases, roughly half of them were convicted of a crime.[10] These conviction rates could improve if prosecutors had a better under-standing of their stalking statutes and the problems that can arise in those cases. Many considerations, including ethical questions, come into play in cases involving stalking behavior that exist during all stages of charging and prosecution. Most con-siderations center on the proper application of state stalking statutes, with issues such as applicability to the defendant's behavior and the victim's fear and behavior at the forefront. Expert knowledge of these issues will help prosecutors to effectively prose-cute the stalking cases that they encounter.

What Is Stalking?

Most state stalking statutes define the term "stalking" as some form of harassing or threatening behavior that is conducted repeatedly against another individual.[11]

Beyond the legal definitions, stalking behavior takes on many different forms, depending on the relationship of the stalker to the victim and on the mindset of the stalker.

The Psychology of Stalking, Clinical and Forensic Perspective, edited by J. Reid Meloy, provides a quick overview for the lay reader of the current findings from clinical and forensic researchers working with stalkers and their victims.[12] Below are *some* of the findings:

- The length of pursuit by stalkers is measured in months or years; this is not a brief encounter.
- The primary motivation for stalking is not sexual, but is, instead, conscious anger or hostility toward the victim (Meloy, 1996). Victims of stalking most commonly perceive that the defendant's sense of control is the primary motivation for stalking (Tjaden & Thoennes, 1997).
- Typical psychological defenses exhibited by stalkers include denial, minimization and projection of blame onto the victim.
- Most individuals who stalk are not psychotic at the time of their stalking. (Note: this fact is important in attacking potential defenses to stalking.[13])
- Research suggests that stalkers are more intelligent than other criminals, which perhaps accounts for their manipulative skills.
- Most stalkers are unemployed or underemployed at the time of the stalking; this is important because stalking is a protracted crime that requires a substantial investment of the stalker's time.
- There is some evidence to consider stalking, at least for some individuals, as a courtship disorder (Feund, Scher & Hucker, 1983). Stalkers often exhibit a history of failed intimate relationships, and usually the stalker is not in a sexual pair bond at the time of the criminal behavior. Stalking for some individuals is a maladaptive response to social incompetence, social isolation and loneliness (Meloy, 1996).
- Stalking marks the far end of a continuum that begins with "obsessive relational intrusions" (Spitzer & Cupach, 1994), which are not, per se, criminal acts.
- Pursuit patterns by stalkers are multiple, varied and most commonly include physical approach behavior and telephoning.

- Although most victims of stalking are women, men are also victims; they are most likely to be stalked by other male acquaintances or strangers (Tjaden & Thoennes, 1997).
- At least one-half of stalkers explicitly threaten their victims, and even though most threats are not carried out, the risk of violence is likely to increase when there is an articulated threat.
- The frequency of violence by stalkers toward their victims averages in the 25-35 percent range, quite a high rate for violence when compared to other criminally violent groups. The *simple obsessionals* (definition to follow), those individuals who have had a prior sexually intimate relationship with the victim, are the most likely group to be violent. (Note: this is an important fact to take into consideration when conducting an accurate lethality assessment.[14])
- The homicide rate among victims of stalking is less than two percent.
- There are no scientific data, as yet, on the prediction of violence among stalkers although certain factors appear to correlate with stalkers who are violent. Many of these factors are similar to correlates of criminal violence in general, such as male gender, prior felony convictions, weapons involvement, prior drug abuse (including alcohol) and psychiatric history.

Apart from current findings in the criminology field, reference is always made to stalker typologies when defining stalking and stalking behaviors. While research in stalker typologies is ongoing, the most frequently cited classification system originated in a study carried out by Dr. Michael Zona (a psychiatric fellow at the University of Southern California Institute of Psychiatry, Law and Behavioral Science) and the Los Angeles Police Department's (LAPD) Threat Assessment Unit.

Published in 1993, Dr. Zona's and his colleagues' comparative study delineates three "types" of stalkers: *simple obsessional, love obsessional* and *erotomania*.[15] In 1998, a fourth type was identified—*false victimization*—based on statistics compiled from data generated by the increasing numbers of new stalking cases handled by the Threat Assessment Unit.[16]

Simple obsessional cases involve interpersonal relationships, such as those between spouses, lovers or co-workers, and are the most likely to turn violent.[17] *Love obsessional* describes cases where there is no prior relationship between the parties, such as a woman who is stalked by an unknown neighbor in her apartment building.[18] When the stalker believes that the victim loves him, it is referred to as *erotomania* stalking.[19] These erotomania situations are less likely to be dangerous because the stalker does not wish to harm the person who loves him and rarely attempts face-to-face contact. The final type of stalking, *false victimization,* is the least common. In a false victimization situation, the stalker poses as the victim of stalking while the actual victim is made out to be the perpetrator.[20] Research suggests that the majority of cases encountered (47 percent) will fall into the *simple obsessional* category.[21] The second largest category is the *love obsessional* at 43 percent.[22]

Prosecutors should attempt to discern the stalking typology present in their case. During the intake phase of the case, identification of the typology will help assess the potential lethality of the defendant and, in the case of false victimization, will help to determine the true victim.

Establishing a working relationship with a qualified expert in stalking typology is key. The expert can assist the intake prosecutor with preliminary assessment and, while not necessarily required to testify at trial, the expert can assist the trial prosecutor in preparing witnesses and identifying viable defenses.

CHARGING CONSIDERATIONS

Many considerations come into play when a prosecutor is deciding whether and how to charge a stalking case. The crime of stalking is legally defined and treated in many ways and a broad range of activity is classified as stalking by state law. Thus, it is extremely important for prosecutors to be knowledgeable regarding the nuances in their state statute and even its legislative history prior to charging a stalking case. In addition, some cases involve victims or defendants of foreign cultures who do not recognize stalking as an illegal behavior, and these cultural beliefs may play a role in pre-trial motions. Finally, there are issues surrounding the stalking victim, specific to stalking cases, which must be considered.

Interpreting the Statute

Before making any charging decisions in stalking cases, prosecutors should carefully analyze their state's statute to ensure that the applicable language in fact prohibits the defendant's behavior.[23] Furthermore, the prosecutor must be able to prove that the defendant's actions satisfy the intent requirement of the statute.

The definition given to stalking varies by state but generally employs language such as, "willfully and repeatedly follows another person," or "engages in a course of conduct which would cause a reasonable person to fear physical injury to himself." Statutes vary greatly, however, in the specificity of the definition. Colorado, for example, sets out seven specific behaviors that constitute harassment.[24] At the other end of the spectrum, Idaho mentions no specific behaviors that comprise stalking, as long as the behavior is willful, malicious and repeated, and serves to alarm the victim.[25] In addition, some states require that the defendant's behavior be that which would likely cause the victim to fear for her safety, while others merely require the behavior, regardless of the propensity to incite fear.[26]

Many states employ a strict stalking definition, which requires that the defendant, in addition to satisfying the "repeated conduct" requirement, make a "credible threat" to the victim.[27] This requirement may cause problems for prosecutors because it is vague. For example, Alabama requires that a "credible threat" be made towards the victim without defining the term, and allows that threat to be either express or implied. A prosecutor with an implied threat that is not very strong should be prepared for a defense argument that the defendant's behavior has not met the requirements of the statute.

Analysis of the defendant's behavior should be accompanied by an analysis of the defendant's intent. Evidentiary issues may arise in stalking cases when the prosecutor is required by the statute to show that the defendant specifically intended by his actions to place the victim in reasonable fear.[28] There are several avenues that a prosecutor can take to show this intent. Specific threats made to the victim that show intent include: statements of defendant's future conduct (e.g., "I'm going to kill you one day."); statements of suicidal intentions (e.g., "If you don't meet with me tomorrow I'm going to shoot myself."); or statements that convey heightened levels of intimidation by the defendant (e.g., "I talked to your co-worker on the phone today, and she gave me your address.").

Any past violent history between the defendant and victim may also be used to show intent. This history can be evidenced by a restraining order between the two parties, particularly if the defendant violated the order, or with past convictions for crimes against the same victim. Prosecutors should discover from the victim, if possible, the method the defendant used to obtain her personal information. Acts such as discovering personal information about the victim through third party contact and looking at the victim's mail may be useful to show the defendant's intent to frighten the victim.

In general, states that do not require that the prosecution prove that the defendant intended to place the victim in fear usually only require proof that the defendant intended to commit the acts that make up the stalking behavior. This allows the prosecution to put into evidence the acts themselves, be they repeated phone calls, following the victim or any of the activities mentioned above, to show that the defendant's course of conduct was intentional and that his actions were not merely coincidental.

The final major component of many stalking statutes relates to the effect of the defendant's behavior on the victim. While 20 states do not require that the defendant actually incite fear in the victim, the rest include a requirement that the victim be placed in reasonable fear or be in fear of the defendant as a result of his actions. The vast majority of the states that require the victim to be in fear set forth an objective standard, meaning that the victim must be in reasonable fear of the defendant's actions. Three states merely require that the prosecution show that the victim was in fear as a result of the defendant's actions. When a prosecutor is required to show that the victim was in reasonable fear, the actions that show the intent of the defendant may be used to show the reasonable fear of the victim, along with actual victim testimony of the effects of the defendant's actions.

CULTURAL CONSIDERATIONS

Occasionally, prosecutors encounter an additional feature in a stalking case where the victim, defendant or both are from cultural backgrounds that regard stalking types of behavior, however misguided, as merely a persistent demonstration of unrequited love or devotion. Prosecutors usually encounter this cultural phenomenon in the defendant, not the victim (as a victim with those cultural beliefs would not be likely to identify the behavior as criminal and, consequently, would not involve the police).

When presented with a victim of a foreign culture who has come forward with allegations of stalking, prosecutors should be aware of how her background may potentially affect her perception of the facts of the case. In cultures where lovers are "pursued" or persistence in inviting a women on a date is seen as accepted courtship behavior, victims may tend to downplay the defendant's indefatigable and repeated actions even while recognizing that they are objectively unsolicited and illegal. Effectively conveying to the victim the types of behavior that encompass stalking, while avoiding the temptation to coach the victim, is the key to building a complete case against the defendant. This tension between the desire to prove the case and the need to avoid overly aggressive or even unwelcome prosecution is the reason that convincingly demonstrating the genuine fear of a victim from a foreign culture can be the main ethical problem that the prosecutor encounters with stalking prosecutions. In states where the victim must be placed in actual fear to satisfy the statute, the victim's failure or refusal to recognize stalking behavior as frightening or unwanted may hinder the prosecutor's efforts to prove the case.[29]

Additional challenges arising in the stalking prosecution of a defendant from a foreign culture are proving intent and addressing the "cultural defense."[30] Defendants from foreign cultures may argue that the behaviors America classifies as criminal are considered "courting behavior" in their own culture. A defense attorney who successfully argues a cultural defense will effectively thwart the prosecutor's ability to prove that the defendant possessed the requisite intent to place his victim in fear. If the statute requires this level of intent the prosecutor may not be able to meet the evidentiary burden for successful prosecution.[31]

Although U.S. courts have thus far refused to recognize a formal "cultural defense," the argument has been made successfully to mitigate criminal responsibility.[32] Prosecutors should be aware of the legal arguments as well as the policy reasons against the "cultural defense." Obviously, to allow one group of defendants to escape criminal liability opens the door for other groups to do the same.[33] The issue then becomes a difficult and never-ending one of where to draw the line. Worse, allowing the use of a cultural defense in stalking cases and associated domestic violence and sexual assault cases would likely create the belief among some cultural groups that the American court system condones violence against women.[34] Most importantly, it allows the defendant to effectively use a defense that is based on his abuse and manipulation of accepted norms in his culture. In reality, no culture and no world religion officially condones violence against women. If the criminal justice system allows the defendant to utilize this cultural defense, it would in effect incorporate cultural myths into America's jurisprudence.

CYBERSTALKING CASES

The Internet is a wonderful resource for information and a quick way to connect people around the globe, but it can also be a means for inciting fear and delivering threats. Regrettably, while criminal justice professionals are making real strides in the tangible world, domestic violence offenders, stalkers and rapists have found in the Internet a new virtual frontier and a new set of tools with which to inflict terror and violence on their victims. This unfortunate development has not gone unnoticed. In a keynote speech on January 10, 2000, Attorney General Janet Reno took note of the enormous benefits of the Internet, and at the same time, warned of the new opportunities for criminal behavior that the Internet and other information technologies bring to society.[35]

Internet violence against women takes many forms, limited only by the constantly enlarging parameters of the ever-developing technology. The dangers are various but quite real: a woman can be stalked through e-mail or she can become a target for sexual assault when her stalker features her on a sexually explicit Web site (unbeknownst to the victim). In addition, an estranged intimate can "steal her identity" and potentially deprive her of credit, job opportunities or the ability to relocate.

Because of the supposed anonymity of chat rooms and bulletin boards on the Internet, women Internet users may at first feel shielded from danger. Likewise, some women may feel immune from cybercrimes because they do not have (or affirmatively decide not to have) access to the Internet. Yet the anonymity of the Web is easily violated. Databases of personal information widely available on the Internet enable a potential stalker to trace a victim's user name to her real name, address and telephone number. They enable a potential rapist to impersonate the victim online, seek out "rape fantasy" enthusiasts and even "invite" partners to the victim's home. The criminal can harass his victim via e-mail, mail and telephone calls or even by appearing at the victim's home.

Probably the most pressing issue for police and prosecutors faced with cases involving stalking and Internet crimes against women is the lack of an adequately trained workforce and state-of-the-art technology to investigate these cases and a lack of prosecutors with relevant experience to try them. Many who work directly on or study stalking and cyberstalking cases report that police and prosecutors are in desperate need of training. Prosecutors need to understand the genuine threat that Internet crime against women poses. They should become familiar with the technology utilized by cybercriminals and be able to gather sufficient information and evidence to successfully charge a cyberstalking case and prove it beyond a reasonable doubt.

What is Cyberstalking ?

It is impossible to offer a comprehensive definition of every type of case that could be classified as cyberstalking or as an Internet crime against women. Anecdotal evidence, however, suggests that the majority of the on-line stalking victims parallel the victims of traditional stalking—they are women.[36] Furthermore, research on this topic identifies a difference in the way men and women communicate online:

> "[M]en are more belligerent online and are more likely to use angry and abusive language. [The researcher[37]] derives such conclusions from the different socialization of men and women. Men tend to behave more aggressively and women more politely."[38] "Chat room cybersex is another area men seemed more attracted to than women. While men and women alike enter such rooms looking for erotic chat, it is men who remark how addicting such sexual entertainment is to them. The addiction grows from the ability to cruise such chat rooms looking for uninhibited erotica—things they would never do or say with their wives or girlfriends."[39]

To facilitate discussion, Internet crime can be divided into three areas:

- Computers utilized to commit traditional crime: examples include stalking, identity theft or impersonating a victim online (e.g., by constructing "her" Web site).
- Computer use that is incidental to offense: examples include sexual assault (meeting victim on-line and arranging a meeting where the victim is sexually assaulted), stalking (stalking victim both in person and online), or drug-facilitated rape (and then videotaping the victim during the sexual assault and later downloading the illicit video clip to the World Wide Web).
- Technology used to attack a computer or computer system: examples include sending viruses, hacking or "spamming."

Legal discussion about the issues surrounding cyberstalking is not mere theoretical postulating on the potential occurrence of a future crime. Rather, it is a very real discussion about existing criminality. Below are recent examples of some Internet crimes against women:

- Murder-Suicide: In Nashua, New Hampshire, Liam Youens, age 21, constructed a Web page to express his love for Amy Boyer, age 20. Youens's Web page contained pictures of the victim and love poetry he had written for her. The offender ambushed and shot Ms. Boyer on the afternoon of Friday, October 15, 1999, as she was leaving to go to work. Youens then shot himself.
- Multiple messages sent via e-mail: In Oakland County, Michigan, Andrew Archambeau pleaded no contest to a stalking charge. He met a woman through a computer dating service and had two in-person dates with her. After the second date, the woman attempted to terminate the relationship, but Archambeau continued to send her e-mail messages and leave phone messages.[40]
- Scanning victim's photographs onto the Web: In New Jersey, "Stephany Willman, a 41-year-old New Jersey woman, could not understand why she was receiving letters from men offering sex. She later learned that her ex-boyfriend had scanned her nude Polaroid photographs onto his computer and uploaded them, along with her home address, to a sexually explicit newsgroup."[41]
- Impersonating the victim by constructing Web sites depicting victim as a prostitute or liking "kinky" sex: In the first case in California to be prosecuted under the state's new cyberstalking law, Gary Dellapenta portrayed a woman—whom he had met at church but who had rejected his romantic overtures on the Internet—as someone with fantasies of being raped. The defendant, a former security guard, posted online the woman's physical description, her address, phone number and instructions on how to bypass her home security system. The woman, who had never been online, discovered the cyberimpersonation only after six men appeared at her apartment responding to her Internet "personal ad."[42]
- Incident to Sexual Assault: In New York City, Oliver Jovanovic was convicted of kidnapping, assaulting and sexually abusing a female Columbia University student that he had met online. Jovanovic's conviction was overturned in December 1999, and a new trial was ordered because the New York trial judge misapplied the state's Rape Shield Law.

Nature and Extent of the Cyberstalking Problem

The Problem Generally

Many in the field of law enforcement and criminology agree that most cyberstalking cases go unreported. Consequently, there is a glaring absence of empirical data regarding the prevalence of Internet crime. In August 1999, Attorney General Janet

Reno advised Vice President Gore on the status of cyberstalking in an official report that stated that "[a]ssuming the proportion of cyberstalking victims is even a fraction of the proportion of [the one percent of all women and 0.4 percent of all men]... who have been victims of offline stalking within the preceding 12 months, there may be *potentially tens or even hundreds of thousands of victims* of recent Cyberstalking incidents in the U.S."[43]

Eric W. Hickey, Ph.D., a professor of criminal psychology at California State University, Fresno, who lectures and consults in criminal and civil cases involving Internet stalking, has studied stalkers for more than 20 years. Hickey has amassed a database of over two hundred stalking victims via interviews. Although he attributes a relatively small percentage to cyberstalking—two to three percent of the total cases tracked—Hickey believes that stalking via the Internet or other electronic communications is one of the least reported forms of stalking crimes. According to Hickey, victims of cyberstalking generally do not report the crimes because they do not realize a crime has been committed. They may feel that the offending person has a broad First Amendment right to communicate via computer, regardless of the potential criminal content of the messages. This attitude reinforces the perception of cyberstalking found in other survey results, where the public and law enforcement, in general, fail to treat electronic stalking as seriously as in-person stalking.[44]

Research indicates that "context" is the determining factor in attitudes on cyberstalking:

> Actions which are characterized as stalking in a non-electronic context are interpreted as more like romance and less like stalking in an Internet context. If a stalker initially communicates with his object through the Internet, then his activities are perceived as isolated incidents only occurring within the electronic medium. When an electronic stalker becomes real, however, physical proximity increases, and electronic activities are reinterpreted as part of a larger stalking campaign. Whether or not we understand cyberstalking as "stalking" depends upon what other kinds of behavior accompany electronic activities.[45]

In his training for law enforcement officials, Hickey emphasizes that stalking behavior is only a part of the whole criminal behavior that transpires. How "stalking" is defined depends upon how law enforcement views offender typologies, victim/offender relationships and victim characteristics. According to Hickey, most serial offenders and sexual predators engage in stalking behaviors. Internet predators include the socially dysfunctional, psychopaths, sexual predators (including pedophiles), child molesters, rapists and other paraphiliacs.

"Stalking and Intimate Partner Femicide," an article in the November 1999 issue of *Homicide Studies*, supports Dr. Hickey's findings, reporting that 65 percent of murder victims and 85 percent of attempted murder victims were subjected to at least one episode of stalking during the year preceding the (murder) attack.[46]

CHALLENGES FACED BY PROSECUTORS AND POLICE OFFICERS

Not surprisingly, identifying and prosecuting cybercriminals has become an international law enforcement problem. The *Technological Crime Bulletin*, published by the Communications Unit of the Royal Canadian Mounted Police[47] recently featured an article entitled, "Electronic Stalkers at Large: Tracking Down Harassment in Cyberspace." This article labels stalking as a "growing concern among members of the computer community" and, consequently, a rapidly growing law enforcement issue.[48]

In the United States, the difficulties in prosecuting Internet crimes against women are further compounded by the fact that identifying and recovering offender information may become increasingly difficult. For example, many computer companies now provide "anonymous re-mailer" service. A Montreal-based computer company called Zero-Knowledge Systems[49] offers its version of the "anonymous re-mailer" in an innovative program called Freedom that is designed to hide the identity of the e-mail sender by replacing any identifying information in the sender's software program with pseudonyms. When an e-mail is sent, it travels to Zero-Knowledge servers where the identity is further erased. Finally, any digital tracks left on the Zero-Knowledge servers are also instantly erased to prevent later access by anyone, including law enforcement.

A second example is Stratfor's Shredder, a software program for Windows 95 that acts like an electronic paper shredder and "automatically overwrites deleted files, including all the backup files that are routinely created by the computer every time a new file is created."[50] Consequently, while computer forensic examiners up until now have been relatively confident that most information in a computer could be recovered even if "deleted" [51]/[52], this type of electronic shredder could make recovering deleted information almost impossible.

Another challenge for law enforcement is the relative ease with which personal data can be accessed online. For example, e-commerce marketing groups collect "cookies" [53] left by the buyer while browsing or shopping online. Marketing groups then sell these vast consumer lists to companies or entrepreneurs; e.g., if a gift is purchased online, not only does the company have information about the buyer, but also about the recipient of the gift. Other areas of potential access are schools and hospitals that, because of funding restrictions, construct inexpensive databases online that lack high-tech security features to make them hacker[54] resistant. Others are department of motor vehicles databases, census databases, credit reports and toll systems databases, such as "E-Z Pay." In addition, otherwise confidential financial records can become vulnerable to hackers during frequent periods of bank mergers, when disruptions caused by reorganizations, lay-offs and corporate restructurings degrade otherwise adequate computer security systems.

In addition, national computer companies have come under a great deal of public scrutiny because of the information gathering systems they implant in their computers unbeknownst to the consumer. A special report in *Business Week*, on April 5, 1999, revealed that:

> In January [1999], Intel came under fire for designing its Pentium III chips with serial numbers that can be identified remotely on the Web. That makes it easier for a user to be tracked. Two months later, privacy buffs hammered Microsoft Corporation because its *Windows 98* software, used on a network, creates identifiers that are collected during registration. The result is a vast database of personal information about Microsoft customers... But fearing a backlash, [Microsoft] has promised to modify the feature.[55]

In addition, some Internet service providers (ISPs) have been reluctant to provide access to records of their subscribers' accounts. This reluctance on the part of some ISPs to cooperate increases the amount of paperwork and time a police officer must devote to investigate each individual cybercrime case. Ordinarily, telephone records can be easily obtained by subpoena, but officers have encountered difficulty when attempting to obtain Internet (dial-up) records in the same manner. Some Internet service providers consider their toll records to be "transactional data," (as opposed to subscriber information) which under the Electronic Communications Privacy Act (ECPA) is available only via a search warrant.[56] This requires police officers to draft affidavits and appear before judges to obtain search warrants in each and every case under investigation—another burden for frequently understaffed and overworked cybercrime investigators.

JURISDICTIONAL ISSUES

A threshold decision to be made in cyberstalking cases is the accurate identification of the correct jurisdiction (and venue) in which the crime occurred. Here law enforcement may be forced to deal with state and federal jurisdictional issues and with international jurisdictional issues as well.

The following are just a few of the jurisdictional issues that may arise:

- A person who e-mails harassing messages to a victim in State A may live elsewhere in State A, in State B, on an Indian reservation or in a foreign country.
- If a cyberstalker lives in a state where the act of physically harassing someone was an element of the offense but the cyberstalker only sent harassing e-mails and did not stalk his victim in person (e.g., did not follow his victim), would the cyberstalker be in violation of the stalking laws in his state?[57]
- Since most states classify stalking (first offense) as a misdemeanor, how many prosecutors' offices will devote the financial resources necessary to extradite a misdemeanor cyberstalker from another state (for a maximum penalty, if convicted, of one year in jail)?[58]
- Assume that your state law reads that a search warrant must be issued in the jurisdiction where the property is physically located. Now assume that an employee of a company is sending harassing e-mails to a co-worker whom he formerly dated. From where would those records be seized if the cyberstalker's "computer was part of a local area network (LAN) whose server—the computer on which these records were stored—was actually located"[59] in a different state, or, worse, if the company was multinational and the server was physically located in a foreign country?

Many of these jurisdictional issues can only be resolved by establishing strong networks of communication between local police departments, prosecutors' offices, federal law enforcement agencies, and U.S. attorneys' offices. These networks can be achieved informally through national multi-disciplinary training and formally by establishing cyberstalking task forces at the state level.

CONCLUSION

An adequately trained workforce, state-of-the art technology to investigate stalking cases and prosecutors with experience in trying cybercases are the most pressing needs for police and prosecutors confronting stalking and Internet crimes against women. Police and prosecutors must understand the characteristics of electronic evidence, how chat rooms operate, where evidence is stored and how to get to it, how to draft search warrants and subpoenas for electronic evidence and how to preserve that evidence once a computer is seized.

Currently there are some efforts in the law enforcement community to self-train specialized electronic investigators. However, public sector financial constraints make it difficult for many police departments and prosecutors' offices to afford the equipment that would make prosecution of these types of cases immensely easier. Nonetheless, many offices are aggressively training their officers and prosecutors even without sophisticated equipment.

A broad range of activity may be classified by state law as stalking and it is extremely important for prosecutors to be knowledgeable about the nuances in their state statute, its legislative history and the applicable caselaw, prior to charging a stalking case. In addition, some cases involve victims or defendants of foreign cultures who do not recognize stalking as an illegal behavior, and these cultural beliefs may cause significant difficulties during prosecution.

In the ever-changing field of crimes against women, it is important to arm law enforcement with the weapons necessary to identify and apprehend Internet predators. With proper training and equipment, law enforcement and prosecution will begin to work together, in teams, to better respond to victims and their advocates and aggressively prosecute offenders they would otherwise be unable to bring to justice.

APPENDIX A
STATE STALKING STATUTES

State	Statute Cite
Alabama	Code of Ala. §13A-6-90
Alaska	Alaska Stat. §§11.41.260, 270
Arizona	A.R.S. §13-2923
Arkansas	Ark. Stat. Ann. §5-71-229
California	Cal Pan Code §646.9
Colorado	C.R.S. 18-9-111
Connecticut	Conn. Gen. Stat. §53a-181c-e
Delaware	11 Del. C. §1312A
District of Columbia	D.C. Code §22-504
Florida	Fla. Stat. §784.048
Georgia	O.C.G.A. §16-5-90
Hawaii	HRS §711-1106.5
Idaho	Idaho Code §18-7905
Illinois	720 ULCS 5/12-7.3
Indiana	Burns Ind. Code Ann. §35-45-10-1
Iowa	Iowa Code §708.11
Kansas	K.S.A. §21-3438
Kentucky	KRS §§508.140, 150
Louisiana	La.R.S. 14:40.2
Maine	17-A M.R.S. §210-A
Maryland	Md. Ann. Code art. 27 §124
Massachusetts	Mass. Ann. Laws ch. 265 §43
Michigan	MCL §750.411h
Minnesota	Minn. Stat. §609.749

State	Statute Cite
Mississippi	Miss. Code Ann. §97-3-107
Missouri	§565.225 R.S.Mo.
Montana	Mont. Code Anno. §45-5-220
Nebraska	R.R.S. Neb. §28-311.03
Nevada	Nev. Rev. Stat. Ann. §200.575
New Hampshire	RSA 633:3-a
New Jersey	N.J. Stat. §2C:12-10
New Mexico	N.M. Stat. Ann. §30-3A-3
New York	NY CLS Penal §240.30
North Carolina	N.C. Gen. Stat. §14-277.3
North Dakota	N.D. Cent. Code §12.1-17-07.1
Ohio	ORC Ann. 2903.211
Oklahoma	21 Okl. St. §1173, 22 Okl. St. §60.1
Oregon	ORS §163.732
Pennsylvania	18 Pa.C.S. §2709
Rhode Island	R.I. Gen. Laws §11-59-2
South Carolina	S.C. Code Ann. §16-3-1700
South Dakota	S.D. Codified Laws §22-19A-1
Tennessee	Tenn. Code Ann. §39-17-315
Texas	Tex. Penal Code §42.072
Utah	Utah Code Ann. §76-5-106.5
Vermont	14 V.I.C. §2072
Virginia	Va. Code Ann. §18.2-60.6
Washington	Rev. Code Wash. (ARCW) §9A.46.110
West Virginia	W.Va. Code §61-2-9a
Wisconsin	Wis. Stat. §940.32
Wyoming	Wyo. Stat. §6-2-506

Appendix B
Requirements of State Stalking Statutes

State	Requires Credible Threat	Requires Specific Intent to Frighten	Requires Victim to be in Fear
Alabama	•	•	
Alaska			•
Arizona			
Arkansas	•	•	
California	•	•	•
Colorado		•	
Connecticut		•	•
Delaware			•
District of Columbia		•	
Florida	•	• (3rd degree)	
Georgia		•	•
Hawaii		•	
Idaho			
Illinois			•
Indiana			•
Iowa			•
Kansas	•	•	•
Kentucky	•		
Louisiana		•	
Maine			•
Maryland		•	
Massachusetts	•	•	•
Michigan			•
Minnesota			•

State	Requires Credible Threat	Requires Specific Intent to Frighten	Requires Victim to be in Fear
Mississippi		•	•
Missouri	•	•	•
Montana		•	•
Nebraska		•	
Nevada			•
New Hampshire		•	•
New Jersey			
New Mexico		•	
New York		•	
North Carolina		•	
North Dakota		•	•
Ohio			
Oklahoma		•	•
Oregon		•	•
Pennsylvania		•	
Rhode Island		•	
South Carolina		•	•
South Dakota		•	
Tennessee			
Texas			
Utah			•
Vermont		•	
Virginia		•	
Washington			•
West Virginia	•	•	
Wisconsin			•
Wyoming			•

APPENDIX C
REQUIREMENTS OF CYBERSTALKING STATUTES

States with harassment statutes that encompass electronic communications:
Alabama (written or electronic harassing communications)
Arizona (harassment/electronic means)
Connecticut (harassment/computer network)
Delaware (harassment/electronic communication)
Hawaii (harassment/electronic mail transmissions)
Illinois (harassment through electronic communications)
Indiana (harassment/computer network or other form of electronic communication)
Minnesota (harassment/electronic means)
Missouri (harassment/via computer)
New Hampshire (harassment/electronic transmission including transmissions generated by computer)
New York (aggravated harassment—first degree covers hate crimes, too/electronic means)

States with stalking statutes that prohibit electronic communications:
Alaska (electronic communication)
California (electronic communication device)
Georgia (computer, computer network)
Maine (computer network)
Massachusetts (electronic mail, internet communications)
Michigan (electronic communications)
Oklahoma (electronic communications)
Wyoming (electronic means)

States with both harassment and stalking statutes that encompass electronic communications:
Pennsylvania (electronic mail, Internet)
Washington (electronic communication)

States with statutes prohibiting unlawful computer communications:
Arkansas (unlawful computerized communications)
Maryland (telephonic and electronic mail misuse/electronic mail)
Wisconsin (unlawful use of computerized communication systems)

States with statutes prohibiting threatening computer communications:
North Carolina (threatening telephonic or computer email communications)
Virginia (threats of death or bodily injury electronically transmitted producing a
visual or electronic message)

ENDNOTES

[1] *Domestic Violence, Stalking, and Antistalking Legislation: An Annual Report to Congress under the Violence Against Women Act*, (U.S. Department of Justice, Office of Justice Programs, National Institute of Justice, 1996).

[2] N.Y. [Stalking] Law §§ 120.45, 120.50, 120.55, 120.60 (Consol. 1999).

[3] Eleven states have statutes prohibiting harassment via computer contact. Those states are: Alabama, Arizona, Connecticut, Delaware, Hawaii, Illinois, Indiana, Minnesota, Missouri, New Hampshire and New York. Eight additional states have stalking statutes that cover electronic communications. They are: Alaska, California, Georgia, Maine, Massachusetts, Michigan, Oklahoma and Wyoming. Pennsylvania and Washington have both stalking and harassment statutes that encompass electronic communications. Three additional states have statutes (not within stalking or harassment) that criminalize computer communications or electronic mail misuse. They are Arkansas (unlawful computerized communications), Maryland (telephonic and electronic mail misuse), Wisconsin (unlawful use of computerized communication systems). Both North Carolina and Virginia's statutes prohibit making threats through e-mail or electronically submitted communications.

[4] H.R.1869 Sponsored by Representative Kelly (introduced 5/19/1999, Related Bill: S. 1660) Most recent summary: 11/10/1999, Passed House, amended. Text: *Stalking Prevention and Victim Protection Act of 1999 - Rewrites stalking provisions of the Federal criminal code. Prohibits: (1) for the purpose of stalking an individual, traveling or causing another to travel in interstate or foreign commerce, using or causing another to use the mail or any facility in interstate or foreign commerce, or entering or leaving, or causing another to enter or leave, Indian country; or (2) stalking an individual within the special maritime and territorial jurisdiction of the United States or within Indian country. Specifies that a person stalks an individual if that person engages in conduct: (1) with the intent to injure or harass the individual; and (2) that places the individual in reasonable fear of the death of, or serious bodily injury to, that individual or a member of that individual's immediate family, or that individual's intimate partner.*

[5] Patricia Tjaden and Nancy Thoennes, *Stalking in America: Findings from the National Violence Against Women Survey*, Office of Justice Programs, National Institute of Justice, U.S. Department of Justice, Washington D.C., (April 1998).

[6] *Id.*

[7] Approximately 77 percent of all women stalked are stalked by someone they know, with approximately 59 percent stalked by an intimate partner. *Id.*

[8] Due to this fact, throughout this article, victims will be referred to as female, and perpetrators as male.

[9] *Stalking in America.*

[10] *Id.*

[11] *Id.*

[12] J. Reid Meloy, ed., *The Psychology of Stalking, Clinical and Forensic Perspective,* Academic Press (1998): 4-6.

[13] "Note" designation was inserted by Diana Riveira, co-author of this article, not by Dr. Meloy, researcher-author of *The Psychology of Stalking.*

14 "Note" designation was inserted by Diana Riveira, co-author of this article, not by Dr. Meloy, researcher-author of *The Psychology of Stalking.*

15 Zona, Michael et al., "A Comparative Study of Erotomaniac and Obsessional Subjects in a Forensic Sample," *J. of Forensic Sciences* (July 1993).

16 *Id.*

17 *Id.*

18 *Id.*

19 *Id.*

20 *Id.*

21 Wayne Petherick, *Cyber-Stalking: Obsessional Pursuit and the Digital Criminal* (visited April 13, 2000) http://www.crimelibrary.com/criminology/cyberstalking/3.htm, citing Geberth, V.J., "Stalkers." *Law and Order*, October (1992): 138-143.

22 *Id.*

23 *See* Appendix A.

24 C.R.S. 18-9-111. The seven behaviors that constitute stalking in Colorado include striking, shoving, kicking or otherwise touching another person; directing obscene language or gestures to another in public; following a person in public; initiating communication in a manner intended to harass, threaten bodily injury or be obscene; making a telephone call or causing a telephone to ring repeatedly with no purpose of legitimate conversation; making repeated communications at inconvenient hours which invade another's privacy and interfere with their use of private property; and repeatedly insulting, taunting, challenging or using offensively coarse language to another in a manner which is likely to provoke a violent response.

25 Idaho Code §18-7905 (1999).

26 The Iowa statute (Iowa Code §708.11 (1997)) requires that the defendant's behavior is that which, "would cause a reasonable person to fear bodily injury to, or the death of, that specific person." The Florida statute (Fla. Stat. §784.048(1998)) merely requires that the defendant "willfully, maliciously, and repeatedly follows or harasses another person..." to be prosecuted for first degree misdemeanor stalking.

27 *See* Appendix B.

28 *See* Appendix B.

29 *See* Appendix B.

30 *See* Taryn F. Goldstein, "Cultural Conflicts in Court: Should the American Criminal Justice System Formally Recognize a 'Cultural Defense'?" *Dick. L. Rev.* 99 (1994): 141.

31 *See* Appendix B.

32 Cultural Conflicts in Court: 143.

[33] *Ibid.* 144.

[34] Nancy S. Kim, "The Cultural Defense and the Problem of Cultural Preemption: A Framework for Analysis," *N.M.L. Rev.* 27: 101, 111 (1997).

[35] On this date, Attorney General Reno also proposed a round-the-clock cybercrime network, regional computer forensic labs, and a secure online clearinghouse for law enforcement to share information about cybercases. U.S. U.S. Department of Justice Press Release: *Attorney General Reno Proposes New Steps to Fight Cyber-Crime.* (Released Jan. 10, 2000) (on file with the American Prosecutors Research Institute).

[36] *Cyberstalking: A New Challenge for Law Enforcement and Industry, A Report from the Attorney General to the Vice President, August 1999*, (visited December 6, 1999) www.usdoj.gov/ag/cyberstalkingreport.htm

[37] The researcher is Susan Herring, an associate professor at the University of Texas, Arlington.

[38] *Id.*

[39] National White Collar Crime Center (Website), "Using the Net as an Investigative Tool."

[40] Michigan, Oakland County Assistant Prosecutor's Office, 47th Judicial District, plea on January 1995.

[41] *Threats, Harassment, and Hate On-Line: Recent Developments*, at 677. Contact the VAWA unit at APRI (703-519-1695) for additional information.

[42] California Case Presses "Cyberstalking" Case, *AP ONLINE*, (Jan. 22, 1999) www.apbonline.com/911/1999/01/22/stalk0122_01.html.

[43] *Cyberstalking: A New Challenge for Law Enforcement and Industry: A Report from the Attorney General to the Vice President, August 1999*, (visited December 6, 1999) www.usdoj.gov/ag/cyberstalkingreport.htm. (emphasis added).

[44] Telephone Interviews with Dr. Eric Hickey, Professor of Criminology, *California State University* (March – April 1999).

[45] *See* Rebecca K. Lee, "Romantic and Electronic Stalking in a College Context," *Wm. & Mary J. of Women & L.* 4:373, (Spring 1998).

[46] *Making the Connection: Stalking and Partner Femicide* (National Center for Victims of Crime, Alexandria, VA) (Winter 2000): 5, citing McFarlane, Judith M.; Campbell, Jacquelyn C.; Wilt, Susan; Sachs, Carolyn J.; Ulrich, Yvonee; Xu, Xiao, "Stalking and Intimate Partner Femicide," *Homicide Studies* 3: no.4 (1999).

[47] *Contact information for the Royal Canadian Mounted Police*: Cpl Michael Duncan, Federal Services Directorate, Economic Crime Branch, Technological Crime Section, Room H-555, 1200 Vanier Parkway, Ottawa, Ontario, K1A 0R2.

[48] Kerry Ramsay, "Electronic Stalkers At Large, Tracking Down Harassment in Cyberspace" *TECHNOLOGICAL CRIME BULLETIN,* (visited Mar. 30, 1999) http://www.rcmp-grc.gc.ca/html/te-crime2x.htm.

[49] Stephen H. Wildstrom, "A Big Boost for Net Privacy," at Technology & You, *BUSINESS WEEK*, April 5, 1999.

[50] *Id.*

[51] Deleted files can be retrieved by computer forensics as long as they are not overwritten. While overwriting information in a 1.44MB floppy disk may be achievable, the task is not so easily accomplished if the offender saved the illicit information to his hard drive.

[52] Some software even offer "panic buttons" which expedite the deletion of a series of designated files in one keystroke. Ezra Gale, "Spooks Spy Shredder," *Cybercrime: Know the Risks,* (visited January 3, 2000) www.zdnet.com/zdtv/cybercrime/features/story/0,3700,2000142,00.html.

[53] A "Cookie" is a "message given to a Web browser by a Web server. The browser stores the message in a text file called *cookie.txt.* The message is then sent back to the server each time the browser requests a page from the server." COMPUTER & INTERNET DICTIONARY: 121. This is the reason, for example, if you visit sites that deal with camping, you will start to see a lot of camping gear ads appear every time you go online.

[54] Hackers are "individuals who gain unauthorized access to computer systems for the purpose of stealing and corrupting data." COMPUTER & INTERNET DICTIONARY: 245.

[55] Edward C. Baig, Marcia Stepanek, and Neil Gross, "Special Report: Privacy, the Internet Wants Your Personal Info. What's in it for You?" *Business Week,* (April 5, 1999): 87 (emphasis added).

[56] 18 U.S.C. §§ 2510-2521.

[57] *See* Barbara Jenson, *Cyberstalking: Crime, Enforcement and Personal Responsibility in the On-line World,* (May 1996) http://law.ucla.edu/Classes/Archive/S96/340/cyberlaw.htm.

[58] *Id.*

[59] *See* Scott Charney and Kent Alexander, Randolph W. Thrower Symposium: Legal Issues in Cyberspace: "Hazards on the Information Superhighway: Article: Computer Crime," *Emory L.J.* 45: 931, 940 (Summer 1996).

THE PROSECUTION OF ROHYPNOL AND GHB-RELATED SEXUAL ASSAULT[1]

Written and edited by Diana M. Riveira, Senior Attorney and Program Manager, and Angela L. Hart, Staff Attorney, American Prosecutors Research Institute, Violence Against Women Program, Alexandria, Virginia, with extensive technical assistance and guidance provided by the following scientists:
Marc LeBeau, Forensic Chemist/Toxicologist, Federal Bureau of Investigation, Washington, D.C., James Tolliver, Ph.D., Pharmacologist, Drug Enforcement Administration, and Christine Sannerud, Ph.D., Drug Science Specialist, Drug Enforcement Administration, Washington, D.C.
APRI wishes to extend a special thank you for their efforts.

Introduction

Of the more than 430,000 sexual assaults that occur annually in the United States, approximately three-quarters are "non-stranger sexual assaults" in which the woman knows the offender.[2] An increasing number of offenders employ drugs such as Rohypnol and Gamma hydroxy butyrate ("GHB") to subdue their victims prior to sexual assaults, particularly at parties, in clubs and bars and on college campuses across the country. The use of GHB and Rohypnol, however, is not limited to teens and college students. Reports indicate that men and women of all ages use it. These drugs are easily slipped into drinks and when consumed with alcohol by unsuspecting victims, the effects are potentially lethal. Rape crisis centers and law enforcement agency personnel report growing numbers of women who believe that they have been drugged and raped. Moreover, many cases go unreported.

Prosecutors and investigators are struggling to understand, investigate, and prosecute sexual assault cases involving Rohypnol and GHB. The challenge that they face is the very nature of the drugs themselves: Rohypnol and GHB result in loss of consciousness and memory. When mixed with alcohol, their effects are increased. Victims often do not remember the attack itself but wake up knowing that something is very, very wrong. Or, they have hazy recollections of the incident, having awakened for a few seconds during the attack and then lost consciousness. Victims of drug-facilitated sexual assault are helpless against opportunistic rapists because of the physically and mentally incapacitating effects of the ingested chemicals.

While Rohypnol and GHB are the current "drugs of choice," other pharmaceuticals that produce similar anesthetic effects are also used to facilitate sexual assaults. Many of these are legally available in the United States and should not be overlooked when conducting investigations.

"Drug-facilitated rape" is generally defined as sexual assault involving the offender's use of an "anesthesia-type" drug which, when administered to the victim (stealthily or not), renders the victim "physically incapacitated or helpless," and thus incapable of giving or not giving consent. For purposes of this definition, we are not referring to common "street drugs" such as crack or heroin. The victims are usually unconscious during the attack and have anterograde amnesia upon gaining consciousness (similar to the effects of a surgery patient coming out of anesthesia).[3]

ROHYPNOL

The most widely publicized drug used to commit drug-facilitated rape is Rohypnol, manufactured by Hoffman-La Roche, Inc., a Swiss pharmaceutical company. Rohypnol, the trade name for flunitrazepam, is a central nervous system depressant, a member of the benzodiazepine family and 10 times more potent than Valium, another benzodiazepine. It is illegal to manufacture, import and sell Rohypnol in the United States, but the drug is legally available for use as a sleeping pill and a pre-anesthetic in more than 70 countries worldwide. The effects of Rohypnol can occur within 15 to 30 minutes after ingestion and last up to eight hours or more depending on the dosage.[4] Generally white, round and smaller than aspirin, a one to two milligram tablet is the typical dose used in drug-facilitated rapes. Ingesting Rohypnol and other benzodiazepines results in[5] sedation, dizziness, motor in-coordination, muscle relaxation, slurred speech, memory impairment, loss of inhibitions and/or loss of consciousness. When Rohypnol is combined with alcohol the effects can be fatal.[6]

Although Rohypnol is generally "slipped into" alcoholic drinks, there have been cases where it was added to non-alcoholic drinks. A Rohypnol tablet placed in a carbonated beverage such as beer or soda produces a large amount of foaming that lasts for several minutes until the tablet dissolves into smaller particles.

Most victims of Rohypnol are unsuspecting, but some victims willingly ingest the drug for recreational use, alone or in conjunction with alcohol and other drugs such as cocaine and heroin.[7] Their victimization lies in the fact that while they know what they are ingesting, they are not consenting to intercourse when the drug incapacitates them. Rohypnol is popular among high school and college students because it is considered a "cheap drunk." In some areas, the drug is associated with gang involvement.[8]

GHB

The Food and Drug Administration (FDA) first issued an advisory on Gamma hydroxy butyrate (GHB) a central nervous system depressant in 1990, declaring GHB unsafe and illicit, except for use under FDA-approved physician supervised protocols.[9] In February 2000, the United States Congress passed a law that scheduled GHB under the Controlled Substances Act as a hazard to public safety.[10] In other countries, GHB is used legally as an adjunct to anesthesia.

GHB is commonly found in nightclubs, at underground RAVE parties and among body builders who use it for its purported anabolic effects. The colorless and odorless drug produces intoxication and euphoric effects but, when taken in sufficient quantities, it can render a victim unconscious within 20 minutes. As with Rohypnol, victims who have ingested GHB have little or no memory of the sexual assault.[11] Because GHB is not commercially available in the U.S. the drug is usually produced in home laboratories. Its users, therefore, may not be aware of the homemade mixture's full potency or the toxicity of its ingredients. Information on the ingredients for GHB, how to obtain the ingredients and "recipes" are widely available on the Internet.[12]

GHB is most commonly found in liquid form, packaged in plastic sports bottles, "spring water" bottles and small "Visine" eye-drop containers.[13] It sells for approximately 10 dollars per capful or "swig."[14] To mask its salty taste, the drug may be mixed with alcohol or fruit drinks. GHB is typically administered in dosages of one to five grams. The effects occur within 15 to 30 minutes and last from three to six hours, depending on the quantity ingested.[15] Ingestion of GHB can result in[16] loss of consciousness, memory impairment, confusion, loss of inhibition, seizures, dizziness, extreme drowsiness, stupor, agitation, nausea, visual disturbances, severe respiratory depression, reduced heart rate and blood pressure, coma and death.

OTHER DRUGS[17]

Many other drugs, including benzodiazepines, are used to facilitate sexual assault and, unlike Rohypnol and GHB, are legally available in the United States. Valium is one example. Over-the-counter sleeping aids, muscle relaxants and antihistamines such as diphenhydramine have also been used to facilitate sexual assault. Thus, it is essential that prosecutors and law enforcement consider the full range of drugs that have sedative and hypnotic effects on victims who unknowingly ingest them, instead of limiting the investigation to the detection of a specific type of drug.

Rape drugs are cruel in their effects: they incapacitate the victim and make it easy for the assailant to overpower her. Victims are robbed of the ability to resist the assault and to remember what happens to them. Because of the properties of these drugs, rapists are able to commit their crimes and remain undetected.

PROSECUTING THE DRUG-FACILITATED RAPE

In the successful prosecution of drug-facilitated cases, the proper collection and testing of urine and blood evidence for a positive toxicology result is extremely important. Many prosecutions, however, are forced to proceed without positive toxicology results because urine and blood samples have been improperly collected, improperly tested, collected after the drug has left the victim's system or not collected at all. In any case, the testimony of expert witnesses such as chemists, toxicologists and pharmacologists is essential. Experts are necessary to explain the positive test results or the possible reasons for negative results, and they must describe the effects of the drug on the victim.

Urine Sample Collection

The length of time Rohypnol, GHB or other rape drugs remain in the urine or blood depends on a number of variables, including the amount ingested, the victim's body size and rate of metabolism, the amount of food in the victim's stomach and prior urination. A urine specimen is preferable to a blood specimen because the drugs and their metabolites remain detectable in urine for a longer period of time.[18] If the victim ingested a rape drug within 96 hours prior to reporting the assault or receiving medical treatment, a urine specimen of at least 30 milliliters but preferably 100 milliliters (a coffee cup size sample),[19] should always be collected and delivered to the crime lab for a "full or comprehensive drug screen." [20]/[21]

Many drugs, including GHB, and most benzodiazepines such as Rohypnol, will be eliminated from the urine in less than 48 hours.[22] A few drugs may be present, however, at trace levels after 96 hours. To sum up, benzodiazepines, e.g., Rohypnol and Valium, remain in the urine for 48 to 96 hours. (Caveat: most benzodiazepines will not be detected after 48 hours). GHB remains in the urine for up to 12 hours. One hundred milliliters of urine will provide enough specimen for a "full drug screen" with sufficient specimen remaining for a re-testing at a second, more specialized laboratory, if necessary.

Collecting the Blood Specimen

If the ingestion of the drug occurred within 12 hours, a blood sample of at least 10 to 20 milliliters should be collected in a gray-top tube.[23] A blood sample taken within this time period may pinpoint the time when the drug was ingested. Since blood is routinely drawn from the victim during a forensic sexual assault examination (and is collected in a purple-top tube) to be used as a reference sample for DNA testing, it is not difficult to add the collection of a second sample. Blood drawn for toxicology screens should be collected separately in gray-top tubes containing preservatives.

Benzodiazepines remain in the blood from four to 12 hours. GHB remains in the blood from four to eight hours. Drug-facilitated rape cases generally do not turn on the blood sample evidence because by the time the victim recovers from the effects of the drugs (approximately 12 hours from ingestion, depending on the dosage), the drug traces are no longer present in the blood.

Prior to ordering a "full drug screen" for the urine or the blood sample, the investigating officer should explain to the victim what the test entails. Obtain her informed consent. In fact, some states require the investigating officer to obtain the victim's consent before ordering a "full drug screen." Some sexual assault community service and support groups that assist victims have expressed serious reservations about "full drug screens" that may reveal that a victim has ingested other recreational drugs (presumably voluntarily).

Crime Lab Capability

Not every crime lab will have the capability to test the sample at levels adequate to detect these drugs. Therefore, it is important to determine whether the lab used by law enforcement in your jurisdiction is capable of carrying out accurate tests or whether the samples must be sent out of state, for instance, to the FBI.

Screening tests for benzodiazepines currently used in most toxicology laboratories will probably not pick up flunitrazepam (Rohypnol) metabolites (e.g., 7-aminoflunitrazepam and N-desmethylflunitrazepam) in urine, particularly if it is present in residual amounts.[24] It may be necessary to conduct a "sensitive confirmatory test" to detect flunitrazepam metabolites in the urine. A sensitive confirmatory test is a gas chromatography-mass spectrometry (GC/MS) assay that is used to achieve detection limits below 10 nanograms per milliliter for the most commonly encountered drugs used in drug-facilitated sexual assaults.[25] This type of testing, if eventually available, may prove helpful because drug metabolites last longer in the hair shaft than in urine or blood. The hair sample, however, cannot be taken until several weeks after the ingestion of the drug because drug metabolites take weeks to appear in the hair growth above the scalp.

Use of Experts

The value of expert testimony in drug-facilitated sexual assault cases cannot be overestimated. Chemists, toxicologists and pharmacologists have historically testified in drug trials regarding their analyses of the particular drug or drugs involved at trial. In a drug-facilitated sexual assault trial the experts will also testify about their analyses of the drug used to rape the victim. In addition, the experts can explain how the particular drug affects the body in general, how the victim's symptoms are typical of someone who has ingested this drug and why a negative toxicological result occurred (if it did).

Different experts may be necessary for different stages of the trial. For example, if actual drugs were seized (the defendant's "stash" of Rohypnol tablets), a chemist can testify about the "solid dosage analysis" (an analysis of any drug found in the defendant's possession or under his control). A toxicologist can testify about the analysis of a sample from the victim and the methods used to test for the drug. Furthermore, he can testify about possible reasons for a negative result (such as the lapse of time between ingestion and collection of the sample).

If further testimony is necessary to explain the properties or effects of the drug, a pharmacologist (or a scientist, e.g., a toxicologist with a pharmacological background) can describe how the drug works in the body. Testimony from a pharmacologist is always important, but it is critical when no blood or urine sample exists, because the pharmacologist will be the only expert who can explain to the judge and the jury what the drug does and how it affected this particular victim. He or she can explain that the symptoms experienced by the victim are "consistent" with the effects of a drug such as benzodiazepine.

The toxicologist or pharmacologist can also neutralize the potential weaknesses of the prosecutor's case by discussing: the absence of physical trauma,[26] the victim's intoxicated appearance and apparent willingness to leave with the suspect, the victim's inability to remember how she got home, the victim's inability to recall other facts and the victim's impaired spectrum of memory versus impaired quality of memory. For example, the victim may not remember the events of the entire night but she may have a clear memory of certain elements of the assault including: a fragmented memory of the rape; lowered inhibitions, disorientation and loss of motor control; and lingering effects of the drug that prevented her from making a report.

Defense Experts

Although expert witnesses employed by the defense in drug-facilitated sexual assault cases are usually not forensic toxicologists, they may be pharmacologists or physicians. It is important to determine the background of the defense experts prior to cross-examination. Pay particular attention to their actual experience in analyzing forensic biological specimens specific to drug-facilitated sexual assaults. The defense experts may not be familiar with the methods of analysis and the protocols employed by forensic laboratories to detect rape drugs in blood and urine specimens. Thus, they will have no basis on which to attack the laboratory's procedures or to make statements about the prosecution expert's methodology in analyzing the specimens.

The defense may also argue that the victim was intoxicated solely from alcohol rather than a rape drug. To further this argument, the defense may call an expert to testify to the similarities between the symptoms of alcohol intoxication and the symptoms of intoxication caused by a drug like Rohypnol or GHB. The prosecution can counter this argument by calling its own expert to explain that while alcohol is a central nervous system depressant, an extremely large amount must be consumed to achieve the same effect as a small dosage of a rape drug. Although every case is different, many victims experience the onset of the drugs' debilitating effects after no more than one drink (alcoholic or non-alcoholic).

Final Thoughts on Working with Experts

Teamwork is critical to the success of drug-facilitated sexual assault cases. Involve the forensic scientist in the case as early as possible. He or she can identify which biological samples are necessary for testing and can help strengthen the case even when a positive toxicological result is not achieved. Secondly, remember that in the majority of cases, the prosecution will not have the benefit of a blood or urine sample, so it is key to work closely with a pharmacologist who can testify that the victim exhibited symptomology consistent with ingesting benzodiazepines or GHB.

Finally, always remember that in the investigation and prosecution of a drug-facilitated sexual assault, the prosecutor cannot win the case alone. A successful trial depends upon the cooperation of the victim, law enforcement, the victim advocate and the expert witnesses. Foster those relationships as soon as possible. Listen to the victim. Always abide by ethical guidelines, but do not be afraid to be creative or aggressive in prosecuting drug-facilitated sexual assaults.

ENDNOTES

[1] Public Law No: 106-172, signed into law on February 18, 2000, schedules Gamma Hydroxybutryic Acid (GHB) (together with its salts, isomers and salts of isomers) under the Controlled Substances Act (CSA) relating to imminent hazards to public safety. The act directs the federal agencies to: 1) develop model protocols for the collection of toxicology specimens and the taking of victim statements in connection with investigations into prosecutions related to possible violations of the CSA, or other state and federal laws that result in or contribute to rape; 2) make a grant for the development of forensic field tests to assist law enforcement officials in detecting the presence of GHB and related substances; 3) submit to Congress annual incident reports of abuse of date rape drugs that occurred during the most recent year; 4) develop a plan for carrying out a national campaign to educate young adults, youths, law enforcement about abuse of GHB; 5) establish within the Drug Enforcement Administration a special unit that shall assess abuse and trafficking in GHB. http://thomas.loc.gov/cgi-

[2] "Violence Against Women: Estimates from the Redesigned Survey," U.S. Department of Justice, Bureau of Justice Statistics, August 1995.

[3] Benzodiazepines and GHB do not produce anesthesia, which is the loss of pain and other sensations. These drugs do cause sedation and sleep (hypnosis). Individuals who are unconscious due to taking Rohypnol or GHB are not in a true anesthetic state. They will respond to pain and other sensations.

[4] DEA Intelligence Report (Rohypnol), July 1995.

[5] Rohypnol Fact Sheet, Hoffman-LaRoche, Inc.; DEA Intelligence Report (Rohypnol), July 1995.

[6] Rohypnol Fact Sheet, Drug Policy Information Clearinghouse, White House Office of National Drug Control Policy, September 1996.

[7] Rohypnol Fact Sheet, Drug Policy Information Clearinghouse, White House Office of National Drug Control Policy, September 1996; DEA Intelligence Report (Rohypnol), July 1995.

[8] Rohypnol Fact Sheet, Drug Policy Information Clearinghouse, White House Office of National Drug Control Policy, September 1996.

[9] FDA Re-Issues Warning on GHB, FDA Talk Paper, Food and Drug Administration, Feb. 17, 1997; DEA Fact Sheet (GHB), August 1998.

[10] Public Law No: 106-172. The Hillory J.Farias and Samantha Reid Date-Rape Drug Prohibition Act of 1999, February 18, 2000.

[11] DEA Fact Sheet (GHB), August 1998.

[12] Refer to <http://www.lycaeum.org/drugs/GHB/kitchen.html> for a sample "GHB recipe" retrieved from the Internet.

[13] *Id.*

[14] *Id.*

[15] DEA Fact Sheet (GHB), August 1998.

[16] DEA Fact Sheet (GHB), August 1998; Training Bulletin, FDA, Office of Criminal Investigations, San Diego, CA.

[17] This article is excerpted from the American Prosecutors Research Institute's video and binder set entitled, "*The Prosecution of Rohypnol and GHB Related Sexual Assaults.*" The video and binder set were prepared under Grant Number 96-WT-NK-K001 from the U.S. Department of Justice, Office of Justice Programs, Violence Against Women Office. *For more information about the Rohypnol video and binder set, please contact the Violence Against Women Unit at APRI, (703) 519-1695.*

[18] Marc LeBeau, et al, "Recommendations for Toxicological Investigations of Drug-Facilitated Sexual Assaults," 44 *J. Forensic Sci.* 227-230 (1999); Marc LeBeau, "Toxicological Investigations of Drug-Facilitated Sexual Assaults," 1 *Forensic Science Communications* (April 1999).

[19] *Id.*

[20] Different jurisdictions utilize the term "full drug screen" or the term "comprehensive drug screen" to signify the same type of test. We will utilize the term "full drug screen" to include both definitions.

[21] Conducting A Full Drug Screen: When conducting a "full drug screen," confirm that the laboratory is testing the urine and blood samples for: benzodiazepines, amphetamines, muscle relaxants, sleep aids, antihistamines, cocaine, marijuana, barbiturates, opiates and ethanol. All other drugs known to be used in drug-facilitated sexual assaults should also be tested for, such as: GHB, ketamine, scopolamine and any other substance that depresses the central nervous system. Remember to obtain informed victim consent before conducting a "full drug screen."

[22] Marc LeBeau, et al, *supra* note 1.

[23] *Id.* The author suggests collecting 30 ml of blood within 24 hours of ingestion of the drug. In the case of the majority of benzodiazepines, however, the drug will no longer be present in the blood after 12 hours. Ten ml is the minimum amount that should be collected; 30 ml is the maximum amount necessary for testing.

[24] Marc LeBeau, et al, *supra* note 1.

[25] *Id.*

[26] While a prosecutor usually uses a sexual assault nurse examiner or emergency room physician to testify as to the absence of trauma in the genital area, they are not the experts best suited to testify in these types of cases. A pharmacologist can explain that one of the effects of these drugs on the victim is unconsciousness or a relaxed state. The victim's body is not tense because she is not able to resist the assault. Thus, the abrasions that are found at times in victims who are conscious during their sexual assault and offer physical resistance to the assault may not appear in a victim who was unconscious during the assault.

COMBATING ELDER ABUSE

By Paul R. Greenwood, District Attorney's Office, San Diego County, San Diego, California

Introduction

Within five years, the term elder abuse will be as familiar as spousal abuse and child abuse are today. Historically, law enforcement agencies have largely ignored cases involving elderly victims. Police officers have tended to stereotype them, prosecutors have been reluctant to allow seniors to testify and judges have underestimated the impact of abuse on elder crime victims. Prosecutors should take heed that the older generation is the fastest growing section of the United States population and prepare now to meet the future needs of the graying society. This chapter is intended to shatter the myths associated with prosecuting elder abuse and will provide practical pointers for prosecutors to use in combating this escalating crime.

Most states have specific statutes in their criminal codes that provide for elder abuse crimes, but because of outdated perceptions about seniors, few prosecutorial agencies take advantage of such laws. Seniors are typically viewed as poor historians, senile, fragile, long-winded and grumpy. Often, police officers write incomplete crime reports where the alleged victim is elderly because of an unfounded belief that the victim is incapable of providing sufficient information that can lead to a successful prosecution. Yet, prosecutors have the responsibility to train and educate officers about the need to thoroughly investigate all cases of suspected elder abuse and to prepare law enforcement agencies for the anticipated influx of such cases in the next five years.

There has been a trend in recent years among prosecutors to develop specialized skills in prosecuting specific types of crime. Vertical units have been established throughout the country to build expertise in prosecuting cases of child abuse, domestic violence, stalking and gang violence. Elder abuse is one more area of criminal law that lends itself to vertical prosecution. The advantages of vertical prosecution units are clear: prosecutors hone skills and specialize in a particular area of law that assists them in anticipating stock defenses and predictable problems that arise with the facts of the case.

This article makes the assumption that the prosecutor is starting an Elder Abuse Unit from ground zero (or would like to create such a unit) and that in the particular jurisdiction where the prosecutor works, police agencies do not have any specialization in investigating crimes against senior citizens.

ELDER ABUSE: PHYSICAL AND FINANCIAL

Elder abuse takes two basic forms: physical and financial abuse. Within those two broad categories lie other subcategories. The main branches of physical elder abuse are:

- Assault and battery, primarily inflicted by predators who target the elderly in the streets for muggings and robberies; family members (typically sons, daughters and grandchildren) who systematically wield aggression against an elderly relative; and care providers who out of a sense of frustration lash out in anger against the victim;
- Neglect as a result of the care provider's willful or deliberate failure to provide basic services of hygiene, medical support or nutrition to the victim;
- Sexual assault usually against a female Alzheimer's patient in a facility by an employee of that facility; and
- Psychological abuse normally inflicted by a family member in the form of verbal threats that may include hints of personal violence if the victim fails to deliver on financial "commitments."

Financial Elder Abuse

- Thefts by care providers and others who gain the trust of the victim, of such personal effects as jewelry and antiques that inevitably end up in the local pawn shop; theft of individual checks from the back of the checkbook; misuse of the ATM card; credit card fraud after the perpetrator has successfully forged the victim's details in a new credit application that has been obtained without the victim's consent or knowledge; and theft of assets such as savings, stocks or real property by use of a power of attorney or quitclaim deed.
- Scams by professionals who target the elderly using such methods as telemarketing fraud, including bogus charity schemes, illegal sweepstakes and false investments; fraud by door-to-door salespeople who convince the elderly victim to engage in services for a new roof, driveway or other home improvement; and fraud by individuals who obtain access to a senior's assets under the false pretenses of exchanging them for a promise of "life time care."

In order for a prosecutor to establish a successful and effective elder abuse prosecution unit, the following areas should be developed:

- Training of the police to perform thorough investigations of all suspected elder abuse crimes;
- Public awareness campaigns to inform the community of the correct channels for reporting suspected cases of abuse;
- Education of key personnel, including Adult Protective Services (APS) caseworkers, emergency room nurses and doctors, paramedics and fire fighters; and
- Outreach on elder fraud to financial institutions such as banks, credit unions and brokerage firms.

POLICE TRAINING

Law enforcement should be encouraged to treat all suspected cases of elder abuse with the same enthusiasm and dedication as any other serious crime. They should undergo training in elder victim interviewing and investigation techniques that emphasize the use of photographs and videotaped interviews. They should learn to spot the red flag indicators of elder abuse. During investigations, law enforcement should routinely make inquiries among neighbors, relatives and close friends of the elderly victims. Officers need to understand and include in their response protocol their duty to cross-report to APS. In financial abuse investigations, officers should not dismiss the matter as "civil" simply because of the existence of a power of attorney.

PUBLIC AWARENESS CAMPAIGN

Although most counties in the United States have a toll-free telephone number that is reserved for reporting suspected cases of elder abuse, the majority of the public is unfamiliar with this number and has heard little of APS. To educate the public about elder abuse reporting, prosecutors should orchestrate community efforts to create billboards, posters and public service announcements on local television and radio. Slogans such as "abuse is getting old" are an effective means of getting the message out to the public. The number of calls reported to APS will undoubtedly increase after such a public campaign.

EDUCATING KEY PERSONNEL

Prosecutors have a unique opportunity to initiate training and establish reporting protocols for personnel who respond to, transport and treat elder victims of abuse and neglect.

After the initial referral is made via the toll-free number, an APS caseworker is assigned to pay an unannounced call upon the senior. This worker requires training to better recognize and assess the red flags of abuse so that they understand at what point they should bring in law enforcement.

Sometimes, an elderly patient will appear at a hospital suffering from injuries sustained from an assault or because of neglect. Emergency room personnel should be able to differentiate between accidental and intentionally inflicted injuries. The victim may be unwilling to explain truthfully the cause of such injuries and it will be up to the nurse to obtain as many details as possible regarding the patient's living conditions and the events leading up to the patient's arrival at the hospital.

The paramedics are usually the first responders to a domestic call for assistance where an elderly person is in need and they are in the best position to recognize abuse or neglect. If the paramedic is not trained to observe the red flag indicators, there is a danger that the police will not be called to the scene. Like paramedics, fire personnel may also be the first responders to the homes of elderly victims. They also require training to spot potential abuse or neglect.

OUTREACH TO FINANCIAL INSTITUTIONS

Banks, credit unions and brokerage firms are common venues for many financial crimes against seniors. The perpetrator will often take the elderly victim into the financial institution to prepare a power of attorney or arrange for a transfer of monies. Outreach to staff at these institutions will help increase their awareness of the various techniques that are used to exploit seniors and encourage them to be more circumspect in approving alterations to existing financial arrangements. For example, a protocol in which a staff member discusses such alterations with the elderly customer in private, away from the elder's companion, might reveal if the elder understands the financial transaction to be undertaken and, if not, help prevent a crime. Several states are enacting laws that provide immunity to banks when reporting a suspected case of financial elder abuse to APS or to law enforcement.

SENIORS AND THE COURT SYSTEM

Faced with their first exposure to the criminal justice system, many seniors experience fear, confusion and feelings of reluctance. A prepared prosecutor's supportive response to a fragile senior victim can help him or her overcome fear, agree to participate and become an effective witness. Some important factors to consider are the logistics of getting to the trial, medical concerns, personal concerns and physical comfort at the trial.

Find out early on in the case whether the senior has special needs for transportation. The prosecutor, through victim/witness services, may need to provide wheel chair assistance, oxygen or an escort. The senior may require special hearing or optical devices for their court appearance.

Find out if the senior is taking medication that could affect his or her ability to testify. Does the elderly witness cope better in the morning or afternoon? Perhaps the elder is physically incapable of coming to court, which will thereby necessitate a request for the court to be convened at the senior's bedside.

The elder may have a hearing deficiency in one ear. The prosecutor should know such information in order to adjust his or her position in court for questioning the witness. The senior may have a problem with incontinence. Again, this issue should be addressed before the court date in order to alleviate any additional worries that the victim might have while giving testimony.

Inevitably, witnesses are kept waiting at court. Prosecutors should be able to provide seniors with a hospitable and friendly environment in which to wait. Therefore, every effort should be made to establish a waiting area exclusively for seniors, consisting of a room with comfortable sofas and recliners, a television, soft lighting, reading materials and crossword puzzles.

PROFILE OF A TYPICAL PHYSICAL ABUSER

In many cases, the physical abuser will be the son of his widowed mother. He is either divorced and has come back to live at home with Mom because of financial pressures caused by the divorce, or he is single and has never left home. His age tends to be late thirties to mid-forties while his mother is usually in her mid-to-late seventies. In the majority of cases, the son is lazy and unemployed. He will have used a variety of excuses as to why he is unable to work, and his mother has accepted such excuses. He is often addicted to alcohol (normally beer), narcotics or gambling. In order to feed his habit, the son extracts money from his mother. There may come a time when the mother refuses to provide any more money, and this tends to be the flash point for violence. The son may grab his mother's arms and shake her, or may push her into furniture or may throw an object at her. Typically, out of a sense of failure or shame, the mother will not immediately call the police. Often, the neighbors hear the altercations between the son and his mother but they also may be reluctant to involve the police.

BARRIERS TO SUCCESSFUL ELDER ABUSE PROSECUTIONS

The Recanting Victim

Many parallels can be drawn between elder abuse cases and domestic violence cases, particularly in the area of the recanting victim. In such cases where the victim is an elderly parent or grandparent and the defendant is the child or grandchild, it is not uncommon for the victim to recant. After the defendant has been arrested and taken to jail pending an arraignment, the elderly victim sometimes receives a telephone call from the incarcerated perpetrator requesting that charges be dropped. The victim is "reminded" that the defendant is the only friend that the victim has and that harm will come to the defendant in jail unless the victim drops the charges.

In such situations, the elder abuse prosecutor will sometimes be able to give the "tough love" speech to the victim. Other times, the prosecutor will need to impeach the victim with prior inconsistent statements made to a paramedic or emergency room nurse or neighbor. Often, the 911 call is the most persuasive evidence of the victim's state of mind at the time of the alleged incident of abuse. There may be injuries that can corroborate the earlier statements of the victim, as well as evidence of prior similar abusive acts.

Deceased Victims

One of the reasons that seniors are targeted for abuse is that many suspects rely on the fact that by the time the crime is detected, investigated and an arrest is made, the victim may already be dead. It is essential that law enforcement videotape the first interview with the victim in order to preserve the victim's account of the criminal act. Florida went so far as to create a statute that allowed for the introduction of a victim's out of court statement as a statutory exception to the hearsay rule. (FLA. Section 90.803). However, in September 1999, the Florida Supreme Court struck down the statute as being unconstitutional because of the defendant's inability to confront the witness.

California passed a similar law that has become incorporated as Evidence Code section 1380 and took effect in January 2000. California's law is narrower than Florida's statute in that only videotaped interviews of elder abuse victims by law enforcement are admissible, at the discretion of the trial judge. It is hoped that other states will adopt similar legislation and that the anticipated constitutional challenges will be overcome. Such a law will allow the introduction of the videotaped testimony of a victim who after the commission of the crime and before the matter comes to trial either dies or becomes incompetent.

Many physical abuse cases can still be proved beyond a reasonable doubt even in the absence of the victim, although the victim's testimony is often crucial when prosecuting a financial abuse case. Testimony may be the only way to establish that the defendant did not have the victim's consent at the time of the transfer of assets from the victim to the defendant.

Evidence Code section 1380 reads in part as follows:

> [a] In a criminal proceeding charging a criminal violation, or attempted violation, of Section 368 of the Penal Code, evidence of a statement made by a declarant is not made inadmissible by the hearsay rule if the declarant is unavailable as a witness... and all of the following are true:
> [1] The party offering the statement has made a showing of particularized guarantees of trustworthiness regarding the statement, the statement was made under circumstances which indicate its trustworthiness, and the statement was not the result of promise, inducement, threat, or coercion. In making its determination, the court may consider only the circumstances that surround the making of the statement and that render the declarant particularly worthy of belief.
> [2] There is no evidence that the unavailability of the declarant was caused by, aided by, solicited by, or procured on behalf of, the party who is offering the statement.
> [3] The entire statement has been memorialized in a video-

tape recording made by a law enforcement official, prior to the death or disabling of the declarant.

[4] The statement was made by the victim of the alleged violation.

[5] The statement is supported by corroborative evidence.

ESTABLISHING A FINANCIAL ABUSE CASE

Sometimes a prosecutor will be faced with a difficult decision as to whether sufficient evidence exists to prove that a suspect has taken property from the victim without consent and with the intent to permanently deprive. Four different scenarios usually surface, the first two of which are fairly straightforward, leaving the second two a tough call.

In the first instance, the victim is able to testify competently that the defendant took money or property from the victim without consent. The victim may be asked to look at a check, to confirm that the signature is not that of the victim, or at bank records, to show that a series of ATM transactions occurred that were unauthorized by the victim.

In the second instance, the victim is incompetent to testify because of dementia, Alzheimer's or Parkinson's disease. The transactions took place at a time when the victim was already in the condition that has caused the incompetency. The prosecution will be able to have the victim evaluated for incompetency and can lay the appropriate medical testimony foundations to establish that the victim would have been unable to provide the necessary consent at the time of the transaction.

In the third instance, the victim is deceased by the time the discovery is made that monies or property have been removed from the victim during the victim's lifetime. Traditionally, such scenarios have led to an immediate decision by law enforcement not to investigate the matter further because of an inability to prove that the victim did not give consent. It still might be possible to prove a case of theft, however, if there is medical evidence that the victim had been diagnosed with dementia or Alzheimer's, and if the transaction in question was made during a period when the victim did not possess the necessary ability to give true consent.

In the fourth instance, the victim is marginally competent to testify although there may be some signs of short-term memory loss. For example, the victim appears to have voluntarily transferred assets to the suspect and appears to understand the nature and extent of the transaction. The suspect may describe the transfer as either a gift or a loan. Again, law enforcement has traditionally refused to investigate such a scenario on the basis that no apparent crime has been committed.

The scenario may further be compounded by the fact that the victim—prior to the transaction—was taken to meet with an attorney to discuss the impending transfer. That attorney will testify that the client understood the significance of the transaction and wished to proceed. While this scenario is the most difficult to investigate as a theft, it is a situation that has become increasingly common. The prosecutor should consider the legal concept of "undue influence" to provide the basis to prove beyond a reasonable doubt that a theft has occurred. Some of the factors that are extremely helpful in determining whether the suspect has exerted "undue influence" on the victim are:

- The length of the relationship between the victim and suspect. The longer the friendship, the less likely it is that "undue influence" can be established;
- The nature of the relationship between the victim and suspect. If the suspect performed certain services for victim without any other evident remuneration, an assessment should be made to determine whether the amount of the transfer is a reasonable exchange for services rendered;
- The prior spending habits of the victim prior to the transfer. If it can be established that the victim had a history of frugal spending, it might be possible to show that this particular transaction was completely out of character and would require some "undue influence";
- The amount of the transfer compared to the amount left for the victim; sometimes, the victim is left with insufficient funds to provide for unexpected emergencies after the transaction has been completed;
- The documentation that accompanied the transaction. If the suspect maintains at the time of the investigation that the monies were given in the form of a loan, then it might be expected that supporting paperwork evidencing a loan was drafted at the same time;
- Whether the attorney that prepared the documentation was introduced by the suspect to the victim;
- Whether the victim demonstrated any changes in behavior prior to the transaction that might point to signs of short-term memory loss, confusion or a decrease in the ability to make wise decisions; and

• The methods used by the suspect to develop the friendship with the victim. Often in cases of "undue influence" the suspect will gradually isolate the victim from other friendships, causing the victim to become increasingly dependent upon the suspect. In one successful method, the suspect persuades the victim that family members can no longer be trusted and that they are driven only by greed.

The prosecutor should consider having the victim evaluated by a recognized expert in the area of geriatric psychiatry to determine if the victim might be at risk for susceptibility to "undue influence." If the expert is able to render a post-evaluation opinion that the victim is susceptible, then the prosecutor may have sufficient evidence to proceed against the suspect.

RED FLAGS INDICATORS OF ELDER ABUSE

The victim may become increasingly withdrawn from the community and much more dependent upon the perpetrator. If an APS caseworker makes an unannounced visit, the perpetrator may insist that "this is not a good time" to see the elder person, giving the excuse that the victim is sleeping or unwell. Even if access is given, the suspect may try to prevent a private conversation between the victim and social worker by leaving the door open or by hovering over the victim. Family and friends who attempt to make telephone calls may be prevented from speaking directly to the victim.

In financial transactions at a bank, the suspect will attempt to control the conversation with the bank official and will endeavor to speak on behalf of the victim. The bank clerk may be told that the elderly customer is unwell or hard of hearing. The suspect will justify the need for a power of attorney or will insist that any withdrawals be made in cash.

CHARACTERISTICS OF SPECIFIC ELDER ABUSE CRIMES

Assaults and Batteries

Often abusers will assault the elderly victims by shaking their arms, causing bruising above the wrists or by slapping their faces or heads. It is unusual for abusers to use guns. They mostly reach for objects close at hand to use in the assault, such as a wooden cane, a bedpan, a pillow, a kitchen utensil or some other blunt object.

Sexual Assaults

Sexual assaults typically occur within a residential facility setting. Management rarely reports such incidents to law enforcement because of their concerns over litigation or publicity and their wish to avoid responsibility for the wrongdoing. The usual victim is an elderly female Alzheimer's patient and the assault may occur in the bathroom area adjoining the patient's bedroom. Should the incident be discovered, often the facility will typically terminate the employment of the perpetrator who is then free to seek alternative similar employment in another facility.

Neglect

Normally the law provides that before an individual can be charged with elder neglect, there must be in existence a duty to care for that elder. Potential perpetrators include paid care providers and adult children who reside with the elderly parent. Factors that are important in determining if the treatment of the senior rises to the level of neglect are:

- The condition of the residence, including hygiene, cleanliness, the existence of proper food and medications;
- The presence of any "decubitus ulcers" (otherwise known as bed or pressure sores) on the elder person;
- The efforts of the suspect to take the victim for medical treatment;
- The prior statements of the victim to others about the level of care being provided by the suspect;
- The stated preference of the victim to live in a certain manner without the intervention of a doctor;
- The presence of malnutrition, dehydration and the fact that the victim is semi-comatose by the time that medical personnel are notified;
- The lifestyle of the care provider, particularly when there is evidence of abandonment of the senior.

Psychological Threats and Intimidation

The perpetrator is usually a relative (child or grandchild) of the elderly victim. The intimidation is often motivated by a desire to instill fear so that the victim will then comply with giving money to the abuser. The verbal abuse can take the form of a threat to cause harm to a pet or a threat to damage the residence. Telltale signs of such abuse may be the existence of an inside lock on the victim's bedroom door. Other associated crimes may be extortion and robbery.

Theft

This crime is escalating against seniors, primarily because the opportunities are widespread and the chances of detection are relatively slim. The classic way for a care provider to rob an elderly person is by stealing jewelry and other valuables and selling them in the local pawnshop. Seniors are encouraged to keep an inventory of all personal effects including photographs. When stealing checks, the suspect will usually start with a check taken from the back of the current checkbook and will then forge the signature of the victim. Once the suspect discovers how easy it is to cash these checks undetected, he or she will then use the box of unused checks that have previously been mailed to the victim by the bank. Sometimes the suspect distributes the checks to co-conspirators.

Many seniors who employ care providers are unable to walk to and from the mailbox. As a result, the care provider collects the mail and is able to decide what mail the senior should know about. When unsolicited credit card applications with the pre-printed name and address of the unsuspecting senior come in the mail, the perpetrator forges the victim's signature and adds his or her name as an authorized joint user of the card. Once the card arrives, the perpetrator then goes on a spending spree and racks up credit in the name of the victim.

A care provider might also encourage a senior to apply for an ATM card through the mail. As soon as the pin number arrives in the mail, he or she has complete access to the checking and savings accounts of the victim. The perpetrator relies upon the fact that the bank will not question the use of the card and the senior will not look at the bank statements.

So-called travelling salesmen often defraud elders by inducing them to contract for bogus repairs to either the roof or the driveway of their home. Once the defective work is done, the suspect may also use intimidating tactics to arbitrarily raise the contract price or alter the check.

Certain telemarketers prey upon the vulnerability and loneliness of elders to persuade them to engage in financial scams. Popular scams involve the promise of a substantial prize after payment of "state taxes," subscribing to worthless investments or writing out checks to bogus charities.

A trusted professional adviser may persuade the elder client to reinvest his or her investments in high-risk investments or impractical annuities that provide the adviser with a substantial commission.

TIPS FOR INVESTIGATING ELDER ABUSE

It is helpful for prosecutors to have a checklist of investigative resources to pursue that can strengthen an elder abuse case. In cases of elder physical abuse, check if there is a 911 tape in existence; contact APS for a possible history of prior reported abuse; talk to the neighbors for any corroborating testimony regarding loud voices or arguments and take photos of the residence. It is equally important to obtain the victim's consent to disclose his/or her medical records; to interview the attending paramedic or emergency room nurse to see if the victim made any spontaneous statements about the cause of the injuries; and to consult a geriatric physician who can identify and differentiate between intentionally inflicted trauma and accidentally caused injuries.

In financial abuse cases it is important to obtain handwriting exemplars, if possible, from both victim and suspect. Perform a credit check on the victim to see if any recent credit card applications have been made in the victim's name and obtain copies of any credit card transaction slips. When dealing with bank fraud, order checks from the bank showing endorsements; thoroughly review all bank statements for the past year; interview bank clerks; request copies of bank surveillance tapes or photos; and if possible execute a search warrant on the suspect's bank accounts. It is useful to conduct a pawn search when valuables have been stolen. Consider obtaining an evaluation of the victim from a geriatric psychiatrist.

Over the next few years elder abuse will become one of society's most widely reported crimes. It is important that prosecutors prepare now to meet the challenge and develop an expertise so that they can aggressively prosecute the growing number of criminals who are preying upon our nation's elderly citizens.

REFUTING THE DEFENSE EYEWITNESS EXPERT IN AN ETHICAL MANNER

By Joseph Sorrentino, Deputy District Attorney, Los Angeles County, Los Angeles, California

Introduction

As every prosecutor already knows, eyewitness testimony is usually the most vital and compelling aspect of trial. However, this standard of the prosecutorial repertoire is under increasing attack from defense attorneys, experts and even, in several different jurisdictions around the nation, the courts. Additionally, expert testimony, a long-time standard for civil litigation, is seen increasingly in criminal trials. This article examines the problems and the opportunities that will arise for prosecutors if, or more likely when, expert testimony about the accuracy of eyewitness testimony becomes more common. The author discusses strategies employed by prosecutors in the California courts to exploit and counter this defense tactic.[1]

LAW AND COGNITIVE PSYCHOLOGY

In an apparent repudiation of the Kelly-Frye analysis in *People v. McDonald*,[2] the California Supreme Court recently sanctioned the use of expert testimony on the reliability of eyewitness testimony in criminal trials, and thus opened a Pandora's box of psychobabble and pseudo-empirical studies with specious results to sway jurors. No one can fathom the mindset of the justices when they decided *McDonald*. From the perspective of the international scientific community, the generalizations propounded by many of these eyewitness experts typically predicated upon a few classroom studies, have about as much scientific validity as tawdry tabloids. However dubious the wisdom, the law—in California, at least—now allows for eyewitness expert testimony upon a showing to the court that certain criteria have been met. This trend, ill-advised as it may be, appears to be spreading.[3]

In California after invoking the right to prosecutorial discovery under state Proposition 115, the first step is to ascertain at the earliest possible phase if the defense intends to call an eyewitness expert. Oppose this energetically. If the court appears inclined to allow this type of evidence, give the court proper notice of an Evidence Code Section 402 hearing and be prepared with a well-researched, well-reasoned brief with points and authorities to exclude the expert. The principle is well established that the trial judge has discretion to prohibit such testimony. In *People v.*

Brown[4] the California Supreme Court reaffirmed that the trial court retains discretion to exclude expert testimony that is unnecessary in a particular case (although appellate deference is not absolute). The subsequent cases of *People v. Walker*[5] and *People v. Sanders*[6] likewise upheld the rule that discretion remains with the trial court to exclude the expert. A standard was articulated in *McDonald* for reference by the trial court to anchor a ruling:

> When an eyewitness identification of the defendant is a key element of the prosecution's case but is not substantially corroborated by evidence giving it independent reliability, and the defendant offers qualified expert testimony on specific psychological factors shown by the record that could have affected the accuracy of the identification but are not likely to be fully known to or understood by the jury, it will ordinarily be error to exclude the testimony.[7]

The critical variable appears to be independent corroboration such as fingerprint admissions, being in possession of the victim's property, etc.

Once the defense's intention to call an expert is known, ascertain the identity of that expert, request an updated resume and insist upon having a bibliography of all the published sources the expert will rely upon in his or her testimony.[8] Unless a bibliography is specified, the expert will be under no constraints in his or her testimony. The prosecutor can anticipate unbridled references to numerous and unspecified studies that validate his or her opinions. Further, unless the published sources are read, the potentially distorted and misleading citations from those sources will remain uncorrected.

Typically, in order to reinforce his or her views, the eyewitness expert will cite the Kassin[9] survey published in 1989 in *American Psychologist*. It attests to widespread professional acceptance of the validity of psychological research on eyewitness testimony and of psychologists giving testimony based on this research in court. In the Kassin study, over 80 percent of all those surveyed endorsed eyewitness expert testimony. Omitted is the fact that out of more than a thousand cognitive psychologists, only 62 percent were queried in the survey and, of those, 90 percent were expert eyewitnesses for the defense and profiting handsomely. Caveat to prosecutor: Do your homework.

Ideally, the investigation into the background of the anticipated expert should include an exhaustive computer search at a major university's science or medical library. This can be instructive. For instance, the astute researcher may find some of the readily available data which acknowledges that cognitive psychology is a new field, one in its infancy.

Equally critical to preparation is the location of transcripts of prior testimony given by the expert at other trials.[10] The transcript will usually reveal a well-developed presentation designed to ingratiate the expert with the jurors and persuade them of the fragility, unreliability and precariousness of eyewitness identification. It will also provide a sworn record for impeachment purposes. Avoid the complacent expectation that the expert will repeat past traps and mistakes.

DIMINISH THE EXPERT'S ETHOS

In his classical treatise *On Rhetoric*, Aristotle underscores that the ethos of a speaker is a compelling element of persuasion. Obviously, then, in an adversarial confrontation the task is to undercut the expert's ethos in the eyes of the jury. Rule number one is to control the cross-examination with simply framed questions amenable to a yes or no answer. If the expert violates the context of the question, have the judge repeatedly admonish him or her. Open-ended questions will invariably lead to a scholarly exegesis calculated to bury the query and make the expert shine. Moreover, maintain a calm and professional composure during cross-examination or it will be your ethos hemorrhaging before the jury.

Clearly, the first vulnerability of the expert is bias: the fact that he or she has been repeatedly called by the defense, has been rewarded monetarily and has not come forward out of a commitment to justice but one of profit. Let it be known to the jury through questioning that this expert has absolutely no empirical knowledge with respect to the matter on trial. He or she has never questioned the witnesses, never been to the crime scene and never conferred with the investigating officer. The expert has no idea how stress would affect any witness in this case and has never tested any of them for their tolerance to stress.

Further, elicit the concession that the expert is not testifying to give an opinion as to whether any given witness testimony is accurate or inaccurate in this case. Make the expert also acknowledge that eyewitnesses can be highly accurate in making identifications. Take the expert down a peg by getting an admission that he or she is not a licensed psychologist as opposed to a clinical psychologist. Erode the expert's ethos by calling to attention a personal lack of published studies in the areas of his or her testimony: the expert has never conducted a weapon focus test, never done a study on the effects of stress on memory and never performed an experiment on the confidence-accuracy factor.[11] Portray the witness as a secondhand expert who relies on hearsay reports by other academics.

Contemplate questions that will make the expert come across as absurdly unreasonable. Ask if the expert believes cognitive psychology (founded circa 1958) has the same empirical reliability as physics (first treatise 2,000 B.C.) or chemistry. Ask a "Columbo" type of question: "Gee, Doctor, according to you, there have been only two weapon focus studies. Are you saying that based on those two studies you can generalize for the six billion people on this planet?" The expert might reply:[12] "Well, I wouldn't say the planet but all the people living in the United States." His answer could trigger another Columbo question: "Oh, so what you are saying here today does not apply to Canada? And how about the millions of recent immigrants to this country from all over the planet?"

REFUTE THE EXPERT BY CITING CONTRARY EXPERTISE

The best way for prosecutors to refute defense experts is to call a prosecution expert, armed with all of the studies with conclusions antithetical to what the defendants have claimed. The prosecutor can go point-by-point with respect to weapons and the impact of stress on memory, etc., and the expert will be able to cite studies that refute the defense expert's claims. However, when unable to afford one or retain one, be prepared to cite the following studies on cross-examination:

- In "Emotional Stress and Eyewitness Memory: A Critical Review" published in 1992 in *Psychological Bulletin,* Volume 112, Dr. Sven Christianson of the University of Stockholm reported that different studies found very different and frequently contrary results on how stress affected memory. Dr. Christianson's article contains a lengthy bibliography of studies helpful to the prosecution.
- The authors conclude, in reviewing 13 different experiments on cross-racial identification, that there is no consistent relationship in a chapter entitled "What Do We Really Know About Cross-Race Eyewitness Identification?" *Evaluating Witness Evidence,* published in 1983 by John Wiley & Sons Ltd.

- In the area of witness accuracy, J.C. Yuille and J.L. Cutshall found that the memory of real witnesses to a crime was as accurate overall four to five months after the crime as it was in police interviews conducted at the scene within two days of the crime.[13]
- The much-cited Loftus[14] study on weapon focus can be refuted by citing a 1990 article entitled "Weapon Focus, Arousal and Eyewitness Memory" by T.H. Kramer and R. Buckout in *Law and Human Behavior,* Vol. 14, 167-184. These two prominent psychologists found that whether or not a weapon was used in the situation made no difference in identification accuracy.
- Professor Ebbe B. Ebbesen and Vladimir J. Konecni of the University of California, San Diego, have made an excellent presentation delineating the full range of issues and citing all the authorities favorable to the prosecution entitled "Eyewitness Memory Research: Probative v. Prejudicial Value." It can be obtained by contacting the professors directly and by gaining their permission to quote it.[15]

Among the earliest vigorous critics of eyewitness expert testimony were Professors M. McCloskey and H.E. Egeth of Johns Hopkins University. In a 1983 article in *American Psychologist,* Vol. 38, 550-563, they wrote, "Where Loftus is willing to draw a sweeping conclusion, for example, effects of stress and weapon focus, confidence and accuracy, we feel there is insufficient evidence to merit such conclusions." Defense experts will selectively cite only those studies that buttress their claims. By skillfully utilizing the opposing literature, the prosecutor can demonstrate that the notions propounded by the defense expert are far from universally accepted scientific norms.

COUNTER THE EXPERT'S CLAIMS WITH COMMON SENSE EXAMPLES

Jurors are easily lost in the turgid, inflated jargon of cognitive psychology. By relating simple, common sense examples the prosecutor can effectively derail an expert's premises. Axiomatic to common sense is how little is known about memory functions. The defense expert's constant contention will be that a traumatic or stressful experience will impair the victim's ability to clearly recall the event. To counter that claim, remind the expert and the jury that many victims of molestation can graphically recall what happened to them years ago. Many rape victims have nightmares in which they still vividly see the attacker's face. Combat veterans have nightmares and flashbacks of battles where they see agonized expressions of buddies. Married couples can vicariously relive the day that they first met 10 or 20 years ago and can see each other the way they looked on that blissful day. Who can forget where they were on the day of a big earthquake or tornado or hurricane, when President Kennedy was assassinated in Dallas or when the Challenger exploded?

Another point to focus on is the variability of human beings and the incredible range of differences in how they might react to the same stimulus. In war, some will be heroes, others will be cowards and most will strive to survive. Of course, ever present is the Lord Jim syndrome, in which the same person will react differently on different days—be a hero one day and a coward the next.

Jurors react skeptically when they are informed that the findings of these experts are all based on classroom studies that overwhelmingly use middle class students from suburbia. Young people growing up in a tough inner city neighborhood may have a different perspective on weapons and on violence. For example, none of the studies have ever used Latino witnesses or subjects who have grown up in a minority community. Furthermore, enormous differences exist between students in a classroom and real crime witnesses. An actual victim can be provoked to anger by the aggression, which creates a motivation to concentrate and scrutinize the attacker's features. No such motivation of revenge or anger exists in a classroom or a simulated scene. A crime victim will be focused on the intruder; a student at one of these classroom studies might be daydreaming about a hot date, be depressed or drowsy, in a prankish mood, inclined to please the teacher or may be only concerned about the reward to be earned for participating.

A participant in a controlled study can conjure countless moods and motivations for students not remotely akin to what a crime victim is feeling. The expert will make much of the fact that the witness cannot give precise descriptions. We all know that at times we cannot describe a person but, if he or she walks in the door, an alarm goes off in our brains and our recognition can be instantaneous. A rape victim will sometimes re-experience the original fear provoked by the attacker, tremble and even break out in a sweat upon seeing the rapist again, even though prior to the occasion she could not precisely describe him.

In closing argument, inject scenes from movies that jurors will have no trouble recalling. Ask the jurors to close their eyes and envision the face of Ingrid Bergman with her hat at the airport in the closing scene of *Casablanca*, or ask them to recall the scene from *Rocky* when, after running up the stairs, he turns and raises his arms facing the city; or Marlon Brando as the godfather, sitting at his desk in a tuxedo at his daughter's wedding. By asking them to conjure up these images from old movies, it obliterates the notion that we lose the ability to recall faces.

ASSAIL THE METHODOLOGY OF COGNITIVE PSYCHOLOGY

The objective of the defense expert is to persuade jurors that based on rigorous, scientific methods certain reliable precepts have been arrived at with respect to eyewitness identification. In voir dire keep a vigil for prospective jurors with a science education because they will quickly dissect the expert's preposterous claims. The first salvo should be to pin the expert down on his ideas stage of validation, i.e. science continuously expands our understanding of natural phenomena by proposing provisional hypotheses of cause and effect. Their validity is explored by sifting through the maze of experimental observations, with the goal of limiting the probability of alternative explications. Predictive power is the penultimate benchmark—if a hypothesis passes these tests it evolves over time into accepted knowledge.

Therefore, analyze the witnesses' methodology. Ask the expert if, in light of the sparse number of studies and their relative newness, he considers weapon focus a provisional hypothesis, a working theory or an established scientific law. Target the most patently untenable categories in the field. Expose the miniscule empirical sample—only a few studies and a few hundred students—that form the predicate for incredibly sweeping generalizations. Highlight the distinction between experiments in the physical versus the social sciences.[16] Molecules are constant and have unvarying properties, in contrast to human beings that manifest a wondrous, mind-boggling range of kaleidoscopic differences. For example, turbulence generates all kinds of reactions in air travelers, from serene calm to boredom to nervousness to compulsive drinking to white-knuckled anxiety to near panic.

Synthetic classroom studies cannot replicate the conditions of an actual crime. Showing a parade of faces to test recollection may have little or no relevance to the very real life scenario of a single gunman. Viewing a simulated scene on film may not be remotely akin to a real visceral encounter. In the vaunted science of cognitive psychology, conspicuously absent are calibrations addressing time frames, distance, angles, lighting and countless other physical variables. For example, in an experiment in which the finding is based on a five-to-ten second exposure, what value does that experiment have when the actual exposure duration in the case lasted for one minute? Or, if in the experiment the subject watched from 30 feet away, how does that relate to a face-to-face confrontation? To what degree does the film actor's aesthetics and sex appeal (or lack thereof) affect the student's concentration? What percentage of the studies involved students? Were they paid? Did they receive academic credit?

It should be pointed out that the expert's confidence accuracy claim conflicts with CALJIC (California Jury Instruction) 2.92,8 that was postulated after years of cumulative trial experience. The law instructs jurors to give added weight to certitude in an identification. Weapon focus can be challenged as debatable dogma and subjective interpretation. How familiar with weapons were the subjects in the studies? Isn't it rather bizarre to predicate, as at least one study has done, a weapon focus finding on a hypodermic needle? How many people in the classroom studies were from the inner city? Isn't survival frequently a matter of cooperation or seeking to please the gunman, which means gazing at his eyes for the state of his intentions? After all, anyone who watches football knows that the defensive back must key in on the quarterback's eyes to fathom his next move.

Remind the jury, by use of recent events, how premature ambitious professionals often are to proclaim new scientific findings. Remember the claim that cold fusion had been created in a laboratory. On March 23, 1989, Stanley Pons and Martin Fleishman of the University of Utah told the world they had done that very thing. Eventually they were absolutely discredited.

Spawned only in the late 1950s, cognitive psychology is still in its infancy, probing and groping to find its way. In the larger realm of psychology there is still no unifying, cohesive, accepted theory of human behavior. Scores of theorists—Freudians, Adlerians, Jungians, Rankians, followers of Frankel, Rogers, Maslov, Pavlov, Watson, Rotter, Horney, Sullivan, and others—are in a seemingly unending battle of babble over the definition of the core of human motivation.

BRING IN HEAVY ARTILLERY: THE PROSECUTION EXPERT

If it appears that the defense will be using an eyewitness expert, go the full measure and have an eyewitness expert lined up for rebuttal. One of these is Dr. Ebbe B. Ebbesen. Cited earlier for his excellent work on eyewitness memory research, Dr.

Ebbesen, formerly at Stanford University and currently at the University of California, San Diego, will only testify for the prosecution. He believes that a balanced scholarly view of all the evidence does not justify any of the generalizations typically made by eyewitness experts testifying for the defense.

In his testimony, Dr. Ebbesen renders ridiculous the claim that a quantifiable measure of stress has been achieved through the galvanic skin test. For virtually all of the studies cited by defense eyewitness experts that purportedly establish a given conclusion, Dr. Ebbesen will cite studies that have arrived at other conclusions. He will cogently demonstrate how the field of cognitive psychology is in serious conflict and disarray. This is contrary to what the defense expert wants the jury to accept. Further, he argues that a generally accepted theory of eyewitness identification reliability does not exist. Before using results from studies that assert eyewitness memory can be applied to real witnesses of real crimes, Ebbesen logically points out that researchers should establish that they have created the same memory processes and motivational states in their test subjects as are experienced by witnesses and victims of actual crimes. Obviously this has not been done (and never will be).

Be creative in using graphic means to illustrate the prosecution's expert testimony. Decide what graphics to use in time to have a technician prepare them skillfully. The use of impressive graphics will enhance the jury's view of the prosecutor's professionalism. Be creative in how the expert's testimony is elicited. Make it dramatic. Make it catch the jurors' attention. Above all, make it accurate.

ADHERING TO ETHICAL STANDARDS

In addition to legal and tactical considerations, there are also ethical considerations in terms of the prosecutor's decisions and actions in a trial involving a defense eyewitness expert. For example, suppose that in the office's expert file on Dr. X a number of transcripts are discovered showing that he has testified inconsistently on the very issue of the case. In addition, the name of a witness is found who can testify that he heard Dr. X say two years earlier that, "This is junk science that I do. I'm only in it for the money." Does the prosecutor have an obligation to disclose the existence of the likely impeaching transcripts or of the potential impeaching witness? According to case law, in California anyway, the prosecutor does have this obligation.[17]

Is the prosecutor legally and ethically obliged to disclose to the other side that a scientific expert will be called in rebuttal? Since the expert is not going to be a part of the case-in-chief and will be testifying only in response to what the defense expert has testified to during the discovery, this is not clear in many jurisdictions. But in order to leave no room for ethical criticism, the defense lawyer should be informed that the prosecution intends to call an expert in rebuttal. On the other hand, if during case research, the prosecutor encounters a study favorable to the defense expert, there is no obligation to disclose such a study since it belongs in the realm of opinion and theory as opposed to exculpatory fact.

ENDNOTES

[1] Note: Readers from the other 49 states should avoid complacency about this topic, as use of these types of experts is spreading throughout the nation.

[2] *People v McDonald,* 37 Cal. 3d 351, __ P.2d __ (1984).

[3] The 3rd U.S. Circuit, Florida and New Jersey all share this problem to some degree.

[4] *People v. Brown,* 40 Cal. 3d 512, __ P.2d __ (1985).

[5] *People v. Walker,* 47 Cal. 3d 605, __ P.2d __ (1988).

[6] *People v. Sanders,* 51 Cal. 3d 471, __ P.2d __ (1990).

[7] *People v. McDonald,* 37 Cal. 3d, at 377, __ P.2d __ at __ (1990).

[8] Obviously, what a defendant is required to disclose prior to trial will depend on the discovery rule in the particular jurisdiction.

[9] Kassin, S., Ellinsworth, P., & Smith, V. (1989) The "General Acceptance" of Psychological Research on Eyewitness Testimony: A Survey of Experts. *American Psychologist,* 44, 1089-1098.

[10] Check around with other prosecutors in the office or in other jurisdictions if a data bank has not yet been established.

[11] Your research will alert you to the best areas in which to concentrate your questions.

[12] As he did in my case.

[13] J. C. Yuille and J.L. Cutshall, *Journal of Applied Psychology,* 71, (1986), 291-301.

[14] Loftus, E.F. (1974) *Eyewitness Testimony,* Cambridge, Mass., Harvard University Press. For a broader analysis of line-ups, see Cutler, B.L. & Penrod, S.D. (1988) Improving Reliability of Eyewitness Identification: Line-up Construction and Presentation. *Journal of Applied Psychology,* 73, 281-290.

[15] Dr, Ebbe B. Ebbesen, Psychology Department C-009, University of California at San Diego, LaJolla, California 92093, (619-534-3000).

[16] Decades of duplication and infinite replications are required in physics or chemistry before a theory becomes a scientific law.

[17] *See Izzazaga v. Superior Court* 54 Cal. 3d 356, 376-77, __ P.2d __ (1991).

THE UNIQUE CHALLENGES OF PROSECUTING SHAKEN BABY CASES

By Rob Parrish, Chief Child Abuse Counsel, Office of the Attorney General, Salt Lake City, Utah

Most prosecutors will tell you, whether they have handled 30 or 300 trials and even if they specialize in the realm of child abuse and homicide, that the first trial involving a shaken baby presents new and incomparable challenges. This article explores the unique features of shaken baby cases, strategies for proving them in criminal prosecution and incentives for successfully meeting the difficult challenges posed by child abuse issues.

It is unclear how many children suffer permanent brain damage, blindness or death as a result of being violently shaken each year. National child homicide statistics are believed to be under reported because they are based on official death certificates, many of which misidentify the child's death as "undetermined" or "natural"[1] when a later criminal investigation and prosecution establish that the child was killed by abuse.[2] We know, however, from direct contact with the families of victims of this tragedy that hundreds and possibly thousands of children are affected each year. For every case that is accurately diagnosed by medical professionals, there are probably several where the medical findings have been so subtle or non-specific that a particular diagnosis cannot be made. The milder shaking of children and infants, never reported or diagnosed, may account for learning deficits, behavioral disorders and other problems in the lives of victims as they grow up.[3]

UNDERSTANDING THE MEDICAL ISSUES

Successful prosecution of a shaken baby case demands that the prosecutor learn the medical dynamics of the syndrome and understand the significance of the injuries caused by shaking. This article is limited in scope to cases where the child suffers permanent brain damage or death.

Medical professionals who specialize in the treatment of abused and neglected children generally agree that the combination of retinal hemorrhages or other ocular damage, intra-cranial bleeding (most often subdural or subarachnoid hematoma) and evidence of direct damage to the tissue of the brain (often described in reports as "diffuse axonal injury") uniquely indicates severe and violent rotational action as a cause. In the absence of a severe automobile accident or some other accident involving equivalent forces, the existence of this constellation of injuries is usually "pathognomonic" (diagnostic) for shaking. "No other condition fully mimics all the features of shaken-impact syndrome."[4]

The only debate among medical professionals on the diagnosis of shaken baby injuries centers on the mere shaking of the infant as the sole cause of permanent damage or death. Dr. Anne-Christine Duhaime and colleagues employed dolls designed to simulate human infant response to conduct biomechanical research on shaken baby syndrome (SBS). They established that the G-forces applied to the doll's head were up to 30 times more severe when the head impacted a surface producing a sudden deceleration, than when it was shaken violently in a whiplash motion.[5] Dr. Duhaime and Dr. Derek Bruce among others believe that the shaking alone is insufficient to cause death or serious injury, arguing that the syndrome should be called the Shaken Impact Syndrome.

The experts who dispute Duhaime's conclusion assert that shaking does produce forces sufficiently violent to explain serious brain injury or death. They argue that the Duhaime model "does not simulate the rotational and shearing forces within the brain on vessels and neurons where the damage occurs, nor does it take into account the possibility that the propensity for damage may be increased by the repetitive nature of the injury rather than the size of the force alone."[6]

Interestingly, this debate within the medical profession has little significance in the courtroom. If the experts who assert that a sudden impact is required in addition to shaking to cause death or permanent injury are correct, then we should assume that a baby who has suffered permanent brain damage or death has been shaken *and* suffered an impact. Defense attorneys argue that if there is no direct medical evidence of impact then there has been no impact. It is fairly simple to explain, however, that a child's head impacting on a soft surface may cause no external damage, fracture or bruise but does cause a severe deceleration of the brain within the skull. Plunkett argues that because of the inability to experiment with live children there is insufficient scientific support for the diagnosis of SBS.[7]

Research is establishing that there are few causes of retinal hemorrhages or evidence of other ocular damage that do not arise from shaken baby injuries; therefore, the importance of this diagnosis cannot be overemphasized. The documentation of retinal hemorrhage, retinal detachment, vitreous bleeding or direct damage to the optic nerve is rare in almost any type of linear fall suffered by a toddler or infant. With respect to SBS, the *hallmark injury* is retinal hemorrhage.[8]

Even in severe auto accidents, retinal hemorrhage or other ocular damage is rare in the absence of a direct concussive injury to the eye itself, and then the findings are usually anterior chamber damage. Although there are anecdotal studies published where physicians claim that CPR has caused retinal hemorrhages, other more representative studies illustrate that the occurrence of retinal hemorrhages from CPR is extremely unlikely, especially when administered appropriately to an infant or young child.[9]

Prosecutors should be aware of the fact that retinal hemorrhages occur in approximately 30 percent of vaginal births as a result of the birth process, although experts generally describe those hemorrhages as different in nature from those associated with traumatic causes. It is important that the prosecutor convey to the jury that birth-related retinal hemorrhages usually resolve within six weeks of birth. Furthermore, there is no evidence that even a very young infant with both retinal hemorrhages and subdural bleeding or other evidence of direct brain injury has suffered *all* of those injuries during birth. Finally, certain diseases cause retinal hemorrhages, such as GA-1, Vitamin K deficiency, meningitis, leukemia, osteogenesis imperfecta (brittle bone disease) and other congenital conditions involving coagulopathy (bleeding disorders). Tests should be conducted to rule out these conditions during autopsy, the clinical treatment of severely injured children or during any related court proceeding.

For those children who die as a result of shaking, there is sometimes an additional finding made during the autopsy of a "diffuse axonal injury," or a direct injury to the tissues of the brain caused by the shearing forces applied during rotational shaking. This finding is often absent in children under the age of five months and may not appear at all in children who have been fatally shaken unless they have been sustained on life support for a significant period of time. When present, it is diagnostic of severe rotational force having been applied to the head. Nothing else accounts for the shearing of the axons within the brain. The absence of a specific finding of "diffuse axonal injury" does not mean that the brain has not been directly injured, only that the changes associated with the healing process cannot be identified microscopically after the fact.

There is some debate in the medical field as to whether SBS can be diagnosed where there are retinal hemorrhages, brain swelling and death but no evidence of intracranial bleeding. Most physicians feel that, at a minimum, there must be ocular findings as well as intracranial bleeding to allow a diagnosis of SBS. However, where there are retinal findings such as bilateral hemorrhage or detachment or folds of the retina and where disease processes have been ruled out, severe trauma can be the only explanation. Where there is intracranial bleeding in the absence of retinal findings, trauma is almost always the cause, but SBS may be more difficult to establish as the cause of the trauma. In one documented case, a two-month-old baby was grasped by the head and his body shaken violently, causing damage to the anterior spinal artery, the base of the brain and the anterior chamber of the baby's eyes. In that case, there was no evidence of retinal damage or bleeding and no upper hemisphere bleeding into the baby's brain.[10]

The onset of symptoms is usually the best way for expert medical witnesses to judge when a particular injury or set of injuries was inflicted upon a child. Studies of children who suffered head injuries in documented accidents have shown that it is highly unlikely that there is any "lucid interval" between a violent shaking and the onset of symptoms such as breathing difficulty, change in level of consciousness, seizure activity or other problems associated with neurological damage.[11] Defense attorneys and their experts often try to expand the time frame in which an injury could have occurred to allow for the possibility of other perpetrators. However, there is no scientifically valid study that proves that there can be a "lucid interval" between a fatal or serious shaking and the onset of symptoms. Common sense would dictate that such a suggestion is ridiculous.

PROVING SBS IN COURT

Given the importance of medical information in the support of a diagnosis of SBS, it is essential that prosecutors carefully consider the qualifications of those professionals whom they call as expert witnesses. Often the best expert witnesses are pediatricians associated with a child protection team at a children's hospital who are specially trained in child abuse recognition and have clinical experience diagnosing the causes of injuries to children. It may also be necessary to use a pediatric neurosurgeon or neurologist to address specific findings relevant to brain damage in shaken baby cases. If the ocular findings are significant, a pediatric ophthalmologist or ophthalmic pathologist may become an important additional witness.

Not all local coroners or medical examiners have the same level of expertise in recognition of SBS. If the child victim has died as a result of the abuse, it may be necessary to call not only the pathologist who performs the autopsy but also a consulting forensic pathologist with specific experience diagnosing child abuse fatalities. In addition to a pathologist, in fatal abuse cases, prosecutors should also use a clinician, such as a pediatrician, who can discuss studies showing that children do not suffer fatal or life-threatening outcomes from routine household accidents and falls.

Medical experts can usually answer the question of what happened to the child that resulted in the specific findings in the case. Furthermore, they can discuss during direct examination why there can only be one reasonable explanation for the combination of injuries that are unique to SBS. The prosecution's experts should also explain what tests have been conducted to rule out disease and natural conditions as factors, and why accidental causes do not explain the child's injuries. The explanations of accidental causes offered by the caretakers and any other conceivable random cause, should all be addressed, so that the door is tightly closed to possible defenses during the prosecution's case-in-chief.

The expert medical witnesses should explain the nature of the violent forces involved when a child is shaken so hard as to cause permanent brain damage or death, illustrating their opinions with clear and concise descriptions of the mechanism of injury. Courtroom demonstrations with a doll may be problematic unless the expert explains that the doll does not represent the victim in weight and size and that the demonstration only conveys the violence of a shaking without replicating how the victim was shaken.[12]

A demonstration with photographs or video that explains the movement of the baby's head during shaking and what occurs to the brain within the baby's skull may more effectively depict the rotational forces unique to SBS and assist in conveying the perpetrator's violent state. Seeing is believing. A video presentation is a superb tool for assisting the jury in understanding how the injury occurs and for creating a powerful, compelling visual image to support the expert's testimony.[13] When the jury watches as the brain rocks back and forth inside the baby's skull, they cannot avoid relating to the otherwise dry, scientific explanations.[14]

The American Academy of Pediatrics determined in 1993 that: "The act of shaking/slamming is so violent that competent individuals observing it would recognize it as dangerous."[15] Although an expert cannot tell what was in a particular perpetrator's mind when the shaking occurred, this general statement—reflecting a consensus of the Academy's Committee on Child Abuse and Neglect—can be the basis for expert opinion. It supports an argument that absent some mental disease or defect, any person would be at least aware of a risk of serious injury or death resulting from the shaking.

The Supreme Court of California resolved the issue of whether the prosecution is required to prove that the defendant knew the exact risks involved with shaking or had only a general intent to engage in the dangerous conduct in the case of *People v. Sargent.* "While defendant denied awareness that his actions were likely to harm Michael, any reasonable person would recognize that shaking a four and one-half month-old infant, who had been born three months premature and had the neck development of a four to six-week-old, with the force equivalent to dropping him out of a second story window, was a circumstance or condition likely to result in great bodily harm or death."[16] This decision is critically important to prosecutors because, as every criminal practitioner knows, absent an admission of guilt it can be very difficult to prove the mental state of the defendant. The court concluded that the prosecution only needed to show this general awareness of the risk, not specific awareness of the exact injuries that could be inflicted upon the baby as a result of shaking. Other courts should follow this logic unless statutory elements of a crime require a showing of specific intent.

Often in SBS cases, the most important aspect of the medical expert opinion is a mix of medical knowledge and investigative fact relating to the timing of the inflicted injuries. It is essential that the prosecutor provide the caretakers' account of the onset of symptoms to the expert medical witnesses to assist them in forming an opinion as to when the shaking occurred. There exists an almost universal consensus among SBS experts that the onset of symptoms for those children who suffer permanent brain injury or death from shaking is virtually immediate. Most experts can express an opinion on the timing of the inflicted injuries based on the onset of symptoms and the evidence of rapid deterioration of the child's neurological function.

Prosecutors should not be concerned, though, when the radiologist who only examines CT scans of the child's brain expresses an opinion that the injury could have occurred within up to 72 hours. Radiographic dating of injuries is less accurate than dating by a neurologist or neurosurgeon who draws upon the medical findings, the onset of symptoms and the rapid decline of the baby's health to form an opinion.

When the child dies, a microscopic examination of tissues and injuries allows for an even more accurate dating based upon the way the body attempts to heal itself. Even in the absence of evidence as to when the baby became symptomatic, EMTs, ambulance crews, life-flight crews and emergency room personnel readily document the rapidly declining health of the child, which can assist experts in pinning down the likely time of infliction of the serious brain injuries.

In some cases, the identity of the individual who inflicted the injury is as easy to prove as the timing of the events, based on the caretakers' statements regarding the child's symptoms. Caretakers who abuse children usually lie about their actions and concoct a fictional account of an accident to explain the injury. On the other hand, caretakers rarely lie about the onset of symptoms or misrepresent who was with the child when the symptoms appeared. All of their statements become relevant when piecing together what happened to the child and when.

If there is no clear indication from the evidence which caretakers were with the child at the time the injury was inflicted, prosecutors and investigators must look to more subtle factors to determinate the identity of the abuser. Sometimes, even the best investigation does not identify who among the possible perpetrators committed the crime, but usually an examination of the details of the case will point with some alacrity to one of several potential defendants. If two partners appear to know what happened to the baby and both tell the same inadequate story to explain the injuries, the likelihood is that both know who committed the abuse and have agreed upon what must be said to cover it up. In many jurisdictions, such partners are equally culpable—one for causing the injury and the other for knowingly permitting the abuse.

Anticipating and confronting defense "theories" is an important part of the prosecutor's case-in-chief. As previously stated, the prosecution's medical expert witnesses should explain why accidental causes, especially the accidental explanations offered by the defendant, do not account for the severe injuries to the child. They should also explain that retinal hemorrhages or intracranial bleeding caused by disease have been ruled out in the case and they should describe the symptoms the baby would have displayed had he or she suffered from the disease prior to the injury.

A favorite defense "theory" in SBS cases will assert that the baby died from normal handling following a previous head injury which, having been aggravated, caused sudden deterioration of the baby's neurological condition and death. This so-called "second-impact theory" has only been shown to apply to adolescents and adults and never to infants or toddlers. Closely associated with the "second-impact theory" is the "re-bleed" theory, a claim that once a child has suffered a head injury, a minor amount of trauma can cause re-bleeding. As Drs. Reece and Kirschner point out:

> It is important to state that there is no evidence to support the concept that re-bleeding of an older subdural hematoma can result from trivial injury and cause an infant to suddenly collapse and die. The subdural bleeding is only significant in that it is a marker for the traumatic episode to the brain that produces all the clinical signs and symptoms. Even if such a re-bleeding should occur, it does not cause traumatic injury to the brain.[17]

Generally, any expert witness called by the defense will attempt to explain that there are other possible causes of individual findings, such as the subdural bleeding or the retinal hemorrhages. Such experts should not be allowed to isolate individual findings as though they occurred in a vacuum but must be challenged to provide an explanation that fits the entire constellation of injuries documented in the child. According to Dr. Duhaime and colleagues, there is no other disease process or accidental or natural cause that mimics all the signs and symptoms of SBS.[18]

As with most child abuse prosecutions where a child sustains fatal or life-threatening injuries, evidence of older injuries indicates that the shaken baby had been abused prior to the final incident. Often, shaking has been accompanied by squeezing of the child and has resulted in rib fractures. When those rib fractures are posterior, near the baby's spine, they are virtually diagnostic of abuse as the cause. Sometimes the long bones are also fractured during violent shaking, when the limbs have been gyrating unrestrained during the whiplash motion. Evidence of prior inflicted injuries to the victim helps to establish the Battered Child Syndrome, to show that the final injuries were not the result of accident, and to establish both the identity and mental state of the perpetrator of the final abuse.[19]

Although the majority of proof in shaken baby cases comes from medical experts and the statements of the caretakers of the child, prosecutors and investigators should exhaust other sources of evidence that might assist in determining the identity of the abuser and the motive. Fellow workers, friends or family members may be able to document that abusers have been under particularly difficult stresses around the times of the injuries. Sometimes abusers have actually made statements to others about their difficulty in caring for the baby or their wish that the baby had never been born. A live-in partner may have been jealous of the attention that the baby received from the parent and have a motive to kill the child to secure all of the affection. Or, it sometimes happens that the act of shaking may have been a single act of violence towards the child for which the perpetrator confesses and expresses remorse. Some form of punishment is nevertheless appropriate in these rare cases if the person's violent attack has caused permanent brain damage to the baby or death.[20]

THE CHALLENGE OF DIFFICULT PROSECUTIONS

As the medical science relating to identification of cause of injuries to children continues to progress, we in the justice system struggle to keep up and to apply scientific conclusions to actual cases where children have been seriously injured or killed. Only if investigators and prosecutors are willing to take on the challenge to learn about the medical issues in SBS cases and spend extra time "wallowing" in the details of a case, can we assure child victims that their abusers will be held accountable. Given the fact that most abusers will continue to inflict injury on children when they are over-stressed, in the absence of an admission of culpability and effective treatment, criminal prosecution is often the only way to remove the danger they present. Putting a SBS case together can be taxing and emotionally exhausting, but the satisfaction of proving a child abuse case and achieving a modicum of justice for that child and his/her family is richly rewarding—and more than ample compensation for the effort.

ENDNOTES

[1] Herman-Giddins ME, Brown G, Verbiest S, Carlson PJ, Hooten EG, Howell E, Butts JD., "Underascertainment of Child Abuse Mortality in the United States," *JAMA*, 1999 Aug 4; 282(5): 463(7).

[2] C.J. Levitt, W.L. Smith and R.C. Alexander, "Abusive Head Trauma," *Child Abuse: Medical Diagnosis and Management*, ed. Robert Reece, Baltimore: Lea & Febiger (1994): 17-19.

[3] *See* R. Reece and R. Kirschner, *Shaken Baby Syndrome/Shaken Impact Syndrome*, National Information, Support and Referral Service on Shaken Baby Syndrome newsletter, (Summer, 1998); R.C. Alexander et al., "Incidence of Impact Trauma with Cranial Injuries Ascribed to Shaking," *Am. J. Dis. Child* 144(6):724-26 (1990); J. Caffey, "The Whiplash-Shaken Infant Syndrome: Manual Shaking by the Extremities with Whiplash-Induced Intracranial and Intraocular Bleedings, Linked with Permanent Brain Damage and Mental Retardation," *Pediatrics* 54(4):396-403 (1974); A.C. Duhaime et al., "Current Concepts: Non-Accidental Head Injury in Infants—the 'Shaken Baby Syndrome,' " *New England Journal of Medicine* 338:25 (June, 1998): 1822-1828.

[4] A.C. Duhaime et al., "The Shaken Baby Syndrome: a Clinical, Pathological, and Biomechanical Study," *Journal of Neurosurgery* 66(3) (1987): 409-415.

[5] M. Gilliland and R. Folberg, "Shaken Babies: Some Have No Impact Injuries," *Journal of Forensic Science* 41(1) (1996): 114–116; J. Haviland and R. Russell, "Outcome After Severe Non-Accidental Head Injury," *Archives of Disease in Childhood* 77(6) (1997):504-507.

[6] *Ibid.*

[7] For a representative article reflecting the views of some defense experts, see Plunkett, "Shaken Baby Syndrome and the Death of Matthew Eappen: a Forensic Pathologist's Response," *American Journal of Forensic Medicine and Pathology* 20:1 (1999): 17-21.

[8] *See* A.V. Levin, "Ocular Manifestations of Child Abuse," *Ophthalmol. Clin. North America* (no number) 3(2): 249-264 (1990); Y. M. Buys et al., "Retinal Findings After Head Trauma in Infants and Young Children," *Ophthalmology* 99(11) (1992): 1718-1723; J. Lancon et al., "Anatomy of the Shaken Baby Syndrome" *Anat. Rec.* 253(1) (1998): 13-18; J. E. Elder at al., "Retinal Hemorrhage in Accidental Head Trauma in Childhood," *J. Pediatr. Child Health* 27(5) (1991):286-289.

[9] *See* M. Gayle et al, "Retinal Hemorrhage in the Young Child: a Review of Etiology, Predisposed Conditions, and Clinical Implications," *Journal of Emergency Medicine* 13:2 (1995): 233-239; A. Odom et al., "Prevalence of Retinal Hemorrhages in Pediatric Patients After In-Hospital Cardiopulmonary Resuscitation: a Prospective Study," *Pediatrics* 99(6) E3 (June, 1997).

[10] *See State v. Teuscher,* 883 P.2d 922 (Ut. App. 1994).

[11] K.Y. Willman et al., "Restricting the Time of Injury in Fatal Inflicted Head Injuries," *Child Abuse & Neglect* 21:10 (1997): 929-940.

[12] *See United States v. Gaskell,* 985 F.2d 1056 (11th Cir. 1993) for a demonstration disapproved; and *State v. Candela,* 929 S.W. 2d 852 (Mo. App. 1996) for an approved general demonstration that included an appropriate disclaimer about not representing exactly what happened in the particular case.

[13] Assuming it is admissible in your jurisdiction, you should make the case that use of video is analogous to photographs, diagrams, charts, etc.

[14] These types of tools are available from commercial vendors; *Mechanism of Injury in Shaken Baby Syndrome,* by Expert Digital Solutions, Inc. (612-942-8630), in Windows or MAC CD-ROM versions, is one example.

[15] American Academy of Pediatrics, Committee on Child Abuse and Neglect, "Shaken Baby Syndrome: Inflicted Cerebral Trauma," *Pediatrics* 92:6 (December, 1993): 872-875.

[16] *People v. Sargent,* 970 P.2d 409 (Cal. 1999).

[17] R. Reece and R. Kirschner.

[18] A.C. Duhaime et al.

[19] *See Estelle v. McGuire,* 112 S.Ct. 475 (1991) on recognizing the admissibility of prior injuries to a fatally injured child and approving opinion evidence concerning the battered child syndrome.

[20] For additional information, the American Prosecutors Research Institute's (APRI) National Center for Prosecution of Child Abuse, in Alexandria, VA, has a valuable manual on the general prosecution of child abuse cases. Contact the center at (703) 549-4253 for prices and availability.

PROBLEMS AND CHARGING CHOICES IN PROSECUTING VEHICULAR FATALITIES

By James J. Dietrich, Assistant State's Attorney, Howard County, Ellicott City, Maryland

Introduction

In the early 1980s, the nation's increased awareness of the prevalence and dangers of impaired driving prompted the passage of tougher impaired driving laws, including harsher penalties for impaired drivers who kill. Today, vehicular homicide statutes (vehicular homicide and vehicular manslaughter) give prosecutors more crimes and penalties to choose from when making charging decisions.

Before the enactment of vehicular homicide statutes, prosecutors sought convictions for vehicular fatalities under traditional homicide statutes (murder, manslaughter and criminally negligent homicide). While these laws were generally effective, prosecutors faced a problem in equating motor vehicles to guns and knives and convincing juries that someone who killed another with a motor vehicle was as criminally responsible as someone who fired a gun or used a knife. Similarly, prosecutors had a difficult time persuading juries that an impaired defendant was just as criminally responsible as someone who committed the same crime while sober.[1] In addition, when impairment rose to the level of intoxication, it could mitigate second-degree murder to manslaughter, thus enabling the most culpable defendants to avoid the harshest penalties.[2]

Vehicular homicide statutes targeted these problems by making driving and impairment elements of the offense that a jury is required to consider when determining if a defendant is guilty of a crime. For this reason, vehicular homicide statutes are valuable tools in the prosecution of impaired drivers who kill, and more importantly, in combination with traditional homicide statutes, they give prosecutors more charging and penalty choices.[3] Many prosecutors have come to depend on the easier-to-prove vehicular homicide statutes, however, rather than risk an acquittal under traditional homicide statutes even when they provide better penalty choices given the nature of the evidence and the sentence sought. More charging and penalty choices have led to more complex and tougher decisions. This article assists in solving these problems and demonstrates that vehicular homicide and traditional homicide statutes together make up a broad spectrum that prosecutors can use to achieve the best outcome.[4]

THE LAW OF CRIMINAL HOMICIDE

A wide range of homicide crimes makes up the criminal homicide spectrum. On one end of the spectrum is capital murder that has the highest culpability level and the greatest penalty. On the other end is criminally negligent homicide that has the lowest culpability level and the most lenient penalty of the homicide crimes. The remaining homicide crimes fall in between into two categories, traditional homicide statutes and vehicular homicide statutes. Traditional homicide statutes include murder (capital, first-and second-degree), manslaughter (voluntary and involuntary) and criminally negligent homicide. Vehicular homicide statutes include vehicular homicide and vehicular manslaughter.

An act that causes the death of a human being is the single, common characteristic that holds the spectrum together. The degree of risk created by the defendant's actions and the defendant's mental state at the time of the killing distinguishes the crimes in the homicide spectrum. Typically, the most difficult issue a prosecutor faces in a traditional homicide case is establishing the identity of the killer. Proving the mental state of the defendant is usually the most difficult issue in vehicular fatality cases because often the defendant is impaired by some intoxicant such as alcohol.

TRADITIONAL HOMICIDE STATUTES AND IMPAIRMENT

Two mental state categories divide traditional homicide statutes: specific intent and general intent.[5] Specific intent crimes focus on the intent of the defendant to cause some future consequence, such as the death of the victim in murder or voluntary manslaughter. General intent crimes focus not on the intention of the defendant but on the degree of risk to human life created by the defendant's physical act. Involuntary manslaughter and criminally negligent homicide are crimes that measure the risk created by the defendant's actions, despite the fact that the defendant never intended to kill anyone.

Vehicular fatality cases commonly involve defendants impaired by alcohol, other drugs or both. In certain instances, that impairment may serve to negate the specific intent to cause a death, particularly if the impairment rises to the level of intoxication. Impairment is not a complete defense to any crime. However, if the defendant's impairment rises to the level of intoxication, the defendant can use that impairment to mitigate specific but not general intent crimes. The defendant's intoxication must negate, not merely affect, the mental abilities, creating an incapacity to form or harbor the requisite mental state. There is no specific blood–alcohol content (BAC) that indicates when a defendant reaches this level. Instead, a fact-finder must take into account a composite of many facts. But as long as the defendant displays any "purpose or rationality" after becoming intoxicated, then intoxication does not negate the specific intent.

The apparent unfairness and inconsistency of the law occurs, for example, when two defendants, one who displays purpose or rationality despite the intoxication and another who displays no purposeful or rational behavior at all because of the impairment, commit the same crime under the same circumstances. The law punishes one defendant more harshly than the other, despite the fact that but for their impairment their criminal actions are the same. Vehicular homicide statutes attempt to solve such problems inherent to this rule of law.

Another problem prosecutors face when prosecuting vehicular fatalities is the treatment of a motor vehicle as a weapon.[6] The law considers a motor vehicle a dangerous instrument, meaning that the danger it poses to others depends on its use. On the other hand, the law classifies a gun as a deadly weapon, meaning that it is inherently dangerous, regardless of its use. The use of a deadly weapon in the commission of the crime enhances the penalties under many assault statutes. Furthermore, a jury will see a defendant who uses a gun or knife as more culpable or dangerous than one who uses a motor vehicle. Vehicular homicide statutes attempt to solve this dilemma as well.

VEHICULAR HOMICIDE STATUTES

Legislatures have passed most vehicular homicide statutes within the last decade. Generally, state legislatures have borrowed the language of general intent mental states from criminally negligent homicide or involuntary manslaughter statutes. Other legislatures have created strict liability offenses which eliminate the requirement to prove the defendant's mental state. Most vehicular homicide statutes feature impairment of the defendant and the use of a motor vehicle as elements of the offense. This statutory scheme solves the problems prosecutors face when charging vehicular fatalities under traditional homicide statutes.

Vehicular homicide statutes remedy the problems inherent in prosecuting vehicular fatalities under traditional homicide crimes by limiting the discretion of the jury.[7] No longer is there a question as to whether a motor vehicle equals a gun or knife as a weapon. Nor can juries use impairment to justify finding a defendant less culpable in the commission of a crime. By making it an element of the offense, legislatures have already determined the weight that juries must give impaired driving. The legislature has also predetermined the level at which causing a death while driving impaired is penalized.

Most vehicular homicide statutes limit the jury's role to determining the following:

- Whether the defendant was operating a motor vehicle on a public way while impaired by alcohol or other drugs;
- Whether the defendant's impairment was the proximate cause of the victim's death;
- Whether the defendant was otherwise negligent or reckless in the operation of the motor vehicle beyond being impaired.

Juries in strict liability jurisdictions need not determine the last factor. Other jurisdictions hold that impaired driving alone is sufficiently reckless or negligent and those jurisdictions do not require a separate showing of the defendant's general intent mental state. In jurisdictions that do require a separate showing, acts of recklessness or negligence usually include: driving on the wrong side of the road, driving at unsafe speeds and/or ignoring traffic signals.

Consider the Illinois vehicular homicide statute governing involuntary manslaughter and reckless homicide:[8]

> A person who unintentionally kills an individual without lawful justification commits involuntary manslaughter if his acts whether lawful or unlawful, which cause the death are such as are likely to cause death or great bodily harm to some individual, and he performs them recklessly, except in cases in which the cause of death consists of the driving of a motor vehicle, in which case the person commits reckless homicide. In cases involving reckless homicide, being under the influence of alcohol or any other drug or drugs at the time of the alleged violation shall be presumed to be evidence of a reckless act unless disproved by evidence to the contrary.

The Illinois statute demonstrates the legislature's recognition that a motor vehicle is a potentially dangerous weapon and uses that fact to create the crime of reckless homicide. The legislature also recognizes that impaired driving increases the risk on the roadways and uses that fact to aggravate the penalty of reckless homicide from a class three felony (two to five years incarceration) to a class two felony (three to 14 years incarceration). Ultimately, vehicular homicide statutes take away any discretion a jury has under traditional homicide statutes on the issues of impairment and driving.

CHOICES

Despite the benefits of vehicular homicide statutes, they have become alternatives to traditional homicide crimes instead of additions to the criminal homicide spectrum.[9] Prosecutors have come to rely on vehicular homicide statutes because they lack the problems that traditional homicide statutes have with driving and impairment. But neither intoxication nor driving is a barrier to charging vehicular fatalities under traditional homicide statutes especially when those statutes may provide a more effective penalty. Prosecutors can use these facts to prove the defendant's mental state.

Traditional homicide and vehicular homicide statutes allow prosecutors in some jurisdictions as many as five crimes and penalties with which to charge vehicular fatalities. These include second-degree murder, vehicular manslaughter, involuntary manslaughter, vehicular homicide and criminally negligent homicide. While the number of options complicates the process, it improves the opportunity for choosing the most appropriate penalty. The next section identifies many factors to consider when making the charging choice in vehicular fatality cases to reach a just and fair outcome.

PRACTICAL CONSIDERATIONS OF CRIMINAL HOMICIDE

The vast homicide spectrum enables prosecutors to charge vehicular fatalities under an array of crimes. This section builds on the legal aspects of homicide law already discussed and addresses the practical considerations in moving through the spectrum. The first part focuses on determining the best possible outcome in a vehicular fatality case and what prosecutors should consider in that determination. The second part examines the charging decision and the facts prosecutors require to correctly assess the degree of risk created by the defendant's actions and the defendant's mental state. Both assessments contribute to the final charging decision and are instrumental in a successful and fair prosecution of a vehicular fatality case.

It is important to note that even though this article addresses "determining the out-come" before examining the facts involved with making the final charging decision, prosecutors will not necessarily address these issues in this order. Nor are these issues by any means exclusive. Instead, consideration of both these issues takes place simulta-neously in a dynamic assessment that will weigh heavily in the final charging decision.

Determining the Outcome

Outcome determination is not simply an assessment of whether a case is a winner or loser. It is an assessment of what penalty will best reflect the defendant's responsibility for the homicide, possibly effect some change in the defendant's behavior and do the most good for society. Choosing the right penalty is not easy because it is based upon so many different factors. Determining the outcome is an opportunity for the prosecu-tor to effectively make the highways safer for other drivers and bring closure to a trau-matic period in the lives of the victim's family.

Prosecutors can also have an impact on the life of the defendant. This is where the myr-iad of homicide crimes and their respective penalties are most useful. The extent of the impact depends on the effectiveness of the prosecutor's choice of penalty. For instance, a penalty that includes alcohol counseling during the jail sentence would be the most helpful for an alcohol dependent person because it treats the addiction while it removes the defendant from the road. But in order to meet this wide range of goals, a prosecutor must take into account all the facts, not just those that he or she will use at trial.

Although there are no hard rules in outcome determination, certain questions can help prosecutors identify the facts needed to choose the most effective penalty:

- If the defendant is impaired: Does the defendant have any prior impaired driv-ing convictions or has the defendant been involved in injury accidents involv-ing impaired driving? If alcohol or drug dependent, what outcome will punish the crime but also help the defendant's addiction? If not alcohol or drug dependent, does the defendant have drinking or drug habits?
- How many people were killed?
- What were the circumstances surrounding the homicide, including the defen-dant's actions several hours before, immediately before, during, immediately after and several hours after the accident? Did the defendant try to cover up the homicide or any involvement in it?

- What was the relationship, if any, between the victim and the defendant? Did the defendant show any remorse for the harm done to the victim or victim's family? What outcome does the victim's family seek?
- What is the feeling of the community about this and other vehicular homicide cases?
- Does the defendant have family and how will incarceration affect the family?
- What kind of driver is the defendant while unimpaired? What kind of person is the defendant in other aspects of life?
- What objectives will punishment of this particular defendant further? Will others be deterred from driving in a manner that places others at a high risk of death or will incarceration simply mean that this one individual will be stopped from driving in that manner again?
- Overall, how egregious or heinous are the facts of the crime?

While determining the outcome, the prosecutor is continually assessing whether the facts of the case will justify the desired charge and outcome. The next section describes what facts to assess and how to determine whether they support the charge.

ASSESSING THE DEGREE OF RISK AND THE DEFENDANT'S MENTAL STATE

Because homicide crimes are distinguished by the risk created by the defendant's actions and the defendant's mental state, an assessment of these issues is crucial in determining the feasibility of the desired outcome. Unlike outcome determination, an assessment of the risk and mental state is a more structured exercise because the prosecutor is looking for the facts to use at trial (for instance, using prior traffic offenses to assess defendant's appreciation of the risk) to prove the statutory elements of the homicide crime. It is important to remember that one fact alone will not necessarily determine the answer to a particular issue. Instead, it is a compilation of many facts from before, during and after the fatality that will shape the charging decision.

Degree of Risk

The degree of risk is based on:

- The likelihood that death or injury will occur to someone other than the defendant, and
- The immediacy and severity of the risk created.

For instance, running a stop sign might create a high degree of risk of death or injury to someone crossing the intersection, but one that is less a risk than traveling 90 miles per hour into heavy, on-coming traffic. As will be shown later, the degree of risk is a fact used in determining the defendant's mental state. Some of the facts to consider when assessing the degree of risk are:

- Road conditions, i.e., weather, including rain, snow, ice or clear conditions; traffic control signals, including stop signs, traffic lights and yield signs; traffic/pedestrian volume on residential streets, city streets, highways and rural routes; the size of the road, be it two-lane, four-lane or a divided highway; and the immediate topography (straight road, a curve or a hill);
- Alcohol amount, including the BAC level; the BAC level over the legal limit; the amount of alcohol consumed; the time of last drink and the length of time over which alcohol was consumed;
- Where alcohol was consumed (at home, in a restaurant or bar, or in the motor vehicle);
- Condition of motor vehicle, including the brakes, lights, tires and windshield;
- Time of day of accident: dawn, daytime, dusk or nighttime;
- Motor vehicle violations, including speeding, disregard of traffic control signals, crossing center line and driving on the wrong side of the road;
- Egregiousness of action causing death to victims, including passengers, pedestrians and other motorists; and
- The number of victims and the age of victims.

Mental State

After determining the degree of risk and establishing that the defendant in fact committed a crime, the prosecutor then assesses the defendant's mental state at the time of the crime.[10] This assessment incorporates three components: defendant's awareness of the risk, defendant's conscious disregard of the risk and the defendant's purposeful or rational conduct.

Defendant's Awareness of Risk

This inquiry helps the prosecutor determine whether the defendant knew of the risk or failed to perceive it despite the degree of risk created. An awareness of the risk depends on whether the defendant had warning of the risk created by the conduct. If the defendant was unaware of the risk, despite the fact that the risk of death was high, criminally negligent homicide may be the best charge. On the other hand, where the defendant was unaware and impaired, vehicular homicide may be a better charge. When measuring the defendant's awareness of the risk, it should be determined whether there had been a warning:

- By others to avoid driving or to stop driving;
- Of the dangers of impaired driving by prior impaired driving offenses, including prior driving offenses involving injury or death; and by prior traffic offenses, citations, convictions, arrests; and/or
- By the degree of risk created by the defendant's actions.

Defendant's Conscious Disregard of the Risk

After establishing the defendant's awareness of the risk, the prosecutor measures the degree to which the risk was ignored. Determination of the defendant's disregard of the risk is unnecessary: if the defendant continued to perform the act that caused the perceived risk, it is assumed that the risk was disregarded. The only question remaining is the degree to which the defendant disregarded the risk.

Ignoring the risk with a conscious disregard for human life constitutes recklessness and an involuntary manslaughter charge would be appropriate. If impairment was involved, then the penalty for vehicular manslaughter would be more just. If the defendant acted with wanton and willful extreme indifference to human life, then the defendant acted with an implied specific intent to kill or a "depraved heart." When the defendant acts with a depraved heart, then second-degree murder is the proper charge. Some of the facts to consider are:

- Failure to brake or stop after being warned of the risk;
- Speeding up after being warned of the risk;
- Driving at all after being warned of the risk; and
- Driving to a place to drink where defendant would have to drive home while aware of the risks of impaired driving.

"DEPRAVED HEART" MENTAL STATE OF THE IMPAIRED DEFENDANT

In cases involving impairment, the prosecutor must assess the defendant's degree of impairment and what effect that impairment had on the defendant's "depraved heart" mental state. Because second-degree murder is typically the only specific intent crime that applies to vehicular fatality cases, the effect impairment had on the defendant's mental state is most important. If a defendant showed any purposeful or rational conduct immediately before, during or after the crash, evidencing some control over the mental faculties, then the impairment did not rise to a level that affected the mental state. The facts used to determine whether the defendant acted with purpose or rationality are:

- Quantity of alcohol consumed;
- Period of time involved;
- Results of BAC tests;
- Defendant's ability to recall significant events;
- Defendant's ability to get into, start and drive a motor vehicle;
- Swerving or braking to avoid people, objects or other vehicles;
- Efforts to avoid arrest after crash;
- Leaving scene of crash (by foot or motor vehicle);
- Not assisting victims due to flight from scene; and
- Assisting victims.

In many cases of second-degree murder, evidence of trying or failing to avoid a pedestrian or other car is a difficult issue. Defendants have two common arguments. First, the defendant, upon seeing the pedestrian or other car, braked and swerved to avoid a collision, indicating that the defendant did in fact value life and did not have a depraved heart. However, trying to avoid killing the victim did not negate the "depraved heart" possessed by the defendant. Instead, having knowingly placed one-self in a position while impaired where it became necessary to swerve to avoid killing someone is evidence of a "depraved heart." The totality of the defendant's actions, from the time of intoxication to the point of arrest, reflected the existence of the "depraved heart" mental state and indicated, despite impairment, control of the mental faculties.

The second argument often made by defendants is that failure to brake despite an obvious risk of death is evidence of a level of intoxication that negated specific intent. The response to this argument is similar to the first in that the totality of the defendant's actions demonstrated whether he was in control of his faculties—not just one moment in time. The impairment did not necessarily negate his specific intent to kill if other evidence demonstrated purposeful conduct from the time the defendant got behind the wheel to the point of arrest.

CONCLUSION

A goal in any criminal prosecution is the eventual reduction in number of criminal acts and a just and fair disposition of impaired drivers who cause those deaths. A basic understanding of the criminal homicide spectrum, informed decision-making and consistent charging of vehicular fatalities goes far in achieving these goals.

Beyond these goals lies a practical use for this article—the education of those who play a part in the prosecution of vehicular fatality cases. Every day judges and victims' families ask prosecutors why they have charged a vehicular fatality in a certain way. Victims' families want to know why the defendant received only three years in jail rather than life imprisonment. Prosecutors now have a basis to analyze their own state homicide spectrums and the communities in which they prosecute in order to develop effective vehicular fatality charging policies. Prosecutors can show judges how a vehicular fatality case fits into the criminal homicide spectrum and demonstrates consistency in charging decisions. Prosecutors can convey to victims' families the obligation of the criminal justice system to ensure that the defendant's actions fit the crime charged, and how, in service of justice, they strive to achieve the fairest and best outcome possible.

This article is based on the APRI National Traffic Law Center's "Problems and Possibilities in Prosecuting Vehicular Fatalities" which provides a more in-depth analysis of charging decisions in vehicular fatality cases. This article can be found on the APRI Web site at www.ndaa-apri.org. A companion presentation packet contains all the material needed to deliver a presentation on vehicular homicide issues, including handouts and color overheads. For more information on these products and "Lethal Weapon: DUI Homicide," a trial advocacy course, contact APRI's National Traffic Law Center at (703) 549-4253 or fax, (703) 836-3195.

ENDNOTES

[1] National Traffic Law Center (NTLC) "Problems and Possibilities in Prosecuting Vehicular Fatalities" monograph, American Prosecutors Research Institute, 1997.

[2] This article uses the term "impairment" to represent any evidence that a person is under the influence of alcohol or other drugs. The term "intoxication" refers to a high level of impairment that mitigates certain homicide crimes.

[3] NTLC.

[4] Because homicide law is so diverse throughout the country, this article represents a national perspective. While the statutory scheme and definitions of any one jurisdiction may not fit squarely into those discussed here, the schemes and terms used reflect homicide law generally on a national basis.

[5] NTLC.

[6] *Ibid.*

[7] *Ibid.*

[8] Illinois vehicular homicide statute: 720 ilcs 5/9-3. Involuntary manslaughter and reckless homicide, 1998.

[9] NTLC.

[10] *Ibid.*

WINNING SEXUAL ASSAULT CASES WITH SEXUAL ASSAULT EXAMINERS

By Tracy Bahm, Senior Attorney, American Prosecutors Research Institute,
Violence Against Women Program, Alexandria, Virginia

The purpose of the sexual assault examiner program is "to create some sensible and humane way
of treating its victims, not just because it is kind and good but because it may better serve the
cause of justice."
—Anna Quinlen, The New York Times, October 19, 1994.

The above quote can only be faulted for stating that sexual assault examiner programs *may* better serve the cause of justice when actually, there is no question that
SANE programs make an incredible difference in achieving justice.[1] They greatly
improve victim cooperation and evidence collection, and they provide prosecutors
with superior factual and expert witness testimony, resulting in increased prosecutions and more convictions.

WHAT IS A SEXUAL ASSAULT EXAMINER?

Sexual Assault Examiners are the specially trained nurses and physicians who function as part of a multidisciplinary team that responds to sexual assault. This article
will use the acronym SANE (Sexual Assault Nurse Examiner) since most examiners
are nurses. However, there are many different but equivalent programs including but
not limited to:

- Sexual Assault Forensic Examiner (SAFE);
- Sexual Assault Response Team (SART);
- Sexual Assault Examiner (SAE); and
- Sexual Assault Nurse Clinician (SANC).

In response to the traditionally dismal treatment of sexual assault victims in hospitals, victim advocates and medical professionals have been the driving forces behind
the development of SANE programs. Typically, a victim would be seen at the emergency department of a hospital where she would have to compete with other critically wounded and ill patients for the doctor's time. More often than not, unless the
rape victim was *obviously* critically wounded, she was given a low priority for med-

ical care. One can imagine the countless numbers of victims who simply walked out of the emergency room before any medical professional treated them. Physicians in attendance often had little (or no) experience or training in completing a rape examination; little (or no) experience or training to meet the emotional needs of a rape victim and little (or no) experience or training in the collection of forensic evidence.[2]

Moreover, because physicians' schedules are typically quite complex, scheduling them as witnesses was and continues to be problematic. Due to their lack of specific experience or training on the unique characteristics of sexual assault, frequently physicians were unable to provide expert testimony about the findings in their examinations. Therefore, the shift of responsibility from doctors or nurses to specially trained nurse examiners (who enter this specialty fully aware that testifying in court is an aspect of forensic evidence collection) is a logical and welcome development for both the medical and the legal professions.

WHAT DO SEXUAL ASSAULT EXAMINERS DO?

The first SANE programs started in the 1970s, but the real boost in the growth of SANE programs came after the formation of the International Association of Forensic Nurses (IAFN)[3] in 1992. In 1995, the American Nurses Association (ANA) officially recognized forensic nursing as a specialty, and SANE has evolved as the largest subspecialty in this field.[4]

While the exact missions and goals of each SANE program vary slightly, their *primary* duties are to assess, document and collect forensic evidence,[5] and to provide testing and treatment for sexually transmitted diseases and pregnancy. SANEs may also treat minor injuries, but they refer patients with more serious injuries to physicians. One of the SANE programs' biggest benefits for victims, by far, is the offering of immediate emotional support and referrals to legal advocacy agencies that provide continued support to the victim throughout the criminal justice process.

THE BENEFITS TO PROSECUTORS

Prosecutors receive three major benefits from sexual assault examiners: excellent treatment of the victim, the best possible evidence collection and the availability of testimony at trial, both factual and expert.

THE TREATMENT OF THE VICTIM

The chances are significantly greater that a sexual assault victim will follow through with both the rape examination and the prosecution of the case if a SANE is involved. Most programs are set up as on-call or on-site programs, so that when a rape victim places the first call to the police or walks through the doors of the hospital the SANE is ready to spring into action. The victim is seen almost immediately in a private setting that will not embarrass or further traumatize her. The SANE is familiar with all the myths about rape: what to say and what not to say so that the victim is treated sensitively and not blamed in any way for the crime she has suffered. The SANE's message to the victim is that she matters and will be treated with compassion. The SANE will also connect the victim with an advocate (victim-witness or otherwise) who will help her through the remainder of the process. Prosecutors who have practiced for any length of time can attest to the value of a cooperative sexual assault victim, one that perceives that her (or sometimes his) feelings are considered and valued.

PROPER AND THOROUGH EVIDENCE COLLECTION

As stated previously, the primary purpose of the SANE is not to provide medical treatment but to collect evidence. However, most Sexual Assault Examiner programs operate from within hospital emergency departments, which ensures that the victim's medical needs are also met. The SANE is much like a very sensitive detective with a medical background, specially trained in conducting physical examinations of sexual assault victims. The examination includes the documentation of injuries all over the victim's body, and not just in and around the genitalia. It includes the gathering of all possible evidence, some of which may otherwise be overlooked in a hectic emergency room environment. The collection of debris from the victim's hair and clothing, for example, could be valuable in corroborating her version of events, as could evidence of injuries on her scalp and knees. A good SANE knows how to look beyond the obvious and inquire about details, like the victim's raspy voice or spots around the eyes that may be evidence of strangulation. The SANE will also be sufficiently comfortable with both the subject matter and the victim to ask the difficult questions that may be critical to the prosecutor's case, like exactly where on the victim's body can the defendant's ejaculate be found? (Rapists sometimes do unusual things).

The timeliness with which the SANE sees the victims is another boon to prosecutors, particularly in those cases that involve more difficult fact patterns, such as drug-facilitated rape cases where the collection of urine and blood samples needs to be done as quickly as possible. Most date rape drugs remain in the victim's system for only eight to 48 hours following ingestion.

Additionally, the SANE is familiar with the rape kit and knows how to properly collect and store evidence. Prosecutors need not worry about tainted evidence, broken chains of custody or incomplete kits if a SANE does the examination and evidence collection.

FACTUAL TESTIMONY

A good SANE will provide a detailed report of the sexual assault examination that documents any and all findings in a factual and neutral manner. He or she knows that a careful and thorough documentation of forensic evidence is essential if it is to be used in court. An effective SANE program includes training on the legal system, the mechanics of a courtroom and what is expected when testifying.

The SANE should be able to testify to any injuries observed, from redness to bruising to tears and what the victim had to say about the assault during the course of the medical examination. Therefore, the SANE should be trained to keep careful notes (ideally, verbatim) during and immediately after the examination. It is not the job of the SANE, however, to appraise the credibility of the victim or to determine what did or what did not happen. The SANE provides a valuable piece of the puzzle but one that on its own, cannot prove the case.

EXPERT WITNESS TESTIMONY

Many SANEs perform hundreds of examinations a year and, based purely on numbers, they qualify as experts. The SANE can educate the jury on a great deal of necessary information—from female anatomy to the human sexual response. Many jurors do not truly understand the female genitalia, and thus it is helpful for the expert to explain how and why, when a female victim is raped, certain injuries often occur because her body is not "ready" for sex. Conversely, the SANE may be able to offer explanations as to why there may be no documented injury to a victim when she had engaged in voluntary kissing with the defendant before he raped her.

Programs differ in their rules on SANEs serving as expert witnesses on the significance or insignificance of particular findings in an exam. In some programs, the nurses can give such testimony; in others it may be the head of the program (a doctor or nurse practitioner) who may be more qualified to render such opinions.

To better maintain the neutrality of the examiner, consider having someone other than the SANE who conducted the examination give the expert opinion. In any case, do not expect that the witness will be able to testify that "defendant X penetrated victim Y with object Z." But, they may be able to say that the level of injury is inconsistent with consensual intercourse, or that the findings are abnormal for a victim of that age, suggesting that the victim had been penetrated with an object. They may be able to explain to the jury why it is that a teenager was raped and still has an intact hymen. Whatever the scenario in the case, it is axiomatic that the prosecutor talks to the SANE before trial. As with any other witness, take the time to meet with the SANE and prepare him or her for testimony. The SANE should be able to provide the prosecution with a thorough understanding of the findings of the examination and their significance.

MAKE A DIFFERENCE

For any jurisdiction that does not have a sexual assault examiner program and is interested in instituting such a program, there are several model programs to emulate. A good starting point is the *Sexual Assault Nurse Examiner Development & Operation Guide*, by Linda E. Ledray. It is available through the Office for Victims of Crime, Office of Justice Programs, U.S. Department of Justice. Call (800) 851-3420 or (800) 627-6872 to order one, or download one from www.sane-sart.com.

As mentioned at the outset of the article, the SANE should be part of a multi-disciplinary team of professionals that includes at a minimum victim advocates, law enforcement officers and prosecutors. Consider involving other members of the community, such as clergy, educators and social service providers to make the team even more capable.

If jurisdictions already have SANE programs but prosecutors remain unaware of their substantial benefits, they owe it to themselves to become part of one of these multidisciplinary teams that are fundamental to the successful prosecution of sexual assault cases. Professionalism requires no less.

REFERENCES & RESOURCES

- *Sexual Assault Nurse Examiner Development & Operation Guide* by Linda E. Ledray. Published by the U.S. Department of Justice. Available online at www.sane-sart.com.

- American Prosecutors Research Institute, Violence Against Women Unit. See website at www.ndaa–apri.org. APRI provides training, technical assistance and research for prosecutors and other criminal justice professionals. Call (703) 549-4253. Note: Video & Binder set on Drug Facilitated Rape available for $30. Available by telephone or on the website.

ACKNOWLEDGMENTS

A special thank you to three sexual assault nurse examiners who have taught me so much about the great work they do:

- Cheryl Graf, ARNP, MSN, SANE; Clinical Coordinator for the Sexual Assault Nurse Examiner Program at Harrison Hospital, Bremerton WA;
- Kate Espy, RN, SANE; Harrison Hospital, Bremerton, WA;
- Donna Gaffney, RN, DNSC, FAAN; International Trauma Studies Program at New York University, New York, NY.

ENDNOTES

[1] Prior to coming to APRI, Tracy Bahm served as a prosecutor for six years in Kitsap County, Washington. While she was there, Kitsap County implemented a Sexual Assault Nurse Examiner (SANE) program.

[2] Linda E. Ledray, 1996. *Sexual Assault Nurse Examiner Development & Operation Guide* (SANE Guide), Office for Victims of Crime, U.S. Department of Justice, Washington D.C. (1996) p. 5.

[3] Web site located at www.forensicnurse.org

[4] SANE Guide, p. 6.

[5] SANE Guide, p. 9.

EFFECTIVE STRATEGIES FOR THE PROSECUTOR

A Judge's View of Appellate Advocacy

By Thomas T. Woodall, Judge, Tennessee Court of Criminal Appeals, Nashville, Tennessee

Introduction

The purpose of this article is to make observations and suggestions to prosecutors regarding practice in appellate courts. Preparation for appellate advocacy in criminal cases begins when the indictment, presentment or other charging instrument is prepared. Presumably, you plan to prevail in every prosecution and should therefore assume that an appellate court will ultimately resolve each case you handle, even though the vast majority of criminal prosecutions in this country are presently disposed of by negotiated plea agreements. My perspective from the bench is heavily influenced by six years of experience as an assistant prosecutor in the 24th Judicial District of Tennessee and six years of private practice as a sole practitioner, which included five years as a contract appellate defender for the Tennessee District Public Defenders Conference.

This is not meant to be a highly academic article. I merely hope to pass on some useful tips for appellate advocacy in criminal cases. Ideally, a reader will examine it in its entirety, deposit what he or she can remember in the brain bank and when the need for a refresher course in appellate advocacy is apparent, return to this article for assistance.

GENERAL CONSIDERATIONS

As previously mentioned, the preparation for appellate advocacy begins with the charging instrument, whether it is an indictment or presentment. For instance, in Tennessee an indictment that fails to charge an offense is a nullity that can result in a reversal of conviction and dismissal of charges. *See State v. Cleveland*, 959 S.W.2d 548, 552 (Tenn. 1997) (holding that a defendant cannot legally be convicted of an offense which is not charged in the indictment or is not a lesser offense embraced by the indictment).

Never forget that what is said on the record in the courtroom by the judge, the lawyers and the witnesses will be the sole record reviewed by the appellate court. Unless your jurisdiction uses audio/visual tapes instead of transcripts for the record of trial proceedings, what is visible to you and other participants in the trial may not be fully conveyed to the appellate court.

For instance, proof of a crime such as aggravated assault may require evidence of serious bodily injury to the victim. Serious bodily injury may include extreme pain and/or disfigurement. Accurate photographs of the scars or the injuries shortly after being inflicted should be presented to allow the appellate court to have a basis for affirming a conviction or an appropriate sentence. To best illustrate my point, I suggest that you read the transcript of a trial handled by another prosecutor. When you read the testimony and arguments of counsel, are you able to clearly visualize the proof of the essential elements of the crime? This procedure will give you an idea of what an appellate court will or won't see when reviewing your case.

When preparing for trial, recognize the weaknesses in your case and anticipate the objections that the defense counsel may make during the course of the trial. More frequently than is justified, I see instances where prosecutors have successfully introduced evidence over an objection, such as a hearsay exception, that causes the trial court to commit error in allowing the testimony. From the record, it is apparent that the same proof could have been introduced through other witnesses or in a different manner without running the risk of having a conviction reversed and a new trial ordered. Alternatively, do you really need the evidence in question? If not, reserve your fire for more pressing matters and avoid inviting error that improves the defendant's chances of appeal and a possible re-trying of the case at some future date.

Exhibits should be clearly labeled and properly described by the witness through whom the exhibit is introduced into evidence. Make sure that bench conferences that are held on the record but out of the presence of the jury are included in the transcript that is sent to the appellate court.

Ideally, in all cases, but most importantly in cases that involve complicated questions of law, do not hesitate to confer with the appellate counsel in your office or your state who will be representing the government on appeal. In Tennessee, elected district attorneys general and their staffs represent the state in prosecutions at the trial court level. However, in criminal appeals the State of Tennessee is represented by the office of the state attorney general in Nashville. I learned early on as a prosecutor to call one of the assistant attorneys general to receive guidance and advice on how to properly address legal issues at the trial court level. I found they were helpful and most appreciative that potential problems on appeal could be avoided by resolving problems before they occurred.

Depending upon the rules in your jurisdiction, you may find that your office should seek an interlocutory appeal from a ruling on a suppression issue or other matter (assuming this is permitted in your jurisdiction). In Tennessee, the state can also appeal from an order of the court that effectively dismisses the criminal charges, i.e., an order suppressing all of the evidence seized by law enforcement officers. You should familiarize yourself with all of the rules that pertain to interlocutory appeals or appeals as of right from orders which effectively dismiss the prosecution. You must be aware of the time limits for filing the proper notice to begin the appeal process and the time limits for filing a transcript with the appropriate court clerk. Make sure that the record is transmitted to the appellate court on time.

WRITING THE BRIEF

Another article in this book deals with writing appellate briefs. Thus, I will emphasize only a brief point or two from my perspective as an appellate judge. Be concise and logical in your arguments. The brief is your one opportunity to make a permanent record of your position on legal arguments on appeal. Some judges take better notes than others during oral argument. When the appellate court is considering the proper disposition of the appeal, the judges will likely rely heavily upon the brief that you file. Do not depend upon a good oral argument to overcome the deficiencies of a poorly organized and poorly drafted brief. Before filing a brief, you should have put in the workmanship necessary so that when you pick it up again to review prior to oral argument, you feel satisfaction and pride that it is your signature at the conclusion of the brief and your work presented to the court.

PREPARATION FOR ORAL ARGUMENT

The most important component of any case in any court, including an appellate court, is *preparation*. Preparation for oral argument in an appellate court is similar to preparation in any aspect of practicing law. The time required for proper preparation generally far exceeds the time actually spent in the courtroom. When I was in private practice, it was not unusual for me to spend two to three hours preparing for oral argument that was limited by court rule to 20 minutes. At a minimum, you should re-read the brief filed on behalf of your adversary and re-read your own brief to re-familiarize yourself with the authorities cited therein. Time constraints may prevent re-reading the entire appellate record, but notes taken when reviewing the record for the first time should be revisited. And remember, preparation time will vary from case to case.

Recognize the weak positions in your case. While it is always important to be objective when analyzing your case, it is especially well advised to be objective in looking at your case in final preparation for oral argument in an appellate court. I have noticed, as both litigator and judge, that most questions directed to you during oral argument relate to the weaknesses in the case. You should strive to distinguish the caselaw or statutes that are favorable to your adversary's position, and be prepared to cite caselaw that has facts and circumstances similar to your case.

Do not despair, however. There will likely be glaring weaknesses in your adversary's case on which you presumably focused in drafting your brief. During preparation for oral argument, you should review your analysis, and be prepared to remind the appellate court of the other side's weaknesses during your oral argument.

Concede points where necessary. I assume that in all jurisdictions, there is the concept of harmless error or the equivalent: if the trial court or the prosecuting attorney did commit error at the trial court level, this does not always equal reversible error.

With the advances in technology that have occurred in recent years, it is *extremely* important to conduct last minute research prior to oral argument. Shortly after graduation from law school, I was a law clerk for one year for Judge Mark A. Walker, presiding judge of the Tennessee Court of Criminal Appeals. As there was not a single computer in the office, he had filed copies of each opinion of the Tennessee Court of Criminal Appeals to date (the court was created in 1967) under his own efficient indexing system. It was extremely rare for a litigant to cite unpublished cases and virtually all cases relied upon were found in the official reporter of Tennessee decisions. Today, however, opinions of the appellate courts in Tennessee and, I assume, across the country, are posted on the Internet as the ink is drying on the "filed" stamp on the cover page of the opinion. Without final research preparation prior to oral argument, you can literally walk into a courtroom and not be aware of case law that is on all fours with your case. When the appellate judges and your adversary are aware of the case and you are not, it is worse. Final research during preparation for oral argument should also bring to your attention cases that distinguish, support, criticize or even overrule cases relied upon by you or your adversary.

I represented defendants in criminal cases on appeal whom I had represented at trial, and, pursuant to my contract with the Tennessee District Public Defenders Conference, defendants who had been represented by another lawyer at the trial level. In both situations, I employed the same procedure in reviewing the record and preparing to write the appellate brief: I outlined the testimony, exhibits, pleadings, orders and judgment, etc. filed with the record. No particular system is universally the best. Whatever is comfortable and works for you in outlining the record should be sufficient. It is almost mandatory, however, to prepare an outline or take notes that are sufficient to allow you to recollect pertinent parts of the record in preparation for oral argument. Do not rely simply upon your summary of the facts contained in the brief when preparing for oral argument. Review your notes carefully in preparation to answer pertinent questions posed by the judges.

Finally, prepare a skeleton outline of points that you want to present to the court during oral argument. Though I did not use the method (or even think of it when I was in private practice), one of the best procedures I have observed was used by an assistant attorney general in Nashville. He made his outline on the inside cover of a file folder that he brought to the podium along with copies of the briefs filed by the parties. This method avoids the necessity of keeping up with and carrying a legal pad to the podium (as I formerly did) and leaves sufficient room on the folder to make numerous notes during the opposing counsel's oral argument.

During your preparation and analysis of weak points in your case, you should anticipate the questions that may be asked by the judges and prepare your answers to these questions. Of course, you will probably not anticipate every question asked or every point made by your opposing counsel during oral argument. However, anticipating 50 percent of the questions asked could improve by 100 percent your presentation and performance during oral argument.

Never be reluctant to practice oral argument prior to court, especially if you have little or no experience in arguing cases in appellate courts. Whether you practice in front of a mirror (which I admit to doing on some occasions) or in the presence of a co-worker or family member, the process helps you become aware of annoying personal habits that distract from your presentation in court.

ORAL ARGUMENT

As you approach the lectern to begin your argument, remember to speak slowly, speak distinctly and maintain eye contact. I know from experience as an advocate that on some occasions, none of the judges on the panel looked at me at various times during oral argument. Always concentrate on looking up at the judges and not looking at your notes for more than a second to glance at an outline. Never read from your brief or outline except to make a short quote from the record or a pertinent case or statute. Hope, but do not assume, that each member of the court has read your brief and does not require an extensive re-reading of the matters contained therein. Learn about your judges.

In the vast majority of criminal cases heard in appellate courts, the government is the appellee. Having argued first, the appellant has set the tone on the issues that will be addressed during oral argument. As appellee, you should take meticulous notes and pay close attention to the questions asked of your adversary by the court. You may need to alter, sometimes significantly, your planned presentation to the court based upon your opponent's oral argument and the questions asked by the court, at which point your prior preparation, or lack thereof, will be readily apparent to the judges.

If you detect that one or more of the judges on the panel has misunderstood the record on appeal, you should take the opportunity during your portion of the oral argument to clarify any misconception. Again, your preparation prior to oral argument will be extremely helpful to you.

Be confident about your analysis and the logic of your argument, but do not be flippant or demean the arguments presented by opposing counsel. Remember that defendants in criminal cases have an absolute right to first tier appellate review and, frequently, cases are presented in which the law may be extremely unfavorable to the appellant's assertions. The lawyer is required to do the best job possible on behalf of the client. Arguments to change or distinguish well-settled law made by counsel for the appellant could appear ridiculous to you, but the judges may believe otherwise. Be confident but not overconfident. Address each issue raised by the appellant seriously. A show of respect for both the court and your adversary will result in enhanced respect for you and your work.

If you are questioned about the contents of the appellate record or the relevance of a certain case, do not guess at an answer. If you do not recall what is in the record or you are not familiar with the case or statute, admit it and immediately offer to submit a supplemental brief to address the question.

I will digress momentarily to point out from personal experience (primarily as an advocate) that appellate courts are sometimes like juries. That is, the court may not agree with what you and your opposing counsel think is important; and conversely, the court could see something that you and your opposing counsel have overlooked as extremely important. Therefore, if you do not know the answer, you should say so and, as recommended, offer to file a supplemental brief. Never tell a court that the subject of a question is not important: it may be distinguishable or inapplicable, but it is never unimportant. It is sufficient that the judge makes inquiries.

I assume that most jurisdictions are similar to Tennessee and have a time limit for each side to present oral argument in appellate courts. If you are presented with numerous questions that sidetrack you and prevent you from bringing important arguments to the attention of the court, do not hesitate to ask the court for an additional period of time to sum up your argument. If you are allowed to reserve rebuttal time by the rules of your jurisdiction, always ask to reserve the time before you begin your argument, and give it back if it is not needed. In most cases, if it is not requested, you may not have the opportunity to make a rebuttal.

Whether you represent the government as the appellant or the appellee, you should be prepared to respond to questions from the court about the policy considerations of the legal arguments of both parties. Opinions released by appellate courts affect more situations than the case being decided. The decision made in your case will affect all similar cases decided in the future. This is especially true if your case is one of first impression or there are potential ramifications to limiting or expanding well-settled law. You should be prepared for questions regarding the possible results of a ruling in your favor.

If error was clearly made in the trial court, admit it but make a good faith argument of "harmless error" if you are in a position to do so. Similarly, if error dictates that a case must be reversed and remanded and the defendant/appellant must prevail, acknowledge this fact.

CONCLUSION
Appellate oral advocacy can be highly rewarding to those who fine-tune their skills in presenting legal issues to the appellate courts. As in trial court litigation, the appropri-

ate and necessary amount of preparation is the key to success. Appellate oral advocacy offers the opportunity to present and argue points of law in cases where the decisions made on the issues will likely have ramifications for cases in the future across your jurisdiction. Your contribution to making needed changes in the law, even in a small way, can be a satisfying reward for work well done. Remember that in almost all jurisdictions, the opinions released by appellate courts list the attorneys representing both the government and the defendant. Perform the work necessary in appellate advocacy so that you will not be embarrassed to see your name on an opinion 20 years in the future. Appellate advocacy should not be viewed as a chore but as a challenge and an opportunity to make a significant contribution to the legal system.

A Prosecutor's View of Appellate Advocacy

By Timothy A. Baughman, Chief of Research, Training and Appeals, Wayne County Prosecutor's Office, Detriot, Michigan

"The best appellate lawyers will know about important milestones across the legal spectrum. They will keep up with new Supreme Court and… Circuit Court decisions… Appellate advocacy is, in essence, a business for legal intellectuals."[1]

Effective appellate oral advocacy is a daunting subject if one wishes to go beyond the commonplace. This is not to say that the commonplace is unimportant, for indeed it is critical: thorough preparation and answering questions from the bench (rather than putting off the questioner) are essential to effective appellate oral advocacy. One hopes these principles are emphasized in first year law school moot court classes and an audience of prosecutors nationwide is not a first year law school audience. So, consequently, the few remarks and suggestions that follow, gleaned from observation of oral advocacy during 25 years of appellate practice, are directed in the main to the prosecutor who is an appellate specialist. The generalist from the smaller office who handles the occasional appeal might also find them useful.

By way of preface, one should bear in mind that it is a law of nature that some people are better speakers than others; some have a gift for oratory, a presence, as it were, that is advantageous in appellate argument. Most of us do not have this ability. I confess that I have no talent for oratory whatsoever (you do not have to take my word for it since I have any number of witnesses who can attest to it), but this does not mean that you and I cannot deliver effective appellate arguments. As Abraham Lincoln admonished in "Notes on the Practice of Law" in 1850, "If any one, upon his rare powers of speaking, shall claim exemption from the drudgery of the law, his case is a failure in advance."[2] Those of us without talent for oratory can certainly be effective oral advocates; those who *are* gifted speakers require more than talent alone.

HONESTY AND CANDOR GO A LONG WAY

"Always do right. This will gratify some people, and astonish the rest."
Mark Twain, speech on February 16, 1901

Twain's suggestion, of course, extends to all areas of practice. What is urged here is that the prosecutor as appellate advocate, and indeed, as public prosecutor in all situations, always tell the truth. Don't misstate it, don't hide it, don't shade it, don't bend it and don't distort it. Just tell it. Telling the truth is not only good and right, it is effective. It has been said "facts that are not frankly faced have a habit of stabbing us in the back,"[3] which is undoubtedly true in appellate argument. Judges will know, sooner or later, that an advocate has failed to disclose an important fact or case or has misstated a fact or the law. As a result, the advocate's cause will have been harmed as well as the advocate's reputation, which can harm future cases. This is especially true for the prosecutor who, as an advocate for justice, is frequently held to a higher standard than the defense counsel.

A reputation with the appellate bench for candor and honesty—that a statement made during argument regarding the facts or the law can be trusted—goes a long way toward rendering oral advocacy effective. Moreover, oral argument is the prosecutor's last chance not only to explain the strengths of the brief, but also to deal with what might be perceived by the judges as its weaknesses and to explain why a damaging fact is not controlling or, when properly viewed, not damaging at all. Oral argument is also an occasion to explain why a detrimental case is distinguishable or, when not distinguishable, simply wrong. One cannot be a successful appellate advocate and persuade disinterested judges of the rightness of a position taken except by dealing in candor and in truth with the facts and with the law. A prosecutor has no interest in doing otherwise.

ENGAGE THE JUDGES

"The acme of judicial distinction means the ability to look a lawyer straight in the eye for two hours and not hear a damned word he says."
Chief Justice John Marshall[4]

To notice that the judges are not paying attention to the argument or appear baffled by it is one of the most disconcerting things that can happen to a lawyer during oral argument. There may be nothing the oral advocate can do to remedy the situation or to prevent it. On many occasions, however, judges are uninterested or uncomprehending because the argument is dull or incomprehensible. A way to engage the judges is to develop a theme for the argument.

Engaging the judges is what the oral argument is all about. The prosecutor errs grievously who prepares the argument with the hope that it can be delivered without untidy interruptions from the judges that arrest the flow of a meticulously well thought-out presentation. The prosecutor should structure the argument to grab the attention of the judges from the outset, in a way that almost demands that questions be asked. Just as seminars on trial advocacy teach the importance of theme development in closing argument to juries, theme development should be the goal of the prosecutor in appellate oral advocacy. As the focus is on legal issues, the process is different from theme development for jury argument and can be initiated by asking, during the planning phase of the argument: what is this case and this issue about; how does it fit into the framework of the law?

A brief example will suffice. In *Michigan v Summers,*[5] the precise legal issue was whether the police were justified in detaining people found on the premises while executing a search warrant. The theme of the oral argument was the need for the police to conduct a "full and safe" execution of the search warrant—that is, to be able to find that which the warrant commanded them to search for and seize and protect themselves in the process. Using this theme was a great help in engaging the United States Supreme Court[6] and establishing a framework within which questions were more readily answered.

Do Not Oversell Your Case

"It's broccoli, dear."
I say it's spinach, and I say the hell with it."
E.B. White, *cartoon caption*

Just as there is room for a well-turned phrase in appellate writing, there is room for an elegant presentation in oral argument. Interesting and engaging, however, does not mean hyperbolic and overblown. Even though theme development in the construction of the argument is encouraged, along with an opening line or statement that compels the judges to sit up and take notice, it is neither appropriate nor effective for the prosecutor to try to make the case into something it is not. If the case does not have far reaching practical consequences, do not say it does. If it will affect few other cases, admit it. If no novel issue of law is presented, do not invent one. The judges will not appreciate it; they will know it is "really spinach."

ANTICIPATION

"Nothing in life is so exhilarating as to be shot at without result."
Winston Churchill, *The Malakand Field Force*

If the argument should be so constructed as to command the attention of the judges and to generate questions, then the heart of effective oral advocacy is to persuasively answer the questions. For those of us who are not brilliant—and even for those who are—there is only one way to effectively answer questions from the bench and that is to anticipate them. Rather than prescience, this requires diligence and understanding. If you know the weaknesses of your case, or those that appear at first blush to be weaknesses, you can expect questions from the bench regarding them. The best way to understand the trouble spots in your case is to know your opponent's argument as well as he or she does, for the strengths of your opponent's case are generally your case's weaknesses.

In the end, to be truly prepared for possible questions requires a mastery of the field of relevant law. Learning only a narrow slice of the field of law involved in the case will not suffice, however, for it is necessary to understand the bigger picture. The judges will want to know how the rule you seek and the result you desire fit into the scheme of things. As Judge Silberman has said, often it is necessary to fit "each new case into a broad and complex mosaic."[7]

Keep Your Cool

"I was gratified to be able to answer promptly, and I did. I said I didn't know."
Mark Twain, *Life on the Mississippi*

Despite your diligence in preparation, a judge might occasionally ask a question to which you do not know the answer. If you should have known, your cause is badly harmed. This error is avoidable by a more thorough preparation. But sometimes, out of curiosity or for reasons that are unfathomable, a judge might ask a factual question that is not pertinent to the issues, and if you do not know the answer it is best to say so. Even if the question involves a matter relevant to your case, it is better to admit that you have no answer than respond poorly.

Stand Your Ground

"I was with you Mr. Scott—until I heard your argument."
Old English Judge

What I call the "Kenny Rogers" principle of appellate advocacy—knowing "when to hold 'em, and when to fold 'em"—applies from the beginning of appellate advocacy and the decision to appeal through the oral argument. It relies upon a clear understanding of when to make concessions and when to stand fast. Sometimes judges ask hypothetical questions that change the facts of the case at issue to determine whether the rule being advocated would apply under the altered facts. Insisting that it would might be the height of folly; acknowledging that it would not might concede the case. Knowing the difference is the art of advocacy. The prosecutor must thoroughly comprehend the case and the law to make concessions where appropriate and to avoid arguing for untenable principles (or demonstrating a poor understanding of what he or she is talking about). On the other hand, when the judges are hostile to the point being made, the prosecutor must sometimes "hold 'em" and stand fast, despite the discomfort caused by the panel's hostility or the fear of a damaged or lost case.

Brevity is a Good Thing

"He draweth out the thread of his verbosity finer than the staple of his argument."
Shakespeare, *Love's Labor Lost*

A common error in oral argument is not to sit down when finished. On innumerable occasions, I have observed lawyers, who having clearly made all the points intended, realized that there was time remaining and felt compelled to continue. The random repetitions of points previously made were far less effective than those originally put forth and detracted greatly from what had been solid performances. Be concise from the outset and once you make the argument, sit down. The judges will appreciate it; and the more concise and interesting argument will be extremely effective.

THE ROUTINE CASE

Although the foregoing remarks apply to high publicity cases or issues of great importance and complexity, they do not suggest that the prosecutor should avoid arguing the *routine* or *mundane* appellate cases that constitute the vast majority.

Appearing before the panel for a two or three minute argument, simply to cite a new case, emphasize a point or stand for questions, is often valuable. Even if the court has no questions, an appearance demonstrates the prosecutor's interest and concern and emphasizes his or her intention not to waste the court's time with a regurgitation of the brief. The judges are able to put names to faces, which furthers the appellate prosecutor's reputation with the court as a trustworthy and sound advocate, particularly when the brief is well-written.

An important distinction should be kept in mind: the prudent oral advocate appropriately tailors the argument to match the court hearing the case. The United States Supreme Court and the state supreme courts literally—and routinely—make new law. These courts take pains to ensure that proposed decisions are proper, and oral arguments before them are expected to cover wide swaths of ground or material, even when the focus is narrow. In the lower level appellate courts, where the focus is narrower, they rarely make new law and more often apply existing law to new cases to decide the merit of the appellant's position. The oral advocate, then, should take pains to consider in advance the power of the particular court hearing the case. Failure to make this consideration can result in disaster.

CONCLUSION

"That leads me to the subject of the quality of the government's appellate advocacy. Sadly, but surely inevitably, it has declined over the last two decades... Too often, even in important cases, the government lawyer is badly outmatched by the private (including 'public interest') lawyers."
Hon. Laurence Silberman

If Judge Silberman is correct and the trend he discerns must be reversed, then prosecutors have a difficult task before them. The public is entitled to vigorous and effective appellate advocacy from the government. That advocacy, of course, must always be principled. Demonstrating that the more things change, the more they stay the same, Abraham Lincoln observed in 1850 that "There is a vague popular belief that lawyers are necessarily dishonest... the impression is common—almost universal." Lincoln advised resistance: "Resolve to be honest at all events; and if, in your own judgment, you can not be an honest lawyer, resolve to be honest without being a lawyer. Choose some other occupation, rather than one in the choosing of which you do, in advance, consent to be a knave."[8] Prosecutors should always keep in mind that an effective argument is honorable, and an honorable argument, thoroughly research and prepared, is effective.

RESOURCES

Robert Martineau, The Value of Appellate Oral Argument: a Challenge to the Conventional Wisdom, *72 Iowa L Ed 1 (1986)*.

Jason Val, Oral Argument's Big Challenge: Fielding Questions From the Court, *1 J App Prac and Process 401 (1999)*.

Raymond Elliget, Jr., Top 10 Appellate Mistakes (Or Why You Need An Appellate Specialist), *72-JAN Fla B J 41 (1998)*.

Bright and Arnold, Oral Argument? It May Be Crucial!, *80 ABA J 68 (Sept 1984)*.

Hon. Karen J. Williams, Help Us Help You: A Fourth Circuit Primer on Effective Appellate Oral Arguments, *50 S C L Rev 591 (1999)*.

ENDNOTES

[1] Hon. Laurence Silberman, Judge of the United States Court of Appeals for the District of Columbia Circuit, ABA Journal, *Litigation*, Spring, 1994.

[2] Lincoln, *Speeches and Writings: 1832-1858* (Library of America: 1989), p 245.

[3] Sir Harold Bowden, *The New Dictionary of Thoughts*, (Standard Book: 1977).

[4] Quoted in American Bar Association Journal, March 1994, p 50. Appellate advocates used to be allotted more time for argument.

[5] *Michigan v Summers*, 452 US 692, 60 L Ed 2d 340, 101 S Ct 2587 (1981).

[6] In the United States Supreme Court, not surprisingly, one may rest assured that the Court is engaged. In my first oral argument there, I received in excess of 100 questions in my allotted 30 minutes.

[7] Silberman, "Plain Talk on Appellate Advocacy," see footnote 2.

[8] Lincoln, *Speeches and Writings: 1832-1858* (Library of America: 1989), p 246.

EFFECTIVE BRIEF WRITING

*By Kenneth T. McCurry, Chief Assistant State's Attorney, Appellate Division,
Cook County State's Attorney's Office, Chicago, Illinois*

The trial prosecutor's goal is a well-tried case and a conviction, yet for the appellate prosecutor it is just the beginning. The appellate prosecutor's most immediate aim is a decision that affirms the conviction and sentence, but effective criminal appellate prosecution offers opportunities that go beyond salvaging hard-fought convictions. They present a chance to establish favorable principles of law for future cases. Of all the areas in criminal prosecution, appellate advocacy is perhaps the purest form of criminal law practice. It is nothing more than the presentation of the facts of a case, and the application of the law pertinent to those facts in a logical, dispassionate fashion.

Effective appellate prosecution, however, requires discipline in the form of a reasoned and orderly argument intended to persuade a reviewing court that a conviction should stand. This article offers some basic suggestions for the appellate prosecutor in that endeavor, including general remarks about preparation and more specific topics on brief writing and oral argument.

PREPARATION

Perhaps the most important preparation for appellate advocacy is a firm grasp of criminal law, both substantive and procedural. The successful appellate prosecutor studies the pertinent jurisdictions and criminal law opinions, noting holdings and statements of law for later use. Abstracting or quoting from the significant decisions with the use of the computer can keep them accessible through a simple word search and avoids the frustration of knowing that you have read a recent case with a certain holding but do not remember the name of the case.

An appellate prosecutor's work also requires a familiarity with the reviewing court's rules of appellate procedure. In addition to covering such matters as appellate court jurisdiction and filing time limits, the rules set out the details of motion practice, the requisite content of briefs and the procedure for oral argument.

Once the defendant has filed a timely notice of appeal, the record on appeal and his opening brief, the prosecutor can begin work on the responsive brief. He or she should first review the opponent's brief to determine the issues raised. The next step is to read the entire record carefully, taking copious notes of testimony, pleadings and argument. These notes will, of course, be necessary in drafting a responsive brief and will be especially helpful for oral argument.

Be particularly vigilant to note matters pertinent to issues raised. Be equally vigilant to note issues that were not raised at trial and are therefore waived. A waiver (and harmless error) argument is often appropriate and effective. The waiver doctrine requires a defendant to raise an objection at trial in order to preserve a contention of error for appeal. The rationale behind the principle is that a party must first give the trial court the opportunity to correct any error at the time it occurs, rather than burden appellate courts with needless labor. Where the defense has failed to voice the appropriate objection, the appellate prosecutor should always argue, at least alternatively, that the issue has been waived for purposes of appeal. While reviewing courts are not strictly bound by the doctrine of waiver and may address an issue that is not properly preserved, by arguing waiver the prosecution offers the reviewing court a reason to affirm a conviction it might otherwise overturn. Always be aware, however, that at oral argument the court's assessment of the importance of facts may differ from your own. Familiarity with the facts is therefore your best weapon.

STATEMENT OF FACTS

Many jurisdictions do not require the appellee to provide a statement of facts in the brief. There are, however, several advantages to providing one. In arguing most issues the facts are at least as important as the law. A good statement of the facts can, therefore, in itself often resolve an issue in your favor. Drafting a statement of facts, furthermore, forces the author to become more acquainted with the case. A prosecution version of the facts is perhaps even more crucial to counteract the account in the defendant's brief, which may be slanted, inadequate or argumentative. At trial, the evidence had been sufficient to convict and therefore, it facilitates the prosecutor's fair and objective narration of the facts. If the prosecution is consistent in all its briefs in offering a fair and accurate statement of facts, the court will eventually grant it more credibility and rely less on the versions of the facts presented in defense briefs.

There are basically two approaches to a statement of facts. In the first, the author recounts the proceedings at trial by summarizing the testimony of each of the witnesses in the order in which they appeared at trial. A second method combines the trial evidence in a chronological, narrative form, setting out a tale that includes the crime, the investigation and the arrest.

A statement of facts that summarizes the trial testimony witness by witness often has the advantage of being easier to draft. The brief writer can simply string together the notes of the report of proceedings, inserting record cites in the appropriate places. The result, however, can be tedious, repetitive and unfocused, due to the fact that only one witness testifies at a time and several witnesses may describe the same event, perhaps from different perspectives. Furthermore, the order in which the witnesses appeared may have depended upon their availability or a cogent trial strategy not particularly apposite on appeal. The statement of facts in your brief need not suffer from the same restraints.

Whenever possible, a chronological narrative of events gleaned from the totality of the trial evidence may be preferable. This approach gives the brief writer a great deal of flexibility and is more likely to hold the reader's interest. More work is required, however, including some thought as to the sequence and the joining of disparate pieces of the evidence into a unified account. The reward is brevity and clarity. When successfully written, the statement of facts will succinctly tie together all pertinent testimony to form a cohesive narrative.

In some cases, both approaches to the statement of facts can be used within the same brief. For instance, where the sufficiency of the grounds for arrest is at issue, evidence from the hearing on the motion to suppress might lend itself to an explicit presentation of the various testimonies, while the trial evidence of the crime itself can be presented as a narrative. Or, in recounting the trial evidence, it is often effective to combine the prosecution's case into a chronological account, but offer the defense case in the witness-by-witness format, which can highlight testimonial inconsistencies or exaggerations.

Regardless of the form the statement of facts takes, it should be brief, clear and objective. Overly lengthy briefs are appellate court judges' chief complaint. Avoid repetition and inclusion of extraneous matters. Longer accounts of trial proceedings germane to an issue on appeal are better left for inclusion in the appropriate argument where they will be repeated anyway. Matters of no consequence—particularly dates—should be omitted altogether.

The statement of facts is no place for argument. Using it to plead your case or attack the defendant's evidence only detracts from the section's effectiveness and raises questions about your own credibility. Evaluations of the strength of the evidence or the credibility of witnesses are a function of the brief's argument section.

A well-organized statement of facts is not unlike a short story. After reading your presentation of the facts, a reviewing court judge should know exactly what the defendant did in the commission of his crime, how he was arrested, what the trial evidence showed and what facts were considered in the determination of the defendant's sentence.

ARGUMENT

As with all persuasive legal writing, the argument section of an appellate court brief requires an organization that clearly and succinctly states your position and logically lays out the facts and rules of law that lead to the intended conclusion. To this end, the argument should first present the issue at hand and each party's position in the controversy. As to each argument, state the defendant's contention of error and the prosecution's response so that the court can readily grasp the issue and the conclusion you will reach.

Many jurisdictions require a statement of the standard of review for each issue raised. Even when not required, it is helpful to discuss the standard of review immediately following a clarification of the issue. The standard of review indicates the amount of deference that the reviewing court should accord a ruling of the trial court. Generally, where witness credibility is not involved, where there is no dispute as to the facts and where the appellate court's function is simply to declare what the law is or to apply the law to agreed facts, the standard is *de novo*. Otherwise, the standard leans more strongly in favor of the trial court, and reversal is called for only when the lower court's ruling was manifestly erroneous or was an abuse of discretion.

The argument itself is nothing more than a statement of the relevant facts, a recitation of the pertinent principles of law and an application of that law to the facts at hand. Each argument may begin with the facts or the law, but a careful account of both is necessary to arrive at the eventual heart of the argument, the application of the law to the facts.

Make sure, first of all, that the defendant has properly stated the facts. If the defendant's argument simply misstates the facts, the prosecutor's primary task is to point this out and apply the law to the correct facts. Otherwise, briefly recount the facts necessary to an understanding of the issue. At this point, it may be best to set out the testimony, argument or pleadings at issue more fully than in the statement of facts, including the context at trial in which the claimed error arose. Your argument may well depend on a single word used or question asked at trial.

Or it might require a broader presentation of the background activity to capture the true meaning of what transpired at trial. For instance, if hearsay is at issue and your argument will be that a response was not admitted for the truth of the matter asserted, an explanation of the entire context of the witness's testimony may be necessary to make your point. If, on the other hand, your response to a claim of improper closing argument is that the remark was invited, it will be necessary to provide that portion of the defense argument or strategy that provoked the comment.

In citing the appropriate law, start with more general principles and work toward the cases closely on point with your case. It is not necessary to recite the facts of each cited case, especially when the case is mentioned for a general rule of law. If there exists, however, a case directly on point and in your favor, summarize the facts of that case and present its holding.

While long quotations from previous cases are unnecessary and tend to be ineffective, freely quote short portions of opinions that apply. When you are fortunate enough to find a controlling case directly on point, all that remains is to distinguish the defendant's cases by pointing out the factual differences favoring the case or cases you have cited.

When no case applies directly to the circumstances at hand, there are several approaches to take in formulating an argument. After first citing the most apt general principles of law, investigate similar situations and apply the law found there by way of analogy. Also look to other jurisdictions for cases on point. Or argue that reason supports the trial court's ruling and that acceptance of the defense argument will lead to an absurd result in your case or in later cases. Issues where the local law is silent or unsettled present the best opportunity to make new and favorable law by arguing from reason and cases from other jurisdictions.

When case law is against the prosecution's position, legal ethics generally require an acknowledgment of that fact. Ethics, however, do not demand capitulation. If the existing law is flawed, suggest that it is time for a reconsideration of previous principles, again arguing that your position is the more reasonable one. While courts adhere to the principle of *stare decisis*, they do not always do so slavishly and can be convinced that change is appropriate.

Often it is advisable to make alternative arguments to support the conviction. While the basis of a trial court ruling may have been a particular theory of law, it is the lower court's conclusion rather than its reasoning that is crucial. For example, where a court has admitted a decedent's statement into evidence on the dubious grounds that it was a dying declaration, an argument that the remark was admissible as a spontaneous declaration may well prevail.

In many cases, it is possible to make the alternative argument that, if error occurred, it was cured at some other point in the trial. Where a defendant contends that his right to cross-examine was unduly limited when the trial court sustained a prosecution objection, point out any instances in the record where the court allowed questioning on substantially the same matters. If the defendant maintains that a jury instruction was inadequate, look to the entirety of the instructions to determine whether they were sufficient to cure any error.

Besides establishing that error occurred at trial, an appellant has the burden of showing that he was prejudiced as a result of the error. Consequently, a prosecutor, whenever possible, should argue that, if indeed there was error, it was harmless. Generally, any error is harmless if without it the outcome of the proceedings would have been unchanged. To establish that an error was harmless, therefore, the prosecutor's task is to convince the court that the evidence was so overwhelming that the claimed error was of minimal consequence. As is the case with a waiver argument, harmless error gives the reviewing court an opportunity to affirm a conviction despite the presence of possible error.

The prosecutor's appellate argument must also refute the significance of case law cited by the defense. Determine first the subsequent history of all cases upon which the defendant relies. It is not unusual for cited cases to have been later reversed, overruled or seriously questioned. If so, point this out to the court. Noting that the force of a defense case has since been blunted can destroy the credibility of a defendant's entire argument. Significant defense cases may also be distinguished on the basis of their facts. Read these cases carefully to find factual differences that would render their holdings inappropriate in the case at hand. Not every case in the defense brief, however, needs to be distinguished, only those which the defendant principally relies upon as dispositive.

Be mindful that the appellant organizes the argument section of his brief in a way most favorable to his case. The defendant may, for example, make a series of arguments each contending that, for different reasons, the evidence at trial was insufficient to convict. In such a case, it might be more advantageous for the prosecutor to combine a response into a single argument addressing each of the defense points. Such an approach avoids the repetition of general principles of law and a statement of the standard of review. As was the case with the statement of facts, the argument should be as brief as possible.

ORAL ARGUMENT

Oral argument represents the final opportunity to offer the prosecution's case and to respond to any particular concerns that the court may express. A successful oral argument is a dialogue between the attorney and the court, not a speech to the court and not simply a repetition of the matters already set out in the brief. Preparation for the argument, therefore, requires a familiarity with the record, a grasp of all significant cases and a thorough understanding of all the briefs. Select only the salient points for the oral presentation and compose an outline dedicated to offering the court some insight on those points.

As appellee, the prosecutor has the advantage of hearing the defense argument and the court's questions to opposing counsel. Those questions indicate the concerns that the court may have with the issues, and they should be addressed in the argument. While a prosecutor should always have a prepared presentation available, he must also anticipate the possibility that the entire argument will be devoted to answering the court's questions. Such arguments, in fact, are often the most successful because they hold the court's interest and truly become a conversational style dialogue with the court. Counsel should answer the court's questions without hesitation or evasion. Few tactics annoy a court more than elusive or vague responses to direct questions. Some responses may well require a measure of deliberation, however, and in those instances, it is best to avoid a hasty answer.

Oral argument is not the time to impress the court with an exhaustive recitation of case-law when the issue at hand concerns the fact of the case. If there are one or two cases directly on point cite only those at argument. When the issue is strictly one of law, however, a quick history of the rule becomes necessary.

There are a few techniques that the prosecutor should avoid at oral argument. Foremost among these is reading a prepared speech to the court. Eye contact with each member of the panel is essential. Besides risking the possibility of boring the court, excessive reading makes it impossible to engage each of the judges individually. When asked a question, listen carefully to the complete inquiry without interrupting the justice. Then answer as completely as possible without evasion. To avoid a direct reply is an admission of ignorance that serves only to irritate the court and destroy credibility. Rather than offer a nonresponsive discourse, when necessary the prosecutor should freely admit that he or she cannot answer the question.

CONCLUSION

During all phases of the appellate process, the prosecutor is an advocate arguing for a favorable interpretation and application of the rule of law. Effective prosecution at this level, however, requires a strict adherence to the rules of the reviewing court and an honest presentation of both the facts and the law. Anything less in either the brief or in oral argument detracts not only from the efforts in a particular case but also from the prosecutor's general effectiveness in all cases before the court.

THE ADMISSIBILITY OF DEMONSTRATIVE EVIDENCE

By David Marshall Nissman, Assistant U.S. Attorney, Office of the U.S. Attorney, St. John, Virgin Islands [1]

Introduction

This article discusses demonstrative and summary evidence, principally under the *Federal Rules of Evidence (FRE)*. However, most of the concepts discussed have applicability to all jurisdictions, particularly as many states have rules of evidence substantially similar to the FRE. In addition, it explores the use of computer animations, a relatively new type of demonstrative evidence sometimes referred to as crime scene re-enactment. Demonstrative evidence includes real evidence comprised of the tangible items that play a role in the case and illustrative evidence comprised of the tangible items that do not play a role in the case. According to *McCormick*, illustrative evidence is, "tendered for the purpose of rendering other evidence more comprehensible to the trier of fact. Examples of types of items frequently offered for purposes of illustration and clarification include models, maps, photographs, charts and other drawings." [2] While *McCormick* refers to tangible items that do not play a role in the case as illustrative evidence, it should be noted that other treatises, such as 1 Fred Lane, *Goldstein Trial Technique* (hereinafter *Goldstein*) and 4 *Weinstein* refer to such evidence as demonstrative evidence. [3]

Demonstrative (illustrative) evidence is sometimes referred to as, "pedagogical (teaching) devices or jury aids (which) are not evidence themselves, but merely tools designed to streamline the presentation of evidence in a complex case." [4] Another way to categorize demonstrative evidence is to include all evidence that conveys a relevant firsthand sense impression as opposed to that type of evidence that merely reports the secondhand sense impression of others, e.g., assertions of witnesses. [5]

It is clear that demonstrative evidence plays a large role in today's trials and trial judges are vested with broad discretion in ruling on the relevancy of evidence. Generally, "[c]ourts look favorably upon the use of demonstrative evidence because it helps the jury understand the issues raised at trial." [6]

Rule 611(a) of the FRE, in conjunction with the "Advisory Committee Notes," basically incorporates by reference those common law principles of evidence that are not specifically addressed elsewhere in the rules. Specifically, the notes provide that Rule 611(a), "restates in broad terms the power and obligation of the judge as developed under common law principles. It covers such concerns as whether testimony shall be in the form of a free narrative or responses to specific questions, *McCormick* § 5; the order of calling witnesses and presenting evidence, 6 *Wigmore* § 1867; the use of demonstrative evidence, *McCormick* § 179 and the many other questions arising during the course of a trial which can be solved only by the judge's common sense and fairness in view of the particular circumstances."[7]

One area of courtroom practice not specifically covered in the rules is the use of demonstrative evidence which, as noted above, the "Advisory Committee Notes" make clear is controlled by Rule 611(a).

DIFFERENCES BETWEEN SUMMARY CHARTS THAT ARE SUBSTANTIVE AND THOSE THAT ARE DEMONSTRATIVE:

Rule 611(A) v. Rule 1006

The law of evidence recognizes two types of summary charts:

- Charts that purport to summarize or show the relationship between (that is, "tie together") other evidence admitted during the trial. This type of chart is demonstrative evidence and its admissibility and accuracy is totally dependent on the admission in evidence and accuracy of the other evidence it purports to summarize (or "tie together"); the underlying evidence might include testimonial evidence and might consist of a combination of phone records, surveillance photos and surveillance testimony. This type of chart is governed by Rule 611(a); and,
- Charts summarizing voluminous records and offered in evidence under Rule 1006. Under Rule 1006, this type of summary chart constitutes substantive evidence and its admissibility is not dependent on the admission in evidence of the underlying records.

Good discussions concerning the distinction between Rule 611(a) charts and Rule 1006 summary charts can be found in *United States v. Bray*.[8] The evidentiary treatment of each can be different and it is critical that the offering party makes the trial court aware under which rule a chart is being offered.

Summary (substantive) evidence admitted in lieu of the underlying documents is "not embellished by or annotated with the conclusions of or inferences drawn by the proponent, whether in the form of labels, captions, highlighting techniques, or otherwise."[9] Demonstrative evidence, in contrast, is sometimes referred to as an argument made that explains a piece or pieces of real evidence.

ADMISSIBILITY OF DEMONSTRATIVE EXHIBITS

Westlaw Query 611(A)/P "Demonstrative Evidence"

FRE 611 (a) will be your principal guide. Rule 611(a) provides that the court shall exercise reasonable control over the mode and order of interrogating witnesses and presenting evidence so as to:

- Make the interrogation and presentation effective for the ascertainment of the truth;
- Avoid needless consumption of time; and
- Protect witnesses from harassment or undue embarrassment.

The rule was intentionally left open ended and a more specific rule governing the mode and order of interrogating witnesses and presenting evidence is neither desirable nor feasible.[10] Consequently, such evidentiary issues as the order of calling witnesses and the use of demonstrative evidence are to be determined "by the judge's common sense and fairness in view of the particular circumstances."[11]

The admission of demonstrative exhibits is thus clearly governed by the sound discretion of the trial court, and evidentiary rulings regarding such evidence will be reviewed under an abuse of discretion standard. *See* for example, *United States v. Jones* (use of videotape of explosion of bomb built as a replica of bomb discovered in marijuana field); *United States v. McIntosh* (demonstrative revolver); *Roland v. Langlois* (replica of carnival ride); *United States v. Paulino* (organizational chart); *United States v.*

Towns (demonstrative gun and ski mask); *United States v. Gardner* (summary chart); *United States v. Scales* (testimonial summary chart).[12]

Of course, the trial court's discretion will not be exercised in a vacuum, and there are at least four other rules of evidence that will play satellite roles with respect to the admissibility of illustrative exhibits—FRE 401, 403, 702 and 901:

- Rule 401 defines "relevant evidence" as evidence having the tendency to make the existence of a fact more probable or less probable;
- Rule 403 balances relevant evidence against potential prejudice, confusion and waste of time;
- Rule 702 governs the use of experts, who will often be laying the foundation for and explaining your exhibits; and[13]
- Rule 901 governs the authentication of evidence.

By definition, a demonstrative exhibit is illustrative and only serves to demonstrate a point relevant to the trial, e.g., fingerprint comparisons and replicas of crime scenes. Strictly speaking, a demonstrative exhibit is not evidence of the crime charged but is evidence that illustrates how the crime was committed or draws relationships from other evidence. The admissibility and use of a demonstrative exhibit may therefore depend upon how well the event depicted by the exhibit is itself authenticated, e.g., authentication of latents depicted in fingerprint comparison chart, authentication as to accuracy of crime scene model.

RULE 611(A) CHARTS

Westlaw Query 611(A)/P Summar!

True demonstrative charts that are offered under the auspices of Rule 611(a) are said to be "pedagogical" or "illustrative" summaries. They should be based on testimony or exhibits already in evidence. Caution: because of Rule 611(a) demonstrative charts are "derivative" charts—that is, they depend on other admitted evidence for their utility—it is error to introduce Rule 611(a) charts that rely on inadmissible evidence or on items for which no proper foundation has been laid. *See United States v. Pelulo* (error to admit summary chart based on inadmissible hearsay; limiting instructions insufficient to cure error); *United States v. Citron* (insufficient foundation for figures used in summary chart rendered chart inadmissible; limiting instructions insufficient);

and *United States v. Drougas* (summaries are inadmissible if they contain information not present in the underlying materials).[14]

It is sometimes useful to identify on the chart the government exhibit number of each item depicted so the jury can easily go to the source material to see for themselves the truth of the point the chart makes. For example, a chart comparing physical surveillance with telephone traffic should depict the name of the surveillance agent reporting the observation, as well as the exhibit number of the corresponding MUD[15] or telephone toll record in evidence. This technique will also provide assurance to the judge that the chart does not contain any reference to a fact not previously established at trial.[16]

The proponent of the Rule 611(a) chart can use reasonable assumptions or conclusions in creating it. *See United States v. Johnson* (organizational chart summarizing witness testimony in light most favorable to government permissible where jury properly instructed and chart maker subject to cross-examination); *United States v. Norton* ("the essential requirement is not that [summary] charts be free from reliance on any assumptions, but that these assumptions be supported by the evidence in the record"); *United States v. Stephens* (use of characterizations in chart permissible if jury properly instructed).[17] There is also no requirement that the summary exhibit contain the defendant's version or theory.[18]

The *Johnson* case in some respects is illustrative of the outer edge of admissibility for demonstrative evidence. The case involved the use of a drug agent to create a summary chart to explain conduct in a drug case. The organizational chart was essentially a summary exhibit reflecting the officer's compilation of testimony already adduced at trial. Specifically, the chart listed three high-level sources of crack, and below them, the names of the four principals including the defendants. Arrows on the chart illustrated a connection to each principal's source, which was any of the three suppliers or one of the other principals. The name of each principal headed a column of other names. Names printed in black represented persons who, based on the testimony, either bought crack from or distributed crack for only one principal. Names printed in red represented persons who worked for more than one principal. The government conceded that the officer prepared the chart in the light most favorable to the government, reflecting the officer's judgment as to the credibility of witnesses.[19]

The Fourth Circuit had difficulty with this evidence and although it ultimately sustained the conviction, other writers have heavily criticized the *Johnson* case as going too far.[20] There may, in fact, be few limits to demonstrative aids as evidenced by *State v. Olson*,[21] a sex case in which the prosecutor created her own "score sheet" listing the elements of the crime on a chart in full view of the jury. The chart contained the particulars of each count, including the operative names of the violated body parts. As the victims testified, the prosecutor got up and put color-coded check marks on the chart. One reasonable inference the jurors may have picked up was that once the chart was filled up with check marks, the defendants were proven guilty. Appropriate objections were made and overruled and the appellate court sustained the convictions. The cases described in this paragraph should be viewed as the outer limit of admissibility and discretion is suggested when planning trial strategy.

If, however, the prosecution establishes that the case is complex and difficult for the jurors to follow without the aid of these types of charts, the courts are more likely to admit the demonstrative charts or summaries.[22]

There is a danger that assumptions or conclusions implicit in a demonstrative exhibit will cause the exhibit to be impermissibly argumentative, misleading or otherwise unfair.[23] If assumptions or conclusions are important to the understanding of the exhibit, it is imperative that the exhibit preparer be made available for cross-examination. *See United Sates v. Drougas* (summary chart admissible after argumentative entries deleted).[24] Also, remember that Rule 611(a) charts are admissible only if the items, events or exhibits depicted are themselves established through other evidence admitted at trial.

Because Rule 611(a) demonstrative charts are truly a summary of other exhibits and/or testimony and have no independent evidentiary value, there may be judicial resistance to sending them back to the jury room. If jury room use is critical, have a proposed limiting instruction handy and give the trial judge case references to increase the court's comfort level.

RULE 611(A) CHARTS-LIMITING INSTRUCTIONS

Westlaw Query 611(A)/P Summar!

By tendering to the court an appropriate limiting instruction, a prosecutor enhances the likelihood of persuading the court to reject defense objections to a Rule 611(a) chart and such a limiting instruction might be critical to preserving the conviction on appeal. *See United States v. Baker* and *United States v. Winn* (limiting instruction given when summary evidence summarized documentary and testimonial evidence before jury).[25]/[26]

A sample instruction to the jury might be:

> Charts and summaries were shown to you in order to make the other evidence more meaningful and to aid you in considering the evidence. They are no better than the testimony or documents on which they are based and are not themselves independent evidence. Therefore, you are to give no greater consideration to these schedules or summaries than you would give to the evidence upon which they are based. It is for you to decide whether the charts, schedules or summaries correctly present the information contained in the testimony and in the exhibits on which they were based. You are entitled to consider the charts, schedules and summaries if you find that they are of assistance to you in analyzing the evidence and understanding the evidence.[27]

RULE 1006 SUMMARY CHARTS

Westlaw Query 1006/P Summar!

In contrast, summaries admitted pursuant to Rule 1006 are not really demonstrative evidence. These summaries concern voluminous writings, recordings or photos—not testimonial evidence. Rule 1006 requires initially that the underlying documents be too voluminous to be conveniently examined in court. The underlying records or data summarized in the chart need not themselves be in evidence; this rule is really designed to provide the jury a practical opportunity to access information derived from documents (or other evidence) which exist in an inconvenient form.

Under Rule 1006, the underlying documents must be made available to the opposing party before a chart summarizing them can be admitted. If a proper foundation is laid for the chart under the rule, it is irrelevant to the chart's admissibility whether the underlying documents are themselves introduced into evidence. *See United States v. Duncan* (chart summarizing voluminous hospital records admissible even though records themselves were also admitted) and *United States v. Bertoli* (underlying documents need not themselves be admitted for Rule 1006 chart to be admissible).[28]

The Rule 1006 summary chart can also be used to show what voluminous documents do not contain. *See United States v. Scales* (if independent evidentiary basis exists for allowing proof of absence of record entries, Rule 1006 summary chart can show same omissions).[29] Because the Rule 1006 chart is itself substantive evidence, the jury should be instructed to consider the exhibit as any other evidence.[30]

FIVE-PART TEST FOR ADMISSIBILITY OF EVIDENCE UNDER RULE 1006

- Underlying evidence is admissible, although not necessarily admitted.
- Underlying evidence is too "voluminous" for "convenient" in-court review.
- Summaries must accurately reflect underlying evidence.
- Intended summary evidence and underlying evidence must be produced in advance of the trial.
- Preparer of summary evidence must be made available for cross-examination.

Underlying Evidence Is Admissible Although Not Necessarily Admitted

If underlying evidence is admissible under some evidentiary theory, the summaries are admissible. *See United States v. Osum* (summaries of documents, independently admissible as business records under FRE 803(6) and medical records under FRE 803(4), admissible without admission of underlying records); *Martin v. Funtime, Inc.* (summaries of personnel records, independently admissible under FRE 803(6), also admissible); *United States v. Meyers* (summaries of surveillance logs admissible as summaries of business records).[31]

The underlying evidence need not be admitted for the court to receive the summaries in evidence. *See United States v. Strissell* (plain language of Rule 1006 makes it clear that there is no requirement that underlying documents be admitted as a precondition to the admission of summaries).[32] On the other hand, see *Fagiola v. National Gypsum Co.*[33] which incorrectly states the underlying evidence must be admitted before summaries thereof are admitted. Note that before the 1975 adoption of Rule 1006, the documents underlying the summary chart had to be admitted into evidence, and the jury was instructed that the documents, not the summary chart, constituted the evidence.[34] On abuse of discretion to receive summaries of inadmissible evidence, *see United States v. Pelullo* (trial court abused discretion when it admitted summary evidence based at least in part on inadmissible hearsay). *See also AMPAT/Midwest Inc. v. Ill. Tool Works, Inc.* (summaries of records prepared for litigation are inadmissible; summaries of business records are admissible); and, *Hackett v. Housing Authority of San Antonio* (trial court abused its discretion by admitting summary evidence based in part on inadmissible hearsay).[35] *See United States v. Johnson* for a case demonstrating that the burden is on proponent of evidence to establish underlying evidence.[36]

When Underlying Evidence Is Too "Voluminous" For "Convenient" In-Court Review

The determination of "convenient" is much more important than the determination of "voluminous," as indicated by *United States v. Osum* (summary of records from three auto accidents sufficiently voluminous to be summarized) and *United States v. Possick* (limited number of phone calls and drug transactions were sufficiently "voluminous" so as to make summary thereof "convenient").[37] The determination of "convenient" and "voluminous" is left to the sound discretion of the trial court. *See United States v. Campbell* (technical material was not readily understandable by the lay reader); *United States v. Scales* (comprehension of exhibits would have been difficult and certainly inconvenient without summary exhibits); and *United States v. Evans* (in complex case, the court has considerable latitude to expedite the proceedings through use of summary evidence, even though underlying data not particularly "voluminous").[38] The summary exhibit or testimony may concern the absence of records or entries on records.[39]

Summaries Must Accurately Reflect Underlying Evidence

The overriding concern of the courts is that summary exhibits be fair, accurate and not misleading.[40] A chart submitted by the prosecution is a very persuasive and powerful tool and must be fairly used since, by its arrangement and use, it is an argument to the jury during the course of the trial.[41] "Fairness," however, does not mean that the summary exhibit must contain the defendant's version of the facts. There is no requirement that a prosecution's summary chart include the defendant's version or theory.[42]

The captions and headings of the summary exhibits should not contain conclusions or assumptions that take on independent significance. Some assumptions are permissible, however, if based on the evidence.[43] *See United States v. Norton* ("The essential requirement is not that the [summary] charts be free from reliance on any assumptions, but that these assumptions be supported by the evidence in the record"); *United States v. Diez* (heading for "Amounts Not Reported"); *United States v. Smyth*, (headings included "Falsified Data" and "Differences Between Original/False").

The Underlying Documents Must Be Produced Prior to Trial

It is better practice to produce underlying documents as part of normal discovery and then brief the court on the law of summary evidence with summary exhibits attached, although mere production of underlying documents may be sufficient.[44] This gives the defense the opportunity to review the underlying documents so as to challenge the foundation for the summary exhibit, if appropriate. Advance notice of summary evidence will endear the prosecutor to both trial court and appellate court. *See Osum* (no abuse of discretion to deny defendant's objection to summary evidence raised for the first time in trial after early notice by government of intent to call summary witness).[45]

Maintain documentation of production of underlying documents and keep copies of the documents underlying all summary exhibits isolated and readily available since the court may, in its discretion under Rule 1006, order their production at any time.

Preparer of Summary Evidence Must Be Made Available for Cross Examination

Any witness who has prepared or has supervised the preparation of the summary exhibit can establish the required foundation. The witness must be in a position to say that he or she has reviewed the summarized records and that the summary exhibit fairly and accurately summarizes their relevant contents. The summary witness need not be qualified as an expert, in most cases. However, the defense is entitled to cross-examine whoever prepared the summary evidence, irrespective of who laid the foundation in the government's case.[46]

SAMPLE INSTRUCTIONS FOR RULE 1006 SUMMARIES

Westlaw Query 1006/P Summar!

"You will remember that certain (schedules) (summaries) (charts) were admitted in evidence. You may use those (schedules) (summaries) (charts) as evidence, even though the underlying documents and records are not here."[47]

If summaries are challenged, add: "However, the (accuracy) (authenticity) of those (schedules) (summaries) (charts) has been challenged. It is for you to decide how much weight, if any, you will give to them. In making that decision, you should consider all of the testimony you heard about the way in which they were prepared."[48]

For unchallenged summaries: "There have been admitted in evidence certain schedules or summaries. They truly and accurately summarize the contents of voluminous books, records or documents, and should be considered together with and in the same manner as all other evidence in the case."[49]

For challenged summaries: "There have been admitted in evidence certain schedules or summaries. Their accuracy has been challenged by (the government) (the defendant). Thus the original materials upon which the exhibits are based have also been admitted into evidence so that you may determine whether the schedules or summaries are accurate."[50]

Where the underlying evidence was not admitted: "The government has presented exhibits in the form of charts and summaries. I decided to admit these charts and summaries in place of the underlying documents that they represent in order to save time and avoid unnecessary inconvenience. You should consider these charts and summaries as you would any other evidence."[51]

Note that when a summary is admitted, but not underlying evidence, no special instruction is required, and the jury is to view the summary exhibit as any other evidence (See Martin v. Funtime; Osum; Possick and Weinstein's Evidence).[52] On whether to give a special instruction concerning admitted summary exhibits is within the sound discretion of the trial court see Possick; United States v. Orlowski and United States v. Robinson.[53]

Where the underlying evidence was admitted: "The charts and summaries were shown to you in order to make the other evidence more meaningful and to aid you in considering the evidence. They are no better than the testimony or documents on which they are based and are not themselves independent evidence. Therefore, you are to give no greater consideration to these schedules or summaries than you would give to the evidence upon which they are based. It is for you to decide whether the charts, schedules or summaries correctly present the information contained in the testimony and in the exhibits on which they were based. You are entitled to consider the charts, schedules and summaries if you find that they are of assistance to you in analyzing the evidence and understanding the evidence."[54]

Note that such an instruction, of course, is markedly different than the form of instruction that should be given for a Rule 611(a) demonstrative summary chart, an example of which is set forth above in that section of this chapter, which discusses Rule 611(a). Further, since true Rule 1006 summaries are themselves evidence, no other limiting or cautionary instruction should be necessary or appropriate. *See Osum* (limiting instruction concerning Rule 1006 summary may improperly prejudice the party introducing the summary, at least where underlying documents themselves are not in evidence).[55]

Finally, summary charts admitted under Rule 1006 are themselves substantive evidence of the information depicted in the charts. Accordingly, there should be a presumption for their use in the jury room.

APPELLATE REVIEW

The admission of summary evidence is committed to the sound discretion of the trial court.[56] Trial courts are given wide discretion relative to the introduction of summary evidence, and their findings will not be disturbed absent an abuse of that discretion.[57] Failure to object at trial to introduction of summary evidence waives claim of error on appeal.[58] Objections must be set forth with particularity.[59]

Purposes and Effects Achieved by Demonstrative Evidence

As noted above, demonstrative exhibits allow the jury to picture events clearly and quickly, an essential goal since there is only a relatively small window of time to teach the case to them. Additionally, aided by illustrative exhibits, jurors may be better able to focus their collective memories and thereby reach a consensus.

Demonstrative exhibits can also "untarnish" the most unsavory of witnesses. Such exhibits make testimonial evidence more compelling and credible, regardless of a witness's "baggage" and they can make the impeachable witness unimpeachable by putting before the jury in black and white (or preferably, in color) indisputable corroboration for that witness.

Demonstrative exhibits can also achieve the impossible by allowing lay jurors to understand the prosecution experts. They help the jurors to follow along and reach the same expert opinion themselves. Do not underestimate the desirability of making a trial an interactive event for the jury. Demonstrative exhibits inspire the jury to solve the crime as the trial proceeds, rather than leaving them to play "go fish" with voluminous exhibits at the end of the trial. It cannot be overemphasized that the jurors are the triers of fact and the prosecutor must maintain their interest.

Some judges have a distinct aversion to publishing exhibits during the trial, calling it a waste of time for the jurors to examine evidence that they will get to see later—often much later. In some instances, offering demonstrative exhibits may be a way to persuade the judge to allow the jury to see critical evidence as it comes in, since demonstrative evidence is most often used during the testimony of a witness.

Demonstrative exhibits also give the prosecutor credibility. Jurors expect that a federal case will be special and illustrative exhibits make the prosecutor and the case look professional. They give the government a chance to "connect" with the jury; the prosecutor and the government's theory take center stage with effective exhibits while the jurors see the exhibits as independent proof of the government's position.

Don't neglect charts and other exhibits in the opening statement. Appropriate use of charts and exhibits begins the process of instilling confidence in the prosecutor and the prosecution's evidence. Additionally, if a particular demonstrative technique is to be used, the prosecutor may wish to explain or introduce it to the jury in the opening statement. To minimize interruptions, get pretrial approval to use charts and exhibits during the opening statement.

At least some courts will—during opening statement or closing argument—allow the lawyers to display charts to the jury that highlight portions of the lawyers' opening or closing. For example, during opening statement one prosecutor uses charts reflecting the names of the defendants, a description of the charges, an outline of key events and other things he will cover during his opening statement. This not only enables him to present the opening statement without notes, it allows the jury to capture the information with two senses—their ears and their eyes. Of course, such charts are not admissible in evidence and are only intended as aids to argument. However, assuming the court advises the jury that the charts are only aids to argument and are not evidence, such use of "inadmissible" charts is appropriate during opening statement and closing argument. Obviously, one should check with the court before showing any chart to the jury.

Practical Considerations:

- Plan ahead: scanning and storing data onto CDs may take time;
- Technology does not replace accuracy, identification and authentication. Double check source materials and exhibits;
- Educate skeptical judges. It is imperative to convince the court that these techniques speed up the trial, assist the jury in focusing on a particular exhibit, are accurate and are nothing more than enhancements to well-accepted techniques (e.g., charts, overheads);
- Provide notice to defense counsel and get advance rulings from the court on "killer" exhibits that are likely to draw objections;
- Practice with the exhibits. And while practicing with the exhibits, check sight lines in the courtroom to make sure every juror has a clear view of the exhibit. Use multiple monitors if practical and have the jury file by the exhibits if necessary;[60] and
- If possible, use a variety of demonstrative evidence techniques: mixing it up will keep it interesting.

Demonstrative Exhibits in the Jury Room

Westlaw Query "Demonstrative Exhibit"/S "Jury Room" or "Deliberat!
There is language in older opinions stating that the "preferred" evidentiary practice is to exclude demonstrative exhibits from the jury room. *See Possick* ("submission of purely demonstrative charts to jury is disfavored; therefore limiting instructions more strongly suggested"); *Carson v. Polley* ("it rarely is error to have illustrative evidence in jury room," but better practice is to leave it out); and *United States v. Cox* ("the better practice is to exclude illustrative evidence from jury room").[61] This language still shows up from time to time in recent cases.[62]

However, the appellate decisions that have articulated this "preference" have generally not overturned convictions despite the presence of demonstrative exhibits in the jury room. Thus, in *Possick* the trial court admitted two DEA charts: one a flow chart showing the organization of the drug ring and the other showing the number of phone calls between the defendant and his subordinates.[63] The trial court overruled defense objections that the charts were argumentative and allowed both charts to go to the jury during its deliberations. The Eighth Circuit noted that in such situations limiting instructions are "strongly suggested."[64] Despite the fact that the trial court inexplicably failed to give such an instruction even when it announced its intention to do so, the appellate court did not find that "this error, if it is error, requires reversal."[65] *See United States* v. *Cox*[66] (no abuse of discretion in allowing bomb replicas to go to jury room where limiting instructions given).

More recent appellate decisions indicate that the decision to allow demonstrative exhibits to be sent to the jury room will be governed, like their initial admission, by an abuse of discretion standard. Thus, juries have been allowed to have access to a broad range of demonstrative exhibits during their deliberations. *See* United *States v. Salerno* (scale model of crime scene); *United States v. Britton* (tape transcripts); *United States v. Berry* (tape transcripts) and *United States v. Cruz-Paulino* (representative sample of cocaine).[67]

Note that just because a judge may be willing to send demonstrative exhibits back to the jury room, does not necessarily make it advisable to ask the court to do so. While such exhibits can be dramatic and can accordingly enhance the case, they can also end up being "play toys" in the jury room, adding to jury confusion or sending the jury off on tangents the government never intended. Also, some appellate decisions, in affirming convictions, have observed that the trial judge was even-handed in sending all the exhibits back—including defense exhibits.[68] Thus, if there are "dueling demonstrative exhibits" offered by both sides, thought must be given as to whether there is greater chance for jury confusion if competing charts are sent to the jury room, as opposed to none.

SECONDARY EVIDENCE SUMMARIES

There is recent case development to suggest that a third form of evidence may be admissible that is a hybrid of FRE 611 and FRE 1006 evidence. The Sixth Circuit has called this evidence a secondary evidence summary.[69] Secondary evidence summaries are a combination of demonstrative and substantive summary evidence. This type of evidence is not prepared strictly in compliance with FRE 1006 but is more than a pedagogical device designed to simplify and clarify evidence. Secondary evidence summaries are admitted not in lieu of the evidence they summarize but in addition to the underlying evidence if the trial court is convinced that the digest so accurately and reliably summarizes complex or difficult evidence that it is of material assistance to the jury in understanding the underlying material. A limiting instruction is necessary with this third type of evidence.

The secondary evidence summary may be admissible even if the underlying records are partially lost or destroyed. In a bankruptcy case, the debtor, a jeweler, made improper transfers of goods to a third party. The third party did not dispute the fact of the transfer but challenged the volume and value of the goods allegedly transferred. The trustee called an employee to testify concerning the value and amount of goods improperly transferred. The witness pieced together records, including photocopies of adding machine tapes that included handwritten notations, which allowed the witness to reconstruct what occurred. The witness then prepared a summary that showed the amount of the transferred goods and the resulting value. There was no foundation to admit the summary based on FRE 1006. However, using the business record hearsay exception FRE 803(6) in connection with FRE 1004(1) (lost or destroyed original records) established a reliable foundation for the admissibility of the evidence.[70] Secondary evidence used in the place of original evidence need meet no threshold standard of quality or reliability; those questions go to weight, not admissibility.[71]

Secondary Evidence Summary: Jury Instruction

Suggested instruction: "Members of the jury, you are instructed that a secondary evidence summary was admitted for your consideration. This summary is not independent evidence of the subject matter that it summarizes and it is only as valid and reliable as you find the underlying evidence to be."[72]

Courtroom Experiments, Simulations and Enactments

Where the evidence is called demonstrative, the standards for putting the material before the jury are generally less stringent than if the evidence is called a re-enactment. Where an experiment purports to simulate actual events (like a crime scene re-enactment), the proponent has the burden of demonstrating substantial similarity of conditions.[73] Because re-enactments are such powerful pieces of evidence, trial courts tend to use a hard line FRE 403 analysis. In the *Gaskell* case, an expert using a doll purporting to resemble an infant demonstrated the force necessary to cause "shaken baby syndrome." In reversing the conviction, the 11th Circuit said,

> [W]hatever slight probative value that inhered in the demonstration was overwhelmed by its unfairly prejudicial effects. The sight of an adult male repeatedly shaking a representation of an infant with the degree of force necessary to manipulate the doll's head in the required fashion was likely to form a strong impression upon the jury… This prejudicial effect was magnified by the fact that the outcome of this trial hinged upon whether the jury believed that the degree of injury suffered by the victim could support defendant's testimony that he inflicted the fatal injuries in a panicked attempt to revive her.[74]

In *United States v. Wanoskia*, a murder trial in Indian country, the defendant claimed that his wife shot and killed herself.[75] The ballistics showed that the gun was discharged at a distance of at least 18 inches away from the entry wound. The prosecution introduced a demonstration that showed that the victim's arms were not long enough to fire the gun from that distance. In affirming the conviction, the Tenth Circuit said, "re-enactments of events can be highly persuasive. The opportunity for the jury to see what supposedly happened can accomplish in seconds what might otherwise take days to accomplish."[76] Because a visual image can imprint on the jury's mind its version of the facts there is a strict threshold requirement for the admission of experimental evidence that requires a substantial similarity of conditions.[77]

COMPUTER-GENERATED EVIDENCE—A CASE STUDY

In the early morning hours of August 13, 1992, Lyndon Frederick called the police to report that he had accidentally shot his girlfriend in the face. When the police arrived, a hysterical Frederick exhorted them to hurry because she was still alive. He was temporarily taken into custody and gave several statements in which he explained how the gun accidentally discharged. He claimed that she was asleep and lying in a prone position when he bent down to kiss her as he was leaving for work. He said that he had picked up his licensed gun from underneath the mattress because he wanted it out of the way when she cleaned the apartment. As he bent down to kiss her he claimed the gun accidentally fired. He concluded his statement by saying, "I loved her a lot."

The police released Lyndon Frederick and their investigation stalled. The view of the territorial prosecution agency designated to handle all murder prosecutions under Virgin Islands law was that the physical evidence would tell them whether Lyndon Frederick was telling the truth. A nationally renowned pathologist, Dr. Vincent DiMaio, was retained to analyze the blood spatter evidence, sometimes referred to as the "wound ballistics" evidence. From that evidence, DiMaio concluded that the victim was sitting up in the bed with her hand stretched in front of her in a defensive position when Frederick, standing in front of her, fired the gun into her face. Because the method of the presentation of this evidence was critical to the case, a computer animation was developed to present it.

The computer animation was generated by sequencing on videotape a series of still images that reflected information supplied by the police, prosecutor and expert witness about the crime scene. The still images were created on a computer, recorded on videotape and when played on a VCR they appeared as an animated movie.

To produce the video, the animator was furnished with all of the pathologist's raw data, i.e., the dimensions of the bedroom, location of entry wound, location of blood spatter, to prepare a draft version of the animation. After communicating with the animator several times and viewing a draft version of the animation, DiMaio then made suggestions for modifications to the imagery based upon his analysis of the facts. Ultimately, they developed an accurate and presentable computer animation.

During the trial, the government offered the computer animation as demonstrative evidence to help explain DiMaio's testimony. Although there were objections both to his expert opinion and the computer animation because it was offered as an aid to the expert's opinion, much like a chart or diagram, the issue was not a close one.

The animation, which lasted less than three minutes, was an incredibly chilling piece of evidence. The jury watched while a video recreation of the defendant stood in front of the victim while she sat on the bed. The animation of the defendant then pointed a gun at her face and fired the fatal shot. During this time the victim raised a defensive hand in front of her face. The bullet grazed her hand and entered her face below her eye. It was clear from both the expert testimony and the animation that the shooting was no accident. In a very real sense, it was as if the victim had returned from the grave to testify and set the record straight.

The defendant was convicted and appealed on many grounds including the claim that the animation was erroneously admitted into evidence. The Third Circuit Court of Appeals affirmed the conviction with an unpublished judgment order.[78]

Computer Animation Techniques

At the time the Frederick case was being investigated in 1994, this computer animation technique was only available through commercial sources. Today, however, federal prosecutors have terrific resources available through the Federal Bureau of Investigation (FBI). The FBI lab has computer animation capabilities and, within certain guidelines, the agency's Investigative and Prosecutive Graphics Unit (IPGU) will respond to requests to develop animations and supply expert witnesses on a case-by-case basis.[79] IPGU is interested in cases with verifiable objective evidence and definable locations. Verifiable facts include medical examiner reports, trajectory and ballistic evidence and crime scene dimensions, among others. Animations are a time-consuming process and should be developed in conjunction with other expert testimony. IPGU is not interested in generating animations based solely on the statements of witnesses.

Generally, animations are grouped in two broad categories: recreations or re-enactments that purport to simulate an event and animations that are not exact re-enactments but illustrate opinion, such as an expert's theory of the case or a scientific principle.[80]

A re-enactment is a series of graphic images created with the aid of a computer that are shown in sequence to reconstruct a visual representation of an event or process. A comparison with a movie film helps to clarify this definition: a movie is actually a series of photographs in which each photograph varies slightly from the last and the image of motion results from viewing the photographs in sequence, at a high rate of speed.

On the other hand, a computer produces the graphic images in a computer re-enactment. Each image represents an object or activity at a certain moment in time, analogous to the individual photographs in a movie.[81] These computer images also vary, one from the next, so that when viewed in sequence the object or activity appears to be in motion.

Re-enactments purport to translate the circumstances of an event into a picture or a motion picture. With sufficient data, a computer can depict:

- A moving vehicle: *See Pino v. Gauthier* (discussing videotaped computer simulation of four possible scenarios of movements of a truck prior to an accident and concluding it was properly excluded from evidence); and *People v. McHugh* (finding re-enactment of car accident admissible provided the proper groundwork is laid and the expert who prepared the re-enactment is qualified);
- An airplane crash: *See Haley v. Pan American World Airways* (referencing videotaped simulation of takeoff and crash used as evidence of the plaintiff's "pre-impact fear");
- A natural disaster;
- A homicide: *See Strock v. Southern Farm Bur. Cas. Ins. Co.* (unpublished opinion; simulation of aggressive movements of a shooting victim); and
- A bomb from bomb fragments in the Unabomber case or the entry of agents into a building in Waco.[82]

As a general rule, the evidentiary foundational requirements for a computer re-enactment are strict and judges are hesitant to admit this powerful evidence when it is offered as a recreation of the event. However, if offered as demonstrative evidence to support the opinion of an expert witness, the rules are more relaxed and the chances of admission increase geometrically.[83] Judges are much more comfortable allowing juries to view this evidence when they can give a cautionary instruction limiting the effect of what otherwise might be incredibly powerful evidence.[84]

In *Douglass v. Delta Air Lines*,[85] the United States and its experts produced simulations of approximately the last 15 minutes of the aircraft's flight. By using the digital flight data recorder information from the aircraft, a computer animation was developed from 40 different parameters such as acceleration, roll, pitch and heading to recreate a descent profile of the aircraft, including a display of information that would have been available to the cockpit crew.[86] The animations also used information from the National Weather Service, statements from witnesses and the audiotape of the cockpit flight recorder played in sync with the re-enactment[87]

The factual basis for a computer re-enactment may vary widely. On one end of the spectrum, known parameters, data and facts derived from an investigation are entered into a computer and based on this input the computer may be able to supply missing information.[88] A computer-generated re-enactment or recreation is a fact-based explanation of what actually happened.[89] At the other end of the spectrum, a computer animator individually designs each image, with a minimum factual basis, using the computer merely as an animation canvas. Such computer illustrations are generally called computer animations.[90]

These computer animations need not recreate actual events but can be used for other purposes, i.e., to illustrate expert testimony, present a theory of how an event happened or demonstrate an abstract principle. In *Datskow v. Teledyne Continental Motors*,[91] the court admitted a computer-generated animation that illustrated the plaintiff's expert testimony regarding how a fire started in the engine of a plane. Seeking to exclude the animation from evidence, the defendants argued that the computer animation was "less an illustration of [the expert's testimony] than a purported recreation of the accident."[92] The court rejected that contention on the grounds that the jury had been specifically instructed that the tape was only being shown "to help the jury understand the expert's opinion as to what happened and that it's not a recreation."[93] In order to further discourage the jury from concluding that the video-animation was a recreation of the accident, the court had ordered that the "voice-over of the radio communications between the actual airport and the airport control tower" be turned off so that the jury could not hear it.[94]

Animations may also be used to illustrate abstract principles, and are particularly valuable in delineating complex technologies.[95] Animations have been used to illustrate the structure of DNA, the production of proteins in cellular organisms and the method of operation of various separation technologies.[96] In each instance, the animation enables the depiction of complicated scientific principles in a simple and understandable way.

Additionally, computers may be used to generate persuasive, eye-catching graphics that highlight and illustrate important points. In *State of Ohio v. Clark*, for instance, prosecutors used computer-generated graphics to disprove the defendant's case.[97] The defense claimed that a murder victim was shot while sitting on the edge of a bathtub, as she grabbed the gun from the defendant. Using AutoCAD software[98] on an IBM compatible computer, the prosecution's crime reconstruction expert, "draft[ed] a three-dimensional reconstruction of the bathroom where the shooting took place and was able to rotate the reconstructed bathroom on the computer rather than having to draft additional drawings."[99] The expert also inputted other key data, including the dimensions of the bathtub, the location of fixtures, the location of the bullet hole and the dimensions of the victim's body.[100] The computer-generated simulation illustrated that the victim could not have been shot in the manner suggested by the defense, because the gun would have to have been located three and one-half inches below the floor of the bathroom where the shooting occurred.[101] The expert, who based his opinions on the recreation, also referred to blow-ups of the computer-generated crime scene during his testimony.[102]

Computers can also compile data and perform calculations that may be too complex or too repetitive to do manually. For example, computer models have been used to calculate antitrust damages. *See Pearl Brewing Co. v. Joseph Schlitz Brewing Co.*[103] (addressing issues regarding discovery of computer program to prove damages in antitrust case). They have been used to calculate how much steam was used to heat a business during a five-year period, *Commercial Union Ins. Co. v. Boston Edison* [104] (admitting computer model that compiled a variety of variables to prove how much steam was used by the plaintiff during a five-year period) and to determine whether a particular device was "perfectible," *Perma Research & Dev. Co. v. Singer Co.*[105] (computer simulation formed basis of expert's testimony that anti-skid device was "perfectible" and thus, that plaintiff should have used its "best efforts" to perfect the device).

The computer-generated re-enactment/animation procedure has been described as a six-step process.[106] The first step is data collection. It includes the collection of any pertinent data, including drawings, sketches and prints, police or accident reports, depositions of eyewitnesses, calculations and analyses by experts, photographs, etc. The second step is creating a storyboard to describe the motion that is to be animated. The third step is creating the computer models. Here the input data describing the various objects in the animation are actually built on the computer. The fourth step is composing the motion script. The fifth step is rendering. The computer takes all input data and renders, or calculates, a still frame containing the image. Once all the frames are rendered the final step is recording those images.[107]

THEORIES OF ADMISSIBILITY

Although few reported cases discuss the admissibility of computer-generated animations, the ones that do usually state that, to be admissible, computer-generated animations must be properly authenticated, relevant and the probative value must outweigh the prejudicial value. In addition, if a computer-generated animation is presented in conjunction with an expert opinion, it must comply with rules regarding the admissibility of expert opinions. One court observed that video animation adds a new and powerful evidentiary tool to the trial scene. *McCormick's* observes that with respect to one party's staged reproduction of facts "not only is the danger that the jury may confuse art with reality particularly great, but the impressions generated by the evidence may prove particularly difficult to limit."[108] Because of its dramatic power, trial judges should carefully and meticulously examine proposed animation evidence for proper foundation, relevancy and the potential for undue prejudice.[109] Some courts use the traditional relevancy and balancing of probative vs. prejudicial impact in determining admissibility.[110]

Additionally, a distinction must be made between demonstrative and real evidence. Real evidence provides the trier of fact with an opportunity to draw relevant first-hand sense impressions and involves production of an object that usually plays a direct or indirect part in the event at issue. Real evidence must also meet a stricter evidentiary standard under the FRE to be admissible.[111] Purely demonstrative evidence, on the other hand, is derivative in nature and only illustrates or clarifies other substantive evidence. Demonstrative evidence has no probative value in itself and such evidence serves merely as a visual aid to the jury in comprehending the verbal testimony of a witness or other evidence. *See Carson v. Polley* ("[i]llustrative evidence is admitted solely to help the witness explain his or her testimony. Illustrative evidence has no probative force beyond that which is lent to it by the credibility of the witness whose testimony it is used to explain").[112] Thus real evidence, possessing independent probative value, may be carried with the jury into deliberations. Demonstrative evidence, possessing no such independent probative value, may not enter the jury room.

Although some courts have imposed additional foundation requirements, when a computer animation is used merely to illustrate the testimony of an expert, all that should be required is a simple foundation demonstrating that the animation is a fair and accurate portrayal of the event that it is depicting.[113] However, when a computer simulation is offered as substantive evidence, the foundation requirements are much greater.

OVERCOMING HEARSAY OBJECTIONS THROUGH THE "CATCHALL" EXCEPTION

Federal Rules of Evidence 803(24)

When computer animation evidence involves data generated through the computer's software, an argument can be made that both the data and the software (as out-of-court statements of the programmer) are subject to hearsay objections.

Proponents of computer animation often employ Rule 803(24), the "catchall" exception, to avoid the hearsay prohibition because computer animations usually do not fit neatly into any of the enumerated hearsay exceptions. This rule provides that exceptions may be found to the hearsay rule for evidence which has equivalent circumstantial guarantees of trustworthiness if the court determines that:

- The statement is offered as evidence of a material fact;
- The statement is more probative on the point for which it is offered than any other evidence which the proponent can procure through reasonable efforts; and
- The general purposes of these rules and the interests of justice will best be served by admission of the statement into evidence.[114]

Rule 803(24) requires the party seeking to admit the evidence to notify the other side of the animation's existence and counsel's intent to enter it into evidence. The Advisory Committee Notes following the "catchall" rule appear to have anticipated the rule's role in adapting the system to new technologies when it states that the provision is intended to "provide for treating new and presently unanticipated situations, which demonstrate trustworthiness within the spirit of the specifically stated exceptions. Within this framework, room is left for growth and development of the law of evidence in the hearsay area, consistently with the broad purposes expressed in Rule 102."[115]

Due to computer animation's exceptional ability to explain important and complex issues easily to the jury and the current trust placed in the technology by judges, Rule 803(24) appears to be a ready gateway to the animation's entry into evidence. As can be seen in the following sections, however, a larger problem lies in the ability of parties to completely bypass even the minimal safeguards afforded by Rule 803(24).

Authentication

Federal Rules of Evidence 901

Computer-generated evidence must be properly authenticated before its admission into court.[116] *See Gauthier* ("'[t]rial court must consider whether the videotape accurately depicts what it purports to represent...'"); *Lopez v. Foremost Paving Inc.* ("similarity between the filmed portrayal and the actual incident is essential in the interest of fairness") and *Bledsoe v. Salt River Valley Water Users' Ass'n* ("[a]lthough the evidentiary use of computer simulations is generally permissible... their use is dependent on satisfying the usual foundational requirements for other demonstrative evidence").[117]

Witness testimony may be used to authenticate computer-generated evidence in the same manner it has been used to authenticate photographs. In *United States v. McNair*, for example, two bank tellers authenticated photographs from a bank surveillance camera by testifying that the pictures accurately represented the robbery and participants.[118] The court held that this was sufficient to authenticate the photographs. *See United States v. Wilson* (bank employee's testimony was sufficient to authenticate photographs of robbery scene where employer had seen robber for several minutes); and *United States v. Oaxaca* (an FBI agent, present when comparison photographs were taken, testified to authenticate the photographs).[119]

The requirement of authentication is satisfied "by evidence sufficient to support a finding that the matter in question is what its proponent claims."[120] As one court has stated, "[a]t a minimum, the proponent must show that the computer simulation fairly and accurately depicts what it represents, whether through the computer expert who prepared it or some other witness who is qualified to so testify, and the opposing party must be afforded an opportunity for cross-examination."[121] The following two sections will describe issues that may arise in connection with the authentication of computer-generated evidence.

Recreations Must Be "Substantially Similar" To Events Represented

For a computer-generated recreation, evidence will generally be admissible only when "there is substantial similarity between conditions existing at the time of the occurrence giving rise to the litigation and the conditions created in the experiment."[122] That means not only that the facts underlying the representation are accurate, but also that all relevant facts are represented. In *Lopez,* the court held that the re-enactment of an accident with toy trucks must be excluded where the re-enactment did not demonstrate the fog on the road or other conditions that had been present during the accident that gave rise to the litigation. "What the jurors observed on the video was a pickup truck suddenly veering across visible and obvious center stripe markings into the pathway of the tractor-trailer rig. The producers of the video made no attempt to portray the fog or the darkness in which the accident actually occurred. The impact on the jurors' minds of this dissimilar simulation of the accident could have been considerable."[123]

COMPUTER-GENERATED EVIDENCE ADMITTED TO ILLUSTRATE A THEORY OR AN OPINION

When computer-generated evidence is used to illustrate an opinion, hypothesis or principle, the proponent need only show that the computer-generated animation accurately depicts the hypothesis. Thus, "[T]ests or experiments that merely illustrate a theory or scientific principle are not required to possess as high a degree of similarity to the actual event as are purported recreations of the event."[124] Similarly, "[F]ilms used to illustrate a principle do not require strict adherence to the facts of the accident if the jury is carefully instructed as to the extent to which they are to use and consider the videotape." [125]

In *Datskow,* defendants challenged the plaintiff's use of a computer-animated video that demonstrated their expert's theory of how a fire began inside the engine of a plane.[126] The defendants claimed that while the video was introduced to illustrate an expert's hypothesis, it was really a recreation of the accident. The court rejected this challenge stating that, "[a]lthough defendant argues that there is no practical difference between recreating an accident and recreating an expert's theory of the accident, the difference is both real and significant; it is the difference between a jury believing that they are seeing a repeat of the actual event and a jury understanding that they are seeing an illustration of someone else's opinion of what happened."[127]

The court also found that the jury had been properly instructed on the purpose of the animation, noting that the animation had only been admitted "to help the jury understand the expert's opinion as to what happened."[128] Furthermore, the court had instructed that the video be played without sound, and that the jury had been instructed that the animation "'was not meant to be a recreation of the accident,' but 'simply computer pictures to help you understand [the expert's] opinion.'"[129]

Additional cases where courts have admitted computer-generated evidence to illustrate an opinion, hypothesis or principle include: *Hinds v. General Motors Corp.* (finding that the trial court did not err in allowing the plaintiffs to utilize the services and computer-generated evidence of "an expert in accident reconstruction… [who] testified to the manner in which the accident occurred and the movements of the [plaintiff's] body… following the collision"); *Harrison v. Sears, Roebuck & Co.* (finding that the trial court did not err in allowing the defendant's engineering expert to "utilize an x-ray of [the plaintiff's] hand" to reconstruct the cause of the plaintiff's injury); and *Caiazzo v. Volkswagenwerk A. G.* (finding that the trial court did not err in allowing the plaintiff to use an accident reconstruction expert to testify and present computer-generated evidence "regarding the manner of [plaintiff's] ejection [from the vehicle] and the kinematic effects of the accident sequence").[130]

Courts will not hesitate, however, to exclude computer-generated recreations when authentication requirements are not met. *See Chase v. General Motors Corp.* (finding that the trial court erred in allowing the jury to view video tests that were so dissimilar to the conditions existing at the time of the accident "in such fundamental and important respects" that prejudice resulted); *Hale v. Firestone Tire & Rubber Co.* (finding that the "district court abused its discretion in permitting the film to be shown when the conditions of the experiment were admittedly substantially different from the conditions of the accident in this case") and *Gladhill v. General Motors Corp.* (finding that the trial court erred in allowing a videotaped demonstration where "the circumstances of the accident, as alleged, are so different from this test as to make the results largely irrelevant if not misleading").[131] Thus, "a film intended for even a limited purpose, such as illustration of a principle or use as a visual aid, must show sufficient similarity to the actual accident in order to be admissible in evidence."[132]

AUTHENTICATION OF COMPUTER TECHNOLOGY

For evidence prepared with the assistance of a computer, FRE 901(b)(9) explicitly provides that a "process or system" may be authenticated with "[e]vidence describing a process or system used to produce a result and showing that the process or system produces an accurate result." Thus, in the case of a computerized reconstruction, a witness may have to explain not only what data was put into the computer but also how the computer program works and whether the equipment is reliable.[133] *See Robinson v. Missouri Pacific R. Co,* (suggesting that possible objection to computer simulation or animation may be "hearsay or lack of foundation when computer software developer has not testified").[134] This evidence may be provided either through the "computer expert who prepared it or some other witness who is qualified to so testify."[135]

ADMISSIBILITY OF COMPUTER-GENERATED EVIDENCE ILLUSTRATING EXPERT OPINIONS

Federal Rules of Evidence 702-703 and 611(a)

In many cases, such as *Ohio v. Clark, Datskow* and *Robinson,* computer-generated evidence is introduced either as the basis for or to illustrate an expert opinion.[136] In these cases, courts may look to evidentiary rules governing the admissibility of expert opinions in order to determine whether computer-generated evidence may form the basis of an expert opinion or may be used to illustrate expert opinion.[137] In *Robinson,* the court noted that, "under Rule 702, we suggest that as 'gatekeeper' the district court carefully and meticulously make an early pretrial evaluation of issues of admissibility, particularly of scientific expert opinions and films or animations illustrative of such opinions."[138]

FRE 611(a), the basis for demonstrative evidence, also comes into play. Since demonstrative evidence is derivative, i.e., it depends on other admitted evidence as a predicate to its use in court, the other evidence, usually the expert's opinion and the underlying evidence he or she relies on, should be introduced before proceeding with a computer animation.[139] *See Bray*[140] for an excellent review of the rules governing demonstrative evidence.

Where the evidence is called demonstrative, the standards for putting the material before the jury are generally less stringent than if the evidence is called a re-enactment.[141] Where an experiment purports to simulate actual events (like a crime scene re-enactment), the proponent has the burden of demonstrating substantial similarity of conditions.[142]

Expert Must Be Qualified and Methodology Must Be Reliable

An expert presenting computer-generated evidence must be qualified under FRE 702, which provides that "[I]f scientific, technical or other specialized knowledge will assist the trier of fact to understand the evidence or determine a fact in issue, a witness qualified as an expert by knowledge, skill, experience training or education, may testify thereto in the form of an opinion or otherwise."[143] It is fundamental that expert testimony be predicated on facts legally sufficient to provide a basis for the expert's opinion.[144]

If the proponent cannot establish the reliability of the scientific method, the expert will not be allowed to testify. The First Circuit recently upheld the exclusion of an expert witness where there was not an adequate factual foundation to establish the scientific reliability of the testimony. In *Schubert v. Nissan Motor Corp.*, the court affirmed the trial court's finding that the proposed testimony was nothing more than ["A conclusory assertion about an ultimate legal issue… that 'relies on another asserted, yet unproved fact, that the pipe and the injury line up.'"][145] Applying the principles established in *Daubert*, the First Circuit found that "No foundation exists for a critical aspect of the expert's opinion proffered in this case."[146] *See also Smelser v. Norfolk Southern Railway* (reversing a district court's decision to admit expert testimony of a biomechanical engineer, holding that his opinion that a shoulder belt but not a lap belt failed in an accident, was not based on good science and should have been excluded, and his opinion testimony as to the cause of an employee's injuries went beyond his expertise and was not reliable); *Dancy v. Hyster Co.* (expert could have, but did not test his theory, and thus had no basis for reaching his opinion); and *Cummins v. Lyle Industries* (expert failed to conduct tests or research to substantiate his opinions).[147]

In *Ohio v. Clark*, where a crime reconstruction expert used AutoCAD software to demonstrate that a murder victim could not have been shot in the manner suggested by the defense, the court conducted an analysis under Rule 702.[148] First, the court determined that the witness was qualified "in the field of crime scene reconstruction using computer-assisted or electronic drafting."[149] Based on this conclusion, the court held that the principles enunciated in *Daubert* did not apply. Second, the court held that the "methodology" used to perform the crime reconstruction was reliable. In reaching this conclusion, the court found that computer-assisted drafting constituted "technical or other specialized knowledge," rather than scientific knowledge, under Rule 702.[150] The holding that *Daubert* did not apply, however, is now suspect in light of *Kumho Tire Co. v. Carmichael*.[151]

In *Robinson,* decided after *Daubert*, the court noted that "in considering proposed evidence based on scientific and technical evidence, the trial judge should observe that the evaluation under FRE 702 is a flexible one and its overarching subject is the scientific validity—and thus the evidentiary relevance and reliability—of the principles that underlie a proposed submission."[152]

In some cases, however, courts have begun to address the misclassification techniques proponents of computer-generated animations have used to introduce such evidence. For example, in *Bledsoe*[153] the court held that the trial court had erred in permitting counsel to employ computer animation during closing argument because it was misclassified. At trial, the proponent argued that the evidence was for demonstrative purposes and the trial court agreed, although it was "a more sophisticated way of presenting his theory as to how the accident happened."[154] However, the court of appeals ruled that the animation should not have been classified as demonstrative evidence because it was more like a depiction of a computer expert's opinion of how the accident happened. Therefore, the court held that counsel was required to lay the foundation for those opinions prior to their introduction, and opposing counsel should have been permitted to cross-examine the expert about them.[155]

Misclassifying the nature of computer-generated evidence prejudicially affects the judicial process in several ways. First, it unduly confuses the jury as to whether the evidence is demonstrative or scientific. Second, it allows an astute party to avoid the trustworthiness requirements of the hearsay rule by entering substantive evidence under the guise of demonstrative evidence. Third, it completely avoids the evidentiary requirements established to ensure the reliability of the novel scientific evidence presented.

Basis of Expert Opinion

Federal Rules of Evidence 703
FRE 703 provides that facts or data upon which an expert bases an opinion need not be admissible "if of a type reasonably relied upon by experts in the particular field." Although no reported cases analyzing computer-generated animations under Rule 703 were found, it would seem that the facts that underlie an expert's comput-

er-animated evidence should either be admissible or facts upon which an expert could reasonably rely.

There is, however, a great deal of data collection, human judgment and speculation at each step of the animation process and with other computer-generated evidence. Therefore, the contention that the computer's process is an objective one is not acceptable. Parties seeking to object to the admission of computer evidence at trial should understand that if the animation is admitted as anything other than substantive evidence—as, for example demonstrative or illustrative evidence—much of the hearsay evidence that underlies the animation will be admitted as well without any scrutiny by the court.[156] Rule 703 states in a relevant part that "[I]f of a type reasonably relied upon by experts in the particular field in forming opinions or inferences upon the subject, the facts or data need not be admissible in evidence."[157] In considering the sweeping admissibility this rule could offer, the Advisory Committee's note states that "[I]f it be feared that enlargement of permissible data may tend to break down the rules of exclusion unduly, notice should be taken that the rule requires that the facts or data be of a type reasonably relied upon by experts in the particular field."[158] What is reasonably relied on becomes a question of fact and is most likely to be resolved by looking at the test for novel scientific evidence found in *Daubert*.

But in considering the data most relevant to computer animations, the Advisory Committee's note goes on to say that "[t]he language would not warrant admitting in evidence the opinion of an 'accidentologist' as to the point of impact in an automobile collision based on statements of bystanders, since this requirement is not satisfied."[159] This last point is very important because every animator, as an expert "accidentologist" or reconstructionist, relies primarily on the facts and data supplied by witnesses in many instances. The Advisory Committee's note thus implies that this practice should not allow the party to evade the exclusionary rules that in this case would be the hearsay doctrine.

Some courts have viewed computer evidence as merely a "mechanical tool" for the presentation of evidence.[160] In *McHugh*, the Supreme Court of New York found that computers were only "receiving information and acting on instructions at lightning speed" in the presentation of factual evidence.[161] This view, arguably, encourages jurors to surrender their role in factual determinations and allow the computer to resolve the factual disputes in the case. In *People v. Mitchell*, James Mitchell was convicted for the murder of his drug addicted porn king brother, Artie Mitchell, despite

James's claim that he acted in self-defense.[162] The prosecution used computer animation "to show [that] the trajectory of the bullets and possible location of the victim [behind a wall] when the shots were fired," established that James could not have seen any threatening gestures made by Artie.[163] The original animation portrayed Artie walking down the hallway with his hands at his sides. Upon defense counsel's objection, the judge ordered that the animation be altered several times, ultimately replacing the human-like figure representing Artie with that of a geometric shape to avoid the risk that the jury might assume as proven fact the position of Artie's hands in the animation. Defense counsel objected because there was no evidence as to how Artie positioned his arms or his body as he walked down the hallway. Mitchell appealed his conviction, claiming that the animation should not have been admitted.[164] The court of appeal noted the trial court's discretion in admitting expert testimony reconstructions so long as there is "preliminary proof that conditions are substantially identical and that the reconstruction is an accurate depiction."[165] Ultimately, the court held that it was error to admit the reconstruction because the reconstruction relied upon inadmissible evidence. Nevertheless, the court affirmed the conviction because it held that the error was harmless.[166]

The *Mitchell* case illustrates the old computer adage: garbage in, garbage out. When analyzing computer animation, each assumption should be challenged before making the decision to offer it as evidence.

Prosecutors should remember that the test for the admission of expert testimony under *Daubert* is not the correctness of the expert's conclusions but the soundness of the expert's methodology. *See Rebel Oil Co. v. Atlantic Richfield Co.* and *Cabrera v. Cordis Corp.* ("Under *Daubert*, a district court may admit expert scientific opinion if it qualifies as 'scientific knowledge,' that is, if it has a "grounding in the methods and procedures of science... [and is] more than subjective belief or unsupported speculation").[167]

CASE NOTES: PROBATIVE V. PREJUDICIAL VALUE

Federal Rules of Evidence 403

Even if computer evidence is properly authenticated and relevant, it may not be admissible because it is unduly prejudicial.[168] "Although relevant, evidence may be excluded if its probative value is substantially outweighed by the danger of unfair prejudice, confusion of the issues, or misleading the jury, or by considerations of undue delay, waste of time, or needless presentation of cumulative evidence."[169] In determining whether to admit demonstrative computer-generated evidence, a court must weigh the danger that the demonstration will prejudice or mislead the jury against the probative value of the demonstration. *See generally United States v. Yahweh* (weighing the probative value of enlarged autopsy photographs against the danger of unfair prejudice) and *United States v. Jamil* (weighing the probative value of a prior conviction evidence against possible prejudice).[170]

Courts appear to be acutely aware of the potential prejudice of inaccurate animations that do not purport to recreate an event, but may, nevertheless be so perceived by the jury. Consequently, evidence may be open to attack if it fails to represent conditions similar to the events at issue in the litigation or if it distorts the facts.

In *Pino v. Gauthier*, the court upheld the trial court's decision to exclude a videotaped computer animation depicting four possible scenarios of a car's movement on a road. The tape was produced by inserting variables into the computer program, such as the vehicle speed, the vehicle weight and the road conditions. The court excluded the video on the grounds that it was "unduly prejudicial," particularly since the opposing party could not alter the variables used to create the images.[171] "[A]lthough the tape tended to establish a fact of *Gauthier's* case, that a cause-in-fact of the accident was the different surfaces of the two west-bound lanes, the limitation placed on opposing counsel to present alternative scenarios based on differing variables would have been prejudicial."[172]

In *Sommervold v. Grevlos*, the Supreme Court of South Dakota affirmed a trial court's decision to exclude the computer animation evidence because of its prejudicial nature and the inaccuracies that it contained.[173] The court found that the animation, recreating an accident involving two bicycles, was not similar enough to the actual events or the testimony to be admissible. The animation misrepresented the speed of the bicycles, wrongly depicted the light that was cast from a nearby streetlight and showed the wrong location of the injuries to riders. In upholding the exclusion of the evidence based on prejudice, the court echoed the trial court's decision that "[A] video recreation of an accident... stands out in the jury's mind. So it emphasizes that evidence substantially over... ordinary... spoken testimony."[174]

In *Datskow*, the court rejected the argument that a video animation was prejudicial. The mere fact that this was an animated video with moving images does not mean that the jury would have been likely to give it more weight than it would otherwise have deserved. As one commentator has observed, "If audio or visual presentation is calculated to assist the jury, the court should not discourage the use of it.... Jurors, exposed as they are to television, the movies and picture magazines, are fairly sophisticated. With proper instruction, the danger of their overvaluing such proof is slight."[175]

In *Shipp v. General Motors Corp.*, the plaintiff claimed a defect in the roof of a car manufactured by the defendant caused her more serious injuries than she would otherwise have suffered.[176] Both plaintiff and defendant wanted to offer videotapes into evidence. The court admitted plaintiff's video and photos of an accident re-enactment using the same model car but excluded video of an accident re-enactment using other model cars. Defendant wanted to admit video of a dummy being thrown from a car to illustrate the impact of not wearing a seatbelt, arguing the video was relevant to show general principles of occupant movement and was not being offered as a re-enactment of the accident. After expressing its suspicion of demonstrations involving cars other than the model involved in the accident, the trial court concluded that the jury "would likely consider it as more than a simple demonstration of general principles."[177] The appellate court affirmed, finding no abuse of discretion.[178]

Conversely, in *Harvey v. General Motors Corp.*, where plaintiff sought damages for injuries sustained when he was thrown through the roof of his car, the trial judge admitted video of rollover tests offered to illustrate vehicle dynamics and not offered as a re-enactment. The trial court explicitly told the jury to note the difference in car models when viewing the video.[179] The appellate court affirmed, recognizing *Shipp* and explaining that "[E]vidence properly excluded in one context is not automatically admitted erroneously in a separate context."[180] *See Swajian v. General Motors Corp.* (appellate court affirmed the exclusion of video as too prejudicial, which showed what occurs when an axle breaks, but allowed oral testimony about the experiments); *Patterson v. F.W. Woolworth Co.* (court admitted expert testimony about a demonstration that took place under different circumstances; affirmed on appeal because conditions need not be exactly similar and trial court minimized the prejudice by permitting the plaintiff's expert to remain in the courtroom to offer rebuttal) and *Edwards v. Liz Claiborne, Inc.* (unpublished opinion; defendant allowed to burn fiber in court which was used to show only a limited part of accident because jury would not be misled into believing it was a re-enactment).[181]

LIMITED ADMISSIBILITY

Federal Rules of Evidence 105

Computer-generated evidence is often admitted for limited purposes, such as to illustrate an expert opinion. FRE 105 provides that "[W]hen evidence which is admissible... for one purpose but not admissible... for another purpose is admitted, the court, upon request, shall restrict the evidence to its proper scope and instruct the jury accordingly." Thus, video or computer animation should be admissible, like a chart or summary, for the limited purpose of aiding the jury in understanding the underlying evidence.

For evidence that is being introduced for limited purposes, proper instructions may be used to overcome objections. In *Datskow*, for example, the court had instructed the jury that the animation, "'was not meant to be a recreation of the accident,' but 'simply computer pictures to help you understand [the expert's] opinion.'"[182] So long as that distinction is made clear to them—as it was here—there is no reason for them to credit the illustration any more than they credit the underlying opinion."[183]

Cautionary Instruction

"The animation you are about to see is not meant to be a recreation of the (event at issue). It is simply an illustration of the expert witness's opinion."[184]

Motions in Limine

If produced correctly, computer animations can be very persuasive evidentiary devices. Unfortunately, they can be just as persuasive, and hence very damaging to the search for truth, if based on incorrect assumptions. It is extremely important to understand the evidentiary and technical assumptions made in order to insure that the animation the prosecution offers is a fair representation of the evidence and so that the prosecution can successfully challenge inaccurate exhibits offered by the defense.[185]

If the defense cannot establish the reliability of the evidence, or if the prosecution demonstrates that the defense exhibit is speculative at best and not based on the evidence, the animation will be excluded. From a standpoint of fundamental fairness, the proponent of the evidence should make early disclosure of computer-generated evidence to give the other side an opportunity to analyze the evidence and to challenge it at a pretrial hearing. The Federal Judicial Center's publication, *Manual for Complex Litigation,* suggests that courts conduct pretrial hearings well in advance of trial to determine whether the evidence (and the accuracy of the underlying source materials) is reliable.[186] The motion *in limine* should challenge the proponent to commit on his/her theory of admissibility. If the proponent claims that the animation will be used as substantive evidence—in effect, as an actual simulation of the event in question—the foundational burden will be much greater and it will be easier to keep the animation from the jury.

ENDNOTES

[1] The author wishes to thank the following prosecutors for their contributions to this article: Mitchell Mars, Assistant U.S. Attorney, ND Illinois, Arnold Huftalen, Assistant U.S. Attorney, New Hampshire, Scott N. Schools, Assistant United States Attorney, South Carolina, John R. Maney, U.S. Department of Justice Tax Division Attorney, and Peter G. Baroni, Assistant States Attorney, DuPage County, Illinois.

[2] 2 *McCormick*, Section 212, at 8-9 (4th Ed. 1992).

[3] 1 Fred Lane, *Goldstein Trial Technique*, Sections 11.155-11.156, at 11-295 to 11-302 (3d ed. 1996) and 4 Weinstein and Berger *Weinstein's Evidence* Section 611.02[2][a], at 611-12.

[4] 4 *Weinstein's* Section 1006.08[4], at 1006-23.

[5] 3 *McCormick* Section 212, 3, *citing Schertzinger v. Williams*, 17 Cal. Rptr. 719 (1961).

[6] 4 *Weinstein's* Section 611.02[2][a], at 611-12.

[7] "Advisory Committee Notes" *Fed. R. Evid.*, 611.

[8] *United States v. Bray*, 139 F.3d 1104, 1110 (6th Cir. 1998).

[9] *United States v. Bray;* Also *State v. Olson,* 579 N.W.2d 802 (Wis. 1998).

[10] 1972 Proposed Rules "Advisory Committee Notes," *Fed. R. Evid.*, 611(a).

[11] *Id.*

[12] *United States v. Jones*, 124 F.3d 781, 786-87 (6th Cir. 1997); *United States v. McIntosh*, 23 F.3d 1454, 1456-57 (8th Cir. 1994); *Roland v. Langlois*, 945 F.2d 956, 963 (7th Cir. 1991);*United States v. Paulino*, 935 F.2d 739, 753 (6th Cir. 1991); *United States v. Towns*, 913 F.2d 434, 445-46 (7th Cir. 1990); *United States v. Gardner*, 611 F.2d 770, 776 (9th Cir. 1980); *United States v. Scales*, 594 F.2d 558, 563-64 (6th Cir. 1979).

13 Note: *Fed. R. Crim. P.* 16(a)(1)(E) requires the government to provide, at the defendant's request, a written summary of a government expert's testimony, the expert's qualifications and the bases for the expert's opinions.

14 *United States v. Pelullo*, 964 F.2d 193, 204-06 (3d Cir. 1992); *United States v. Citron*, 783 F.2d 307, 316-17 (2d Cir. 1986); *United States v. Drougas*, 748 F.2d, 25. See also *United States v. Kim*, 595 F.2d 755, 763-64 & n.43 (D.C. Cir. 1979).

15 "Message Unit Detail," or record of local calls.

16 *United States v. Radseck*, 718 F.2d 233, 237-39 (7th Cir. 1983).

17 *United States v. Johnson*, 54 F.3d 1150, 1157-59 (4th Cir. 1995); *United States v. Norton*, 867 F.2d 1354, 1362-63 (11th Cir. 1989); *United States v. Stephens*, 779 F.2d 232, 238-39 (5th Cir. 1985). See also *United States v. Bertoli*, 854 F. Supp. 975, 1056 (D. N.J. 1994) and *United States v. Diez*, 515 F.2d 892, 905 (5th Cir. 1975).

18 *United States v. Radseck,* 718 F.2d 239; *United States v. Ambrosiani*, 610 F.2d 65, 68 n.2 (1st Cir. 1979).

19 *United States v. Johnson*, 54 F.3d 1157 (4th Cir. 1995).

20 "Summarizing Prior Witness Testimony: Admissible Evidence, Pedagogical Device, or Violation of the Federal Rules of Evidence?" *Fla. St. U. L. Rev.* 24 (1996) 161, 177.

21 *State v. Olson*, 579 N.W.2d 802 (Wis. 1998).

22 *United States v. Rollack,* 173 F.3d 853, 853 (4th Cir. 1999); *United States v. Justus*, 162 F.3d 1157, 1157 (4th Cir. 1998).

23 *State v. Starr*, 998 S.W. 2d 61 (Mis. 1999); *State v. Raso,* 728 A.2d 231 (NJ 1999). See also *United States v. Gaskell*, 985 F.2d 1056 (11th Cir. 1993).

24 *United States v. Salerno*, 108 F.3d 730, 745 (7th Cir. 1997); *United States v. Paulino*, 935 F.2d at 753 (6th Cir. 1991); *United States v. Radseck*, 718 F.2d at 239. See also *United States v. Drougas*, 748 F.2d 8, 25-26 (1st Cir. 1984).

25 *United States v. Baker*, 10 F.3d 1374, 1412-1413 (9th Cir. 1993); *United States v. Winn*, 948 F.2d 145, 157-159 (5th Cir. 1991).

26 Note: Be sure to have the court give a limiting instruction regarding the demonstrative exhibit at the time it is offered and during the jury charge, especially if the exhibit will be going back to the jury.

27 *See* Sand, Seifert, Loughlin and Reiss, *Modern Federal Jury Instructions. See also United States v. Johnson*, 54 F.3d 1150, 1159-61 (4th Cir. 1995) (giving instruction cited in text); *United States v. Paulino*, 935 F.2d 739, 753 (6th Cir. 1991) (same); *United States v. Cox*, 633 F.2d 871, 873-74 (9th Cir. 1980) (same).

28 *United States v. Duncan*, 919 F.2d 981, 988 (5th Cir. 1990); *United States v. Bertoli*, 854 F. Supp., 1050-51.

29 *United States v. Scales*, 594 F.2d, 562.

30 *United States v. Osum*, 943 F.2d 1394, 1405 n.9 (5th Cir. 1991); *United States v. Atchley*, 699 F.2d 1055, 1069 (11th Cir. 1983); *United States v. Smyth*, 556 F.2d 1179, 1184 (5th Cir. 1977).

31 *United States v. Osum,* 943 F.2d 1394, 1405 (5th Cir. 1991); *Martin v. Funtime, Inc.,* 963 F.2d 110, 116 (6th Cir. 1992); *United States v. Meyers,* 847 F.2d 1408, 1412 (9th Cir. 1988).

32 *United States v. Strissell,* 920 F.2d 1162, 1163 (4th Cir. 1990); *United States v. Meyers,* 847 F.2d 1408, 1412 (9th Cir. 1988); *United States v. Skalicky,* 615 F.2d 1117, 1121 n.5 (5th Cir.), *cert. denied,* 449 U.S. 832 (1980); *United States v. Clements,* 588 F.2d 1030 (5th Cir. 1979), *cert. denied,* 440 U.S. 982 (1979).

33 *Fagiola v. National Gypsum Co.,* 906 F.2d 53, 57 (2d Cir. 1990).

34 *United States v. Scales,* 594 F.2d at 564; *Gordon v. United States,* 438 F.2d 858, 876-77 (5th Cir. 1971), *cert. denied,* 404 U.S. 828 (1971).

35 *United States v. Pelullo,* 964 F.2d 193, 204 (3d Cir. 1992); See also *AMPAT/Midwest Inc. v. Ill. Tool Works, Inc.,* 896 F.2d 1035, 1045 (7th Cir. 1990); *Hackett v. Housing Authority of San Antonio,* 750 F.2d 1308, 1312 (5th Cir. 1985) *cert. denied,* 474 U.S. 850 (1985).

36 *United States v. Johnson,* 594 F.2d 1253, 1256 (9th Cir.) *cert. denied,* 444 U.S. 964 (1979).

37 *United States v. Osum,* 943 F.2d, 1405; *United States v. Possick,* 849 F.2d 332, 339 (8th Cir. 1988).

38 *United States v. Williams,* 952 F.2d 1504, 1519 (6th Cir. 1991); *United States v. Campbell,* 845 F.2d 1374, 1381 (6th Cir. 1988); *United States v. Scales,* 594 F.2d 558, 562 (6th Cir.), *cert. denied,* 441 U.S. 946 (1979); *United States v. Evans,* 572 F.2d 455 (5th Cir. 1978); *See also United States v. Stephens,* 779 F.2d 232, 239 (5th Cir. 1985); *United States v. Shirley,* 884 F.2d 1130 (9th Cir. 1989); *United States v. Meyers,* 847 F.2d 1408, 1412 (9th Cir. 1988); *United States v. Lemire,* 720 F.2d 1327, 1350 (D.C. Cir. 1983).

39 *United States v. Scales,* 594 F.2d, 562.

40 *United States v. Dorta,* 783 F.2d 1179, 1183 (4th Cir. 1986), *cert. denied,* 477 U.S. 905 (1986); *Scales,* 594 F.2d, 563; *United States v. Drougas,* 748 F.2d 8, 25 (1st Cir. 1984).

41 *United States v. Conlin,* 551 F.2d 534, 539 (2d Cir.), *cert. denied,* 434 U.S. 831 (1977).

42 *United States v. Ambrosiani,* 610 F.2d 65 (1st Cir. 1979), *cert. denied,* 445 U.S. 930 (1980); *Myers v. United States,* 356 F.2d 469 (5th Cir.), *cert. denied,* 384 U.S. 952 (1966).

43 *United States v. Norton,* 867 F.2d 1354, 1362-1363 (11th Cir.), *cert. denied,* 491 U.S. 907 (1989); *United States v. Diez,* 515 F.2d 892, 905 (5th Cir. 1975), *cert. denied,* 423 U.S. 1052 (1976); *United States v. Smyth,* 556 F.2d 1179 (5th Cir. 1977).

44 *United States v. Foley,* 598 F.2d 1323, 1337-1338 (4th Cir. 1979).

45 *United States v. Osum,* 943 F.2d at 1405.

46 *United States v. Bertoli,* 854 F. Supp, at 1051.

47 No. 4.12, *Eighth Circuit Manual of Model Criminal Jury Instructions* (1996).

48 *Id.*

[49] Instruction No. 3.29, *Seventh Circuit Criminal Jury Instructions* (1980).

[50] Instruction No. 3.30, *Seventh Circuit Criminal Jury Instructions* (1980).

[51] Sand et al, *Modern Federal Jury Instructions.*

[52] *Martin v. Funtime*, 963 F.2d 110, 115-116 (6th Cir. 1993); *Osum*, 943 F.2d 1394, 1405 n.9 (5th Cir. 1991);. *Possick*, 849 F.2d 332, 339 (8th Cir. 1988); and 5 Weinstein & Berger, *Weinstein's Evidence*, ¶1006[7], 1006-15.

[53] *United States v. Possick*, 849 F.2d at 339; *United States v. Orlowski,* 808 F.2d 1283, 1289 (8th Cir. 1986), *cert. denied*, 482 U.S. 927 (1987); *United States v. Robinson*, 774 F.2d 261, 275 (8th Cir. 1985).

[54] Sand et al, *Modern Federal Jury Instructions.*

[55] *United States v.* Osum, 943 F.2d 1405, n.9.

[56] *United States v. Williams*, 952 F.2d 1504, 1519 (6th Cir. 1991); *United States v. Campbell,* 845 F.2d 1374, 1381 (6th Cir.), *cert. denied*, 488 U.S. 908 (1988); *United States v. Marchini*, 797 F.2d 759, 766 (9th Cir. 1986), *cert. denied*, 479 U.S. 1085 (1987).

[57] *United States v. Gaitan-Acevedo*, 148 F.3d 577, 587 (6th Cir. 1998); *United States v. Francis*, 131 F.3d 1452, 1454 (11th Cir. 1997); *United States v. Petty*, 132 F.3d 373, 379 (7th Cir. 1997); *United States v. Tannehill*, 49 F.3d 1049, 1056 (5th Cir. 1995); *Bristol Steel & Iron Works, Inc. v. Bethlehem Steel Corp.,* 41 F.3d 182, 189 (4th Cir. 1994); *United States v. Baker*, 10 F.3d 1374, 1411 (9th Cir. 1993); *United States v. Williams*, 952 F.2d 1504, 1519 (6th Cir. 1991); *United States v. Collins,* 596 F.2d 166 (6th Cir. 1979); *United States v. Honea*, 556 F.2d 906 (8th Cir. 1977).

[58] *United States v. Miller*, 600 F.2d 498 (5th Cir.), *cert. denied*, 444 U.S. 955 (1979).

[59] *United States v. O'Brien*, 601 F.2d 1067, 1071 (9th Cir. 1979).

[60] *United States v. Salerno,* 108 F.3d 730, 744 (7th Cir. 1997).

[61] *United States v. Possick*, 849 F.2d 332, 339-40 (8th Cir. 1988); *Carson v. Polley,* 689 F.2d 562, 579 (5th Cir. 1982); *United States v. Cox*, 633 F.2d 871, 873-74 (9th Cir. 1980).

[62] *United States v. Salerno,* 108 F.3d 730, 745 (7th Cir. 1997).

[63] *United States v. Possick*, 849 F.2d 339.

[64] *Id.*

[65] *Id.*, 340.

[66] *United States* v. *Cox*, 633 F.2d, 873-74.

[67] *United States v. Salerno*, 108 F.3d 730, 745 (7th Cir. 1997); *United States v. Britton*, 68 F.3d 262, 264 (8th Cir. 1995); *United States v. Berry*, 64 F.3d 305, 307 n.1 (7th Cir. 1995); and *United States v. Cruz-Paulino*, 61 F.3d 986, 997 (1st Cir. 1995). See also *United States v. Tannehill*, 49 F.3d 1049, 1056 (5th Cir. 1995) (summary charts); *United States v. Crowder*, 36 F.3d 691, 697 (7th Cir. 1994) (tape transcripts); *United States v. Winn*, 948 F.2d 145, 158 (5th Cir. 1991) (chronological chart); *United States v. Pinto*, 850 F.2d 927, 935 (2d Cir. 1988) (wiretap summary chart); *United States v. Possick*, 849 F.2d at 339-40 (organizational chart and phone traffic chart); *United States v. Cox*, 633 F.2d at 873-74 (bomb replicas); *United States v. Downen*, 496 F.2d 314, 319-21 (10th Cir. 1974) (blackboard chart summarizing government's theory of the case).

68 *See Salerno*, 108 F.3d at 744–45; *United States v. Hofer*, 995 F.2d 746, 749 (7th Cir. 1993).

69 *United States v. Bray*, 139 F.3d 1104, 1112 (6th Cir. 1998).

70 *Sicherman v. Diamoncut, Inc., (In re Sol Bergman Estate Jewelers, Inc.)*, 225 B.R. 896, 50 Fed. R. Evid. Serv. 889 (1998).

71 *United States v. Matta-Ballesteros*, 71 F 3d. 754 at 4 (9th Cir. 1995), *cert. denied*, 519 U.S. 1118, 117 S.Ct. 965 (1997).

72 *United States v. Bray*, 139 F.3d 1104, 1112 (6th Cir. 1998); *United States v. Citron*, 783 F.2d 307, 317 n. 10 (2d Cir. 1986).

73 *United States v. Birch*, 39 F.3d 1089 (10th Cir. 1994); and *United States v. Gaskell*, 985 F.2d 1056 (11th Cir. 1993).

74 *United States v. Gaskell*, 985 F.2d at 1060.

75 *United States v. Wanoskia*, 800 F.2d 235 (10th Cir. 1986).

76 *Id.*, 238.

77 *Id.*

78 *Government of the Virgin Islands v. Lyndon Frederick*, 94–7153 (3d Cir. 12/6/1994), *reh'g denied*, 46 F.3d 1116 (3d Cir. 12/16/1994), *cert. denied*, 116 U.S. 48 (1995).

79 The Investigative and Prosecutive Graphics Unit (IPGU) chief is Richard Berry. Visual Information Specialist Carl Adrian produces the computer animations. These gentlemen may be reached at (202) 324-4220.

80 William F. Lee, "Using Computer-Generated Evidence at Trial," *PLI/Litig. & Admin. Practice Course Handbook Series* No. H4-5214159 (1995) 523; and Kathlynn G. Fadely, "Use of Computer-Generated Visual Evidence in Aviation Litigation: Interactive Video Comes to Court," *J. Air L. & Com.* 55(1990) 839.

81 Lee, *PLI/Litig. & Admin. Practice Course,* 523.

82 *Pino v. Gauthier*, 633 So.2d 638, 652 (La. App. 1 Cir. 1993), *cert. denied*, 634 So.2d 858 (La. 1994); *People v. McHugh*, 476 N.Y.S.2d 721 (Sup. Ct. Bronx Co. 1984); *Haley v. Pan American World Airways*, 746 F.2d 311, 315 (5th Cir. 1984); *Strock v. Southern Farm Bur. Cas. Ins. Co.*, 998 F.2d 1010 (4th Cir. 1993); and *Hinkle v. City of Clarksburg*, 81 F.3d 416, 424-5 (4th Cir. 1996).

83 *Hinkle v. City of Clarksburg*, 81 F.3d 416 (4th Cir. 1996); *Robinson v. Missouri Pacific R. Co.*, 16 F.3d 1083, 1086 (10th Cir. 1994); *Edwards v. Atro Spa*, 891 F. Supp 1074, 1085, 1088 (EDNC 1995); *Datskow v. Teledyne Continental Motors*, 826 F. Supp 677 (WDNY 1993).

84 *See* §12.18.

85 *Douglass v. Delta Air Lines*, 709 F. Supp. 745 (W.D. Tex. 1989).

86 *Id.*, 759.

87 *Id.*

88 Mark Barrish, Sixth Annual Computer Law Symposium, "Evolution in Intellectual Property Disclosure of Computer Re-Enactments During Pretrial Discovery," *Hastings Comm./Ent. L.J.* 691, 694 (1994).

89 *Id.*

90 *Id.*

91 *Datskow v. Teledyne Continental Motors*, 826 F. Supp. 677, 685 (W.D.N.Y. 1993).

92 *Id.*

93 *Id.*

94 *Id.*

95 Lee, "*523 PLI/Litig. & Admin. Practice Course.*"

96 *Id.*

97 *Id.*, 819 re: *State of Ohio v. Clark*, 655 N.E.2d 795 (Ohio App. 8th Dist. 1995).

98 The brand name of one manufacturer's example of this technology.

99 *Id.*, 812-13.

100 *Id.*

101 *Id.*, 801.

102 *Id.*, 799-800.

103 *Pearl Brewing Co. v. Joseph Schlitz Brewing Co.* 415 F. Supp. 1122, 1134 (S.D. Tex. 1976).

104 *Commercial Union Ins. Co. v. Boston Edison*, 412 Mass. 545 (1992).

105 *Perma Research & Dev. Co. v. Singer Co.*, 542 F.2d 111, 115 (2d Cir.) *cert. denied*, 429 U.S. 987 (1976).

106 David W. Muir, "Debunking the Myths About Computer Animation in Securities Litigation, 1992," at 591 (*PLI/Litig. & Admin. Practice Course Handbook,* Series No. H444, 1992).

107 *Id.*

108 *McCormick.*

109 *Robinson v. Missouri Pacific R. Co.*, 16 F.3d 1083, 1088 (10th Cir. 1994) (quoting 2 McCormick on *Evidence* 19 (4th ed. 1992).

110 *People v. Serrano*, 539 N.Y.S. 2d 845 (1989); *People v. McHugh*, 476 N.Y.S. 2d 721 (1984); *Datskow v. Teledyne*, 826 F. Supp 677, 685 (WDNY 1993).

111 *See generally, Fed. R. Evid. 401, 403, 901 and accompanying adv. comm. notes.*

112 *See Carson v. Polley*, 689 F.2d 562, 579 (5th Cir. 1982).

113 *Strock v. Southern Bureau Casualty Insurance Co.*, 998 F.2d 1010 (4th Cir. 1993); *Nachtsheim v. Beech Aircraft Corp.*, 847 F.2d 1261 (7th Cir. 1988).

114 *Fed. R. Evid.* 803(24).

115 *Fed. R. Evid.* 803(24) adv. comm. notes.

116 *Fed. R. Evid.* 901(a).

117 *Pino v. Gauthier*, 633 So.2d 638, 652 (La. App. 1 Cir. 1993) (*quoting Malbrough v. Wallace*, 594 So.2d 428, 431 (La. App. 1st Cir. 1991), *writ denied*, 596 So.2d 196 (1992)); *Lopez v. Foremost Paving Inc.*, 796 S.W.2d 473, 480 (Tex. App. 1990); *Bledsoe v. Salt River Valley Water Users' Ass'n*, 880 P.2d 689, 692 (Ariz. 1994); *Loy v. Arkansas*, 832 S.W.2d 499 (Ark 1992).

118 *United States v. McNair*, 439 F. Supp. 103, 105 (E.D. Pa. 1977), *aff'd*, 571 F.2d 573 (3d Cir.), *cert. denied*, 435 U.S. 976 (1978).

119 *See United States v. Wilson*, 719 F.2d 1491, 1495-96 (10th Cir. 1983); *United States v. Oaxaca*, 569 F.2d 518, 525 (9th Cir. 1978), *cert. denied*, 439 U.S. 926 (1978).

120 *Fed. R. Evid.* 901.

121 *Bledsoe v Salt River Valley Water Users' Ass'n.*, 880 P.2d, 692. *See also Pino* 633 So.2d. at 652; and *Lopez*, 796 S.W.2d. at 480.

122 *Lopez v. Foremost Paving Inc.*, 796 S.W.2d 473, 480 (Tex. App. 1990).

123 *Id.*

124 *Datskow v. Teledyne Continental Motors*, 826 F. Supp. 677, 686 (W.D.N.Y. 1993); *Natchscheim v. Beech Aircraft Corp.*, 847 F.2d 1261, 1278 (7th Cir. 1988); *Gilbert v. Cosco Inc.*, 989 F.2d 399, 402 (10th Cir. 1993).

125 *Lopez v. Foremost Paving Inc.*, at 480 (*citing Lovesky v. Carter*, 773 P.2d 1120, 1124-1146 (Haw. 1989)).

126 *Datskow v. Teledyne Continental Motors*, 826 F. Supp., 686.

127 *Id.*, 686-87.

128 *Id.*

129 *Id. See also* Chapter 12, "Tape Transcripts and Summary Evidence Charts," at 12.18.

130 *Hinds v. General Motors Corp.*, 988 F.2d 1039, 1042 (10th Cir. 1993); *Harrison v. Sears, Roebuck & Co.*, 981 F.2d 25, 28 (1st Cir. 1992); and *Caiazzo v. Volkswagenwerk A. G.*, 647 F.2d 241, 248 (2d Cir. 1981).

131 *Chase v. General Motors Corp.*, 856 F.2d 17, 19 (4th Cir. 1988); *Hale v. Firestone Tire &; Rubber Co.*, 756 F.2d 1322, 1333 (8th Cir. 1985); and *Gladhill v. General Motors Corp.*, 743 F.2d 1049, 1051 (4th Cir. 1984).

132 *Lopez v. Foremost Paving Inc.*, 796 S.W.2d, 480. (*citing Ford Motor Co. v. Nowak*, 638 S.W.2d 582, 590 (Tex. App. 1982).

133 *Bledsoe v. Salt River Valley Water Users' Ass'n*, 880 P.2d 689, 692 (1994).

134 *Robinson v. Missouri Pacific R. Co.*, 16 F.3d 1083, 1089 (10th Cir. 1994).

135 *Bledsoe v. Salt River Valley Water Users' Ass'n* 880 P.2d, 692.

136 *Ohio v. Clark*, 655 N.E.2d 795 (Ohio App. 8th Dist. 1995); *Datskow v. Teledyne Continental Motors*, 826 F. Supp. 677 (W.D.N.Y. 1993); *Robinson v. Missouri Pacific R. Co.*, 16 F.3d 1083 (10th Cir. 1994).

137 *Fed. R. Evid.* 701-705.

138 *Robinson v. Missouri Pacific R. Co.*, 16 F.3d, 1089.

139 *United States v. Pelullo*, 964 F.2d 193, 204-06 (3d Cir. 1992); *United States v. Citron*, 783 F.2d 307, 316-17 (2d Cir. 1986).

140 *United States v. Bray*, 139 F.3d 1104 (6th Cir., 1998).

141 *Datskow v. Teledyne Continental Motors*, 826 F. Supp. 677, 686 (W.D.N.Y. 1993); *Natchscheim v. Beech Aircraft Corp.*, 847 F.2d 1261, 1278 (7th Cir. 1988); *Gilbert v. Cosco Inc.*, 989 F.2d 399, 402 (10th Cir. 1993).

142 *United States v. Birch*, 39 F.3d 1089 (10th Cir. 1994); *United States v. Gaskell*, 985 F.2d 1056 (11th Cir. 1993).

143 *See also Daubert v. Merrill Dow Pharm., Inc.*, 509 U.S. 579, 113 S. Ct. 2786 (1993); *Kumho Tire Co. v. Carmichael*, 526 U.S. 137, 119 S.Ct. 1167, 1173 (1999).

144 *Damon v. Sun Co., Inc.*, 87 F.3d 1467, 1474 (1st Cir. 1996).

145 *Schubert v. Nissan Motor Corp.*, 148 F.3d 25, 28 (1st Cir. 1998).

146 *Id.*, 30.

147 *Smelser v. Norfolk Southern Railway*, 105 F.3d 299 (6th Cir. 1997); *Dancy v. Hyster, Co.*, 127 F.3d 649, 652 (8th Cir.1997), *cert. denied*, ___ U.S. ___ , 118 S.Ct. 1186, 140 L.Ed.2d 316 (1998) and *Cummins v. Lyle Industries*, 93 F.3d 362, 369-371 (7th Cir.1996).

148 *Ohio v. Clark*, 655 N.E.2d 795, 816 (Ohio App. 8th Dist. 1995).

149 *Id.*

150 *Id.*, 820.

151 *Kumho Tire Co. v. Carmichael*, 526 U.S. 137, 119 S.Ct. 1167, 1173 (1999).

152 *Robinson v. v. Missouri Pacific R. Co.*, 16 F.3d 1083, 1089 (10th Cir. 1994).

[153] *Bledsoe v. Salt River Valley Water Users' Ass'n*, 880 P.2d 689 (Ariz. Ct App. 1994).

[154] *Id.*, 691.

[155] *Id.*

[156] *Fed. R. Evid.*703.

[157] *Id.*

[158] *Id.*, "Advisory Committee's Note."

[159] *Id.*

[160] *People v. McHugh,* 476 N.Y.S.2d 721, 722 (1984).

[161] *Id.*, 723.

[162] *People v. Mitchell,* (Cal. App. First Dist. Div. 2), Marin County Superior Court No. SC-12462-A (1994), 1.

[163] *Id.*,11.

[164] *Id.*, 1-2.

[165] *Id.*, 27.

[166] *Id.*, 32.

[167] *Rebel Oil Co. v. Atlantic Richfield Co.,* 146 F.3d 1088,1096 (9th Cir.1998); and *Cabrera v. Cordis Corp.*, 134 F.3d 1418, 1420 (9th Cir. 1998).

[168] *Fed. R. Evid.* 403.

[169] *Id.*

[170] *United States v. Yahweh,* 792 F. Supp. 104 (S.D. Fla. 1992); and *United States v. Jamil,* 707 F.2d 638 (2d Cir. 1983).

[171] *Pino v. Gauthier,* 633 So.2d 638, 652 (La. 1st Cir. 1993) 652.

[172] *Id.*

[173] *Id.* 738. RE: *Sommervold v. Grevlos,* 518 N.W.2d 733 (S.D. 1994).

[174] *Id.*

[175] *Datskow v. Teledyne Continental Mo*tors, 826 F. Supp. 677, 685 (W.D.N.Y. 1993) (*quoting* 1 J.Weinstein &; M. Berger, *Weinstein's Evidence* P 403 [5] 403-88 (1992 ed.).

[176] *Shipp v. General Motors Corp.,* 750 F.2d 418, 422 n.4 (5th Cir. 1985).

[177] *Id.*, 427.

[178] *Id.*, 418.

[179] *Harvey v. General Motors Corp.*, 873 F.2d 1343, 1355 (10th Cir. 1989).

[180] *Id.*, 1356.

[181] See *Swajian v. General Motors Corp.*, 916 F.2d 31, 36 n.2 (1st Cir. 1990); *Patterson v. F.W. Woolworth Co.*, 786 F. Supp. 874, 880 (8th Cir 1986); *Edwards v. Liz Claiborne, Inc.*, ___ WL ___ (E.D. Pa. 1984), *aff'd*, 760 F.2d 256 (3d Cir. 1985). *See also Shekell v. Sturm, Ruger &; Co.*, 716 F.2d 911 (9th Cir. 1983) (unpublished opinion) (new trial ordered in product liability case where gun misfired because a live drop demonstration using a different gun was done only for effect and was likely too prejudicial); *Wolf v. Procter & Gamble Co.*, 555 F. Supp. 613, 626-27 (D.N.J. 1982) (toxic shock syndrome case where court permitted expert to perform courtroom experiment to explain his testimony, allowing any distinctions between the testing circumstances and the human body, that may be prejudicial, to be brought out during cross-examination).

[182] *Datskow, v. Teledyne Continental Motors*, 826 F. Supp 677 (WDNY 1993).

[183] *Id.*, 685.

[184] *Hinkle v. City of Clarksburg*, 81 F.3d 416 (4th Cir. 1996); *Robinson v. Missouri Pacific R. Co.*, 16 F.3d 1083, 1086 (10th Cir. 1994); *Edwards v. Atro Spa*, 891 F. Supp 1085, 1088 (EDNC 1995); *Datskow v. Teledyne Continental Motors*, 826 F. Supp 677 (WDNY 1993).

[185] *State v. Starr*, 998 S.W.2d 61 (Mo. 1999); *Sommervold v. Grevlos*, 518 N.W.2d 733 (S.D. 1993); *Pino v. Gauthier*, 633 So.2d 638, 652 (La. 1st Cir. 1993).

[186] Federal Judicial Center, *Manual for Complex Litigation* 3d, Section 21. 446 (1995).

THE PROSECUTOR AND THE ART OF PLEA NEGOTIATION

By John Brigham, Senior Attorney, American Prosecutors Research Institute, Alexandria, Virginia

Introduction

The United States Supreme Court, among others, has recognized that plea negotiation plays an indispensable role in our criminal justice system and in *Brady v. United States*,[1] the Court unequivocally approved the practice. In some form and at some stage during the life of the criminal prosecution, plea negotiation is practiced in every jurisdiction in the United States. Plea agreements, discussions or negotiations (wise prosecutors are careful to avoid the pejorative term "plea bargain") are necessary for one overriding reason: the community and the criminal justice system lack the resources to dispose of all or even most criminal cases by any other means.

The percentage of criminal cases that finally end in agreement or settlement has been estimated at over 90 percent.[2] There are good reasons for this. Negotiated guilty pleas save time and money, they create an opportunity for the prosecutor to handle more cases and they concentrate resources on the highest priority cases. Nonetheless, they are not intended to create an atmosphere in which expediency displaces the purpose of the criminal justice system.

GENERAL CONSIDERATIONS FOR NEGOTIATING PLEAS

The purpose of the criminal justice system is to serve the interests of justice by protecting the community and holding the defendant accountable for criminal conduct. This purpose is best served when the prosecutor pursues four goals:

- Adequate protection of society from individuals who pose a danger to persons or property;
- Appropriate punishment of individuals who violate the law;
- Deterrence of the individual defendant at bar and the members of the general public from posing a similar danger in the future; and
- When appropriate, rehabilitation of individuals so that they can become law-abiding participants in society (assuming that rehabilitation is a primary responsibility of the prosecutor).

The mission of the criminal justice system is not served when the settlement of a case fails to hold a defendant responsible for the criminal allegations that accurately describe the specific nature of the defendant's criminal conduct. The values embodied in our statutes are undermined when a defendant is allowed to bargain with the system without assuming responsibility for the criminal conduct.

Saving time and money may provide justification for the concept of plea negotiations in general, yet alone they are inadequate and unacceptable reasons for plea negotiations in every criminal case. Moreover, defendants have no *right* to a plea agreement (statutory, constitutional or otherwise) absent an agreement with the prosecutor. Nor can the prosecutor in any way be required to negotiate a plea in every, or indeed, in any case.[3] Before entering into a plea negotiation, the prosecutor should determine that valid and articulable reasons exist to negotiate the case and that the defendant is unwilling to plead guilty as charged in the indictment.

PARTICULAR CONSIDERATIONS FOR NEGOTIATING PLEAS

Ultimately, the responsibility for all dispositions of criminal cases by prosecutors rests with the elected prosecutor. The primary duties, however, rest with the prosecutor processing the individual case who sees that it is resolved in a manner consistent with office policy and the overall purpose of the criminal justice system. Within the context of an office's specific plea policy, there are several questions to ask and concepts to consider when negotiating pleas. Each of them is discussed briefly below in no particular order of significance.

The Severity of the Crime

What was the nature of the criminal conduct? What were the physical, emotional and economic damages to the victim and the lasting effects of the criminal act or acts? How many people were victimized? What penalty does the law provide and the crime deserve? Was the victim selected at random or because of a particular vulnerability or helplessness? Does the crime feature any aggravating, horrifying or heinous aspects?

Participation of the Defendant

How aggravated or violent were the acts? Was the crime premeditated or acted out on the spur of the moment? Was he the ringleader, or did he play a relatively insignificant part? Did he talk other young, impressionable persons into criminal acts? Did someone of overreaching personality or intelligence lead the defendant into the crime? What was the *mens rea*?

Background of the Defendant

Is he a war hero with no prior arrests or is he a habitual or professional criminal? How many previous convictions; how many arrests? What is his psychiatric history, if any? How long has he been engaged in illicit activity? Is he part of organized criminal activity?

Expectation of Rehabilitation

If granted probation, is the defendant likely to be regularly employed? Will he support his dependants; can he? What kind of opportunity has he had in the past? Can he be reformed? What kind of influences will he be subjected to if not confined? Can he handle probation? Will a prison sentence serve a useful purpose to society? Is he the kind of recidivist that can be expected to re-offend if not confined? Will probation with special conditions or a special program be necessary? Does he have those around him who can and will assist him if he is granted probation or a short sentence? Most significantly, was he on bond, bail, early release, parole, probation or other legal restraint at the time of the offense?

Judicial Economy and the Effort Required to Make the Case

How difficult is it to apprehend this type of offender? Might the case require extradition from another jurisdiction? Will it require testimony from out-of-state witnesses? Did the police or investigating agency spend many laborious hours gathering the evidence? Was the manner in which the offense was committed difficult to detect? If so, a stronger punishment may be warranted to deter others. What are the desires of and recommendations from the police officers involved with the case? What recommendations does the parole or probation officer have?

If this case is partially amenable to a negotiation, should the prosecutor require the defendant to plead to the offense as charged in the indictment and leave the final sentence outside of the negotiations and agreement, to be determined later, after formal argument, by both sides and by the court? Does the offense fall within sentencing guidelines? Will the defendant formally waive his right of appeal and/or his Fourth Amendment search and seizure protections in the event of his re-arrest?

Most jurisdictions require the final agreement to be committed to writing and made a part of the record in the case; the prosecutor should decide if the recitation of the evidence and testimony will be by way of stipulation or if it will also be submitted in written form.

The Kind of Offense Involved

What type of consequences that threaten society does this offense involve? Is this a case of first impression in your jurisdiction, or is it part of a larger and more serious trend? Is the defendant likely to re-offend in the future or, worse, re-offend with a more serious crime?

The Jury's and the Court's Reaction

How would the jury react if there were a trial on the merits? How would the jury view the prosecution's potential witnesses? What would be the probable verdict; what would be the probable sentence? What is the likely attitude of the court? Would the case be a good one but for the views of a particular judge? What would be the probable outcome of any pretrial or evidentiary hearings? Will the proposed plea agreement be accepted or rejected by the court? Perhaps most importantly, is this case one that, despite valid reasons in favor of a negotiated agreement, calls out for the considered evaluation (whatever that may be) of a jury composed of 12 members of the community?

Treatment of Co-defendants

What disposition occurred with the co-defendant(s)? What penalty did the co-defendant(s) receive? Was this defendant equally or more culpable? Should this defendant receive the same, a greater or a lesser sentence?

The Current Attitude of the Defendant

Is the defendant willing to admit guilt, save society the cost and expense of trial and spare the victims and witnesses the traumatic experience of reliving the crime? Is the defendant willing to testify against others? Did the defendant cooperate with the police; did the defendant lead police to stolen goods, contraband or other evidence and other defendants? Has the defendant threatened or intimidated witnesses since arrest? Has the defendant fled to avoid arrest or indictment? Has the defendant offered to pay restitution or medical bills? Is the defendant truly regretful and remorseful for having committed the crime?

Victim Concerns and Input

Victims of crime have a statutory right to participate in the criminal justice process in every state in the nation. Victims should and, in many jurisdictions must, be consulted regarding all plea negotiations. They should be educated about all the advantages of plea agreements, and in particular, the important fact that guilty pleas effectively prevent any successful appeal or post-conviction attack on that plea and sentence. This is a significant advantage of negotiated plea agreements, one that few victims have reason to know and one that the prosecutor has the duty to forcefully articulate.

However, victims must not be permitted to control the outcome of plea negotiations. A victim's family may properly feel that their relative's death justifies a full-scale trial and/or a more severe sentence; they may wish for more than a plea. While their feelings are entitled to full consideration, it would be a mistake to grant the victim or the victim's family a veto power over the prosecutor's tactical decisions.

On the other hand, the fact that a homeowner may not want to testify, and having received insurance proceeds may wish to drop a burglary charge, should have little influence on the outcome. Alternatively, a wife may wish her abusive husband to complete a batterer's program in lieu of a guilty plea or a trial. If the husband is unlikely to re-offend, her position might be important to the prosecutor's successful disposition of the case and to the public's perception of the correctness of that disposition.

The Timeliness of the Defendant's Offer to Plead Guilty

Negotiated pleas are intended to maximize judicial and prosecutorial resources. Has the offer to plead guilty been tendered under conditions consistent with this result? Has the state expended considerable time and resources preparing for trial, defending motions, etc? To what extent have victims, witnesses and police been inconvenienced and how many times have they been subpoenaed in connection with the case? Once a case has progressed to the trial stage, plea negotiations are usually not advantageous absent a significant benefit to the state.

It is vital to keep in mind the singular attribute of plea negotiations and agreements. They are efficient means to achieve satisfactory and just results and they exist for that reason alone. Often, however, the amount of time consumed by negotiation may exceed the time that an actual trial would require. For this reason, many prosecutors believe that the longer and more protracted the negotiations, the less likely that a satisfactory agreement will actually be reached (this is sometimes known as the inverse rule of plea agreements).

Additionally, the prosecution should evaluate the integrity and caliber of the defense counsel. Is the defense attorney a trustworthy opponent and a reliable negotiator? Can he or she be relied upon to adhere to the terms of the agreement? Does the defense attorney have the requisite trust of and control over the defendant? Is the prosecutor wasting time because the defense attorney actually lacks the ability to "deliver" the client; is the defense attorney truly empowered to negotiate on the defendant's behalf; will the defendant actually do what the defense attorney says he will? In other words, is the prosecutor wasting time in fruitless and theoretical negotiations instead of preparing for trial?

The Strength of the State's Case

Are the witnesses available? What are the known defenses and which defense witnesses will appear? How strong is the state's evidence; how good are the state's witnesses? Are there evidentiary problems, such as a motion to suppress that has been granted? What are the chances of conviction at trial on the primary charge or on a lesser-included charge; in the event of a conviction, what is the likelihood that the jury will recommend or the court will actually impose a meaningful punishment?

The Necessity of Having a Trial for the Sake of Upholding Confidence in the Criminal Justice System

Sometimes a crime may be so deplorable or shocking that any plea negotiation, no matter how advantageous to the prosecution, would have adverse and negative connotations. A satisfactory agreement, in some circumstances, may be an impossibility. How did the community react to the seriousness of the crime? Is this the kind of case that should not be compromised in any way by either side and is deserving of a full-scale trial? Should an example be made in this instance and, if so, is this the case the prosecutor should rely upon to achieve that purpose?

FINAL THOUGHTS

It is impossible to overemphasize the fact that most lay people regard the concept of pleas and plea negotiations (plea "bargains") with great suspicion, even hostility. Historically, there are valid reasons for this popular prejudice. Nevertheless, all prosecutors know that without pleas the system would literally collapse (assuming, of course, that the numbers of judges, attorneys and venire members remained static). Furthermore, there is much to be said for hearing the defendant's response to the judge's question, "Are you pleading guilty because you are, in fact, guilty?" The answer to that question should be, "Yes, your honor." These words, alone, are often deeply satisfying to the victim or to the victim's family. Getting to that point and hearing those simple yet healing words can do wonders for the victim's state of mind and for the prosecutor's job satisfaction.

There is also another and equally compelling reason, sometimes, to actively avoid plea negotiations. Simply put, the elemental fact is this: the first, most basic and fundamental job of the prosecutor is to try cases, not to negotiate them. It is professional suicide to gain a reputation as a prosecutor who is reluctant to go to trial. Professionally speaking, sometimes it is better to go to trial and lose than it is to take a plea and "win." If the defense bar knows that you have taken and will continue to take the tough cases to trial and that you are fully prepared to mount the best prosecution you can, regardless of the obstacles against you, then the number of cases your office disposes of with successful pleas will actually increase. The converse is true. If you flinch from making the hard calls or from trying the hard cases, you will get few offers for easy pleas. A reputation for being shy is no reputation at all. Avoid it at all costs. Your trial skills, your comprehensive trial preparations and your courtroom tenacity are the foundation for an esteemed professional reputation; lose that and you will get no pleas at all. Nor will you deserve to.

For all these reasons, crafting intelligent, fair and appropriate plea agreements is one of the prosecution's most critical responsibilities. Prosecutors further the ends of justice when they do it correctly, and in the process, educate the society they serve.

Author's Note: The impetus for this article and some of the opinions expressed were the work of Barbara LaWall, County Attorney, Pima County, Tucson, Arizona.

ENDNOTES

[1] *Brady v. United States*, 397 U.S. 742, 90 S.Ct. 1463 (1970).

[2] *Johnson v. Commonwealth*, 214 Va. 515, 201 S.E. 2d 594 (1974), citing the *A.B.A. Standards Relating to Pleas of Guilty*, 1, 2 (Approved Draft, 1968).

[3] *Weatherford v. Bursey*, 429 U.S. 545 (1977).

PUBLIC POLICIES AND SPECIAL TOPICS

POLICE LIABILITY: THE PROSECUTOR'S ROLE AND ETHICAL DUTIES WHEN DEADLY FORCE IS USED

By Grover Trask, District Attorney and E. Michael Soccio, Chief Deputy District Attorney, Riverside County, Riverside, California

Introduction

Police liability and allegations of police misconduct are relatively rare. Nevertheless, these unfortunate situations will from time to time occur. If it happens in your jurisdiction it may take one of several forms. General misconduct, assault and battery and unreasonable force, misappropriation of funds, unlawful arrest, search and seizure, resisting arrest, perjury, evidence tampering, high-speed pursuit and civil rights violations are some of the situations that you as the prosecutor may have to deal with. Perhaps the most difficult police liability case of all, however, is the officer-involved deadly force and shooting situation.

In such a case you may very well find yourself in the perhaps uncomfortable position of investigating and, if required, prosecuting "one of your own." This may be an unenviable and usually thankless task but sometimes it is a necessary one. Perhaps your office can avoid it, perhaps not. This chapter presents a scenario and a few guidelines that may help to steer you through the morass in the event that it does occur.

CASE STUDY

John Scott lived in a two-story apartment in a residential neighborhood, and as landlord, attempted to evict some troublesome tenants. Twice on the day of the event, Mr. Scott had called the police to complain of disturbances caused by these tenants. Officer Henrich was among the police officers that spoke with Mr. Scott, in person, and when later that day a neighbor called the police and reported hearing gunshots in front of Mr. Scott's building, Officer Henrich and his partner responded to the call. Upon arrival, they were informed that the man who allegedly fired the shot was acting "crazy" and had entered a nearby apartment. With weapons drawn, the officers immediately approached the apartment, banged and kicked the door, and yelled, "Police. Police officers. Open up."

A man who would later be identified as John Scott opened the door holding a gun pointed at them. It was later determined that Scott had a blood alcohol content of

---

.31. Believing that Scott had raised his weapon, Officer Henrich fired a shot. Officer Henrich's partner, assuming the suspect had fired his weapon, then fired four shots into the doorway. One of his shots killed Mr. Scott, who had never fired his weapon. *See Scott v. Henrich*, 39 F. 3d 912.[1] The police department's initial press release stated that the officers fired only after they had been fired upon by the suspect. This announcement was later retracted.

Assume now that the police chief calls you, the prosecutor, to say that he has begun an administrative review and a criminal investigation of the shooting, the findings of which he will submit to your office. He does not specify when that will happen nor he does request your assistance. You also receive calls from the victim's family and the press demanding answers and action against the officers. What is your role in this highly public affair? What do you do?

THE PROSECUTOR'S DILEMMA

Rarely is a situation more distressing to the community than one in which a protector—in this case, the police officer on duty—uses deadly force against a member of the community. Society looks to the prosecutor for reassurance that law enforcement's actions were legal and appropriate, and therefore, the prosecutor is obliged to determine the truth and dispense justice under the glare of their intense scrutiny.

Prosecutors routinely engage in assessing crimes, finding truth and charging crimes. A shooting case, however, presents a unique ethical challenge: how to police the police and ensure public confidence in the process. When a law enforcement officer uses deadly force and kills a citizen, every social and political interest group, including criminal justice professionals and the media, along with the victim's family and supporters and every opinionated citizen, brings pressure to bear on the prosecutor's office to "do the right thing." The right thing, however, will be defined differently by each interested party.

While it is easy to say the prosecutor must be unbiased and neutral in his investigation and judgments, it can be quite difficult to put into practice. Any decision made affects future police behavior and hence, community safety. A ruling against law enforcement could cause the agency to react less aggressively and decrease response times and call-out times that could degrade protection of the public. A finding that a shooting is not criminal in nature often results in at least one segment of the community feeling alienated. It also reinforces stereotypical beliefs about "cover-ups," including the perception that the prosecutor is "in bed" with the police.

THE PROSECUTOR'S ETHICAL CHOICES REGARDING NEUTRALITY

Adequate safeguards already exist through state and federal law and collective bargaining agreements to ensure the rights of the police officer who fires his or her weapon while on duty. The investigating prosecutor is expected to know and respect these rules and regulations and failure to do so is rarely a problem in police liability cases. The difficulty more often flows from the inevitably close working relationship between prosecutors' offices and law enforcement agencies. Prosecutors and the public presume that law enforcement acts appropriately in most situations. The ethical challenge, therefore, stems from the temptation to reach this comfortable conclusion prematurely. Every effort should be made to independently and thoroughly investigate the case and review the evidence before reaching a final conclusion.

The Prosecutor's Duty to Investigate

Investigative duties have been recognized as an integral part of the prosecution function in most jurisdictions throughout the United States. For example, in California "the prosecutor's authority to investigate alleged police officer criminal misconduct cases stems from the executive branch of government, e.g., Cal. Const., Art. III, sec. 3, and the investigation and gathering of evidence relating to criminal offenses is the prosecutor's responsibility and rests solely within his or her discretion." *Triple A Machine Inc. v. State of California*; and *Hicks v. Orange County Board of Supervisors.*[2] See also ABA Prosecution Standard 3-3.1(a), declaring that, "… the prosecutor has an affirmative responsibility to investigate suspected illegal activity when it is not adequately dealt with by other agencies".[3]

A prosecutor should investigate suspected illegal activity when such activity cannot be adequately dealt with by other agencies. In their criminal investigations of police officers, prosecutors are governed by the same ethical considerations applicable to other prosecution functions.

Furthermore, the prosecutor has a "public duty to prepare a complete prosecution."[4] That duty (and authority) is so vital to the public order that it will not be subjected to prior restraint by a court "except under extraordinary circumstances."[5] The United

States Supreme Court noted in *Imbler v. Pachtman*[6] that the prosecutor's responsibilities "cast him in a role of an administrator or investigative officer" as well as an advocate.

However, do not forget that, depending on the specifics of the particular situation, the wisest and fairest approach may be to request the appointment of an outside or special prosecutor, one not from your office. Perhaps your office simply cannot fairly and effectively conduct an investigation or perhaps a conflict of interest—real or perceived—prevents your involvement. In fact, your jurisdiction may already have established procedures in place for requesting outside investigators and, if necessary, prosecutors. If so, and depending on the complexities of the problem, this is an option you should consider.

Although police agencies often look to the prosecutor for legal advice concerning investigations even when a legal advisor is attached to the police department, the degrees of coordination and cooperation vary from jurisdiction to jurisdiction. Actual prosecutorial control over an investigative effort is generally limited to investigators employed by the prosecutor. Law enforcement personnel conduct most officer-involved investigations, creating the potential for inter-agency policy issues and conflicts that should be addressed jointly by both offices before the investigation begins. It is the ethical duty of the prosecutor to maintain cooperative but independent control over the review and the ultimate charging decision on police officer misconduct cases.

The Prosecutor's Decision to Charge

The prosecutor's sole legal role in any criminal case is to determine criminal responsibility, not civil liability. In a police liability (criminal) case, the threshold ethical and legal inquiry for this determination requires an independent review into the facts of the incident with or without the cooperation of the responsible law enforcement agency. The prosecutor may wait until the law enforcement agency completes its own criminal review of the incident. The prosecutor's findings are then made in reliance upon the agency's investigation.

Another method available to deal with police criminal responsibility cases is the creation of a call-out team. This is a joint effort by the police department, the prosecutor and other allied law enforcement agencies. Other jurisdictions turn over the entire criminal investigation to the prosecutor. The wiser approach, especially in controversial shootings, is for the prosecutor to initiate a separate criminal investigation independent of the law enforcement agency's review. This assumes, of course, that your office has the latitude, the ability and the resources to undertake this responsibility.

Once the prosecutor's investigation has been completed, the legal question in reviewing the case for criminal liability is whether the officer's acts fall within the state laws of criminal liability. In blunt terms: did the officer commit a crime? To effectively answer the question it is strongly recommended that the prosecutor clearly and affirmatively convey to law enforcement agencies and the public the prosecutor's role and oversight responsibilities:

- To investigate shootings by law enforcement officers engaged in the performance of their duties for the purpose of assessing criminal responsibility;
- To oversee the events attendant to the shooting, as a neutral fact-finder, ensuring fairness and integrity for the participants in those shootings and the community as a whole;
- To properly apply the law relating to police use of force to the current investigation, regardless of who was involved; and
- To assure the public and law enforcement that the final determination regarding criminal responsibility will be as fair and just as humanly possible.

It is important that the prosecutor assigned to the criminal investigation clearly understands that the purpose is *not* to decide whether or not the officers were civilly negligent or may have violated any other state, federal statute, or administrative policy. This is beyond his or her authority and duty.

THE GENERAL THEORY OF CRIMINAL RESPONSIBILITY

While charges of murder certainly are available in the case scenario presented earlier in this article, the charging in most officer-involved incidents will focus on a theory of criminal negligence. The difference between criminal and civil negligence as it relates to state criminal statutes and case law is at the center of the inquiry. Generally, there are few reported state appellate cases on point and the prosecutor will want to analyze federal case decisions for guidance as to the threshold issues of criminal responsibility. A review of these federal cases will also help identify what the courts have found to be reasonable or unreasonable under specific fact patterns. (See endnotes 10,11 and 12.)

In most states criminal negligence is conduct that is more than the failure to exercise ordinary or reasonable care. For example, in California, criminal negligence is conduct that is aggravated, reckless and flagrant. In addition, the facts must be such that the consequences of the conduct could have been reasonably foreseen and were not the result of a mistake in judgment or inattention.

In any officer-involved shooting where a death has occurred, the prosecutor investigating the officer's criminal responsibility decides whether there is sufficient evidence to conclude that the officer's actions occurred with either malice aforethought or with criminal negligence and without legal justification or excuse.

In making a charging decision against a police officer, prosecutors should be guided by national and state standards. The prosecutor should file a criminal complaint only if the following four basic prosecutorial filing guidelines are satisfied:

- Based on a complete investigation and a thorough consideration of all pertinent, available facts, the prosecutor is satisfied that the evidence shows the accused is guilty of the crime to be charged beyond a reasonable doubt;
- There is legally sufficient, admissible evidence of a *corpus delicti*;
- There is legally sufficient, admissible evidence of the accused's identity as the perpetrator of the crime charged; and
- The prosecutor has considered the probability of conviction by an objective fact-finder hearing the admissible evidence. The admissible evidence should be of such convincing force that it would warrant conviction of the crime charged by a reasonable and objective fact-finder after hearing all the evidence available to the prosecutor at the time of charging and after hearing the most plausible, reasonably foreseeable defense that could be raised under the evidence presented to the prosecutor.

APPLYING THE "OBJECTIVE REASONABLENESS" STANDARD

Because of the complexity of the legal analysis required to review police criminal responsibility cases and lack of state decisional law, prosecutors should review the seminal federal cases involving officer shootings and liability cases. This review is beneficial in understanding the application of the objective reasonableness standard to making any charging decision against a police officer.

The U.S. Supreme Court in *Graham v. Conner*[7] set the legal standard for reviewing a civil rights claim alleging police use of excessive force, including deadly force, in the course of arrest, investigatory stops or other "seizure" of a person. The objective reasonableness standard applies in any criminal analysis when following criminal charging standards. While a state's definition of criminal negligence may vary, the underlying theory of criminal responsibility deals with the Fourth Amendment objective reasonableness inquiry: whether the officers' actions are objectively reasonable in light of the facts and circumstances confronting them without regard to their underlying intent and motivation. The U.S. Supreme Court held that the reasonableness of a particular use of force should be judged from the perspective of a reasonable officer on the scene, rather than with 20/20 vision of hindsight.[8]

The objective reasonableness standard has not been given a precise definition or mechanical application by the courts. However, the U.S. Supreme Court has held that to determine whether a Fourth Amendment seizure is reasonable the extent of the intrusion on the suspect's rights should be weighed against the governmental interests in effective law enforcement.[9] Therefore, the proper analysis for a prosecutor is whether the force that was used to affect a particular seizure was reasonable viewing the facts from the perspective of a reasonable officer on the scene. If the conduct is unreasonable under the court's objective reasonableness standard, then the prosecutor should determine whether the conduct reached the level of criminal conduct defined by state statute. The professional responsibility of a prosecutor in reviewing these cases requires a clear understanding of these legal standards.[10]

Proper application of the objective reasonableness standard requires careful attention to the facts and circumstances of each particular case, including the severity of the crime at issue, whether the suspect poses an immediate threat to the safety of the officers or others and whether he is actively resisting arrest or attempting to evade arrest by flight.[11]

OUTSIDE PRESSURES AND WHAT TO DO ABOUT THEM

An additional complication in office-involved shootings or allegations of excessive force is the sometimes not so subtle political pressure that the prosecutor may face from various sources. The following five guidelines are recommended to mitigate outside pressures:

- *Initiate and complete a thorough independent investigation.* The more information gathered and the more truly independent the investigation conducted, the more likely it is that truth, and therefore justice, will prevail. These cases create a difficult challenge for the prosecutor because the officer is often the only surviving eyewitness. In many instances, and under the direction of the police union attorney, the officer will not provide a statement to the prosecutor's investigator. It therefore becomes critical for the prosecutor to examine medical reports, all available physical evidence and any spontaneous statements made by the officer. In addition, police experts should be consulted to determine whether the officer's story (if given) is factually consistent with other known facts. If other witnesses are available, detailed statements should be taken. Uncooperative and reluctant witnesses should be subpoenaed before the grand jury. When discrepancies and inconsistencies occur, prosecutors should be prepared to look at the circumstantial evidence that, if believed, would tend to support or discredit the police officer's version of the facts.

- *Give the information to the public.* Open communication with the public is essential in maintaining confidence that the investigation will be thorough, factual and complete. The prosecutor should dispense all relevant, accurate and non-privileged information that will not jeopardize the ongoing investigation as soon as possible and on a regular basis. Any misinformation provided by the police or other institutional source should be corrected and explained immediately upon discovery. While no information should be released that would jeopardize the integrity of the investigation, certain "gossip" and other misinformation left uncorrected will only jeopardize the final conclusions of the complete investigation. For example, in the case study for this article the information regarding the fact that the alleged suspect did not fire his weapon should be released and then explained. Some of the media as well as certain individuals in the community at large may already have formed a fixed position on guilt or innocence. The release of accurate information may help alleviate some misperceptions advanced through public gossip. However, and most importantly, the general public deserves to know the truth—no matter what it is—so they can have faith in the integrity of the process. The prosecutor's role is not to defend the police or lobby for the victims. However, public understanding improves when citizens are given regular updates and accurate facts.

- *Work with the media.* Media attention requires a clear and direct plan of action. The best plan allows for continuous release of all non-privileged information, provided that does not compromise the investigation. The prosecution may be accused of withholding vital information, protecting the police and perhaps even being involved in a "cover-up." When a good working relationship with the media is established, such accusations will be less likely, or at least minimized. There will be information that cannot be given to the media until the investigation is completed, but nothing will ensure more suspicion or accusations of a cover-up than hiding the facts from reporters. Remember their institutional bias: to look for mistakes, misconduct, incompetency, conspiracy or cover-up, no matter how implausible. All media, whether print, broadcast or electronic, should have equal and fair access to the information. Their perception of the magnitude of and public interest in the newsworthy event will determine the level of news coverage. A public affairs contact person within the prosecutor's office can handle most cases. This person may be the prosecutor or a subordinate. When the matter rises to the level of a national issue that remains in the headlines for months, it is recommended that the prosecutor meet with his or her state or national associations and outside media consultants for strategic assistance and planning.

- *Address issues with the victim's family and community support groups.* Emotions run high in police shootings and are often generated by the concerned family and friends of the victim and/or suspect. This is only natural. Their loss and knowledge of the victim may be the force to counter the police version of events. It is as important for the prosecutor to address these issues as it is to work with the media. Family members and supporters should be shown courtesy and respect. The prosecutor should meet with the victim's family members and their support group to apprise them of the state of the investigation, to answer whatever questions he or she can and to attempt to maintain the integrity of the investigation. Like the police, they have vested interests in the outcome and they are responding primarily from an emotional position. A prosecutor should take care not to favor a particular viewpoint or constituency. Nothing ensures a negative result more than favoritism or alignment with a particular faction. Finding that a shooting was "good" will most likely anger family and friends of the victim. It may also offend any personal injury lawyers involved in the matter. The intent of meeting with these groups is not to win them over (this may be an impossible goal) but rather to learn from them and to provide them with information.

- *Protect the rights of the police officer under investigation while maintaining professional independence.* Law enforcement and prosecutors are normally a team, but in an officer-involved shooting involving death or injury, the working relationship can dramatically change. Prosecutors who once had collegial working relationships with law enforcement might be viewed with suspicion, and as a result, inter-agency cooperation may suffer. The mere fact of an investigation by the prosecutor's office can be viewed as an offense to police personnel: a devaluation of their character, their honesty and their oath to protect the public. The prosecutor should be cognizant of law enforcement's aversion to the public and media criticism that in-house investigations of personnel can evoke. Tensions concerning the conduct and scope of the investigation could prove problematic and further degrade the interagency rapport. While cooperation and mutual respect are required, fairness demands impartiality in the decision-making process. The challenge to the prosecutor is to reassure those being investigated that their rights will be protected and that despite the media attention and the emotional stress generated by an officer-involved shooting case, they can have faith that the prosecutor will be fair and competent.

CONCLUSION

While no prosecutor can ever know the whole truth about any case, his/or her responsibility is to conduct the most thorough investigation possible; to recognize any potential bias or flaws in any officer-involved shooting investigation; and to conduct the investigation in a fair and impartial manner. This ethical duty is a burden but it can also be an asset and a shield. Prosecutors should realize that they cannot answer all questions or solve all issues for every interested party who is seeking a specific result or answer.

Avoid the temptation to believe that every group with an interest in the case should be placated. A decision regarding an issue as weighty as criminal responsibility will never be met with complete approval by all members of the community, every victim, every victim's family or every police officer. The prosecutor should have the strength, the integrity and the courage to face and accept the criticism that is inevitable in police misconduct cases. In assuring fairness to all those concerned, it is the prosecutor's fundamental obligation to be guided solely by his or her sense of public responsibility to ensure the attainment of justice.[12]

ENDNOTES

[1] *See Scott v. Henrich*, 39 F. 3d 912. The family sued civilly on the premise that the officers used excessive force by creating an unreasonable risk of armed confirmation when they stormed the door without first trying to defuse a potentially deadly situation. The court held officers were not required to avail themselves of the least intrusive means of responding to an exigent situation before approaching and knocking on the door where a suspect was firing his weapon. While this case was a civil lawsuit in federal court, it does give the prosecutor some ethical insights into factors to review for criminal liability.

[2] *See Triple A Machine Shop, Inc. v. State of California* (1989) 213 Cal.App.3d 131, 144-146; *Hicks v. Board of Supervisors* (1977) 69 Cal.App.3d 228, 241 and cases cited therein. "The investigation and gathering of evidence relating to criminal offenses is the prosecutor's responsibility and rest solely within his or her discretion." *Triple A Machine Shop, Inc. v. State of California, supra*, 213 Cal.App.3d at pp. 144-145. *See also People v. Superior Court* (Aquino) (1988) 201 Cal.App.1346, 1350 (stating that "investigation and the gathering of evidence relating to criminal offenses is a responsibility which is inseparable from the district attorney's prosecutorial function").

[3] NDAA-NPS 2d. Nos. 8.3, 39.1; ABA Standard 3-3.1(a): "A prosecutor ordinarily relies on police and other investigative agencies for investigation of alleged criminal acts, but the prosecutor has an affirmative responsibility to investigate suspected illegal activity when it is not adequately dealt with by other agencies."

[4] *Pachaly v. City of Lynchburg* 897 F.2d 723, 728) (4th Cir. 1990).

[5] *Manchel v. County of Los Angeles* 245 Cal.App.2d 501, 505-10 (1966); *see also Dix v. Superior Court* 53 Cal.3d 442, 451 (1991).

[6] *Imbler v. Pachtman* 424 U.S. 409 (1976).

[7] *Graham v. Conner,* 490 U.S. 386 (1989). Under the Fourth Amendment, police may use only such force as is objectively reasonable under the circumstances.

[8] *Graham v. Conner*, 490 U.S. 386, 397, 109 S.Ct. 1865, 1872, 104 L.Ed.2d 443 (1989). An officer's use of deadly force is reasonable only if "the officer has probable cause to believe that the suspect poses a significant threat of death or serious physical injury to the officer or others. *Tennessee v. Garner*, 471 U.S. 1, 3, 105 S.Ct. 1694, 1697, 85 L.Ed.2d 1 (1985); *see also Graham*, 490 U.S. at 396, 109 S.Ct. At 1872 (one of the factors in determining reasonableness is "whether the suspect poses an immediate threat to the safety of the officers or others"). All determinations of unreasonable force "must embody allowance for the fact that police officers are often forced to make split-second judgments, in circumstances that are tense, uncertain, and rapidly evolving, about the amount of force that is necessary in a particular situation."

[9] *See Scott v. United States*, 436 U.S. 128 (1978); and *Bell v. Wolfish*, 441 U.S. 520 (1979).

[10] The "reasonableness" of a police officer's excessive force or "seizure" depends not only on when it is made but also on how it is carried out. Said the court:

> 1. Determining whether the force used to effect a particular seizure is "reasonable" under the Fourth Amendment requires a careful balancing of "the nature and quality of the intrusion on the individual's Fourth Amendment interests" against the countervailing governmental interest at stake. Id., at 8, 105 S.Ct., at 1699, quoting *United States v. Place*, 462 U.S. 696, 703, 103 S.Ct. 2637, 2642, 77 L.Ed.2d 110 (1983). Our Fourth Amendment jurisprudence has long recognized that the right to make an arrest or investigatory stop necessarily carries with it the right to use some degree of physical coercion or threat thereof to effect it. See *Terry v. Ohio*, 392 U.S., at 22-27, 88 S.Ct., at 1880-1883. Because the test of reasonableness under the Fourth Amendment is not capable of precise definition or mechanical application," *Bell v. Wolfish*, 441 U.S. 520, 559, 99 S.Ct. 1861, 1884, 60 L.Ed.2d 447 (1979), however, its proper application requires careful attention to the facts and circumstances of each particular case, including the severity of the crime at issue, whether the suspect poses an immediate threat to the safety of the officers or others, and whether he is actively resisting arrest or attempting to evade arrest by flight. See *Tennessee v.*

Garner, 471 U.S., at 8-9, 105 S.Ct., at 1699-1700 (the question is "whether the totality of the circumstances justifies a particular sort of... seizure").

2. As in other Fourth Amendment contexts, however, the "reasonableness" inquiry in an excessive force case is an objective one: the question is whether the officers' actions are "objectively reasonable" in light of the facts and circumstances confronting them, without regard to their underlying intent of motivation. See *Scott v. United States*, 436 U.S. 128, 137-139, 98 S.Ct. 1717, 1723-1724, 56 L.Ed.2d 168 (1978); see also *Terry v. Ohio, supra*, 392 U.S., at 21, 88 S.Ct., at 1879 (in analyzing the reasonableness of a particular search or seizure, "it is imperative that the facts be judged against an objective standard"). An officer's evil intentions will not make a Fourth Amendment violation out of an objectively reasonable use of force; nor will an officer's good intentions make an objectively unreasonable use of force constitutional. See *Scott v. United States, supra*, 436 U.S., at 138, 98 S.Ct., at 1723, citing *United States v. Robinson*, 414 U.S. 218, 94 S.Ct. 467, 38 L.Ed.2d 427 (1973).

[11] Officer-Involved Shootings: As with any major incident, officer-involved shootings present a number of immediate and long-term issues within the scope of the criminal, administrative and civil investigations. Below is a partial list of some of the more frequent authorities and guidelines applicable to many of the most common issues that might arise. Please note that this is intended only as a quick reference and should not serve as a substitute for the actual authority or the advice of competent legal counsel.

Statements Involving Officer(s)

1. Public safety information (e.g., outstanding suspects, location of rounds, etc.) may be immediately coerced (ordered) without presence of attorney if need is compelling. *Ward v. City of Portland*, 857 F2d 1373 (9th Cir. 1988). (Note: Case modified 2/89).

2. While it may be advisable to give a voluntary statement to criminal investigators, department should not order any such statement without specific requests from involved officer. (Fifth Amendment; *People v. Gwillim* 223 Cal.App.3d 1254 (1990) and *Gwillim v. San Jose* 929 F2d 465 (9th Cir. 1991); *U.S. v. North* 920 F2d 940) (D.C. Cir. 1990); *In Re Grand Jury Subpoena: HBPD* (9th Cir. 1996) 75 F3d 446.

3. Interview for administrative investigation includes right to representation (California Government Code (GC)), GC § 3303h) and should commence with *Lybarger* admonishment, 40 Cal.3d 822 (1985), (GC § 3303 e, h).

4. Consider short-term delay (3303d).

5. Maintain confidentiality (California Penal Code (PC), (PC § 832.7 *et seq.*). Limited civil privilege except for discipline or impeachment (after *in camera*) (GC § 3303f).

6. Not required to, but may, provide material before interview. *Pasadena P.O.A. v. Pasadena*, 51 Cal.3d 564 (1990), (3303g).

7. Officer may consult with attorney prior to submitting Department Report (D.R.), which should be limited to elements of pre-shooting crime to be prosecuted. *Long Beach P.O.A. v. Long Beach*, 156 Cal.App.3d 996 (1984).

8. Record officer injuries for cross-complaint.

9. Single supervisor for all reports.

10. Avoid preamble re: "coercion" and limit elements to crimes to be prosecuted.

Blood Testing

1. Generally not taken as part of criminal investigation unless voluntary. (Fourth Amendment).

2. With properly implemented policy and testing procedure, may be ordered as part of administrative investigation. *Skinner v. Railway Labor Exec.*, 109 S.Ct. 1402 (1989).

Media

1. Coordinate a single press release among all involved agencies limited to GC § 6254(f).

2. Absent good cause, must release names of officers. *N.Y. Times v. Superior Court* (1997) 52 Cal.App.4th 97.

3. May release internal information. *Bradshaw v. L.A.*, 221 Cal.App.3d 908 (1990). PC § 832.7(d).

Civil Investigation

1. Any "attorney work product" must be separately protected to maintain privilege.

2. Officer's conduct will be reviewed by objective standard of reasonable officer under similar circumstances known to him at time. *Graham v. Conner*, 109 S.Ct. 1865 (1989).

3. Department policy and training must be adequate (*Tennessee v. Garner*, 105 S.Ct. 1694 (1985)) and without "deliberate indifference" to the rights of citizens. (*Canton v. Harris*, 109 S.Ct. 1197 (1989)). Encourage reasoned discretion rather than absolutes (Evidence Code § 669.1).

4. Look into situation leading to shooting. *Alexander v. S.F.* 29 F3d 1355 (9th Cir. 1994) (created risk of deadly force).

5. Officer must not place self in harm's way (i.e., is vehicle already moving?). *Estate of Starks v. Enyart*, 5 F3d 230 (7th Cir. 1993).

[12] The following is a list of some of the more significant case decisions frequently relied upon in the area of use of force cases. The brief summary of each case is intended for quick reference only and should not be cited as the "rule of the case." Each case should be considered in conjunction with applicable state statutory provisions.

Federal Civil Rights Actions

- *Farrar v. Hobby* 113 S.Ct. 566, 506 U.S. 103 (1992) – No attorney's fees for nominal damages unless truly "prevailed."

- *Romberg v. Nichols* 48 F3d 453 (9th Cir. 1995) – Plaintiff must "succeed" with result sought at outset of trial, not just "prevail" with nominal damages.

- *Monell v. NYC Dept. of Social Services* 436 U.S. 658, 98 S.Ct. 2018 (1978) – Public entity liability must be based on official custom, policy, or practice of Constitutional deprivation (no respondent superior).

- *Pembaur v. Cincinnati* 475 U.S. 469, 106 S.Ct. 1292 (1986) – Single deliberate choice of alternatives made by official with final authority sufficient to establish policy. (See *St. Louis v. Praprotnik* 485 U.S. 112, 108 S.Ct. 915 (1988)- Department head must be only authority for state policy for agency).

- *Bryan County, OK v. Brown* 520 U.S. 397, 117 S.Ct. 1382 (1997) - Risk of constitutional violation from inadequate hiring process must be "plainly obvious." Standard to impose municipal liability is a rigorous one of "deliberate indifference" as opposed to mere indifference.

- *Daniels v. Williams* 474 U.S. 307, 106 S.Ct. 662 (1986); *Davidson v. Cannon* 474 U.S. 347, 106 S.Ct. 668 (1986) - No 1983 violation of due process based on mere negligence.

- *Canton v. Harris* 489 U.S. 378, 109 S.Ct. 1197 (1989) - Inadequate police training is actionable under § 1983 only where it can be shown to have been a policy reflecting "deliberate indifference" to constitutional rights. (E.g., availability of other programs, unsatisfactory training, or mistake of single officer not sufficient). *See also Merritt v. County of Los Angeles*, 875 F2d 765 (9th Cir. 1989).

- *Grandstaff v. City of Borger* 767 F2d 161 (5th Cir. 1985) - Policy of "reckless disregard" by failure to take disciplinary action (i.e., ratifying) for bad shooting and *Laraz v. City of Los Angeles* 846 F2d 645 (9th Cir.1986) - Police chief's failure to sustain complaints of excessive force or discipline officers may lead to municipal liability.

- *DeShaney v. Winnebago Co.* 489 U.S. 189, 109 S.Ct. 998, (1989) - Under the Fourteenth Amendment, the state assumes no obligation to protect an individual from even foreseeable harm from outside sources and no "special relationship" is created unless the individual is in actual custody or confined care.

- *Johnson v. Barker* 799 F2d 1396 (9th Cir. 1986) - Not all tortious conduct by state officials (e.g., defamation, false imprisonment, malicious prosecution) is actionable under § 1983, absent some showing of a constitutional deprivation without due process.

- *Oklahoma City v. Tuttle* 471 U.S. 808, 105 S.Ct. 2427(1985) - Single acts of police misconduct are not, by themselves, sufficient to show official policy.

- *Harlow v. Fitzgerald* 457 U.S. 800, 102 S.Ct. 2727 (1982) - Individual officer entitled to qualified good faith immunity if conduct does not violate a clearly established statutory or constitutional standard.

- *Anderson v. Creighton* 483 U.S. 635, 107 S.Ct. 3034 (1987) - Immunity determined as matter of law based upon objective standard.

- *Hunter v. Bryant* 502 U.S. 224, 112 S.Ct. 534 (1992) - Good faith immunity for reasonable belief in probable cause.

- *Cornwell v. City of Riverside* 896 F2d 398 (9th Cir. 1999) - Federal law does not prohibit city payments of officer's punitive damages. (GC § 825b).

- *Trevino v Gates* 99 F3d 911 (9th Cir. 1996) - Policy of city council to consider payment of punitive damages of each individual case deemed not unconstitutional.

Use of Force

- *Alexander v. San Francisco* 29 Frd 1355 (9th Cir. 1994) - Entry into house of disabled person on administrative warrant (not arrest warrant), following armed threats, created risk of deadly force, which was unreasonable.

- *Estate of Starks v. Enyart* 5 F3d 230 (7th Cir. 1993) – If officer is already in front of vehicle before it accelerates (vs. stepping in front of moving vehicle) shooting may be justified.

- *Tennessee v. Garner* 471 U.S. 1, 105 S.Ct. 1694 (1985) – Authority to use deadly force must be based upon reasonable belief that suspect is armed or poses an actual or threatened danger rather than classification of offense (i.e., misdemeanor/felony).

- *Forrett v. Richardson* 112 F3d 416 (9th Cir. 1997) – Use of deadly force on desperate fleeing felon requires only probable cause of violent crime or threat of same. Officer need not be threatened and suspect need not be armed.

- *Graham v. Conner* 490 U.S. 386, 109 S.Ct. 1865 (1989) – Excessive force no longer under substantive due process analysis, but now under Fourteenth Amendment test of reasonable objective standard of similarily situated officer.

- *Scott v. Henrich* 39 F3d 912 (9th Cir. 1994) – Officers need not consider or avail themselves of lesser alternative levels of force. Test is one of reasonableness, not escalation. *See* also *Forrett* above – all alternatives need not be examined.

- *Edson v. Anaheim* 63 Cal.App.4th 1269 (1998) – Unlike civilian battery, burden is on plaintiff to prove that officer's use of force was "unreasonable." (Adopts federal standard in state court actions.)

- *Forrester v. San Diego* 25 F3d 804 (9th Cir. 1994) – Pain compliance on demonstrators ok, least painful and least intrusive method not required, test is reasonableness under totality of circumstances.

- *Reynolds v. San Diego County* 84 F3d 1162 (9th Cir. 1996) – Officer is entitled to good faith immunity if facts show officer's perception of immediate threat is reasonable (despite experts).

- *U.S. v. Reese* 2 F3d 870 (9th Cir. 1993) – Objective reasonableness standard (*Graham*) now applied to criminal police use of force; "reckless disregard" now sufficient for requisite intent; supervisor has duty to prevent unreasonable use of force on one in custody.

- *Hammer v. Gross* 932 F2d 842 (9th Cir. 1991) – Only reasonable force may be used to force blood from misdemeanor DUI suspect and may not be done if alternative is available (e.g., breath – consider video)

- *Maddox v. Los Angeles* 792 F2d 1408 (9th Cir. 1986) – Negligent application of chokehold is not a violation of § 1983; no negligence *per se* despite LAPD moratorium; no due process violation since officers sought medical care.

- *Nava v. City of Dublin* 121 F3d 453 (9th Cir. 1997) – Whether or not carotid hold constitutes deadly force, individual may not obtain injunction against future use without showing likelihood of future harm to him rather than general public. (See *City of Los Angeles v. Lyons* 103 S.Ct. 1660 (1983)).

- *Reed v. Hoy*, 909 F2d 324 (9th Cir. 1989) – A police officer has no duty to retreat from resistance or threatened resistance and may use reasonable force to effect an arrest, prevent escape, or overcome resistance (see also PC § 835a).

Use of Canine

- *Robinette v. Barnes* 854 F2d 909 (6th Cir. 1988) - Despite suspect's death, appropriate use of a properly trained police dog to apprehend a felony burglary suspect is not deadly force nor is it constitutionally unreasonable.

- *Chew v. Gates* 27 F3d 1432 (9th Cir. 1994) - Note: 3-way split opinion. Canine law is not clearly established and supports good faith; question of K-9 as deadly force is jury question under *Garner*.

- *Mendoza v. Block* 2 F3d 1357 (9th Cir. 1994) - Use of K-9 falls within objective reasonableness test based on seriousness of crime, risk to officers, and flight of suspect.

- *Fikes v. Cleghorn* 47 F3d 1011 (9th Cir. 1995) - Test is reasonableness based on totality, not just three factors. Controlled K-9 is not deadly force unless applied as such.

- *Quintanilla v. City of Downey* 84 F3d 353 (9th Cir. 1996) - Use of canine is tested under reasonableness standard of *Graham*, not deadly force standard of *Garner*.

- *Vera Cruz v. City of Escondido* 139 F3d 659 (9th Cir. 1997) - Burden on plaintiff to show that use of K-9 under totality of circumstances presented reasonable probability of death. (Use of fleeing suspect with knife reasonable under *Graham* not *Garner*).

- *Andrade v. City of Burlingame* 847 F.Supp. 760 (N.D. Cal. 1994) - When K-9 escapes from unit and bites suspect, no Fourth Amendment seizure occurs since instrument (K-9) was not intended method of seizure.

- *People v. Rivera* 8 Cal.App.4th 1000 (1992) - Use of police dog to search for and bite felony suspect is not necessarily an arrest requiring probable cause, but might only constitute a detention requiring reasonable suspicion.

- California Civil Code § 3342(b) - No strict liability for police or military dog used to apprehend criminal suspect, investigate crime, execute a warrant or defend a peace officer or other person if agency has written policy governing use of dog. (Note: Exemption does not apply if victim was not suspect).

Arrest/Detention

- *Barry v. Fowler*, 902 F2d 770 (9th Cir. 1990) - Although PC § 836 may prohibit arrest for misdemeanor not in presence, Fourth Amendment permits any arrest based upon probable cause in 1983 action.

- *Whren et al v. U.S.* 517 U.S. 806, 116 S.Ct. 1769 (1996) - When probable cause exists for traffic stop, officer's subjective motivation or deviation from police practices is irrelevant (drugs observed in plain view by vice detectives admissible).

- *Orozco v. County of Yolo*, 814 F.Supp. 885 (E.D. Cal. 1993) - Transporting witness to police station and holding for questioning constitutes an "arrest" requiring probable cause.

- *Hayes v. Florida*, 470 U.S. 811, 105 S.Ct. 1643 (1985) - No hard line rule for length of field detention, must balance law enforcement purpose with reasonable time to effectuate.

- *Michigan v. Summers*, 452 U.S. 692, 101 S.Ct. 2587 (1981) - OK to retain occupants of residence during service of search warrant.

Course and Scope

- *White v. County of Orange* 166 Cal.App.3d 566 (1985) - County held liable for negligent entrustment when deputy stopped female with patrol car and threatened rape/murder if no date was made (i.e., absent authority as police officer, plaintiff would not have stopped).

- *Mary M. v. City of Los Angeles* 54 Cal.3d 202 (1991) - Employing agency may be held vicariously liable for on duty criminal acts (sexual assaults) of its officers if officer exercises "unique power and control." But see *Lisa M. v. Mayo Hospital* 12 Cal.4th 291 (1995).

- *Henrikson v. City of Rialto* 20 Cal.App.4th 1612 (1993) - City not liable for off duty accidental shooting by officer who was socializing rather than engaging in law enforcement activity.

- *Thorn v. City of Glendale* 28 Cal.App.4th 1379 (1994) - No vicarious liability when on duty arson investigator uses badge to gain access to start fire.

- *McInerney v. San Francisco* 668 F.Supp. 1352 (N.D. Cal. 1986) - Off duty officer was not acting under color of law when he identified himself only when police were going to be called to landlord-tenant dispute.

Liability to Third Persons

Pursuits

- California Vehicle Code (VC), VC § 17004.7 (Effective 1/1/88) - Every agency which adopts a conforming pursuit policy will thereafter be entitled to immunity for injuries caused by suspect vehicle; but not those caused by police unit.

- VC § 17004 - Public employee not liable for authorized operation of emergency vehicle en route to emergency call or while pursuing suspected violator.

- VC § 17001 - Public entity liable for negligence or wrongful conduct of employee while driving within course and scope.

- PC § 13519.8 (1995) - Mandates post pursuit training for all officers and establishes specific "guidelines" for policies.

- *Payne v. City of Perris* 12 Cal.App.4th 1738 (1993) - Agency must include factors in pursuit policy to apply 17004.7.

- *Kishida v. State of California* 229 Cal.App.3d 329 (1991) - Immunity of 17004.7 applies even if officer did not adhere to department policy.

- *Hooper v. Chula Vista* 212 Cal.App.3d 442 (1989) - Immunity of GC § 845.8(b) extends to injuries to suspect fleeing from police even if officer's unit collided with suspect.

- *Thomas v. City of Richmond* 9 Cal.4th 1154 (1995) - No duty not to pursue or to discontinue pursuit; agency liability under 17001 will only look to unreasonable negligence in actual conduct of pursuit.

- *Kisbey v. State* 36 Cal.3d 415 (1984) – Immunity of § 845.8(b) for liability for injuries caused by escaping person or person resisting arrest applied when suspect fled from car stop and collided with plaintiff's vehicle.

- *Brower v. County of Inyo* 489 U.S. 593, 109 S.Ct. 1378 (1989) – Police roadblock intended to terminate one's movement may constitute seizure if unreasonable.

- *Lewis v. County of Sacramento* 118 S.Ct. 1708 (1998) – Pursuit with no intent to physically harm suspect or worsen their legal plight does not give rise to constitutional deprivation under Fourteenth Amendment.

Special Relationship

- *Mann v. State of California* 70 Cal.App.3d 773 (1977) – No duty to stop for stranded motorist, but liability for negligence after special relationship created. (GC § 820.25 – Immunity for discretionary assistance or departure).

- *Davidson v. City of Westminster* 32 Cal.3d 197 (1982) – No special relationship duty to warn potential rape victim during surveillance (i.e., no special relationship unless risk to specifically identifiable plaintiff increased or some detrimental reliance created).

- *Foremost Dairies, Inc. v. State of California* 190 Cal.App.3d 361 (1986) – No special relationship duty to warn general motoring public when CHP unit with flashing amber lights positioned at entrance to hazardous area fails to prevent collision.

- *Baker v. City of Los Angeles* 188 Cal.App.3d 902 (1987) – Absent an expressed or implied promise to render additional aid, a voluntarily assumed duty does not extend beyond the initial act. A special relationship created by one officer does not extend to or obligate the entire department indefinitely.

Intoxicated Persons

- *Lahto v. City of Oxnard* 171 Cal.App.3d 285 (1985) – No policy duty of special relationship duty to arrest drunk driver.

- *Harris v. Smith* 157 Cal.App.3d 100 (1984) – No special relationship duty to arrest drunk driver previously stopped by officer and released after FST.

- *Hucko v. San Diego* 179 Cal.App.3d 520 (1986) – No duty for officer to recognize signs of drunkness during stop and no liability when released driver is injured in subsequent collision. (Cert. denied.)

- *Sunnyvale v. Superior Court* 250 Cal. Rptr.214 (1988) – No duty owed to passenger who is told to re-enter vehicle operated by intoxicated driver who is cited and released to drive (i.e., no duty to arrest GC § 846).

- *Truong v. James* 168 Cal.App.3d 833 (1985) – No duty to arrest (GC § 846) and no liability when drunk driver is injured after being entrusted to tow truck driver. (Cert. denied).

- *Jackson v. Clements* 146 Cal.App.3d 983 (1983) – No liability for injuries to complainant when he is released by officer (i.e., no increase of risk).

Negligence

- *Williams v. State of California* 34 Cal.3d 18 (1983) - No duty to investigate traffic collision or aid motorist.

- *Lopez v. San Diego* 190 Cal.App.3d 678 (1987) - No liability for police negligence or failure to act absent a direct connection to an increased risk of harm to the injured third party.

- *Bastian v. County of San Luis Obispo* 199 Cal.App.3d 520 (1988) - Officer creates peril by knowingly altering accident scene, duty to warn even without special relationship.

Providing Police Protection

- California Government Code § 845 - No liability to provide police protection or, if provided, failure to provide sufficient protection.

- *Escamilla v. City of Santa Ana* 796 F2d 266 (9th Cir. 1986) - Absent special relationship, undercover officers had no duty to intervene in bar fight to prevent murder (negligence not actionable under § 1983).

- *Antique Arts Corp., v. City of Torrance* 39 Cal.App.3d 588 (1974) - Discretionary immunity applied to dispatcher's delay in sending units to silent alarm.

- *Von Batsch v. American Dist. Telegraph* 175 Cal.App.3d 1111 (1985) - No special relationship or duty created when officers responded to silent alarm and failed to discover suspects who later killed employee after officers told employees "no break-in."

- *Sullivan v. City of Sacramento* 190 Cal.App.3d 1070 (1987) - (1) No duty for dispatcher to send units despite return call to victim during rape; (2) Decision to call victim was immune as discretionary (§ 820.2) despite department policy prohibiting same.

- *Watts v. County of Sacramento* 136 Cal.App.3d 232 (1982) - No duty to intervene in civil dispute and no liability for negligent investigation.

Fireman's Rule (bar to recovery)

- *Lipson v. Superior Court* 31 Cal.3d 362 (1982) - Rule applies only to recovery for injuries caused by the very misconduct that created the risk that necessitated the officer's presence.

- *Rose v. City of Los Angeles* 159 Cal.App.3d 883 (1984) - Rule does not apply when officer's injury was caused by separate and independent act which was not the original circumstance to which the officer was called.

- *City of Redlands v. Sorenson* 176 Cal.App.3d 202 (1985) - Police officer pursuing suspected violator is not barred from recovering against the suspect when the officer is injured while ramming the suspect vehicle.

- *Gibb v. Stetson* 199 Cal.App.3d 1008 (1988) - Bailiff could recover for injuries in altercation since defendant knew of officer's presence.

- California Civil Code § 1714.9 - Third person liability to officer if defendant knew or should have known of officer's presence or defendant violates law designed to protect officer.

- California Labor Code § 3852 - Separate right of action for officer beyond worker's compensation.

Prisoners: California GC § 844.6(a)

- Public entity not liable for injury caused by prisoner.

- Public entity not liable for injury to any prisoner.

- (b-d) No immunity for injuries caused by vehicle (i.e., jail only), dangerous condition, or due to public employee's negligence or wrongful act or omission.

- California GC § 845.6 - Liability for failure to summon medical care for prisoner upon actual or constructive notice of immediate need for care.

But see

- California GC § 855.8 - Immunity for failure to diagnose or treat 5150 or addiction.

- California GC § 856 - Immunity for determination to confine 5150 or addict.

- *Ward v. San Diego* 791 F2d 1329 (9th Cir. 1986) - § 1983 liability of strip search is contrary to "clearly established statutory or constitutional rights" (i.e., no strip search of arrestee for minor offense absent individual suspicion of contraband). See PC § 4030.

MEDIA RELATIONS FOR PROSECUTORS

By Paul Logli, State's Attorney, Winnebago County, Rockford, Illinois

Introduction

Winston Churchill once described Russia as, "a riddle, wrapped in a mystery, inside of an enigma." Many prosecutors have used similar terms to describe the workings of their local media. Just when prosecutors believe they can confidently deal with any media-related issue, they are often confronted with a situation that quickly convinces them that they have not yet begun to truly fathom the depths of the media's perceived excess, bias and inaccuracy.

Many prosecutors experience a cycle of emotions involving their relationships with the media. Newly elected prosecutors may have an initial fear of the media that gives way to the thrill of seeing the prominent placement of their quotes in the paper and their images on the local television screen. Early success with the media gives a sense of confidence. All that disappears, however, when they fall victims to the front-page stories or top-of-the-newscast features that portray them as stupid, incompetent or crooked. Eventually, the feeling of betrayal turns into utter exhaustion or burnout at the prospect of ever having to come into contact with a reporter again.

At one moment it appears that the media can inspire and inform and at the next frustrate and confuse. The media can help build the public's trust in the criminal justice system and, a day later, destroy all confidence in the competence of police, prosecutors and courts. Nevertheless, in spite of their on-again/off-again relationship with the media, prosecutors cannot afford to retreat into anger, self-pity or futile attempts to avoid media contacts.

After all, media organizations have a job to do: it is their responsibility to inform the public of the progress, conduct and results of all matters pertaining to the criminal justice system and public safety. The media holds public officials, including prosecutors, accountable for the wise exercise of their judgment. Therefore, the making of decisions at all crucial stages and the results of actions that initiate, advance or terminate any prosecution are fair game for coverage and comment.

At the same time, prosecutors are vested with important responsibilities as gatekeep-ers for the criminal justice system. In that regard, they must work closely with local law enforcement agencies, charge and prosecute cases when evidence of guilt is suf-ficient to support a conviction and competently administer their offices. The media wishes that the functioning of these duties be visible to the public, yet the prosecu-tor is obliged to maintain the confidentiality of investigations and to only permit the release of information regarding pending cases as ethical guidelines and rules of court permits. The contrasting motivations can supply a constant source of tension.

Somewhere in the midst of the media's desire to disclose everything, and the prose-cutor's responsibility to preserve the integrity of investigations and the fairness of tri-als, there exists a middle ground upon which a media policy for a prosecutor's office should be based. It is in the prosecutor's best interest to have an informed public that can observe the workings of the criminal justice system with confidence that the process is efficient, honest and capable of producing a just result. To achieve this desirable goal, prosecutors must work with the media. There is no alternative.

GENERAL ELEMENTS OF A SUCCESSFUL MEDIA POLICY

The following recommendations represent guidelines for the development of good prosecutor/media relations in the areas of prosecutorial conduct and a well-defined media policy for all members of the office.

Be aware of and work with deadlines. Return a reporter's calls as quickly as conven-ient. Failure to cooperate with deadlines can generate several days of negative press when a well-timed but concise statement of facts might convince the media that you are trying to respond to their concerns. This is especially true when a major or controversial case is breaking.

If you or a member of your office does not know an answer to a media question, admit it. Then be prepared to find out the answer and get back to the reporter. At the very least, point the reporter in the right direction for finding the requested information.

Look at each contact with the reporter as an opportunity to reach the public. Prosecutors work hard every day to make their communities safer for everyone. When they are successful in their work, people are held accountable and punished appropriately or given the opportunity for a meaningful rehabilitation. If prosecutors ignore the media they ignore the opportunity to let their story, much of which is positive, be told to the public.

When dealing with reporters, especially inexperienced reporters, take time to teach. The terminology and procedures unique to the criminal justice system can be confusing. More errors are likely in a news story if the reporter lacks a clear idea of how the system works.

In all cases, be truthful. Do not lie or tell half-truths and never equate putting a "spin" on the story with telling anything other than the truth. "Spin" may contribute an angle or nuance to the response but it can never divert us from telling the truth.

The prosecutor's attitude must be one of helpfulness. Do not expect the media to do all the work, without assistance, and then act disappointed when they get the story wrong.

Develop a working relationship with the beat reporters. Knowing an editor or even a publisher is useful, but it is the beat reporters and their evaluation of you as a person and a source that will most influence the slant of their story.

If you disagree with a story or a report, go first to the reporter and discuss your concerns. If those contacts fail to achieve your purpose, then it is appropriate to contact the reporter's supervisor or editor. In a similar vein, do not hesitate to compliment a reporter when you believe that his or her story is accurate and balanced.

Although we may be tempted, it is never advisable to engage in battle or even guerrilla warfare with an opponent who buys ink, videotape or audiotape by the case. In spite of our belief that we may be getting a "raw deal" from the media, the fact remains that the media is a force in our community and represents the public's right to know. They must be dealt with in a manner consistent with these considerations.

Most of the time, a prosecutor's office serves the community well. Now and then, however, mistakes are made. If you are caught in the middle of a mistake, admit it, promise to change the conditions that brought about the error and move on to the next case. Allowing negative information to dribble out, instead of confronting the problem forthrightly, keeps an embarrassing story alive. Simply put, don't screw up on a slow news day but, if you do, face up to it and move on.

THE CRIME SCENE

Often a prosecutor or an assistant prosecutor is expected to go to a crime scene. There may be little information available at the scene yet there may be great media interest. Early on in an investigation, it is a good idea to allow the police to release all appropriate information. A prosecutor should be careful when releasing information during the early stages of an investigation for fear of compromising the confidentiality or progress of an investigation. However, since the police often look to the prosecutor for advice on how to handle the media, especially at a crime scene, the following considerations may be helpful:

Control the site, if possible, to keep the media and others away from the scene. If this is impossible, avoid at all costs the videotaping of scenes of police restraining the reporters. This looks bad on the six o'clock news. If a shoving match occurs, law enforcement will lose, both on and off camera.

If the media insists, you must realize that in most cases they have the right to be there. Also, videotape evidence may later prove helpful to your case: to observe details, to identify witnesses, to spot missing evidence and to illustrate the scene for the jury. However, potential witnesses should be separated from the scene and interviewed without media influence or interference.

Consider setting up a media command post away from the scene, especially when the incident is ongoing. Emphasize that all relevant information will be released at the command post and no information will be given out at the scene.

Be prepared early on to give a brief, factual description of the event. Never offer a personal opinion but provide the reporters with the basic facts that they probably already know but are trying to confirm. A 60-second briefing up front can prevent a week of bad press implying that law enforcement was either incompetent or, worse, intentionally trying to conceal important information from the public.

THE INVESTIGATION

As the investigation proceeds, the prosecutor and the police should coordinate the release of all information. A convenient rule of thumb is that prior to arrest the police can release information in concurrence with the prosecutor. After the arrest, the prosecutor should take charge of the release of all information to the media. If police and prosecution both appear at the customary press conference announcing charges, then the prosecutor should impress upon the police spokesperson that all pertinent ethical rules should dictate the conduct of the conference. For instance, both bar association and National District Attorneys Association (NDAA) considerations prohibit commenting on the contents of confessions made by defendants, whether they did or did not talk to the police. The disclosure of confessions or statements is probably the ethical rule most often violated by prosecutors and police during press conferences when announcing the arrest of a suspect.

During the investigation, information should be released sparingly and only then to aid the investigation of the case or the apprehension of the suspect. At the commencement of the actual prosecution, adherence to ethical guidelines must control the release of all information.

PRESS CONFERENCES

Although prosecutors and police departments are making greater use of fax machines and web sites to disseminate information, press conferences are still an efficient way to get a story out to all the media. Subjecting a prosecutor to numerous individual contacts with the media is inefficient because it is time consuming and can result in the release of information that may be somewhat inconsistent.

Press conferences are best held between ten o'clock in the morning and two o'clock in the afternoon. Broadcast outlets then have adequate time to edit stories to have them in good shape for the evening newscast. Similarly, newsrooms come to life in the afternoon and are busy throughout the evening until the post-midnight press run prepares the morning edition.

Lead off the press conference with a statement. It need not be prepared. A handout that includes information such as the identity of the defendant, the actual charges and the punishment the defendant faces upon plea or conviction insures that every reporter at the conference has the same accurate information. Keep the opening statement short and then provide plenty of time to answer questions.

Strongly consider using prepared visual aids at the press conference. Reporters like visuals, as do cameras and audiences. Charts, posters, photos, displays, videotapes and PowerPoint presentations help to make press conferences more memorable.

Ideally, at the conclusion of the press conference the police should defer all further questions regarding the case to the prosecutor's office. Failure to do so simply allows the media to play one source against the other. When that happens, either side can be tricked into confirming anonymous leaks that may have been provided by an unauthorized third party. Although reporters want the entire story of a case early on, it is best to advise them that they will learn the facts of a case as they develop in court for it is important that all parties to a criminal case maintain the integrity of the investigation and subsequent prosecution.

THE PRESS RELEASE

Press releases—the most basic form of communication with media outlets—continue to be an effective tool. Increasingly, many news organizations are tightening budgets and have discontinued assigning reporters to "cover" traditional beats. A press release is therefore effective in getting out your day-to-day story. E-mail and programmable fax machines conveniently permit the simultaneous delivery of press releases to the media on a timely basis. Effective press releases should be confined to one page and include a good lead paragraph that tells the conventional "who, what, when, where and why of a story."

The cover page of the press release should clearly state who is making the announcement, the name and position of the individual who can be contacted for follow-up information and a contact phone number. If the press release announces a later news conference, then mail or fax the advance notices to news directors or editors. When announcing a news conference a day or two in advance of the event, it is advantageous to call each news organization the morning of the event to remind the assignment editor of the event and to encourage a reporter's attendance.

THE INTERVIEW

Radio, television and newspaper reporters constantly bombard prosecutors with requests for interviews. A successful interview, as is true of a successful trial, is an outcome that depends entirely on good preparation. Find out the subject of the interview in advance of the appointment. If a reporter hesitates to provide that information, beware: this may indicate that the reporter is interested in more than a "puff piece," and the prosecutor should insist on knowing the topic to be covered. Obviously, a prosecutor can be more helpful and knowledgeable if allowed to pull case files, statistics, etc.

Once the topic is known, anticipate the likely questions and determine what points you want to make. If it is a domestic violence story, for instance, and there have been several controversial prosecutions of late, then be prepared to answer questions about those cases. In addition, know what points you want to make, in general, about your office's handling of domestic violence cases. For instance, describe the increased domestic violence resources in the office; the training provided to the assistants assigned to those cases; and the number of victim advocates or witness coordinators that work with the Domestic Violence Division. Even if the reporter does not ask questions eliciting such information, include it in your answers. If the points can be made within a 10 to 15-second "sound bite," there is less chance that they will be edited out of the answers.

Prior to going on camera for a television interview, check your appearance. Looking haggard is all right but it is wise to dress conservatively, comb your hair, wipe your brow and avoid the "deer caught in the headlights" look.

Whenever possible, select an appropriate location. The reporter's choice of location may not be ideal. Some days a pretty picture is appropriate; on others, the grim reality of the jailhouse steps is needed. Try to avoid the "walking" or "ambush interview," it evokes a trapped or defensive demeanor. Be confident and look confident.

At the time of the actual interview, speak to the reporter before beginning the dialogue to confirm the subject matter. Keep in mind the points you wish to make during the interview, make them and then repeat them. Many prosecutors believe that limiting the message to no more than three main points helps to keep the interview and the reporter on track.

If you don't like the question, answer the question that you believe the reporter should have asked. Answer questions thoroughly and then be quiet. Be cautious when you find yourself doing all the talking and the reporter has grown strangely silent. You may be getting yourself into trouble. On the other hand, do not let the reporter upset you. Stay calm.

Off the record conversations should not be recorded. When going off the record with a reporter, do not assume that the camera or tape recorder is really off. Even if it is, be aware that mistakes happen. For this reason, many prosecutors' offices follow the maxim that *no* conversation or interview is ever really off the record.

Be aware of your behavior during breaks and as the camera sets the atmosphere for the story. If the interview concerns a serious matter, do not let yourself be observed (or worse, videotaped) making jokes or laughing in anticipation of the questioning.

During the interview, look at the interviewer and not at the camera. If more than one reporter is conducting the interview, your eyes should focus on the reporter asking the question. If you allow your eyes to shift between the reporters and the other people in the room, you may appear "shifty" or unfocused. This applies not only to interviews but also to press conferences.

A pause before answering will convey careful deliberation and control and allow time for composing thoughts. Rushing through an answer on television may resister a lack of confidence or lack of control. Editors will remove the pauses from the final cut, regardless.

Never say "no comment" during any interview or press conference. Explain why you are unable to answer a question by referring to the ongoing investigation, the pending litigation or the ethical considerations that restrict your response. Or explain that the question is premature, that the facts are being assembled and that the eventual complete answer will be forthcoming and accurate. If by chance the interview becomes combative, then your demeanor should be that of a cooperative public official. Be firm but stay calm.

Finally, a good broadcast interview is based on an understanding and appreciation of the "sound bite." "Sound bites" are those 10-to-15 second, clever and succinct answers generated by practiced speakers that are inevitably quoted by the media. In a typical broadcast, 15 seconds is a considerable amount of time; most news stories on television or radio last between 30 to 90 seconds in total. If the answer is longer than 20 seconds, it will be edited or cut out entirely.

Colorful language or a catchy phrase will almost guarantee that a particular "sound bite" will make the evening news. Avoid dry, technical or obscure terms and avoid negatives, especially double negatives. Try to use active not passive voice. Instead of saying, "We are not insensitive to the victim's concerns," say, "We are sensitive to the victim's concerns." The positive twist of a phrase imparts confidence and energy, especially if it is delivered in a normal tone in a short, direct sentence. In any event, be human and relate to the average citizen. A broadcast interview is an excellent opportunity to impress your citizens that you are competent, compassionate and effective.

Lastly, if you don't like what you just said, stop and start again. Few interviews are live. Television crews usually have plenty of tape, so it is usually better to stop and improve the message than it is to appear on the six o'clock news saying something that you regret. Repeating an answer can, however, be an inconvenience to the television crew, so it is best to reserve the option for worthy occasions.

TRIAL AND POST-TRIAL

During a trial, ethical considerations should completely control a prosecutor's public pronouncements. Daily press conferences on the steps of the courthouse are ill advised and can compromise efforts to ensure a fair trial. On the contrary, silence is golden. If you must respond to a reporter's question, then the official record should control your comments. For example, it is appropriate to tell a reporter that jury selection has begun and that it is projected to last several days. It would not, however, be appropriate to comment on the strength of your case, or that a witness performed well or that your cross-examination reduced a defense witness to quivering pulp.

The conclusion of a trial presents another important opportunity to communicate with the public. If you win, it is appropriate to briefly state your appreciation of the work of the judge or jury and your personal belief that the verdict was consistent with the law and the facts you were able to prove. Expressing your belief that justice was done, and once again displaying sympathy for the victims of the crime, makes for a complete and appropriate response to a reporter's questions.

Facing the loss of a trial, on the other hand, offers a greater challenge. It is certainly appropriate to express disappointment with the verdict but neither appropriate nor ethical to criticize the judge or jury. You may comment that you presented the best case possible given the facts you had to work with but that the jury or judge apparently did not find the evidence sufficient to convince them of guilt beyond a reasonable doubt.

THE BIG CASE

Recent criminal acts have thrust some local prosecutors into the national media spotlight. In the event of a major catastrophe or heinous crime, it is not uncommon for a local prosecutor to become a central media figure on a national or even an international stage. The major news story may initially last several days and require a prosecutor to work with others in providing accurate information. A prosecutor must be able to present a complete picture of the case without drowning the public in unnecessary or possibly prejudicial details. Too much public information can cause problems if and when trial approaches. Throughout the crisis, a prosecutor should be a team player, collaborating with police, coroner's staff and other public officials who meet regularly and share information freely. Whenever possible, only one spokesperson should communicate with the media. Otherwise, be sure that everyone speaking to the media is "on the same page."

At all times, express concern for the victims of the crime or catastrophe. The media can serve as a useful partner in keeping the public informed, calm and confident that the criminal justice system is handling the situation well.

FINAL CONSIDERATIONS

Radio and television are the most effective way of getting through to the greatest number of people. Recent polls indicate that a large majority of the people in our society relies on television for the daily news. A much smaller number of people rely on newspapers to keep in touch with local, national and international events. Newspapers, however, are more important in getting through to the decision-makers in a community and continue to monopolize editorial opinion and comment.

In the age of the Internet, a prosecutor's office may consider using a Web site to communicate with the public. To be effective, however, the information on the Web site must be current and of good quality. Furthermore, the Web site is by no means a passive method of communication, as is the case with radio and television in that people must seek it out. Create a Web site that will be worth the journey that the audience must undergo to visit it. Web sites should be more than a public relations tool. They should contain current information such as court dockets, case dispositions and recent press releases, as well as a current roster of all office personnel and the best means of contacting them.

Finally, use your own experience and the information from this chapter and other sources to draft a media policy for every member of your office. Make sure the policy is followed—especially after business hours and on weekends. A good relationship with the media helps prosecutors foster public confidence in the criminal justice system. It encourages citizen cooperation in the solution of crimes, supports the vital work of the police and encourages witnesses and victims to become involved in the prosecution of a case. A bad relationship plays into the hands of those who condemn the criminal justice system at every turn. As attacks increase on the fairness, credibility and competence of police and prosecutors, sometimes maintaining good media relations becomes the highest priority.

A FINAL WORD ON ETHICAL CONSIDERATIONS

Prosecutors must conduct their affairs and those of their office in a manner consistent with the ethical rules of conduct for lawyers (especially those that pertain specifically to prosecutors). Most states have adopted rules regarding the conduct of prosecutors and their relations with the media that are consistent with the model rules of the American Bar Association. In addition, the NDAA has developed national prosecution standards, a portion of which addresses a prosecutor's relationship with the media. The texts of both are set out in the appendix to this article. It is imperative, however, that prosecutors be familiar with the ethical guidelines that apply within their jurisdictions. There is no substitute for a prosecutor's familiarity with cases that have been handed down by the courts in regard to prosecutor/media relations. The following list of court decisions is representative of cases regarding particular areas of media relations. It is against the backdrop of these ethical considerations and court decisions that the prosecutor must maintain an open, ethical and legally proper relationship with the media.

COURT DECISIONS UPHOLDING RESTRICTIVE RULES OF CONDUCT FOR ATTORNEYS IN REGARD TO MEDIA CONTACTS

Chicago Council of Lawyers et al. vs. William J. Bauer and Terrance McCarthy, 522 F.2d 242, 371 F.Supp 689 (7th Cir. 1975).

Hirschkop and American Civil Liberties Union of Virginia et al. vs. Snead, 594 F.2d 356, 421 F.Supp. 1137 (4th Cir. 1979).

Gentile vs. State Bar of Nevada, 501 U.S. 1030, 111 S.Ct. 2720, 115 L.Ed. 2d 888, (1991) (General rules upheld, but specific contempt finding vacated).

MEDIA'S RIGHT TO OBTAIN COURT DOCUMENTS

Bludworth vs. Palm Beach Newspapers, Inc., 476 SO. 2d 775 (Fla.App 4 Dist. 1985).

State vs. Tallman, 537 A.2d 422, 148 Vt.465 (Vermont 1987).

Cox Arizona Publications, Inc. vs. Collins, 852 P.2d 1194, 175 AZ 11 (Arizona 1993).

GAG RULES AND PRIOR RESTRAINT

Chase vs. Robson, United States of America, 435 F.2d 1059, 309 F.Supp. 430 (7th Cir. 1970).

State vs. Schaefer, 599 A.2d 337, 157 Vt. 339 (Vermont 1991).

PROSECUTOR'S CONDUCT

U.S. vs. Troutman, 814 F.2d 1428 (10th Cir. 1987).

In the Matter of Death of Manners, 542 NYS 2d 485, 143 Misc 2d 945 (Co.Ct. 1989).

In the Matter of Westfall, 808 S.W. 2d 829 (Mo.banc 1991).

Marrerro v. City of Hialeah, 625 F.2d 499 (5th Cir. 1980).

In RE Rachmiel, 449 A.2d 505 (Sup. Ct. of N.J. 1982).

In RE Conduct of Lasswell, 673 P.2d 855 (Or. 1983).

People v. Phillips 169 Cal.App. 3d 634, 215 Cal. Rptr.394 (1985).

In RE Burrows, 618 P.2d 1283 (Or. 1980).

In RE Zimmerman v. Bd. of Pro. Responsibility, 764 S.W. 2d 757 (Tenn. 1989).

Latimore v. Widseth, 7 F.3d 709 (8th Cir. 1993).

Wilson v. Layne, 119 S.Ct. 1692 (1999); *Hanlon v. Berger*, 119 S.Ct. 1706 (1999).

OTHER ETHICAL ISSUES
Sheppard v. Maxwell, 86 S.Ct. 1507, 384 U.S. 333 (1966).

APPENDIX

American Bar Association Model Rules of Professional Conduct

Rule 3.6 Trial Publicity

(a) A lawyer who is participating or has participated in the investigation or litigation of a matter shall not make an extrajudicial statement that a reasonable person would expect to be disseminated by means of public communication if the lawyer knows or reasonably should know that it will have a substantial likelihood of materially prejudicing an adjudicative proceeding in the matter.

(b) Notwithstanding paragraph (a), a lawyer may state;

    (1) The claim, offense or defense involved and, except when prohibited by law, identity of the persons involved;

    (2) information contained in a public record;

    (3) that an investigation of a matter is in progress;

    (4) the scheduling or result of any step in litigation;

    (5) a request for assistance in obtaining evidence and information necessary to the investigation;

    (6) a warning of danger concerning the behavior of a person involved, when there is reason to believe that there exists the likelihood of substantial harm to an individual or to the public interest; and,

    (7) in a criminal case, in addition to subparagraphs (1) through (6):

        (1) the identity, residence, occupation and family status of the accused;

        (2) if the accused has not been apprehended, information necessary to aid in apprehension of that person;

        (3) the fact, time and place of arrest; and

        (4) the identity of investigating and arresting officers or agencies and the length of the investigation.

(c) Notwithstanding paragraph (a), a lawyer may make a statement that a reasonable lawyer would believe is required to protect a client from the substantial undue prejudicial effect of recent publicity not initiated by the lawyer or the lawyer's client. A statement made pursuant to this paragraph shall be limited to such information as is necessary to mitigate the recent adverse publicity.

(d) No lawyer associated in a firm or government agency with a lawyer subject to paragraph (a) shall make a statement prohibited by paragraph (a).

Rule 3.8 Special Responsibilities of a Prosecutor

The prosecutor in a criminal case shall:

(e) exercise reasonable care to prevent investigators, law enforcement personnel, employees or other persons assisting or associated with the prosecutor in a criminal case from making an extra judicial statement that the prosecutor would be prohibited from making under Rule 3.6;

(f) except for statements that are necessary to inform the public of the nature and extent of the prosecutor's action and that serve a legitimate law enforcement purpose, refrain from making extra judicial comments that have a substantial likelihood of heightening public condemnation of the accused.

NATIONAL DISTRICT ATTORNEYS ASSOCIATION NATIONAL PROSECUTION STANDARDS

Protection of Rights of Accused and Public

33.1 Balancing Interests

The prosecutor should strive to protect both the rights of the individual accused of a crime and the right of the public to know in criminal cases.

33.2 Media Relations

The prosecutor should seek to maintain a relationship with the media that will facilitate the appropriate flow of information necessary to educate the public.

LIMITATIONS ON MEDIA CONTACTS—THE PROSECUTOR

34.1 Limits on Information

Prior to and during a criminal trial the prosecutor should limit comments on pending matters to:

      1. The accused's name, age, residence, employment, marital status, and citizenship;

      2. The substance or text of the charge, such as a complaint, indictment, infor-

mation, and, where appropriate, the identity of the complainant;

3. The identity of the investigating and arresting agency and the length of the investigation;

4. The circumstances immediately surrounding the arrest, including the time and place of arrest, resistance, pursuit, possession and use of weapons, and a description of items seized at the time of arrest or pursuant to a search warrant; and

5. Matters which are of public record, or disclosure of which would serve the public interest.

34.2 Bars on Information

The prosecutor should not release certain types of information and should be aware of the dangers of prejudice in making pre-trial disclosure of the following:

1. Statements as to the character or reputation of an accused person or a prospective witness;

2. Admissions, confessions, or the contents of a statement or alibi attributable to an accused person;

3. The performance or results of tests or the refusal of the accused to take a test;

4. Statements concerning the credibility or anticipated testimony of prospective witnesses;

5. The possibility of a plea of guilty to the offense charged or to a lesser offense or other disposition; and

6. Opinions concerning evidence or argument in the case, whether or not it is anticipated that such evidence or argument will be used at trial.

34.3 Public Responses

Standard 34.1 and 34.2 do not preclude the prosecutor from making reasonable and fair responses to comments of defense counsel or others.

Limitations on Media Comments—The Police

35.1 Law Enforcement Policy on Information

The prosecutor should inform local law enforcement agencies of the state, court, constitutional and case law provisions, as well as professional codes and standards, concerning fair trial/free press issues, and should encourage them to adopt policies which will protect both the rights of the individual and the ability of the prosecution to proceed.

VICTIM ISSUES FOR PROSECUTORS

By Bill Ritter, Jr., District Attorney, 2nd Judicial District, Denver, Colorado

Introduction

In the past two decades, the role of the prosecution has assumed many different aspects. Perhaps no development has been more dramatic than the phenomenon of crime victims acting as agents of change within the criminal justice system. Through the efforts of thousands of victims, victim advocacy groups and victim service providers, tremendous changes have occurred in substantive criminal laws, sentencing laws and, most recently, in the codification of rights afforded to victims of crime at both the state and federal level throughout the criminal justice process. Today, the legitimacy of the concept of victims' rights is accepted almost everywhere; it is even the new status quo. However, this development was not preordained when first espoused and the wide degree of acceptance it received would have seemed unlikely a mere 10 years ago.

Throughout the growth of the movement, victims and victim advocacy groups have provided opportunities for prosecutors to march with them in lock step, advocating changes and bringing about vast improvements. At the same time, increased victim advocacy has challenged prosecutors to look critically at their policies and practices, with an eye toward making the system "user-friendly" to victims. The process has not been without some degree of resistance on their part and a fair amount of pain.

THE HISTORY OF THE VICTIMS' RIGHTS MOVEMENT

The changes began slowly. In the 1970s, grassroots women's groups started rape crisis centers and opened safe houses for victims of domestic violence. In 1975, the U.S. Department of Justice began to fund prosecutor-based victim/witness services at the state and local level. Also in 1975, the National Organization for Victim Assistance initiated the present-day model of introducing concerned professionals to the criminal justice system to improve the services offered to crime victims. By the late 1970s, victim services were rapidly emerging in police departments, prosecutors' offices and corrections' agencies throughout the United States. Today, victim/witness services are the rule, not the exception.

The emergence of Parents of Murdered Children (POMC) in 1978 and Mothers Against Drunk Driving (MADD) in the 1980s brought a new and different level of victim advocacy to the forefront. POMC and MADD touched the hearts and souls of citizens across America with the emotional and compelling message that violent crime is not just something that happens to "someone else, somewhere else." POMC provides peer support to families who have suffered the tragedy of having a child murdered. MADD's missions include advocating stiffer penalties for drinking drivers, scrutinizing prosecutors' plea-agreements and participating in "court watch" programs to monitor sentencing practices. More than any other organization, MADD brought true political activism to the victims' rights movement. MADD's members spoke with one voice, and prosecutors and legislators listened.

Borrowing from the lessons learned from these activists, other victim-oriented groups began grassroots advocacy movements for specific issues such as domestic violence, child abuse and sexual violence. These groups engaged prosecutors, the police, courts and legislatures to improve every aspect of the system from the victims' perspective. They were met with a variety of responses, both positive and negative. The most effective tools developed as a result are the multi-disciplinary task forces and the protocols that determine how agencies, particularly the police and the prosecution, should behave in a given situation. Slowly, methodically, they have made inroads across the country.

At the same time that these victim groups were making their presence felt, prosecutors were coming to grips with the benefits of victim assistance services. The responsibility for victim contact, long considered within the sole purview of the prosecutor, became a responsibility shared between the victim advocate and the prosecutor. Not every jurisdiction could afford what was then considered the luxury of a victim assistance program. Frequently, resources were just too scarce. Over time, however, victim advocates became an absolute necessity in most jurisdictions, and prosecutors could only hope that their funding sources would continue to support them.

While victim groups accomplished a great deal in the 1980s, they did not rest on their laurels. Even though a 1990 Bureau of Justice Statistics study concluded that, nation-wide, prosecutors were becoming more responsive to crime victims, too many victims continued to feel ignored. Most victims' complaints focused on prosecutors' failure to advise them of significant developments in their cases and to consult with them about decisions, particularly concerning plea negotiations and agreements. Worse, even when prosecutors did all they could to include victims in the process, courts often disregarded victims' rights to be present and to address the court during critical stages of the case. This author has been present on numerous occasions when victims were denied the right to speak at a sentencing hearing by judges who valued docket efficiency above true justice for victims. No doubt other prosecutors have had similar experiences.

Victims' responses to these and other issues within the criminal justice system were not passive. They formed more powerful local and national organizations. They took the fight directly to state legislatures and demanded statutory rights for victims of crime. In some states, they took their case directly to the people, via referendum. Constitutional amendments that provided victims of crime with actual rights in the criminal justice system were placed on ballots throughout the country and the voters' response was overwhelmingly positive in nearly every instance. At this writing, 32 states have enacted some form of constitutional protection for victims of crime. Today, consideration of victims' rights is not an option for most prosecutors; it is mandatory.

It deserves mention that many prosecutors were directly involved in the movement to enact victims' rights measures. In fact, they frequently led the way. Those prosecutors who did not, who resisted the movement toward victims' rights or remained ambivalent about the issue, appeared to be primarily concerned with two issues: the additional financial burdens that serious consideration of victims' rights would necessarily impose and the impact of the penalties that were contemplated for prosecutors who failed to comply. However, more than a decade has passed since the first victims' rights protections were enacted, and prosecutors' worst fears about sanctions against them for failure to comply have largely failed to materialize. The push for victims' rights and better communications with victims has inarguably required increased efforts from prosecutors but most would agree that the benefits of this change have been well worth the price.

Without question, in the last 20 years victims have gained substantial power throughout the criminal justice system. Some form of statutory victims' rights is now found even in the 18 states that do not have a constitutional amendment for this purpose. It may be only a matter of time before all 50 states have constitutional victims' rights amendments. A debate continues in Congress regarding a proposed amendment to the U.S. Constitution that would likewise provide for constitutional rights for victims throughout the country. Regardless of the results of that initiative, the reality of victims' rights is that this is a movement that is here to stay. The question then is, what is left for prosecutors to do about victim issues that has not been already accomplished through statutes and constitutional amendments? The answer is—plenty. These programs must be honored, administered and improved. Accomplishing this will require leadership, by prosecutors.

THE PROSECUTOR'S ROLE

Prosecutors play a critical role in making sure that the rights provided to crime victims by statute or constitutional amendment are, in fact, delivered. Knowing precisely what these rights are is crucial. All prosecutors, whether their jurisdictions are large or small, urban or rural, should take the following basic steps to ensure full justice for victims:

- Undertake a study of the constitutional and/or statutory rights for victims of crime provided for in their respective states; and
- Review all internal policies relating to crime victims. This review should include a study of available training for prosecution staff and should consider what protocols might be required to ensure full implementation.

Most statutory and constitutional amendments that create victims' rights do so for select categories of crime, i.e., crimes of violence and the more serious property crimes like home burglary. Many of these measures mirror the provisions enacted in Colorado in 1990. Essentially, they require police and/or prosecutors to do the following:

- Inform crime victims of the status of their case at critical stages of the process;
- Allow victims of crime the right to be present at critical stages of the process;
- Seek input from victims of crime regarding plea bargains and other critical decisions; and
- Permit victims the right to be heard at critical stages of the process.

These rights, especially when they are grounded in a constitutional amendment, typically include the means for victims to redress actual or perceived wrongs. In Colorado and many other states, a prosecutor's failure to provide these rights can ultimately result in an injunction against him or her, or even a finding of contempt of court. Happily, however, the usual course of action is more often a non-judicial demand for compliance. The remedies for non-compliance vary, but they generally establish a procedure for victims to publicly air their grievances.

Over the past decade, in Colorado anyway, complaints of prosecutor missteps have been rare, and the board that reviews these cases has so far informally resolved the matter or found in favor of the prosecutor. However, the National Institute of Justice recently published research in *The Rights of Crime Victims—Does Legal Protection Make a Difference,* which indicates that compliance with victims' rights provisions, although improving, remains a challenge for some prosecutors.[1]

Although providing victims the rights afforded by law is the bare minimum of the prosecutor's overall responsibilities, doing so may not be as simple as it sounds. Scarce resources are serious impediments for many prosecutors' offices. Whether prosecutors choose to implement the protection of basic rights through a victim advocates' program, through utilization of ever-improving technology or through a combination of both, considerable resources are required. Many offices already scratch and claw for funding to adequately support trial attorneys. Therefore, developing a comprehensive program for victim advocacy may, because of fiscal constraints, be an afterthought. That is a mistake, for even though doing so may take a great deal of political advocacy on the part of the chief prosecutor, funding authorities and taxpayers alike must be educated about the need to fully fund prosecutor programs that fulfill *all* of their responsibilities to crime victims.

TRAINING FOR PROSECUTOR STAFF

Without question, the next important prerequisite for prosecutors' offices that fully comply with their legal responsibilities to crime victims is to ensure adequate training for prosecutor staff. Providing training for victim advocates may be a given in those offices fortunate enough to have functioning victim assistance programs but training efforts should not stop there. Trial attorneys and investigators should also receive training that enhances their understanding of victims' issues and heightens their sensitivity to the victims' plight. Despite the recent success of the victims' movement, neither law schools nor university-based criminal justice programs do much to prepare law students or criminal justice professionals to deal with individuals who have been victimized by crime.

Currently, the best available option is to engage the real experts in the field to properly train prosecutors, investigators and victim advocates. Some of these experts may include other prosecutors but specialized organizations exist to provide services to victims of crime. Do not hesitate to call upon them. They have a great deal to teach, and prosecutors should be willing to draw upon their expertise.[2]

A formal training plan should recognize the significant volume of information prosecutors would require as they progress in understanding and responsibility. This
training, which can be provided in phases, might include such content as: statutory
responsibilities, appropriate responses to those in trauma, the impact of trauma on a
victim's capacity to cooperate, how to work with a victim advocate, crime-specific
dynamics in areas such as domestic violence (the cycle of violence, etc.), homicide,
sexual assault, cultural issues and problems in victimization. Every prosecutor's office
should encourage a corporate culture that clearly values compassionate treatment of
crime victims. Again, this attitude is really no longer optional; it is mandatory in virtually every jurisdiction in the country.

Apparently, some prosecutors are still mistaken in the belief that compassion towards
victims of crime means that a prosecutor somehow cares less about winning cases or
seeking justice. This view is incorrect. What it does mean, simply stated, is that prosecutors should never unduly traumatize victims for lack of sensitivity to their suffering. Additionally, prosecutors cannot and should not demand or assume that victims
will appreciate their hard work, nor should they be surprised when victims lash out
because cases cannot be filed or charges are dismissed.

Having said that, more often than not a victim's reaction to the disposition of a case
has less to do with the number of years of penitentiary time the defendant receives
than the level and quality of interaction with the prosecutor or victim advocate
throughout the process. Unless the prosecutor's office is committed to effective staff
training, this important lesson can go unlearned. Victims are re-traumatized, this time
by the system, and the healing process for victims deteriorates, as does the prosecutor's
relationship with the community.

Effective prosecutor training must focus on the real benefits of improved victim
communication and victim input. Research conducted by the American Prosecutors
Research Institute (APRI)[3] points to a clear improvement in victim satisfaction with
the system when the prosecutor encourages victim involvement. Sixty-seven percent
of victims were satisfied with the handling of their cases when they were allowed to
present Victim Impact Statements versus a mere 18 percent who were satisfied when
the prosecutor did not encourage and facilitate this right. In another study, the
National Institute of Justice found that victims were not informed of plea negotiations in nearly 50 percent of the violent crime cases surveyed, even when statutes in
their jurisdictions required notice.[4] Clearly, this is an unacceptable situation or

should be. Office procedures should never allow prosecutors to accept victim exclusion from a system that requires victim inclusion.

In 1998, the Office for Victims of Crime (OVC), U.S. Department of Justice, published a document entitled, *New Directions from the Field: Victims' Rights and Services for the 21st Century. New Directions* discusses recommendations for prosecutors' offices to consider when designing procedures to achieve full justice for victims. While state statutes may cover many of these recommendations, they merit re-statement:

- Prosecutors' offices should notify victims in a timely manner of the date, time and location of the following events: charging of defendant, pretrial hearings, plea negotiations, trial, all schedule changes and the sentencing hearing. Timely notification of advanced scheduling should be provided, orally or in writing, in relevant languages. Statutes should require prosecutors to verify these notifications with documentation in case files or through another mechanism.
- Prosecutors should establish victim/witness assistance units to ensure that victims of crime receive at least a basic level of service, including information, notification, consultation and participation. Prosecutors' offices should develop and incorporate into performance evaluations written definitions of the roles and responsibilities of prosecuting attorneys, victim/witness professionals and other relevant staff and volunteers.
- Prosecutors should use the full range of measures at their disposal to ensure that victims and witnesses are protected from intimidation and harassment. These measures include ensuring that victims are informed about safety precautions, advising the court of victims' fears and concerns about safety prior to any bail or bond proceedings, automatically requesting no-contact orders and enforcing them if violated and utilizing witness relocation programs and technology to help protect victims.
- Prosecutors should advocate for victims to have their views heard by judges regarding bail, continuances, plea agreements, dismissals, sentencings and restitution. Policies and procedures should be put into place in all prosecutors' offices to ensure that victims are informed in a timely manner of these crucial rights in forms of communication they understand.
- Prosecutors should make every effort, if the victim has provided a current address or telephone number, to consult with the victim on the terms of any negotiated plea, including the acceptance of a plea of guilty or nolo contendere.
- In all cases, particularly those involving sexual assault, the prosecuting attorney

should confer with the victim or survivors before deciding not to file charges or before deciding to seek dismissal of charges already filed.

- Prosecutors should establish policies to "fast track" the prosecution of sexual assault, domestic violence, elderly and child abuse and other particularly sensitive cases to shorten the length of time from arrest to disposition. Prosecutors should encourage judges to give top priority to these cases on the trial docket and should try to ensure that the case goes to trial when initially scheduled.
- Prosecutors' offices should use technology to enhance the implementation of victims' rights.
- Prosecutors should adopt vertical prosecution for domestic violence, sexual assault and child abuse cases.
- Prosecutors should work closely with victim service providers as well as victims of domestic violence to establish appropriate prosecution policies and support research to assess the effectiveness of proceeding without victim testimony in domestic violence cases.
- Victims' rights and sensitivity education should be provided to all prosecutors during their initial orientation and throughout their careers.
- Prosecutors' offices should establish procedures to ensure the prompt return of victims' property, absent the need for it as actual evidence in court.[5]

Every prosecutor should study these recommendations with an eye toward the feasibility of implementing them. Because jurisdictions vary in size, caseload and staffing, some degree of creativity will be necessary in this process. The resulting strain on resources may also require prosecutors to identify the recommendations that can be implemented in the short term and those that must wait.

INTERAGENCY AND COMMUNITY COLLABORATION

In considering the *New Directions* recommendations, prosecutors will find great benefit in drawing on true collaboration from the community. Inviting all of the stakeholders in the community to the table requires some risk-taking but the payoffs can be substantial. A tremendous benefit is derived from breaking down the barriers that the formalities of the profession too often create.

By using community collaboration, the prosecutor can become a powerful catalyst for the creation of varied responses to crime and criminal victimization. These responses (also know as protocols) establish a common ground of understanding of each institution's or agency's role and appropriate situational behavior from those organizations in response to particular crimes.

In Denver, Colorado, protocols exist for response to domestic violence, child abuse, sexual assault on a child, sexual assault, victimization of disabled persons and victimization of the elderly. There is an effort underway to amend Denver's sexual-assault protocol to improve the response to non-stranger, sexual assault cases. Each protocol requires that all stakeholders—agencies, community groups and social welfare organizations—meet to create a matrix of integrated and coordinated services to crime victims and their families. This process typically requires months of regular meetings. In Denver, once distant, cautious and perhaps even antagonistic relationships have in time become collegial and supportive.

While developing protocols, additional benefits are achieved by the elimination of communication barriers, the education of each entity or agency about the functions and limitations of the others, the establishment of understandable expectations and the development of mutual trust and respect. When implemented, the protocol will create an objective standard with which to measure the quality of victim services and when concerns or disputes arise, a means to analyze and resolve the problems. Lastly, when the protocol is signed, a public ceremony can attract significant attention from the media and the public.

VICTIM SERVICES IN THE 21ST CENTURY

Prosecutors should also evaluate the role they might play in providing seamless delivery of services and support for crime victims. OVC is currently funding two model programs for this purpose: an urban site in Denver, Colorado, and a rural site in Vermont. Building seamless service is a lofty goal based on the belief that there should be no "wrong door" for crime victims to enter when they call upon the justice system for assistance.

At the heart of these efforts is a commitment to reach out to under-served or unserved people in our communities, many of whom allow crimes to go unreported. The targeted populations include, among others, racial minorities, the disabled, the elderly, non-English speakers and gays and lesbians. These model sites emphasize computerization as a way to improve communications and case management by agencies and service providers. Interdisciplinary cross-trainings are essential for improving working relationships, especially among criminal justice professionals, community service providers and allied professionals. OVC has established a technical assistance and training program to support local jurisdictions that have an interest in similar program development.

Prosecutors must use every opportunity to stand shoulder to shoulder at public events with the victim advocates in their community. Each year, National Victims' Rights Week, Sexual Assault Awareness Month, Domestic Violence Awareness Month, Red Ribbon Campaigns and many other community events create a platform for prosecutors to publicly demonstrate their commitment to crime victims' rights. Joint participation at forums like these enhances vital partnerships between public service and community-based agencies.

Finally, prosecutor ethics deserve mention in the context of crime victims' rights. At present, there are no victim-specific ethical standards for prosecutors. Considering the continued growth of victims' rights in the criminal justice system, however, prosecutors should reflect on what, if any, ethical guidelines are needed to frame their legal responsibilities to victims. The over-arching ethical mandate—to seek justice—is their compass, but greater specificity on how that broad directive intersects with victims' rights or victims' interests might be helpful.

Prosecutors have come a long way since 1982, when a President's Task Force on Victims of Crime documented how the criminal justice system treated victims with institutional disinterest. Nearly two decades later, a follow-up report still maintains that the system appears to hurt more than it helps.[6] But, where victims believe they have been afforded a full voice in the process, it is usually a prosecutor who gets the credit.[7] Unless prosecutors understand victims' need to be listened to and to be heard, victims will continue to feel they are outside the process looking in. If the last two decades have taught us nothing else, they have taught us that victims deserve a voice in the process and they have a right to one. In fact, they insist on it. We must strive to ensure that their voice is heard.

LINKS
- Office for Victims of Crime, U.S. Department of Justice: http://www.ojp.usdoj.gov.ovc
- National Center for Victims of Crime: http://www.nvc.org/
- National Organization for Victims of Crime: http://www.try.nova.org/

• Violence Against Women Office, U.S. Department of Justice:
http://www.ojp.usdoj.gov/vawo/

ENDNOTES

[1] National Institute of Justice, *The Rights of Crime Victims—Does Legal Protection Make a Difference* (Washington, D.C.): 1998.

[2] *See* links to recommended organizations (listed above).

[3] In conjunction with MADD.

[4] E.K. Alexander and J.H. Lord, *A Victim's Right to Speak, A Nation's Responsibility to Listen*, National Center for Victims of Crime, Mothers Against Drunk Driving and American Prosecutors Research Institute Grant from USDOJ/OVC, (1994): 40.

[5] Office for Victims of Crime, U.S. Department of Justice, *New Directions from the Field: Victims' Rights and Services for the 21st Century* (Washington D.C.): 1998.

[6] *Ibid.* Executive Summary: vii-xx.

[7] Or the blame when victims have no voice in the process.

DOMESTIC VIOLENCE
POLICIES AND PRACTICES

By Pamela Paziotopoulos, Assistant State's Attorney, Cook County, Chicago, Illinois

ENGAGING VICTIMS SAFELY IN THE CRIMINAL JUSTICE SYSTEM

Historically, prosecutors and law enforcement officials *reacted* to violent crimes committed but none of their training focused on crime *prevention*. The prosecutors' mentality was reactive rather than proactive. No protocols existed and no methods were available to apply techniques to avoid further violence. Today, however, prosecutors realize that there is no time to wait when the crime concerns domestic violence. Prompt intervention is essential before the violence escalates.

It is this reactive mentality that has made it difficult for law enforcement, prosecution and the judiciary to address domestic violence issues and, in particular, stalking cases. Initially, prosecutors were puzzled by domestic violence crimes. With other offenses, prosecutors have evidence such as medical records, paramedic reports, photos of crime scenes, photos of victim's injuries and independent witnesses' testimony. However, in many domestic violence cases, there are no physical injuries (and therefore no pictures), medical records or paramedic reports and no crime scene photos. The evidence is often limited to eyewitness accounts and the victim's testimony.

Additionally, the role of the prosecutor in a domestic violence case is often confusing and creates complex questions. For example, securing an appropriate sentence for an offender may result in serious negative ramifications for the victim and her children. If the abuser's incarceration may leave them completely destitute, what has been accomplished?

Oftentimes victims fail to appear in court. Nationwide, in rural and urban settings alike, the typically low in-court appearance rates of domestic violence victims discourage prosecutors from pursuing these cases. If victims do attend the proceedings, they are often reluctant to cooperate. They may refuse to testify or even recant.

Prosecuting a domestic violence case without the victim's testimony is a possibility and a daily reality in many jurisdictions, assuming there is enough independent evidence to convict the offender. Many prosecutors have done it. In fact, some discover positive results when the victims recant because juries will often see the defendants for what they are—controlling and manipulative. Although that difficult practice can be effective in holding the offender accountable, the following article explores methods to *engage* the domestic violence victim in the judicial process and to secure the victim's safety when the case is prosecuted, with or without her testimony.[1]

Due largely to the efforts of the advocacy communities throughout the country, prosecutors now attempt to define success in this area in terms of victim safety instead of rates of conviction. The following article describes policies and practices employed by the Cook County State's Attorney's Office that are proving to be effective in reducing domestic violence and keeping victims and children safe while holding the offender accountable for his actions. The Cook County State's Attorneys Office handles approximately 55,000 domestic violence cases a year in the City of Chicago and another 15,000 in the suburbs. Allocating sufficient resources to these cases is challenging but not impossible. Moreover, the role of the prosecutor has been enhanced to include the additional responsibility of introducing victims to the collateral services they will need to participate safely in a criminal prosecution.

THE DOMESTIC VIOLENCE PROSECUTOR

Prosecutors at the misdemeanor level typically rotate through different courts every few months. However, prosecutors[2] of domestic violence cases are required to make long-term commitments—a minimum of two years—to the Cook County State's Attorney's Domestic Violence Division (the division) in order to develop a thorough understanding of the issues and to give victims vertical prosecution. Although extensive training is a part of the process, prosecutors also need considerable time in court actually prosecuting these cases to become truly proficient.

In addition, prosecutors participate in roll-call training with the police department which enables them to develop relationships with the officers that bring the cases into their courtrooms. They also instruct various community groups on the victim assistance services offered through the division. This level of requisite training and community involvement may seem burdensome in light of the prosecutors' heavy caseloads, but the additional responsibilities actually help diminish the possibility of burnout. The result of this high level of sacrifice and dedication is a division that is truly expert in the prosecution of domestic violence cases.

TARGETING HIGH RISK CASES

Prosecutors around the country are often disappointed with the poor cooperation and participation of domestic violence victims in the criminal justice system. As part of their efforts to better serve victims (and improve prosecutions, not incidentally), Chicago developed the Target Abuser Call Program (TAC). TAC focuses on high-risk (for violence) misdemeanor domestic violence cases. TAC results have been promising—strikingly improving what were previously considered acceptable outcomes for domestic violence cases in the jurisdiction. Roughly 80 percent of TAC victims follow through with the program, meaning that 80 percent actually appear for the first court date and participate further in the prosecution process.

Funded by the Violence Against Women Grants Office at the U.S. Department of Justice, TAC is providing tremendous insight into domestic violence prosecutions. Most importantly, TAC members have learned that to aggressively prosecute these cases the victim must be provided with as much collateral support as possible. Merely handing a victim a brochure with a list of referrals is not enough. Prosecutors have to make sure that they actually connect the victim with the services they endorse. Otherwise, the outcome is failed prosecutions.

The experience of TAC has illustrated that an effective and responsible domestic violence prosecution is a team effort. Comprised of four agency partners: the prosecutor's office, an advocacy agency, a (civil) legal service provider and an abuse treatment provider, the TAC partnership provides a comprehensive legal strategy for victims. Achieving victim safety is accomplished through round-tabling cases from all agency perspectives, discussing prosecution issues, advocacy issues, civil issues, etc. The result is a far-reaching, comprehensive civil and criminal plan for the victim. Note that this concept can be adopted by any prosecutor's office, even one without a grant from the Justice Department, provided that the agencies in local communities make the necessary commitment.

Not every domestic violence case is appropriate for TAC. They are chosen based on a variety of factors. The program is both victim and offender oriented, targets high-risk misdemeanor cases and contemplates the defendant's domestic violence history and the circumstances of the pending criminal case. In addition, numerous other lethality indicators are considered during this process.[3]

The TAC Team

Each of two *prosecutors* assigned to handle these high-risk cases has been with TAC for over five years. They have prior felony trial experience that, in a misdemeanor setting, lends considerable weight and real credibility to the program. The prosecutors are responsible for securing the protection order for the victim rather than delegating it to another prosecutor or a different court. The cases are vertically prosecuted.

The *victim specialist* provides on-going, extensive support to the victim during the pendency of the case. This specialist explains the court process and acts as a valuable liaison between the prosecutors and the victim.

The *investigators* present themselves at the doorstep of the victim's home with information in hand that explains the benefits of the program. They deliver an information sheet with the names, phone numbers and roles of the various members of the team and, of course, they also collect all additional evidence that may be helpful to the prosecution.

The *advocate*, who is from an independent advocacy agency, provides free and confidential services. The advocate's duties include referrals to counseling, shelter, crime victim's compensation and other services. Most importantly, the advocate maintains extensive contact with the victim for post-trial follow-up.

The *civil attorney* provides free representation in civil court, as needed. Many noncriminal legal issues that are not part of but have a significant impact on the criminal case affect domestic violence victims, including child custody, paternity, visitation, child support and protective orders.

The *social service liaison* monitors the compliance (or non-compliance) of offenders who have been court-ordered to the Social Service Department for counseling services. The liaison reports to the team on any counseling issues the defendant may have and monitors his compliance with other court orders.

The services that the partners provide as a team are already available for victims but on a fragmented basis. The TAC actors and their agencies are all available to the victim every step of the way. Remarkably, the high victim participation rate that results from this coordinated approach is mirrored by a high conviction rate. Although the number varies from month to month, the TAC team achieves approximately an 85–90 percent conviction rate.

Prior to the inception of TAC, prosecutors worked with victim advocates, civil legal providers and social service agencies in a decentralized mode that did not yield the results that TAC has achieved. The fact that TAC meetings require each of the team members to analyze every case and present the unique perspective and recommendations of his or her particular agency—in concert with the other TAC members—is the unique aspect of TAC. The TAC process is coordinated, multi-disciplinary and cohesive. The result is a comprehensive civil and criminal plan for the victim.[4] The following sections will explore methods that TAC has developed that can be applied to all cases.

ENHANCING THE NOTIFICATION PROCESS

The division prosecutes domestic violence cases and, just as importantly, provides support and information to the victims. More than 1200 victims, from a variety of income levels, ethnic groups and neighborhoods, come each week to the dedicated domestic violence courthouse. Until recently, there was no format through which the office could provide domestic violence victims with the vital information and critical resources they urgently need to end the violence in their lives. Few victims possess this information when they enter the court system.

In addition to these issues, the victim, upon arrival at the courthouse, is also trying to understand what is, to the layman, a bewildering legal process. The following discussion details methods to de-mystify the system for victims, provide them with the collateral support necessary to proceed with a successful prosecution and, just as importantly, to leave the courthouse with a comprehensive plan for their safe and successful return to (violence-free) civil society.

The first notification to victims of their court dates is the subpoena. It is clear that serving subpoenas in the traditional manner may cause the victim to show up. But, it does not adequately engage domestic violence victims in the process, either to further their understanding of the system or to answer any of their immediate needs.

Our investigators are specially trained on the issues facing domestic violence victims. They conduct reactive and proactive investigations, from the initial complaint through the post-trial stage. When they serve a victim with a subpoena, they also hand her a victim information folder that answers many of the common questions asked by domestic violence victims. It is an excellent reference for victims as their cases progress through the legal system. The folder contains information on the roles of the prosecutors, information on orders of protection and what to do if they are violated, a list of community resources, a thorough explanation of the cycle of violence, myths and misconceptions about domestic abuse, an extensive description of the courthouse process, and a safety plan.

This notification process has markedly improved our attempts to safely engage victims in the system. Under the former system, victims merely received notification of their court dates, without any other type of material. Not surprisingly, most would immediately seek to drop charges, express serious reservations about prosecuting and show great reluctance to cooperate with the prosecution. Since the notification process has been enhanced, most victims are more informed when they arrive at the courthouse and are thus more likely to complete the process. This method has proven that it can successfully reduce many of the fears and misconceptions victims have about the court system.

THE RESOURCE CENTER

Located in the domestic violence courthouse, the resource center is available for use by all victims whether they are in court for the first or the fifth time. The prosecutor's office oversees the center and staffs it with a resource coordinator who is a former victim witness specialist. Financial support for funding and staff, however, comes through collaborative relationships with public and private service providers, community organizations and other professionals.

Financial independence is a common issue facing many domestic violence victims; they depend upon their abusers for financial support and lack the skills and training necessary for employment. Further, most prosecutors have seen how domestic violence victims frequently receive or have received public assistance. The prosecutors in the Cook County State's Attorney's Office believe that victims of domestic violence are not necessarily on welfare because they do not want to work but because factors associated with domestic violence often prevent them from working. In addition the lack of access to financial resources and independent living skills prevents many victims from leaving abusive situations and perpetuates the pattern of violence.

The resource center exposes victims to resource information and services that can ultimately enable them to make the informed life choices they must adopt to reduce the level of violence in their lives. Through this program, victims have an opportunity to listen to regularly scheduled court orientation presentations, participate in support groups and take the initiative to develop individual comprehensive plans.

Successfully communicating with domestic violence victims can be a difficult, complicated task. The center is accessible to the victims while their cases are pending as well as after the trial. Since its inception, most victims have availed themselves of the system. Through court orientation presentations, group discussions, informational materials, individualized referrals and community information presentations, victims can now make choices, through cooperation with the justice system, that allow them to hold their abusers accountable. Although most prosecutors' offices throughout the country include victim witness specialists who undoubtedly perform some of the services offered at the center, Chicago prosecutors have learned that a designated center for *all* these services, centrally located at the courthouse, is immensely beneficial.

LETHALITY INDICATORS AND INTERVIEWING TOOLS

Prosecutors are fact-finders but they are specific in their skills. When sitting down to interview a witness they tend to limit their questions to the particular incident that is going to trial. Typically, they begin the dialogue with who, what, when, how and why questions. Often, because of their heavy caseloads, severe time constraints and pressure from the judiciary to expedite the process, they favor quick results even though they know that domestic violence cases are often only smaller parts of larger, more complicated domestic problems.

In order to improve domestic violence management skills (and results) prosecutors need to re-think their approach to domestic violence cases. Domestic violence cases often appear innocuous and straightforward when compared to other crimes, and especially so where no physical evidence or additional witnesses are available for corroboration. However, they may begin small and then explode into something much larger and more serious. For example, when the offender is charged with phone harassment, or when he violates a protection order by showing up at the victim's house, it may not be readily apparent to the prosecutor, let alone to the court, that the case could quickly escalate into a homicide.

After a domestic violence homicide occurs, coworkers may often be heard to say things like "Who could have possibly predicted something like that?" or, "Who can blame the judge for giving a low bond on his case... it was after all just a phone harassment charge." To limit the potential for this kind of tragedy, prosecutors should present the court with as much information as possible about domestic violence cases at the bond hearing, at trial (if evidentiary laws permit) and especially at sentencing. If other dangerous factors between the parties in the case have been identified, the court should have all that information to determine an appropriate sentence.

The identifiers discussed in this section are designed to obtain information to be used when appropriate and when the law permits. Most likely, a prosecutor will seek to admit this information in a pre-trial negotiation setting, motion in limine or in an aggravation or mitigation hearing. Most importantly, even if the prosecutor chooses not to introduce to the court the following identifiers, when present, they will still enable him or her to gain tremendous insight into the nature and violence level of the particular case and of domestic violence cases in general.

The time available to interview the victim is often quite limited. Although there is usually sufficient time to interview a victim thoroughly enough to proceed, most cases require better background information on all their aspects. This necessitates a refining of the interview process.

To re-shape and effectively design questions to pose to domestic violence victims and to develop "lethality instruments and factors" for offender assessment, the division convened a multi-disciplinary advisory group made up of law enforcement, investigators, prosecutors, politicians and domestic violence specialists.[5] The research also involved numerous discussions with various members of the domestic violence community and threat assessment professional agencies. What follows is a summation of their conversations and training. Although they collected numerous identifiers from these discussions, only a few of the more severe indicators are cited here. Of course, this data is supplemental to such information as the offender's prior criminal record, police reports and other court documents.

The advisory group searched for ways to gain insight into domestic violence cases to determine how close an offender is to acting violently against the victim or another. Some experts in the field subscribe to the philosophy that everything in the criminal justice system that moves the offender closer to a conviction can be construed as a risk to the victim. Again, how does one seek justice and also implement the goal to "keep victims safe"?

The first question asked at the beginning of the interview with the victim is "Have you conveyed to the offender that you intend to leave this relationship or have you left?" The answer to this question will help determine the status of each case. For example, if the victim has never told the offender that she is going to leave and does not plan on announcing it, then that fact is taken into consideration when evaluating the case and again when planning a recommendation to the court for sentencing. However, if the victim conveys that she intends to leave, the prosecutor should be sure that before she exits the courthouse an advocate or victim witness specialist has helped her design a safety plan. Also, take note that the single most dangerous moment for a domestic violence victim comes when she leaves the relationship or informs the offender that she intends to leave him. From that point on, the prosecutor will see a pattern of behavior generally referred to as "stalking." When the offender no longer has immediate access to the victim (when they are no longer living together), he tends to act out his controlling behavior in public rather than in private. This behavior manifests itself in the form of phone harassment, violations of orders of protection, appearing at the victim's workplace, etc.

The next inquiry, assuming that the victim has announced her decision to leave, is to learn more about how the offender has handled her decision. What was his response to that change in the relationship? Did he prevent her from leaving? Has he ever prevented her from leaving? (Ask about behavior such as tearing the phone out of the wall, following her to a friend's place, becoming obsessed with finding her if she has gone, etc.) Experts characterize this as interfering with the victim's "help-seeking behavior." Violence is known to escalate because the perpetrator is fearful of losing control over the victim. Therefore, an abuser will increase the level of violence to increase the victim's fear. Abusers cannot tolerate the exercise of another's free will.

After determining this important fact, there are numerous other lethality indicators that must be identified. Depending on resources and staff availability, consider assigning a victim witness specialist, an investigator or other individual in the office (in addition to or as a substitute for the prosecutor), the responsibility for conducting this assessment. Keep in mind, however, the possibility that if an independent advocate rather than a prosecutor or prosecutor's office staffer administers these questions they may, depending on local laws, be restricted from releasing the information they garner due to confidentiality or privacy restrictions.

Lethality Assessment Factors

Symbolic Violence

As stated previously, prosecutors have a habit of restricting evidence collection to items that are directly relevant to the specific case or offense they are currently prosecuting. However, they should also inquire about the existence of symbolic violence, e.g., violence to property the victim treasures or that is particularly important to the victim. For example, has the offender broken the piano that she played every evening? Has he destroyed any photographs? Another common example of symbolic violence might be a package of dead roses sent to the victim. And do not neglect to ask about injuries or cruelty to pets, which are unfortunately common, and may be an indication of future violence.

Children

The age of the children will provide insight as to how the violence is affecting them. Keep in mind that children younger than five years old will most likely not be in school or active outside the home. Therefore, they do not have the opportunity to share what they have witnessed with anyone outside the home. Further, when children become teenagers they begin to intervene in the abuse and are often injured in the process.

Mental Illness

It is important to ask if the defendant has ever suffered from a mental illness, has been hospitalized or is currently taking any medication. Police officers, among others, have noted that it is imperative to note exactly what medications the offender is taking and what he is being treated for during this time period. Often when asked, the offender will not reveal this or may not be able to do so because of his mental condition.

Suicide

It is not enough to merely inquire whether the defendant has ever attempted suicide. Prosecutors should inquire as to the specificity of the plan and whether or not the offender has also conveyed a desire to kill the victim or children. Obviously, the more concrete the details and specificity of the plan, the higher the risk to the victim.

Guns

The recent acquisition of a gun is often a more ominous indicator of violence than long-term possession of a firearm. Ask if the offender has access to a gun and how often he handles it. The goal is to determine to what degree the weapons are a part of this person's persona. Be extra careful of an offender who is emotionally attached to his weapon, will not even walk down the street to buy a newspaper without it. Also, examine what other kinds of paraphernalia he keeps. What does he collect (knives, explosives, other weapons)?

Substance Abuse

Many domestic violence offenders have problems with alcohol or drugs. The prosecutor should examine exactly how the domestic relationship is affected by the substance abuse. It is especially important to ask if the offender has recently increased his usage.

Fear

One can speculate about how lethal the situation may be, but only the victim holds the true answer to this question. Do not forget to ask simple questions such as "Are you afraid of the offender?" and, if so, "Why?" If the victim has ever visited a shelter before, it will be a good indication of real fear, because hiding from the offender is an excellent indication of real danger. In addition, her fear is likely to escalate greatly if she has ever been hospitalized because of an injury caused by the offender.

Orders of Protection

Although experts tend to disagree about whether court orders really protect victims or merely serve to infuriate offenders and make matters worse for their victims, the fact remains that if they are used, the prosecutor should ascertain how the offender has reacted to the order. If he has violated it, then many experts believe one should assume that the offender has little or no regard for the punitive powers of the criminal justice system. A protective order will not act as a deterrent to such an individual. In that case, the prosecutor must establish safeguards for the victim *before* the court issues the order, especially if the offender has reacted negatively to such orders in the past.

Offenders Who Resist Arrest

Many domestic violence cases are coupled with charges for resisting arrest. These cases should be highlighted since the logical inference is that law enforcement and/or the courts will not deter this individual. If he resists arrest at the scene, makes remarks to the police officers and fights with the police officers, then it is likely he will resist obeying any court orders. One caveat here: often-volatile offenders may act in a calm and cool fashion. That does not necessarily mean that these individuals are not as dangerous as those that act out violently when police are present.

Threats
It is especially important to evaluate threats. Examine the communication pattern. Look at the defendant's recent behavior. How has he communicated his threats? What is the content of those threats? Even otherwise simple love notes can be scrutinized as threats if the victim has terminated the relationship.

Location of Violence
If the violence was conducted in a public place, it is likely that it will be repeated. This is because the offender is confident enough (or desperate enough) to move the exercise of his power and control from the home (a private domain) to a public domain, despite the risk of escalating the jeopardy to himself.

The Three Ds
Desperation—a change in the abuser's behavior as a result of his perception of the victim's changed behavior. She may escalate her attempts to gain independence; he may not be able to accept this.
Decreased focus—the abuser's world zeroes in on the victim.
Depersonalization—the offender has wiped the victim clean of any identity as a human being. He feels he can do whatever he wants to her because she belongs to him. She is just a thing.

Physical Violence
This is a common but vital question: "Has there been any physical violence?" If the answer is no, then ask: "Has he ever pushed you around or punched you?" Victims define physical violence in a surprising number of ways. The victim may also know if the offender has abused former girlfriends or ex-wives. If at all possible, try to determine how the prior relationships ended. These questions can be asked quickly and it is important to know if the prior victims were able to leave the relationship easily or whether they also suffered. Were there prior protective orders? What were the results? If the other women had a difficult time leaving, then there is a good possibility that this victim will face the same (or greater) difficulties.

Strangulation

The ultimate in symbolic violence is removing the victim's voice. Often, this is the last step before homicide.

Surveillance/Control/Monitoring

What kind of stalking behavior does the offender exhibit? Even if not enough exists to charge the offender with the crime of stalking, it is still noteworthy to learn if the offender has followed the victim or has acted in any other persistent manner (not respecting the word "no").

Stress and Stressors

What kinds of stressors are present in the offender's life? His arrest report may indicate that he is employed. However, after a few questions, it may be determined that is he on probation at work or has recently experienced a demotion. What is the status of his social circle? Has he recently experienced any personal losses (the loss of a parent, the loss of a friend)? This, coupled with the anticipated loss of his girlfriend, wife or children, can lead him to a state of hopelessness. He will be most dangerous when he begins to spiral downward and then out of control.

Defendant's Admission

Obviously the defendant's words on the scene are particularly insightful. An informal study conducted by the chief judge of the Cook County Domestic Violence Courts revealed that offenders who admit their guilt are more eager to participate in treatment, counseling and to start on the road to recovery. However, offenders who insist on a trial and are then found guilty are more likely to violate any conditions of the court and to ignore mandatory counseling.

CONCLUSION

Incorporating the foregoing research into the preparation of the case will enable the prosecutor to make more informed decisions. It will also (and, more importantly) be helpful in making the appropriate referrals and community links for victims. By introducing this information into the case, the prosecutor will notice remarkable stiffening of the punishment meted out to offenders and will have the necessary data to design more effective and comprehensive legal and safety plans for victims. This is the best way to give real meaning to the often-repeated goal: keep victims safe while holding offenders accountable.

ENDNOTES

[1] Although the writer knows full well that not all domestic violence victims are female, a great majority are. Therefore, for the purposes of this article, I will often refer to the "victim" with the feminine pronoun. My apologies to those who may be offended by this usage.

[2] Assistant State's Attorneys.

[3] *See* section on lethality instruments.

[4] Note: it does not take a million dollar grant from the federal government to implement this, but it does require a formal commitment or memorandum of agreement to partner with other agencies. Every prosecutor's office has similar agencies in its jurisdiction. Understandably, however, your office may not be able to apply this method to every domestic violence case, just as Chicago cannot.

[5] The group included numerous members of the Cook County State's Attorney's Office; Mr. Tom Cronin, Ms. Karen Huels, Ms. Debra Kirby, Ms. Mary Jensen, Mr. Scott Keenan of the Chicago Police Department; Ms. Leslie Landis of the Mayor's Council on Domestic Violence; Mr. Bob Martin of Gavin De Becker, Inc.; Ms. Gael Strack of the San Diego Prosecutor's Office; Mr. Scott Hampton of the Stafford Guidance Center in New Hampshire; Mr. Bryan Vossekul and Ms. Nancy Fogarty of the United States Secret Service; and Ms. Barbara Hart, an independent consultant and noted expert in the field of domestic violence.

THE EFFECTS OF DIVERSITY IN THE OFFICE

By Patricia L. Gatling, Deputy District Attorney, King's County, Brooklyn, New York and Majorie Heidseick, Legal Assistant, New York Law School

"A prosecuting attorney assumes high duty, and has imposed upon him grave responsibilities. He may be the means of much good or much mischief. Interests of vast magnitude are entrusted to him; confidence is reposed in him; life, liberty, character and property should be protected by him. He should guard, with jealous watchfulness, his own reputation, as well as that of his profession and the court."[1]

Introduction

Most prosecutors would agree that the profession has withstood many changes since 1972, when the New York State Bar Association published the above statement of prosecutors' ethics. Most notably, the references to prosecuting attorney as *he* and *him* have become obsolete. Notwithstanding, the subtext of the drafter's message was as clear then as it is now: the reality is that the occupation of prosecutor continues to be dominated by the *he* lawyers of the profession.

In 1972, there were female prosecutors in offices throughout the State of New York but their roles and contributions to the profession went largely unnoticed by one of the largest and most influential bar associations in the nation. Equally disappointing is that today there has been minimal effort to diversify many prosecutors' offices across the country. Many offices remain dominated by white men, creating an imbalance of women and minority lawyers. I would argue that this is unfair, because society needs and deserves full and fair representation of all ethnic groups and both sexes, for both the population served and the society at large, for practical reasons which will be discussed in this article.

In contemporary society, prosecutors are charged with a dual role. On one side, they are representatives and enforcers of the law, and on the other side, they are educators, watchdogs and crime preventors. In either set of circumstances, it is incumbent upon prosecutors to understand the communities they represent and treat them equally at all times.

For innumerable reasons, communities across the country—and especially inner-city neighborhoods—have evolved into enclaves of people representing a hodgepodge of racial, ethnic and religious backgrounds. Like it or not, these people often view law enforcement—including prosecutors—with hostility and resentment. As these neighborhoods and communities continue to attract people from all corners of the world, it becomes crucial for the prosecuting arm of law enforcement to be aware of and educated about the inherent differences that potentially affect the judicial process.

On diversity, author Ben Wattenberg has concluded:

> ... the United States is in the process of becoming the world's first "universal nation." Certainly, America is in the process of assembling an array of ethnicities and races unlike anything previously assembled. And, if we are wise we will choose to make that a virtue. We will realize that the differences various groups bring to the table represent a potential gold mine of fresh ideas, if only we learn to be open to them.[2]

THE PERCEPTION OF BIAS IN THE CRIMINAL JUSTICE SYSTEM

Supreme Court Justice Sandra Day O'Connor remarked in 1993, that "When people perceive... bias in a legal system, whether they suffer from it or not, they lose respect for the system as well as for the law."[3] Perception often becomes reality; and in the case of the American judicial system, the perception among many is that the system exists to protect the majority and prosecute the minority.

Society admires and seeks truly skilled prosecutors with the ability to observe and absorb societal and demographic changes from the well of the courtroom. Given their exposure and experience, prosecutors must be more sensitive and more willing to accommodate the changing face of the American landscape.[4] Prudent prosecutors look beyond the immediate mission and take the daily interaction with those unlike themselves as an opportunity to learn and absorb information about those they are charged with serving and protecting. An essential class, and one missing from law school curriculums, is that of effectively interacting with minority populations; it is only learned through real life experience.

The relationship between race and crime in America is an integral part of the criminal justice system.[5] People of color have historically viewed the criminal justice system as an oppressive and insensitive institution that further burdens their community. Many prosecutors have been confronted with criminal cases motivated or at least explained by the perception of troublesome racial, ethnic, religious or cultural differences. Past discrimination by law enforcement, compounded by what many Americans regard as historically unfair treatment in the courts, has fostered a negative perception of the judicial system by many people of color. Accordingly, there is a widely held belief in minority communities that they will not receive justice in a court of law. Today, this opinion remains deeply rooted and is passionately voiced despite 50 years of legal decisions and efforts aimed at eliminating discrimination in the legal system. In order for prosecutorial agencies to reflect the needs and, perhaps most importantly, to gain the support of the communities that they serve, it is crucial that chief prosecutors aggressively diversify their offices. Practicality notwithstanding, it should be morally mandated.

While legal decisions and laws have certainly improved access for people of color to public and private establishments such as schools, restaurants, hotels, etc., they have not been as successful at leveling the proverbial playing field of the real world. For people of color, equal access does not mean equal treatment in their daily existence.[6] Those with whom they come in contact usually determine equal treatment.

It is well known that members of minority groups are arrested, charged and convicted in greater percentages than their majority counterparts. This reality, compounded by daily life experiences, the negative relationship with law enforcement and the fact that in a demographically changing America, prosecutors' offices remain dominated by a white male hierarchy, all support the perception that bias exists in the criminal justice system. Disparate sentencing (studies show people of color receive longer sentences than similarly situated non-minorities)[7] and harsher treatment of juvenile offenders of color,[8] further contribute to the prevailing belief that equal justice under the law does not apply to racial minorities.

In criminal courtrooms across the nation the outlook can be daunting for people of color. The accused is typically a person of color who is often arrested, prosecuted and sentenced by a courtroom of white men and women. Often the jury may not be from the defendant's own community. What is the impact of this unbalanced and demoralizing set of circumstances in the judicial system? Even if every agent in the criminal courtroom involved in the dispensation of justice acts fairly, ethically and beyond reproach, the fact remains that the perception of bias exists within certain segments of the community. Based solely upon appearance, people of color could thereby conclude—and many do—that the law exists only to serve and protect the majority, not the minority.

The Utah Bar Association's study of bias in the courts concludes that, "the perception of bias even if it is groundless is as damaging as actual bias."[9] As Justice Frankfurter said in *Offutt v. United States*, "… justice requires the appearance of justice."[10]

To date, 30 states and several federal circuits have commissioned reports on diversity in their respective legal systems. Consequently, they have established diversity task forces to address the issues of gender, racial and ethnic discrimination (real and/or perceived) and its impact on fairness in the courts.[11] Court diversity studies in Florida, Washington and Utah address in detail the integral role of prosecutors in the criminal justice system.[12] Of the three state studies, only Florida and Washington examine the area of the exercise of prosecutorial discretion and its impact on fairness in the criminal justice system.[13] The studies—both empirical and anecdotal—highlight and verify what prosecutors already know, that is, that the dominant role played by prosecutors in the dispensation of justice has a great effect on equal treatment and perceptions.[14] The studies also explore and identify key stages of impact in the prosecution process, such as arrest, charging decisions and bail requests, as well as plea and sentencing recommendations. All of the reports concede that bias does indeed exist, and therefore adversely affects people of color in the justice system.[15]

It is important to note that the goal of one of those studies, the Florida Racial and Ethnic Bias Study Commission, was not to determine whether the justice system was biased against minorities, but whether or not "racial or ethnic considerations adversely affect the dispensation of justice to minority Floridians."[16] It is significant that the Florida inquiry sought to identify the "policies and practices, which treat minorities unjustly, irrespective of whether the basis for mistreatment is malevolence, undue benevolence, or indifference."[17]

Without focusing on prosecutorial discretion, most of the state commissions utilizing lawyer surveys drew conclusions similar to the Florida, Washington and Utah studies regarding the issue of the perception of bias in the administration of justice.

All concluded that the opinions of black lawyers on these issues differ sharply from those of their white counterparts.[18]

When queried about the existence of discrimination in the courts, the majority of non-minority lawyers responded either that they never witnessed any discrimination or that none existed in the courts. Conversely, lawyers of color and minorities responded that discriminatory practices were routine in the courts.[19] It is clear that the issue of whether race negatively affects the work of the courts depends on the racial perspective of the viewer, as well as the perceptions and experiences of the individual. Even the Supreme Court in *Crawford vs. United States* conceded, "the naturalness of bias or prejudice is such an elusive condition of the mind that it is most difficult, if not impossible, to always recognize its existence."[20]

In conclusion, on the issue of real and/or perceived bias, empirical studies and anecdotes notwithstanding, Sir Walter Moberly, an English educator said it best: "the most pernicious kind of bias consists of falsely supposing yourself to have none."[21]

RECRUITING AND HIRING
The first step in the process of diversifying a prosecutor's office must be a firm and resolute commitment by the chief prosecutor that translates into a management priority and an administrative goal of the agency. The second step may require the creation of institutionalized diversity training for all levels of management. An unambiguous training program can positively heighten race and gender awareness throughout the agency. The third step is the creation of a multi-cultural work environment.

Since the mid-1960s, many privately held U.S. companies have developed initiatives targeting the recruitment and hiring of people of color. CEOs and managers in many of these companies assert that cultural diversity is critical to their future survival. They believe and understand that companies cannot continue to ignore the impact that demographic changes in the U.S. will have in the workplace and on their businesses.[22]

The Hudson Institute's Workforce 2000 Report identified several key demographic trends in the United States that will dramatically impact organizational life in the twenty-first century:[23]

• The population and workforce will grow slowly;
• The average age of workers will increase;

- More women along with more minorities will enter the workforce; and
- Immigrants will, for the first time since World War I, contribute the largest increase in the workforce.

The report concludes with the observation that, "although white males will continue to maintain a numerical edge in the next decade, they will constitute a shrinking percentage of the new entrants into the color pool. The new workforce will comprise greater diversity of gender, race, age, culture and language." [24]

The importance of the Hudson report cannot be underestimated in that it statistically *confirms* what most prosecutors *know* anecdotally: in many jurisdictions—irrespective of the size—there are growing multi-cultural populations that are entitled to and, in fact, demand justice, without bias. For practical reasons, however, prosecutors' offices should turn to the corporate world and borrow a page from the corporate policy on diversity. Corporate presidents and chief prosecutors are confronted with similar challenges in their responses to the issue of diversity with one significant difference. Corporations are motivated and respond to policies—or the lack thereof—that affect profitability, whereas chief prosecutors respond to a moral obligation and a need to maintain credibility in the communities they serve.

THE HIGHER CALLING TO DIVERSIFY

In a conversation regarding the recruitment of minority prosecutors, a chief prosecutor not long ago complained that he could not find any applicants. While some may view his frustration as unresponsive to the need to diversify, it also begs the question: where had he been looking?

Until recently, it was unremarkable for a prosecutor's office to lack a diverse staff. Even today, the goal of diversifying is often not a priority in many prosecutors' offices, perhaps because the identification of potential applicants of color requires the prosecutor to become proactive and undertake an aggressive recruitment approach. The truth is, without *actively* recruiting people of color they are difficult to hire. Prosecutorial agencies, assuming they hope to diversify, must develop and adopt comprehensive strategies to locate minority candidates and to address those issues that may prevent qualified candidates of color from applying.

Prosecuting agencies across the nation are conservative in culture. These offices may require aggressive efforts to shift to a culture of inclusion. It is therefore incumbent upon the chief prosecutor to develop and distribute a non-discrimination policy to all legal and non-legal staff.

While most offices have a non-discrimination policy, it is not always prominently displayed and distributed to the entire staff under the chief prosecutor's signature. The presumption amongst many prosecutors is that a colleague will not discriminate in hiring practices because discrimination is morally reprehensible, not to mention illegal. This belief, however, is not easily conveyed to minority communities. A potential minority candidate might view the lack of a published non-discrimination policy as an indication that people of color need not apply.

Historically, many people of color who have been excluded from government institutions are reluctant to apply for employment in a prosecutor's office. Placing advertisements in newspapers to encourage applicants of color stating, EEO/Equal Opportunity Employer or "women and minorities encouraged to apply" is no panacea. It alone may not be sufficient to attract minority applications. A successful recruitment campaign requires the development of a strategy that recognizes the history of mistrust between people of color and law enforcement and one that embraces cultural differences.

First, it is prudent to explore the subtle messages that have been conveyed to the public about the agency (e.g., its reputation as a fair employer). Begin with current employees who are minorities and people of color. Consult them about this issue. Employees can be an agency's greatest advocate or its worst nemesis. They are the ambassadors who voice their observations and experiences to countless people each day. Staff should be considered a promotional source that can vouch for the genuine or counter the superficial efforts of the agency's minority recruitment initiatives.

The next step is a thorough review and analysis of the agency's practice in charging, sentencing and plea agreement policies that perhaps adversely affect minorities and people of color. An agency cannot expect to attract candidates of color if it practices questionable or ill-defined charging and plea policies. Furthermore, professional growth and development is important to minorities, just as it is for non-minorities. Both are drawn to the prosecutorial profession to, among other things, enhance their careers. This requires a philosophy and practice of operation that fosters participation of *all* and a system that is just to *all*. The perceived lack of such practices is a red flag to minority employees that career growth in your office will be retarded. For example, if non-minorities hold all positions of power in the agency, the not-so-subtle message of "no room at the top" for people of color is conveyed, implying an absence of real commitment to diversify. Hence, the advancement of qualified and respected people of color and minorities, presently within the organization should be an important component of any strategy.

Establishing and aggressively building support networks for people of color and minorities will further assist with recruitment and retention goals. Whether formal or informal, support networks (e.g., mentor initiatives) encourage better knowledge and understanding of work place systems and cultural differences among employees.

Cultural diversity training can contribute to the creation of a multi-cultural and ethnic-friendly environment. The motto of the Lotus Corporation, for example, is: "... at Lotus, we speak diversity."[25]

Community outreach initiatives serve as useful recruiting vehicles in the identification and recruitment of people of color. Like staff employees, members of the local community are in the unique position to encourage or discourage potential applicants, depending on the strength of the relationship the chief prosecutor has with them. As a caveat, chief prosecutors who are genuinely committed to the goal of diversity should not be discouraged by the uneasy relationship that has traditionally existed between law enforcement and minority communities. The changing public perception of prosecutors, as evidenced by television shows like "Law and Order," coupled with the fact that "prosecutor" clinics are becoming part of the curriculum in law schools, has persuaded a growing number of minority law students to pursue careers in prosecution. Additionally, the traditional reasons for seeking a career in prosecution, such as the opportunity to serve the public, litigation experience and exposure to complex legal issues continue to be strong motivations.

Many high-profile trials are first won (or lost) in the court of public opinion. When a community perceives—rightly or wrongly—that a prosecutor is culturally insensitive, the judicial system, including all levels of law enforcement, pays a heavy penalty. A mistrust of law enforcement will fester amongst members of the minority community and consequently, will bolster the belief that the laws are unjust. As a result, citizens' inclinations to abide by the laws may ebb, thus leading ultimately to failure of the entire criminal justice system. The potential for damage is great; the potential to strengthen your community is also great.

TEN-STEP PLAN FOR THE RECRUITMENT OF MINORITIES AS PROSECUTORS

- Formulate and publicize a non-discrimination policy;

- Establish recruitment goals;

- Develop long-term recruitment and retention strategy;

- Diversify upper-level management;

- Create minority support networks within the office;

- Publicize commitment to diversity to the general community;

- Establish and institutionalize "sensitivity" training for upper-level management and assistant prosecutors, if necessary;

- Interface with local and national minority bar associations;

- Establish a relationship with minority law school associations in area law schools; and

- Maintain a pool of minority applicants; send recruiters to public interest job fairs, law schools that demonstrate a strong commitment to increased minority enrollment and historically black law schools.

ENDNOTES

[1] New York State Bar Association's Committee on Professional Ethics (1972) (emphasis supplied).

[2] Ben J. Wattenberg, *The First Universal Nation* (New York: The Free Press, 1990).

[3] Judicial Improvements and Access to Justice Act, Pub. L. No. 100-702 Stat 4642 (1988) Ninth Circuit Task Force on Gender Bias, The Effects of Gender in the Federal Courts (1993), address of Justice Sandra Day O'Connor.

[4] Ellis Cose, *A Nation of Strangers* (William Morrow and Company, Inc., eds., 1992).

[5] Andrew Hacker, *Two Nations* (Macmillan eds., 1992).

[6] *Brown v. Board of Education*, 347 US 483 (1952).
Heart of Atlanta Motel, Inc. v. U.S., 379 US 241 (1964).
Katzenbach v. McClung, 379 US 294 (1964).
U.S. v. Lopez, 514 US 549 (1995).

[7] District of Columbia Task Force on Racial/Ethnic Bias in the Courts, Final Report of the Task Force on Racial and Ethnic Bias and the Task Force on Gender Bias in the Courts, 64 *George Washington Law Review* 173 (1996).

[8] Research Sub-committee, Washington State Minority and Justice Commission, Racial and Ethnic Disparities in Prosecution and Sentencing, 32 *Gonzaga Law Review*, 577 (1996/1997).

[9] Utah Task Force on Racial and Ethnic Fairness in the Legal System, 11 *Utah Bar J.* 38 (1998).

[10] *Offutt v. U.S.*, 348 US 11 (1954).

[11] Information Service of the National Center for States Courts, Part I: Materials from States and Individual Task Forces and Commissions on Racial and Ethnic Bias in the Courts (1997).

[12] Florida Racial and Ethnic Bias Study Commission, *Report and Recommendations of the Florida Supreme Court Racial and Ethnic Bias Study Commission* (Florida Supreme Court, 1991), Juvenile Justice: The Need for Further Reform; Utah Task Force On Racial and Ethnic Fairness in the Legal System, 11 *Utah Bar J* 38 (1994); Washington Minority and Justice Commission (November 1995), Racial and Ethnic Disparities in the Prosecution of Felony Cases in King County.

[13] Florida Study, Washington State Study, *Ibid.*

[14] *Ibid.*

[15] *Ibid.*

[16] Florida Racial and Ethnic Bias Study Commission, Report and Recommendations of the Florida Supreme Court Racial and Ethnic Bias Study Commission (Florida Supreme Court, 1991) pg. 607.

[17] *Ibid*, pg. 606.

[18] District of Columbia Task Force on Racial/Ethnic Bias in the Courts, Final Report of the Task Force on Racial and Ethnic Bias and the Task Force on Gender Bias in the Courts, 64 *Geo. Wash. L. Rev.* 173 (1996).

[19] *Ibid.*

[20] *Crawford v. U.S.*, 212 U.S. 183 196 (1902).

[21] Task Force on Gender, Racial, and Ethnic Fairness in the Courts (2nd Circuit) (1997).

[22] Melanie G. Fine, *Building Successful Multicultural Organizations* (Westport, Conn: Quorum Books 1995).

[23] Hudson Institute, *Workforce 2000* (Johnson & Packer, 1987).

[24] *Ibid.* pg. 126.

[25] *Ibid.*